To the Bomb and Back

To the Bomb and Back

*Finnish War Children
Tell their World War II Stories*

Edited by
Sue Saffle

berghahn
NEW YORK · OXFORD
www.berghahnbooks.com

Published in 2015 by
Berghahn Books
www.berghahnbooks.com

© 2015 Sue Saffle

All rights reserved. Except for the quotation of short passages for the purposes of criticism and review, no part of this book may be reproduced in any form or by any means, electronic or mechanical, including photocopying, recording, or any information storage and retrieval system now known or to be invented, without written permission of the publisher.

Library of Congress Cataloging-in-Publication Data

To the bomb and back : Finnish war children tell their World War II stories / edited by Sue Saffle. — First edition.
    pages cm
  Includes bibliographical references and index.
  ISBN 978-1-78238-658-2 (hardback) —
  ISBN 978-1-78238-659-9 (ebook)
  1. World War, 1939–1945—Children—Finland. 2. World War, 1939–1945—Evacuation of civilians—Finland. 3. World War, 1939–1945—Personal narratives, Finnish. 4. World War, 1939–1945—Children—Sweden. 5. Children—Sweden—Biography. 6. Children—Finland—Biography. 7. Finns—Sweden—Biography. I. Saffle, Sue. II. Title: Finnish war children tell their World War II stories.
  D810.C4485 2015
  940.53'161—dc23

                                                              2014033560

British Library Cataloguing in Publication Data

A catalogue record for this book is available from the British Library

Printed on acid-free paper.

ISBN: 978-1-78238-658-2 hardback
ISBN: 978-1-78238-659-9 ebook

To my husband Michael, who has introduced me to much of the world, including sublime Finland. Without his patience, steadfast support, and editorial expertise, this book would never have come to fruition.

And to Finland's surviving war children: may their voices in this volume help to create a greater awareness of children in war and conflict throughout the world.

Contents

List of Figures	x
Foreword	xii
Kai Rosnell	
Acknowledgments	xiv
Introduction	1
1. The Work of Sorrow	28
Marja Hultin Barron	
2. Unanswered Questions for a Finnpojke	34
Martti Kalervo Broström	
3. A Desire to Scream	39
"Emmi Eskola"	
4. Horseshoes and Licorice Drops	42
Juha Hankkila	
5. The Last Summer in Sweden	52
"Karina Heino"	
6. Farting in Swedish	55
Veijo Holopainen	
7. Sugar Beets and Spettecaka	59
Soile Kiema Ilvesoksa	
8. Dragons in a Handbag	63
Veikko Inkinen	
9. A Good and Bad Hand	71
Eric Jaakkola	
10. The Red Shoes	78
Anita Jakobsson	

11.	Bread in a Suitcase *Rauni Janser*	85
12.	The Lucky Stain *Rauno Juntunen*	96
13.	Paper Dolls *Sirpa Kaukinen*	107
14.	The Woman in the Broad-Brimmed Hat *Kirsti Kettunen*	113
15.	Swedish Toys *Helena Nyqvist Koivisto*	122
16.	Goodbye to the Bombs *Anne-Maj Korpela*	128
17.	Someone's Daughter *"Leena Korpi"*	133
18.	To the Bomb and Back *Eeva Lindgren*	142
19.	A Blonde Curly-Haired Girl *Mirja Luoma*	150
20.	Fishing with Ragnar *Pekka/Peter Louhimo*	152
21.	Black Birds *Seppo Mälkki*	166
22.	Terror of the Dark *Marita Merilahti*	175
23.	Funeral Games *"Eine Miller"*	180
24.	The Woman in Black *Helena Nilsson*	186
25.	Understanding Backwards *Veijo Pönniäinen Paine*	195
26.	A Happier War Child Story *Virve Kaisu Kyllikki Palos*	204
27.	No Easy Choices *Ossi Rahkonen*	213

28.	God natt, sov Gott *Lea Rehula*	221
29.	A Lifelong Exile *Kai Rosnell*	225
30.	Take the Bed Down! *Gertrud Rullander*	231
31.	Waiting for the Time to Pass *Irma Saarinen*	241
32.	Children's Prayers *Kaarina Siilasto*	245
33.	"Send the Little Ones!" *Bodil Nordman Söderberg*	249
34.	A Tale of Two Sisters *Marja Tähtinen*	255
35.	Swedish Fish *Rolf J. E. Tarvala*	259
36.	Horses in the Kitchen *Jorma Törmänen*	268
37.	Rita, not Rauha *"Rita Trent"*	273
38.	Repairing the Clock *Kaj Wanne*	284
39.	Soldier Boy *Norman Westerberg*	294
Appendix. A Swedish War Child Administration Form		310
Bibliography		312
Index		314

Figures

4.1. Juha Hankilla at age four, around the time he was sent to Denmark. Courtesy Juha Hankilla. 43

8.1. Veikko Inkinen at age four, around the time he was sent to Sweden. Courtesy Veikko Inkinen. 64

9.1. Eric Jaakkola at age six, just before he and his sister were sent to Sweden. Courtesy Eric Jaakkola. 73

12.1. Rauno Juntunen at age five, when he was sent to Sweden. Courtesy Rauno Juntunen. 97

13.1. Sirpa Kaukinen at age five, with her own Christmas tree in Sweden. Courtesy Sirpa Kaukinen. 110

14.1. Kirsti Kettunen as an infant in her mother's arms with her family in rural Finland, prior to being sent to a children's home or orphanage in Finland. Courtesy Kirsti Kettunen. 114

15.1. Helena Nyqvist Koivisto (left) with her foster mother and foster siblings. Courtesy Helena Nyqvist Koivisto. 123

18.1. Eeva Lindgren's father in uniform during World War II. Courtesy Eeva Lindgren. 143

20.1. Pekka/Peter Luohimo fishing with his Swedish foster father Ragnar. Courtesy Peter Luohimo. 158

21.1. Seppo Mällki (right) at age three, with his foster sister and brother in Sweden. Courtesy Seppo Mällki. 167

21.2. Finnish boy soldiers of 1942. Seppo Mälkki's brother Jorma (second row center) forged his signature at age fourteen in order to join the Finnish Army. Courtesy Seppo Mälkki. 172

22.1. Marita Merilahti (right) with her Swedish foster sister in 1943. Courtesy Marita Merilahti. 177

25.1.	Facsimile of a letter written on toilet paper by Veijo Paine to his mother from Haparanda, Sweden, where he was receiving medical care. Courtesy Veijo Paine. 200
26.1.	Virve Palos at age three. Courtesy Virve Palos. 205
27.1.	Ossi Rahkonen at age three, sitting in his father's lap during his father's leave from the front. Courtesy Ossi Rahkonen. 216
29.1.	Kai Rosnell (right) at age nine, standing next to his Swedish foster brother Berndt, who holds an accordion. Fall 1944. Courtesy Kai Rosnell. 227
30.1.	Gertrud Rullander at age seven. Courtesy Gertrud Rullander. 238
38.1.	Kaj Wanne's father Ilmari Vanna, an officer in the Finnish Army during World War II. Courtesy Kaj Wanne. 288

Additional photo section follows page 160.

Foreword
Kai Rosnell

More than eighty thousand Finnish children were sent away from Finland during World War II to Sweden and Denmark to escape the dangers of war. This huge operation is part of modern Finnish history but has been hidden in silence for over fifty years. Since the 1990s many books have been written by and about these "war children," both fiction and fact. A few of them have been written and published in the United States. I can only express my gratitude, on behalf of all of us who took part in the world's greatest child exodus, that our true stories, our fates, now will be known to the American people.

I have known Sue Saffle for many years and have attended several of the same conferences in Reading, England, and elsewhere. I am deeply impressed with her research and the papers she has given—they have been excellent. She is truly devoted to our cause and she has the skill to convey our true feelings about the whole war child project.

Yli 80,000 suomalasta lasta lähetettiin Suomesta toisen maailmansodan aikana sodan vaaroja pakoon Ruotsiin tai Tanskaan. Sotalapsitoiminta on osa Suomen nykyhistoriaa, mutta sitä on piilotettu tai siitä on vaiettu yli 50 vuoden ajan. 1990-luvusta lähtien näistä sotalapsista on kirjoitettu monta kirjaa, sekä fiktiota että faktaa. Joitakin kirjoja on julkaistu USA-ssa. Edustan niitä sotalapsia, jotka olivat osa tätä maailman suurinta lastensiirtoa, ja haluan ilmaista suuren kiitollisuuteni siitä, että meidän tosikertomukset, meidän kohtalot, nyt voivat tulla tutuksi myös amerikkalaiselle yleisölle.

Olen tuntenut Sue Safflen monta vuotta. Olen ollut hänen kanssa monessa kokouksessa Readingissä ja muualla, ja hänen erinomaiset tutkimuksensa ja luentonsa ovat tehneet minuun syvän vaikutuksen. Sue Saffle suorittaa tehtävänsä antaumuksella ja hänellä on kyky välittää todelliset tunteemme.

Mer än 80,000 finska barn sändes bort från Finland till Sverige och Danmark under andra världskriget, undan krigets faror. Krigsbarnsverksamheten är en del av Finlands moderna historia, men har förtigits eller gömts undan i över 50 år. Från 1990-talet har många böcker skrivits om och av dessa krigsbarn, både fiktion och fakta. Några har skrivits och givits ut i USA.

Jag vill uttrycka min tacksamhet, som representant för alla de krigsbarn som var en del av världens största barnförflyttning, för att våra sanna berättelser, våra öden, nu kan bli kända även för den amerikanska publiken.

Jag har känt Sue Saffle i många år; jag har bevistat flera konferenser i Reading och andra ställen, och jag är djupt imponerad av hennes forskning och de föreläsningar hon givit—de har varit utmärkta. Hon är hängiven sin uppgift och har förmågan att förmedla våra verkliga känslor.

Kai Rosnell, Knivsta, Sweden
War child and secretary of the War Children´s Association in Sweden
Editor in chief, *Finska Krigsbarn*

Acknowledgments

I want to thank all the war children who have so generously shared their stories and even their homes with me; the latter include Rauni Janser, Anne-Maj Korpela, "Leena Korpi," Veijo Paine, Virve Palos, and Gertrud Rullander. I also want to thank Seppo Mälkki for his delightful tour of Stockholm and Helena Nilsson for an equally enjoyable tour of Ystad. Special thanks go to Kai Rosnell, Veikko Inkinen, Sinikka Ortmark Almgren, Brita Stenius-Aarniala, Tapani Rossi, and Dr. Peter Heinl, all of whom read my introduction and offered valuable suggestions; and to Pertti Kavén and Seppo Mälkki for their insights and answers. I am also grateful to those who have helped me with translation: Kenneth Granlund, Mari Lehtimaki, Anne-Maj Korpela, Virve Palos, and—above all—Millie Wiggert, a dear friend who has translated several of the Finnish works quoted herein.

I would like to thank Virginia Polytechnic Institute and State University, especially the College of Liberal Arts and Human Sciences and the Department of English for support that enabled me to attend conferences in England and the United States, where I gave papers on the Finnish war children. I also want to thank Martin Parsons for providing a venue at Reading University for discussions by international authorities concerning children and war. Thanks also go to Kelly Bellanger and Jen Mooney, who gave me practical advice; and to Virva Kirijarvi and Janna Rehnstrom, for their encouragement and support. *SA-kuva-arkisto,* the Finnish Wartime Photograph Archive (often identified simply as "SA-kuva" and referenced as such in the photo credits below), kindly extended permission to reprint images from its impressive collection. Finally, I would like to thank Elizabeth Berg of Berghahn Books for her thoughtful and cordial help with the present volume.

In a more general way I would like to thank sheer good fortune and my wonderful parents for an idyllic childhood free from the horrors of war. Finally, I want to thank my husband Michael and son Thomas for their love and enduring companionship.

Introduction

> We look at the world once, in childhood. The rest is memory.
> Louise Gluck

> A child's world always has had odd dimensions, as narrow as the backyard or a corner of the kitchen, but as broad as the imagination.
> Reed Karaim

> We have each of us a life story, an inner narrative—whose continuity, "whose sense, is our lives. It might be said that each of us constructs and lives "a narrative," and that this narrative is our identities.
> Oliver Sacks

> Perhaps the most common myth about war is that it ends when the textbooks say it does, when the cease-fires begin and the documents are signed.
> Ann Hagedorn

Breaking the Silence

Until relatively recently, the stories of Finland's estimated 80,000 or more *sotalapsi* or *krigsbarn* ("war children" in Finnish and Swedish, respectively) were shared primarily among themselves. Most of these children were sent to Sweden for safekeeping during World War II, but some 4,000 were transported to Denmark and elsewhere. While the majority of stories that follow relate the experiences of children sent to Sweden, there are a few that describe the experiences of those sent to Denmark or who remained in Finland throughout the war, as well as the story of one little girl who during Finland's difficult postwar years was sent to the United States, where her childhood was blighted by confusion, servitude, and humiliation. Considering the number of such children, a number rivaling Finland's approximately 89,000 military casualties,[1] it is surprising that more has not been written about "the world's largest child transfer," now perceived as "a great social-historical mistake."[2]

As an identifying label, "war children" has generally come to refer only to children sent to other countries in wartime (and, of course, to the adults they later became), but for the purposes of the present volume I would like to extend the definition to include children who lived on the home front during the war. It is important to see that even those children who were not separated from their biological families and native language also often endured great emotional trauma and hardships. Aura Korppi-Tommola writes about "the forgotten group of those Finnish children that stayed in Finland" whose "life stories have been subordinated to adults' memories and to the experiences of the children that were evacuated to Sweden or Denmark."[3] While statistically it may be true that there is "evidence for greater vulnerability and individual weaknesses" among evacuated children than those who remained behind, it is important to remember that a vast number of these were also brutalized by war and their families' often desperate circumstances.[4]

In 2001, while living in Finland, I was introduced to a war child and became fascinated by what she described as the mass evacuations of Finnish children during the "Winter," "Continuation," and "Lapland" Wars (1939–1945), fought by Finland mostly against Russia, Finland's principal historical oppressor. Although I had read many books on these wars, I had seen nothing in English about the Finnish child transports, which puzzled me. Similar wartime transports—from Central Europe to other countries during 1919–1922; from Spain to England and the USSR in 1937; from London to the English countryside ("Operation Pied Piper") throughout World War II; from Europe to various countries during the 1930s and 1940s (the "Kindertransports" of Jewish children); and the "Peter Pan Children" of Cuba, sent to the United States after the Bay of Pigs fiasco, to name a few examples—have been widely researched and written about.[5] Yet there appeared to be virtually nothing in English concerning the Finnish war children. Even more perplexing was the discovery that there appeared to be extremely little written on this subject in either Finnish or Swedish, though nearly all other events relating to Finland in World War II have been exhaustively researched and written about.

Not until 1977 was the silence broken when former war child Annu Edvardsen published her revealing history and memoir, *Det får inte hände igen: Finska Krigsbarn: 1939–45* (This Must Never Happen Again: Finnish War Children, 1939–45).[6] Today considered the first real work published about the Finnish war children, this book created a sensation and inspired other war children to come forward. Among them was Sinikka Ortmark Almgren, who related her war child story in *Du som haver barnen kär* (Thou Who Hast the Children Dear), which appeared in 1989.[7] The momentum grew and several other war children came forward to share their stories. As of 2004 some "seventy works [nearly all of them written in Finnish or Swedish] from the genres of fiction and autobiography" had been located by Irene Virtala.[8] Since then, more have been published by war child associations that grew up in the 1990s in Finland, Sweden, and Denmark. According to Pertti Kavén, who also helped to break the silence in 1985 with his acclaimed *70,000 små öden* (70,000 Small Destinies),[9] one of the reasons for the prolonged silence surrounding the child transfers is that criticisms of them were officially censored by the Finnish government "because it was thought that they would offend the Swedes." Kavén further writes that the "censorship organ used child transports as a means of active propaganda aimed at improving the relations between the two countries."[10] Another concern both during and after the war years was that, "had they [i.e., Finnish government officials] not allowed the child transfers, Finland might not have received any other war-related help from Sweden."[11]

Later, during the Cold War years of the 1950s and 1960s, Finns were officially discouraged from discussing *any* of their war experiences for fear of Russian reprisals. Former war child Kai Rosnell—whose story is included in the present anthology—has written that, "after some discussions in the Finnish Parliament in the early [1950s], the war children were never mentioned in Finland; they were forgotten." Nor were they "mentioned in history books until the end of the 1990s, so a whole generation of Finnish youngsters grew up without knowing anything of this part of their history."[12] I have also been told by many former war children who returned to Finland—upwards of 15,000 never returned or, after returning, found their way back to Sweden—that they felt their burdens were relatively insignificant in light of the enormous personal and material losses experienced by surviving parents and siblings. After the war Finns were busy rebuilding their devastated country, and many Finnish parents refused to discuss their children's expatriate experiences out of shame, guilt, or due to their own overwhelming war traumas.

Veikko Inkinen—a war child whose story is also included here—has another theory: namely, that "Finns have an underdog psychology. Many of us believe that the last thousand years have been a long series of catastrophes or dangerous mistakes. There is little sentimental feeling toward things gone. Why should anyone dwell in useless memories?" Regarding the postwar years he adds, "Why remind the Russians that we had made war with Hitler against them? The war, war veterans, and war children were subjects better to avoid speaking about."[13] Finally, the trauma of the initial separation from their biological parents and native language (at the time of the war Finland's Swedish-speaking minority was about 12 percent of the population, and some war children came from this group), compounded by the often worse trauma of forced repatriation and postwar separation from their Swedish foster parents and second acquired language, was simply too painful for many to address until psychologically and emotionally unavoidable.

In her own war child memoir, *Att inte höra till* (Not to Belong), Ann-Maj Danielsen describes how, after decades of repression, she felt "confronted with memories [that had been] dormant for over fifty years [but which suddenly] created an almost unbearable chaos and confusion in [her] life." She writes that

> for a long time, I was convinced I was getting ill and that I was even about to lose my mind. Without understanding the reasons, I slipped into a surreal parallel world that, aside from the usual life with work, family, and spare time, also contained nightmares robbing me of my night's rest. Also, there were all these scary glimpses and memories that wouldn't let go, but very vividly made me understand that these weren't just nightmares sprung from unreal fantasies.

Danielsen describes how, despite her efforts to suppress disturbing glimpses of her past, "one painful memory after another rolled up like a movie from my subconscious mind. When I finally realized that I couldn't get away from nightmares or flashbacks, I instead forced myself to try to finally understand what all of this meant." Once she began to write about her early childhood, Danielsen's memories "came crashing down": her departure at age five for Sweden, the five years spent with her caring foster parents, and her forced return to an extremely hard life in the Finnish countryside. There she lived with her family in a wooden shed with newspaper on the walls, lice, little food, no heating or plumbing, and a tyrannical father who had been psychologically damaged during the war.[14]

Like Danielsen, most of the war children I have corresponded with since 2001 claim that their wartime experiences haunted them in later life. Many underwent years of therapy to deal with troubling memories and general feelings of emptiness and rootlessness. And although not all experienced irrational feelings of guilt, others have struggled to deal with this additional emotional burden. In a text written for Waltic, an International Writers Conference in Stockholm in 2008, Almgren wrote: "We lonely war children were expected to be nice, obedient, and grateful. Some of us found a loving family, others didn't. ... But most of us are plagued by guilt from feeling rejected by our parents as well as from having deserted both them and our Swedish foster parents." Other war children have sought healing through sharing their stories in the safe context of war child associations. Today, according to Kavén, there are fifteen such associations in Finland with a combined membership of 1,193, six associations in Sweden, and one in Denmark. Though this is a small percentage of war children still living in Finland, Sweden, Denmark, and elsewhere (there are an estimated 30,000 to 40,000 living in Finland alone), it nevertheless points to the collective imperative that gave rise to these associations. Inkinen was the first chairman of Hämeenlinna's war child association and feels the sharing of stories to be so central to emotional healing that he has personally coached many members in how to write their memoirs. As he puts it, this is the "best and safest" way to deal with childhood trauma.

Part of my purpose in collecting these stories—and they are as various and unique as the war children themselves—is to bring them to an English-speaking audience. Although several anthologies of stories, mostly sponsored by war child associations, have appeared in Finnish and Swedish, I believe mine to be the first anthology of its kind in English. As such, it fills a void in the English literature on World War II by some of the war's last surviving eyewitnesses and its most invisible victims.

It goes without saying that the Finnish war child transports would never have occurred in peacetime; therefore, a very brief summary of Finland's three wars—which together span most of Europe's World War II—appears below.

First, however, a note on this anthology's title: *To the Bomb and Back*. This was the name given to a game that Eeva Lindgren played with her friends in wartime Finland. Eeva is one of those who remained in Finland for the duration of the war and remembers the nearly constant bombardments by Soviet planes with special vividness. After a bomb had created a colossal crater in her neighborhood, she and other children had racing contests to and from the crater. They called these contests *"Pommille ja Takaisin!"* (To the Bomb and Back!).

Having heard and read dozens of war child stories, it seems to me that every child of war had his or her "bomb" to contend with: living under constant threat of enemy attack and near-starvation in Finland; being put on a train in the middle of the night to suddenly find one's mother has vanished; encountering an entirely alien culture where no one can explain what is happening; having to learn a new language in Sweden and again in Finland after several months or years away; discovering the shocking news that one has another long-forgotten "family" to which one must now immediately return; being brutalized in one's native land, host country, or both; being "sold" without explanation to a foreign family to work as an unpaid laborer; and/or suffering terrible homesickness in Sweden or, later, in Finland. These describe just a few of the traumas war children commonly describe, and it must be emphasized that most war children experienced multiple traumas. Sadly, many experienced the majority of them. In part, through writing about their often very painful pasts, the majority of contributors to this anthology all seem to have made it "back" from their own personal "bombs" and to have achieved greater peace of mind, although it has often been a long and arduous journey.

Finland at War: 1939–1945

For Finland, World War II meant three distinct wars. The first was the fabled Winter War (*Talvisota*), which lasted from November 1939 to mid-March 1940: three-and-a-half months during which Finns proved themselves "Davids" in their valiant struggle against the Soviet "Goliaths." The second was the so-called Continuation War (*Jatkosota*), which lasted from July 1941 to September 1944 and was fought in concert with Nazi Germany as a cobelligerent against the Soviet Union.[15] The third and final war was the Lapland War (*Lapinsota*), which began in September 1944 and was reluctantly waged: as part of the ruinous armistice agreement with the Soviet Union at the end of the Continuation War, Finland was compelled to drive German troops out of Lapland, which was ultimately accomplished in April 1945.

In 1939, Finland, like her three Baltic neighbors to the south—Estonia, Latvia, and Lithuania—had enjoyed only brief independence from Russia and was still a young nation. Although it had declared its independence on December 6, 1917, independence was not realized until May 1918 after a bloody civil war that created bitter divisions but resulted in the expulsion of the Bolshevik army. In 1939 Finland did not want to give up its hard-won independence. Nor did it want to give up any of its territories. The Winter War came about because Finland refused to agree to territorial demands made by the Soviet Union.[16] As a consequence of Finland's noncompliance, Russia broke off diplomatic negotiations and began its attack along Finland's eastern border.[17] Russia believed its conquest of Finland would be swift. Both Finns and Soviets were in for a surprise, however. Eloise Engle and Lauri Paananen describe how, at the beginning of the war,

> Finns along the 800-mile-long border found themselves being attacked from every road.... Trees cracked and crashed into the deep snow sending clouds of white ice and slush, black rocks and debris mushrooming into the air. Overhead, airplanes roared low over the treetops, spraying machine-gun fire and dropping bombs. There was no nightmare with which the Finns could compare the scene. Nothing in their memories or wildest imaginations had prepared them for this.[18]

Finland had begun its preparations to resist in September through October 1939, but only on November 30 of that year did the Winter War begin when 450,000 Russian troops crossed Finland's eastern borders, and Russian planes rained incendiary bombs on helpless civilians in Helsinki and other major Finnish cities. Nevertheless, the Soviet strategy to defeat this small country of 4 million people in two weeks and install a puppet government failed abysmally. Soviet aggression united the once-divided Finns and aroused a determination among them that became famous as

"The Spirit of the Winter War." As Finns withstood aggression from their neighbor to the east, their country became a magnet for the world press. Even Winston Churchill was moved to declare that "Only Finland—superb, nay, sublime—Finland shows what free men can do."[19] Unfortunately, the grossly outnumbered Finns eventually lost 16,000 square miles of territory in eastern Finland known as "Karelia" (and today part of the Russian Federation), and some 420,000 Karelian Finns had to be evacuated. When a peace agreement was finally reached on March 12, 1940, 25,000 Finnish troops had been killed and 45,000 wounded. Astoundingly, Soviet casualties were far greater, with 200,000 dead and 400,000 wounded.[20]

From March 1940 to June 1941 the Finns enjoyed an "Interim Peace," during which time they looked for new allies. Unfortunately, only Germany was willing to assist in any significant way, though for its own purposes. On June 29, 1941, when Finland attacked the newly expanded Soviet border, the Continuation War began. In an attempt to recapture lost lands, Finns advanced rapidly with the aid of the Germans. Their battle cry was: "A Greater Finland; Free White Sea Karelia!"[21] Although Finland regained Karelia in 1941, it lost it again in 1944 during this far more disastrous second war. Four hundred thousand Karelians were once again displaced and had to be evacuated inland. During the ensuing Lapland War, other massive evacuations of Finns living in the northern territories occurred, while Finland's embittered former allies pursued a scorched earth policy, resulting in the ruination of many towns and cities. According to Korppi-Tommola, by 1945 some "88,000 men [had been] killed in action [... leaving] 30,000 war widows and more than 50,000 war orphans."[22]

In addition, "Infant mortality was high.... although the bombings and enemy fire caused the direct deaths of 337 children, the main cause of death was disease, especially diphtheria. Altogether, 44,181 children under 15 years of age died during the years 1940–1945."[23] But many also died of hunger. In 1943 Thérèse Bonney reported that "Of the 800,000 children in Finland, approximately 20 per cent are starving. In the northern part of the country 60 per cent have tuberculosis. In Salla, scene of one of the biggest battles of the first war between Russia and Finland, the rate of this disease has risen as high as 80 per cent." Bonney also writes that "about 10 per cent of the children are stillborn. Another 10 per cent are premature. Few hospitals or clinics are available for the children: they are filled [instead] with wounded soldiers." Newborns fortunate enough to survive were often wrapped in paper and slept in cardboard cradles, due to wool and cotton shortages. Most were dangerously malnourished as, according to Bonney, "Milk production has declined 40 per cent, because Finland has 200,000 fewer cows than in 1939."[24]

Three years earlier, Martha Gelhorn published a touching story about a young Finnish woman who filled in as a "fireman" in Helsinki while the men were at the front. In 1940 this woman had just been to a bomb site where she found "more children buried under the bombed houses since the first afternoon raid." Amid the rubble she found one small girl alive. Angrily but eloquently, this woman expressed the feeling that "you always love one child, you always pick one child out of many, one wounded soldier, one weary old woman: you have to fix your mind on someone, the heart cannot hold everything."[25]

It is against this grim backdrop that tens of thousands of Finnish children were sent to Sweden and some four thousand to Denmark for safety. Statistically these children, 7–8 percent of all Finnish children up to fourteen years of age, stood a far better chance of survival abroad. But survival came at a heavy emotional and psychological cost for many, if not most, of the children. In 1939 psychoanalyst John Bowlby warned about the consequences of sending children to the British countryside and separating them from their mothers. In 1943 Anna Freud and Dorothy Burlingham also discussed the long-term consequences of such separations and stated that what children fear most is not hunger, disease, or death—the very calamities Finland and Sweden endeavored to spare Finnish children. Instead, they fear separation from parents and families. Unfortunately, Bowlby's and Freud's research came too late to enlighten the architects of the Finnish war child transports, nor were their warnings relevant to the transportation of those Jewish children who would certainly have been murdered had they not been moved to safety.[26]

A saying circulated in Finland, a country still known for its black humor, at the end of the war: "The East took our men, the Germans took our women, the Swedes took our children. But at least we are left with our war debt."[27] As part of the peace agreement, the USSR demanded $300,000,000 in gold from Finland. This equaled 5–7 percent of the Finnish GNP at the time: a staggering sum which, according to several sources, helped the USSR rebuild its entire infrastructure after the war. At the same time, however, Finland was burdened with a problem far more elusive and difficult than that of reconstruction and reparation. Thousands of war-traumatized children, many greatly in need of healing and relief from often unimaginable sufferings, were gradually returning to Finland's lakes, mountains, and shores.

The War Child Transports

By far the greatest number of children was transported to Sweden during the Continuation War. During the Winter War some 10,000 children were sent abroad, along with 3,000 adults—mostly young mothers as well as ailing and elderly women. Throughout the Continuation War, however, approximately 65,000 children—anywhere from two months to fourteen years of age—were sent abroad.[28] The number of children sent privately to Sweden (which is to say, outside of official transports) is believed to have been around 5,000. Due in part to the enormous difficulties of postwar reconstruction, efforts to bring the war children home continued long after the war, the last official transport occurring in 1949, four years after the war's conclusion. An estimated 15,000 children were lost to Sweden permanently either through adoptions, the biological family's choice, or other circumstances. An estimated 3,000 were formally adopted; 4,000 remained foster children in Sweden; 7,000–8,000 children and young people who were repatriated found a way to return to Sweden, where many settled permanently.[29]

The idea of sending Finnish children to Sweden was the brainchild of Maja Sandler, wife of Sweden's then-foreign minister, and Hanna Rydh, president of a prominent Swedish women's organization. According to Rosnell, Sandler was inspired by three previous child transports: the thousands of children sent from Germany and Austria to Denmark, Holland, Sweden, and Switzerland during World War I; the relocation of thousands of Spanish children sent abroad during the Spanish Civil War during 1936–1937; and the seemingly successful "Pied Piper" operation in Britain, by means of which children were sent from British cities to the countryside at the outset of World War II. Shortly after 1918, Sweden itself had accepted more than 21,000 Austrian and German child refugees, creating an important historical precedent.[30] During World War II, Switzerland also offered to take some 100 Finnish children, but the Finnish War Children's Transport Committee rejected this offer, due to the distance involved. In 1944 Hungary also offered to host Finnish children, but this proposal was rejected for similar reasons.

Initially, Finland resisted the idea of sending children to Sweden, preferring any material and military assistance their neighbor could give. But initiatives in Sweden, associated with the slogan *Finlands sak är vår* (Finland's cause is ours), seemed unstoppable, and the Centrala Finlandshjälpen (Center for Help for Finland) was born. Influential Finns were approached, including pro-Swedish Gustav Mannerheim, who had won the civil war for the Whites in 1918—and who, as "Finland's George Washington," was made commander-in-chief of the Finnish armed forces in 1939 at age 72. Thus, early in December, the Nordic Assistance Center in Finland was formed, and Swedish families were encouraged to host Finnish children without compensation—although it is important to note that Swedes were given extra ration coupons for agreeing to this (a fact referred to in several of the stories here).

There may also have been an ulterior motive in the drive to "import" Finnish children. According to Swedish historical statistics on population numbers, the Swedish birth rate during 1930–1940 was significantly lower than that of 1910–1920. In 1940, for instance, there were only 445,195 Swedish children aged 0–4 years of age, compared with 619,518 children of the same ages in 1910. All this may have been a concern for the Swedish government and for many childless couples, which figure prominently among the foster parents referred to in war child stories. As Alva Myrdal, a well-known Swedish author and politician put it, "The Finnish war children were like a gift from heaven to Sweden."[31]

The first wave of children, mothers, and the elderly was sent from Finland to Sweden on December 15, 1939, just two weeks after the outbreak of war with the Soviet Union. The evacuations were arranged by the Red Cross, and the children were given tags to wear, each tag identifying the child as well as the name of the family to which that child was assigned in the event that a family had been pre-chosen. In the beginning this program was aimed at poor Karelian children, and many of the stories in this volume feature families who had been deprived of their homes and property in Karelia. The general belief was that evacuation would be brief. Before the Continuation War commenced, war children were even referred to as "summer children," suggesting only a few months' absence from home. As the war dragged on, however, criteria were relaxed and eventually nearly all children, from infants to fourteen-year-olds, were allowed to go, including many who were handicapped or ill. During the ensuing Continuation War, some 72,000 children in all were evacuated by ship, train, or plane to Sweden and Denmark.

In the beginning, ship travel was more common, aboard the hurriedly prepared SS *Arcturus* or SS *Heimdall,* both of which sailed frequently from Turku to Stockholm. However, this mode of travel was deemed unsafe after a boatload of children was attacked by a Soviet submarine in January 1940. Although no children were killed, many sailors died, and after the Russians began to mine the Gulf of Bothnia, rail transport became more common. Unfortunately, this mode of travel was also fraught with danger. In March 1940 a tragic collision of two trains travelling north to the border town of Haparanda in Sweden killed fifteen children and several mothers and caretakers.[32]

Rail travel took place only at night because of the possibility of air raids, and train-car windows were blacked out.[33] Despite this precaution, many war children vividly recall having to rush out of the train to hide in the forest when Soviet bombers targeted their trains. Journeys that had been short in peacetime often became interminable ordeals with children sleeping on boards placed crosswise over seats or even in overhead baggage racks. Once they arrived in Tornio on the Finnish-Swedish border, children had to change onto Swedish trains in Haparanda because of different track gauges. For the majority, however, train travel soon resumed, with stops in towns where couples had either committed to taking a child or where they selected children according to their whims and preferences.

Inkinen remembers the ordeal of being chosen at random when one day, "women began to move around the beds [in the holding center] and to touch us." Several of the women, he writes, were "stroking my hair and feeling my hands and feet. Some removed the blanket ... to see me more clearly, perhaps to make sure I wasn't deformed or ill ... I remember that I was so afraid that I forgot to cry." According to many accounts, the first chosen were usually blonde curly-haired little girls. Mirja Luoma luckily fit that description and acknowledges her good fortune, since "Swedish couples seemed to prefer" pretty little girls. Many older boys or visibly malnourished and less conventionally attractive children, however, traveled from station to station, yet were never chosen: an extremely humiliating experience. "Eine Miller," for example, remembers being left alone in a large room after all the other children had been selected by foster parents. She recalls that, at the time, she believed she hadn't been chosen "because I was very pale, skinny, and ugly."

Many children fell gravely ill during journeys that often lasted ten days or more. According to Kavén, more than a few of the evacuees died of diphtheria contracted during transfers. As many as 20 percent of those who had been well when they left Finland were so ill by the time they arrived in Sweden that they had to be hospitalized.[34] Veijo Paine was one such unfortunate child, contracting a grave illness during his transportation by railway to Sweden.

At various hospitals, schools, garrisons, and even at the Hotel Anglais in Stockholm, children were often placed in quarantine and subjected to frightening medical exams, boys and girls having sometimes to stand nude to wait in line for checkups and vaccination shots. Like many war children, Soile Ilvesoksa was deeply frightened of the blood tests. Helena Nilsson also relates how terrifying it was to stand in a long line of screaming children, waiting for injections. Children with lice had their heads shaved or were treated with sabadil vinegar—and later, in 1944, with DDT. Their clothing was either burned or placed in heated chambers to eradicate lice, while the children were being bathed or washed. According to Inkinen, the delousing and burning of clothes may have been unnecessary but carried out because some Swedes believed Finns to be "dirty," due to their proximity to Russia. Those children diagnosed with infectious diseases, such as Marita Merilahti, were kept in isolation in Swedish hospitals for weeks and even months. According to Kavén and Tapani Rossi, who published a book in 2008 on the Swedish care of sick Finnish children, some 3,000 war children were saved in this way from various diseases and malnutrition.[35] Nevertheless, medical care at the hands of strangers was often experienced as traumatic.

Another great trauma for many war children was their separation from siblings (although, as Rossi states, this was often done when one of the siblings was ill and had to be hospitalized or quarantined to prevent contagion). Often the last thing older children heard their mothers tell them was to "watch out for" and "never be separated from" their younger sister or brother. Unfortunately, most Swedish parents preferred single children, and siblings were almost always divided. Juha Hankkila and his older brother were sent to Denmark in 1941, and Juha remembers being "separated immediately" and meeting his brother only once during his five years in Denmark. He describes this as "A terrible thing. Why couldn't we have been placed in the same village?" Even many siblings who happened to be placed in the same town or within short distances of one another seldom met or never saw each other until they were reunited in Finland. Nor were many introduced to other Finnish-speaking war children. Compounding these traumas, at least in many cases, was the total absence of anyone who could explain what was happening to the children in a language they could understand.

Wartime evacuation would be traumatic in the best of circumstances. Consider, for instance, "Operation Pied Piper," in which thousands of British children were evacuated to the countryside. Dozens of these children have written memoirs about their often very challenging experiences. Yet none of them lost their language in the process, while the vast majority of Finnish war children lost their language not just once but *twice*. Like the German Jewish children sent to England during the war, they could understand nothing upon arrival.[36] In other words, both upon arriving in Sweden and again upon returning to Finland, children were effectively rendered both deaf and dumb; they were forced to navigate strange new worlds without the benefit of adult explanation and guidance. Although female Finnish interpreters escorted the children during transports, it was not always possible for the larger transports to obtain enough women translators. And although the larger quarantine centers also had interpreters on hand for the children, there were often far too few to meet the demand. As Rossi also points out, the farther from Stockholm the children traveled, the fewer Finnish or bilingual escorts there were to accompany them.[37] Unfortunately, many of my war child correspondents did not benefit from such assistance and only remember how bewildering it was to be surrounded by strangers, speaking a strange language.

As former war child Brita Stenius-Aarniala has written, language is not merely a tool with which to communicate. It defines us: "Finnish is my skin, my air, my snowfall, my rage and my sorrow. In this language I heal my deepest wounds, and in it I mold and plant my feelings. My Finnish language is the very origin and foundation for whom I am."[38] Often, foster parents lacked Swedish-Finnish dictionaries, as well, though more educated and considerate foster parents attempted to bridge the language gap through such aids. Luckily, Martti Brostrom's foster and later adoptive parents, as well as Peter Louhimo's foster parents, had such dual language dictionaries to ease the transition. But learning the language, customs, and habits of an unfamiliar culture required time. Furthermore, most war children, especially those who were too young to understand their "abandonment" (sometimes referred to by war children as the "Betrayal of the Mother"), were desperately homesick and lonely. Marja Tähtinen suffered such terrible "homesickness" that she attempted to escape Sweden on a kicksled, was discovered, and was forced to wear her name tag for many weeks after.

Worse: many children believed their ordeal was "punishment" for displeasing their Finnish parents in some way, especially if they had been singled out from several siblings before being sent abroad. Undefined feelings of guilt often underscored not only their first banishment from Finland, but also their second banishment from Sweden. Somewhat older children who understood the reasons for their evacuation, and even voiced their desire to leave the ravages of war behind, experienced a different kind of guilt. Marja Barron "felt guilty" when she parted with her mother, because she believed that while she would be "in a safe place," her mother and brother would continue to be exposed to the chaos and hazards of war. It is also important to note that, upon their arrival in Sweden, many war children moved several times and were handed from one set of caretakers to another. Some of the least fortunate were sent to children's homes or a series of children's homes. According to Rossi, about 12,000 children were placed in orphanages in Sweden, some functioning as temporary housing while foster families were found, and some functioning as convalescent homes. Just as the quality of foster care varied from family to family, however, so too did the care children received in these holding centers. Some orphanages or children's homes had Finnish women employees, so that the children could at least keep their language. But with every move, of course, the initial trauma was intensified and compounded. The more times a child was moved and disoriented anew, the greater the collective trauma, which profoundly impacted many war children in later life.

Complications surrounding the war child transports didn't end with the last shipment of children returning to Finland. After World War II ended in 1945, and in spite of efforts on the part of the Finnish government to repatriate all evacuees, it proved impossible to bring home some 15,000 war children who remained in Sweden and some 500 who remained in Denmark. Due to the 1931 Treaty on Adoption in Nordic countries—a treaty that, in effect, protected the interests of foster parents in participating host countries—the written document signed by biological parents, which stated that their child or children would not be left abroad permanently, had no authority after 1945.[39] All legal procedures relating to adoption were thus carried out according to legislation in the host country. Many children were adopted against the will of their Finnish parents, who often fought tireless and futile legal battles to retrieve them. Tragically, although it was official Finnish policy that all war children be returned to Finland before 1950, many Finnish and Swedish parents were still fighting as late as 1956 for custody of these children. According to Rosnell, "there were hundreds of cases like that, in which [each] Finnish mother was left to grieve the loss of her child for the rest of her life."[40] As Korppi-Tommola has written, "Poor Finnish parents who did not speak Swedish and did not have legal advice, should have been supported legally. When looking back from today's perspective, these Finnish parents were not fairly treated."[41]

War Trauma Among the Finnish War Children

The endless variety and range of war child experiences invites comparison with an indifferently rotating roulette wheel. For those fortunate children sent to loving families, Sweden is often remembered as paradisiacal. But for those placed in homes where they felt unloved or valued merely as unpaid field hands, maids, or babysitters, Sweden is remembered as hell on earth. Marja Tähtinen, the little girl who tried to escape Sweden on a kicksled, was referred to by her foster mother as her "little cellar maid" and forced to do tiring domestic chores as an unpaid servant. "Rita Trent" was virtually given away at age eight to an American couple who immediately changed her name and put her to work cleaning their house. Soile Ilvesoksa was also eight when she was sent to Sweden and was put to work weeding fields of beets.[42] A small number of evacuees were even denied schooling and/or sufficient food and clothes.

Worse than functioning as unpaid labor, though, was physical and/or sexual abuse endured by some war children. According to a recent study by a Swedish war child association, at least 3–4 percent of all war children must have been abused—this based on statistics relating to any general population of children.[43] A one-year-old boy who was sent to a children's home was beaten with a leather strap and kept in a dark room both day and night. Others, mostly young girls, were raped by either their foster fathers or other caregivers. When 80,000 children are sent to largely unsupervised homes, one can understand how such abuse could occur. Eric Jaakkola was sent to Sweden at age six, together with his five-year-old sister. While Eric was sent to a loving family with which he bonded completely, his sister Airi suffered. Upon arrival at her foster parents' home,

Airi's clothes were given to her new foster sister, and Airi herself was forced to sleep in the attic. She was often spanked and punished by being locked in the bathroom where she was made to eat her meals.

The vast majority of war children are believed to have been treated decently, however. Lea Rehula and her sister Eila were twelve and ten, respectively, when they were sent to Sweden and placed with the same nurturing family. "Karina Heino," Peter Louhimo, "Eine Miller," Helena Nilsson, Veijo Paine, Ossi Rahkonen, Gertrud Rullander, and many others whose stories appear in this volume remember their time spent in Sweden as completely happy and even the "best time" of their lives. Many bonded so tightly with their foster families that it was the involuntary return to Finland that proved most traumatic. For these children, especially those who were very young when they were evacuated, it was the second banishment they remember as their worst childhood experience. Often these children had possessed no photos of their biological parents, nor had they communicated over months or years, so that their real mothers and fathers were virtual strangers to them upon their return. Not surprisingly, many children loathed their Finnish parents whom they even perceived as abductors or kidnappers. When her mother demanded her daughter back, Barron "was furious and never got over it." Paine "had hateful feelings toward my mother, which intensified after our departure" from Sweden. He "blamed her for taking me away from the Westers, but especially *Pappa*, the only father I had ever known. At the same time, I felt guilty for all of the hardship and anguish she [his mother] had experienced," Paine writes in his story.

Unless returnees had siblings who had also been sent to Sweden, they often endured intense longing for their foster families in complete isolation, without recourse to a sympathetic ear or even someone who could speak Swedish. Often, returning evacuees were taunted by siblings and schoolmates for their inability to speak Finnish, their strange accents, or their "different" clothes. Many were called *hurri*, a perjorative term for Swedish-speaking Finns, and were ridiculed for being "stupid." Seppo Mälkki admits that he was "bullied in Finland by my contemporaries, due to my having lived in the neutral and, therefore, more prosperous Sweden." For this reason he was "made fun of" and treated as "a kind of misfit." Gertrud Rullander remembers being spat upon by her schoolmates and having her ski equipment, a gift from Sweden, broken and burned by her contemporaries.

In addition to all this, the dwellings to which returning children were taken were often extremely primitive in comparison with their Swedish foster homes. Barron thought that her Finnish home "looked small and poor, and even smelled weird." Veijo Holopainen spent several years in Sweden, as did his sister, and like many war children he relates what "a shock it was for both of us to go from a comfortable life in Sweden to an extremely poor one in Finland."

Rosnell points out that the age of the child when he or she was sent to Sweden was extremely important to his or her experiences, and he writes that older evacuees with clear memories of their families and former life often adjusted better to their evacuation, while younger children were greatly traumatized. Here too, however, there were exceptions. Virve Palos was only two when she was sent to Sweden, having been placed by private arrangement with long-standing friends of the family. Both her foster parents and Finnish mother corresponded regularly. Virve's mother also visited her in Sweden, so that when Virve returned to Finland she recognized her mother at once and does not recall any particular trauma attached to her return. As she herself acknowledges, however, her circumstances were especially favorable.[44]

In contrast to Virve's case, Rosnell points out that the vast majority of children sent to Sweden when they were infants or toddlers

> soon forgot their biological family. They had no memories of them, and many Swedish foster parents encouraged this process by not telling the children where they had come from. Many Finnish boys and girls grew up in Sweden believing their [Swedish] fathers and mothers were their biological ones. To them it was a shock when they were told they were Finnish, or when they were summoned back to Finland, or when they eventually found out the truth by themselves.[45]

In *Krigsbarn erinran* (War Children Recalling Memories), Almgren's Swedish collection of Finnish war child stories, one author who signs herself only as "Anja" describes how at age two-and-a-half years old she was sent to Sweden and was abused by her mentally ill foster mother before being reassigned to loving foster parents with whom she bonded. Hoping to adopt Anja, they kept her biological family secret, so that after seven years in Sweden, "the shock was great when a letter came from Finland where my biological mother wrote that she wanted me back." Imagine going from a loving family and a large farm to a "home consisting of one room where seven people lived."[46] Even for somewhat older children who might have remembered their Finnish families, the news of having to rejoin them could come as a cruel blow. Sirpa Kaukinen was five when she left for Sweden in 1944. A year later she was cutting paper dolls when her foster parents gently informed her that she would soon have to return to Finland. Describing the scene, she writes that "to the amazement of myself and my family, I began cutting and cutting until the good tablecloth fell to either side of the table in two pieces. I started to cry, and *Mamma* pulled me into her lap, and everyone began crying."

Upon repatriation, such traumas might have been alleviated had biological parents been able to discuss their children's experiences abroad.

Kavén—who, like "Anja," was two and a half when sent to Sweden—continues to lament the impossibility of speaking with his real father and mother after his return because they apparently felt guilty about what they had done. "I did not want guilt," he writes, but "only to know and understand" the reasons why he had been sent away. "It is sad," he writes, "that we have not been able to grieve over this matter together." Instead, Kavén recalls that, "As a child, I felt that my sisters had a closer relationship with my parents than I, and I felt myself to be an outsider."[47] Rauno Juntunen experienced similar feelings of envy and alienation from his biological parents upon his compulsory return to Finland: "In Sweden I got love and care from my foster parents. Here [in Finland] I many times watched how the five-year-old [younger] brother could climb and sit in our father's arms [and] I wondered why I couldn't be treated the same way, sit and hug." Like Kavén, Juntunen never felt as close to his Finnish parents as he did to his foster parents; additionally, his living circumstances in Finland were very primitive in contrast to Sweden. Luckily for him, Juntunen returned to Sweden permanently quite soon thereafter. In describing his final departure from Finland he writes, "I was not sorry at all leaving the house which had been my home for two and a half years."

Peter Heinl, a celebrated psychiatrist and therapist in Great Britain and Germany who specializes in war-related trauma, discusses the catastrophic impact of "polytrauma": the "network of causally related traumas or a cluster of coinciding, concomitant or sequentially occurring traumas" in many of his patients, mostly those who, as children, lived in Germany during World War II. About these war children, Heinl writes that many of his patients "had suffered more in their short [childhood] lives than many adults, during their whole lifespan." In adulthood their "trauma[s] had not simply faded away nor had the (post-)war children simply 'grown out' of them. Quite the contrary, the polytrauma had remained virulent even after the passage of decades." Heinl discusses the "collective catastrophes" often experienced by war children, which "tend to shift the axis of normality and to distort the measuring stick of perception of what constitutes a trauma."[48]

That trauma may even be inherited by the offspring of war children or those intimately impacted by war. Heinl and other psychoanalysts and therapists have witnessed the "transmission of early traumatic experiences across generations, the so-called transgenerational effect."[49] I myself have been contacted by two offspring of Finnish war children who felt that their parents' war traumas had clouded their own childhoods and in one case even damaged the lives of grandchildren two generations removed. In both cases the former war children (whose stories are not related here) had been moved several times between shifting sets of caretakers and had clearly experienced the "polytrauma" or the effect of "collective catastrophes" that Heinl describes.

Heinl himself laments the fact that even after 1945, child psychiatry and child psychotherapy were still "in their infancy." In addition, in the aftermath of war, "traumatized families, and indeed societies, are hardly able to muster the resources for a sophisticated psychological support if existential issues such as housing, clothing, food, and heating are at stake." He agrees with Rosnell on the importance of the age a child was when he or she was evacuated and writes that "A given trauma impacting the mental world of a tiny baby, of a six-year-old child, or of a fifteen-year-old adolescent, may produce rather differing long-term consequences."[50]

For infants and very young children, loss of a parental figure is especially traumatic and can result in a lifelong inability to create lasting relationships.[51] Virtala reminds us that there is an important mirror stage in children's development, which is necessary to build a harmonious base from which to start the identity process. If children do not have positive reflections from their mothers during these early years, they will seek that mirror for the rest of their lives.[52] She adds that "When Finnish war children were removed during this important phase of life, they were subjected to this trauma."

Virtala notes too that, as Anna Freud observed of British child evacuees, often very young children will attempt to cope with their loss through important "transitional objects." In reading Finnish war child literature, Virtala sees an "endless variation in the transitional objects." These "objects" may be activities or places as well as inanimate things, including "Finnish magazines, swimming in the Gulf of Bothnia toward home, a secret hut [to replace] their home in Finland, nature sites like a cave or a brook."[53] Maternal deprivation, as Bowlby has described it, can result in a seemingly endless search for a substitute that will always prove inadequate.[54]

Literature can also be used as a coping or rescuing mechanism. Rauni Janser describes how, after having been placed with her Swedish foster family, she immediately came to the conclusion that her foster mother was a "witch" who might be fattening her to kill like the rabbits she kept in cages in the yard. But on the morning after her first night in this frightening new place, she awakened to find a man, lying on a bed on the other side of the room. He smiled at her and suddenly she knew that she was not the prisoner of a witch, since witches in such stories as *Hansel and Gretel* "don't have husbands." Historian and Brothers Grimm authority Maria Tatar explains that "fairy tales register an effort on the part of both women and men to develop maps for coping with personal anxieties, family concerns, social frictions, and the myriad frustrations of everyday life."[55]

Food was also something many war children turned to, to alleviate their sorrows and homesickness. In *The Uses of Enchantment*, Bruno Bettelheim identifies bread as a metaphor for mother love, an idea expressed about food generally and frequently by the war children who often became attached to their new foster mothers through the medium of food and being fed.[56]

In contrast with those war children who bonded with foster mothers through food, Juha Hankkila describes the comfort he derived from eating delicious pancakes or custard slices he received on the sly from neighbors and the village baker because his foster mother was stingy with food as well as affection.

It is doubtful, however, that most war children found sufficient compensation for the loss of their biological families and native language in transitional objects or even in plentiful food and hugs from their foster parents. Many studies have shown that most, if not all, war children were injured for life. Pentti Andersson has concluded that "compared to non-evacuees, Finnish refugees exhibit a significantly higher level of PTSD" symptoms on the Post-Traumatic Stress Disorder Checklist.[57] Andersson also compares the Finnish war children to "Jewish children who came to Sweden from Nazi concentration camps" in terms of their "forced displacement … loss of parental figures of origin, loss of spoken language, and loss of family history." Both groups of war children had no survival strategy other than living with their own fear of rejection. He concludes that such trauma "led to permanent consequences in adult life."[58] Former war child Mona Serenius describes how as an adult she

> locked away the child which I carried inside me, behind walls, back into the shelter. Partly, I believe, to protect this vulnerable living core from more hurt, but also because I could not endure the overwhelming feelings of sorrow and hate, love and guilt, hidden within this child. [… Her life] felt like a series of compartments, with no connection between them [… like] Russian dolls, with many colourful but empty shells, one within the other, hiding … a small solid core deep inside it.[59]

As the result of sequential ruptures in their childhood routines and surroundings, many Finnish war children never really felt they "belonged" in any one place in particular and have suffered from the emptiness that Serenius describes. Many of them have lived their adult lives in states of suspended animation and experienced difficulty trusting other people or retaining relationships.

As Heinl explains, the more a child was moved, the more he or she was traumatized, and many war children were frequently transferred from one foster family to another. Bodil Söderberg remembers that just as she was getting over her homesickness and developing a fondness for her foster Swedish mother, they "took the steamboat to Uddevalla one day. At the boat dock was a strange lady and a little girl whom I had never met. This was how they had planned to do the transfer to the other family!" Söderberg writes that she had "a sort of meltdown and screamed and cried so hard" that her first foster mother said the little girl could stay with her after all.

Official Recognition of Mistakes Made, Attempts at Redress, and Ongoing Studies

After the first appearance of war child memoirs in the 1970s and 1980s, more followed in the 1990s. War child societies actively encouraged the sharing of stories, and public acknowledgment and interest spread. In September 1994, one popular Finnish newspaper ran on its first page the headline printed in capital letters: "THIS MUST NEVER BE REPEATED." The article that followed was written in response to a psychological study that had been recently published, which announced that war children who had repressed their memories, often for decades, had suffered throughout their lives from disproportionately high rates of divorce, suicide, alcoholism, affective disorders of various kinds, and self-punishing guilt.

Only in 2005 was the plight of the war children officially recognized when, in apparent acknowledgement of wartime mistakes made by both countries, Sweden's King Gustav XVI and Tarja Halonen, then president of Finland, presided jointly over the installation of a statue named *Ero* (Separation) on the Finnish-Swedish border where the vast majority of war children crossed into Sweden. Other commemoration plaques have been erected in honor of the war children in both Finland and Sweden. Also, in 2005 the film *Den bästa av mödrar* (Mother of Mine) won international recognition, further increasing public interest.[60] In *Mother of Mine*, director Klaus Härö relates the touching story of ten-year-old Heikki, who is transported "with an address label tied around his neck, together with 600 other children in the cargo hold of the ship *Arcturus*," to Sweden in 1944. In an interview published in 2005 in the *Svenska Dagbladet*, Härö provides another explanation as to why the child transports and experiences of the Finnish war children only began to be discussed in the mid-1980s and 1990s:

> When the war was over, there was so much misery to deal with that people felt the war children should keep quiet and be thankful for how good they had it during the war compared to everyone else. Later, when things started going well for Finland during the 1950s, people didn't want to talk about the war anymore, they wanted to forget, so the war children never got a chance to share their experiences, either the good or the bad ones.[61]

Several documentaries on the war children have also appeared in recent years. One film director, Erja Dammert, was interviewed for Helsinki's chief newspaper, the *Helsingin Sanomat*. In that interview, which appeared on November 11, 2003, Dammert remarks on the widespread insensitivity of adults during the prewar, war, and postwar years. Dammert claims she read that "in the 1930s, children sometimes underwent surgery without anaesthesia, because it was believed that their emotions were not sufficiently developed" to feel pain! She also lists egregious errors relating to the war child transports, adding—significantly—that "there is much that adults could learn from the survival mechanisms of children."

Some resolute former war children are doing more than "learning." Kai Rosnell—frequently referred to this introduction and a journalist by profession—has dedicated his retirement to the cause of the war children. For fourteen years since 1999, Rosnell has edited *Finska Krigsbarn*, a quarterly magazine published for Sweden's nationwide association of war children, and has contributed innumerable articles to it. More than that: he has led investigations on behalf of many dozens of war children who desired to find lost relatives and has, through intense digging and detective work, reunited hundreds of war children with their long-lost families. He has reunited not only Finnish war children who wanted to rediscover their Finnish families, but Swedes who wanted to be reunited with former foster children. Rosnell has also challenged the laws in both Finland and Sweden that make it difficult for abused war children to seek compensation even when they have the clearest evidence of prolonged sexual or physical abuse. In accordance with the Convention of Children's Rights, he has even helped some former war children discover the paternity of fathers who abandoned them. As of October 2013, and thanks in part to Rosnell's efforts, the Finnish Supreme Court of Justice is working to effect changes in the law.

Rosnell has never received remuneration for his work on behalf of war children, but in December 2012—and in recognition of his extraordinary service—Sauli Niinistö, president of the Finnish Republic, awarded Rosnell the First Class Medal of the White Rose of Finland with Golden Cross. Tapani Rossi, who has also dedicated his retirement to the cause of Finnish war children, received the same decoration on the same day for his outstanding accomplishments on their behalf.

Keeping their cause alive, war child associations in Finland, Sweden, and Denmark continue to collect as many stories and memoirs as possible. Still other efforts include the War Child Memory Project sponsored by the Central Organization of War Child Associations in Finland. This project, currently being conducted by Stenius-Aarniala and Inkinen, involves collecting hundreds of stories or fragments of stories from war children otherwise unlikely to have recorded their reminiscences for posterity. Stenius-Aarniala and Inkinen created and circulated a questionnaire that is greatly facilitating this process. Almgren, who is frequently quoted here, has worked to make November 20, the date on which the General Assembly of the United Nations adopted the Convention on the Rights of the Child, to be known as "A Day for the Children of War" in Sweden, England, and elsewhere. Her goal is to make this an internationally observed occasion on which to remember all war children: past, present, and future.

Tiina Kinnunen and Markku Jokisipilä have referred to the recent, European-wide "memory boom" in all matters relating to World War II and to burgeoning "memory communities," such as the war child associations that exist today in Finland, Sweden, and Denmark. "For many" war children, Kinnunen and Jokisipilä remind us, "writing either for folklore collections or with the aim of publishing one's reminiscences, functions as a route to the therapeutic catharsis of traumatic emotions."[62] In other words, despite the decades-long Finnish war censure, many war children have themselves taken steps toward healing as autobiographers and members of associations. In a speech delivered in 2002 about her own memoir, Serenius talked about the "extraordinary experience" of sharing her story "with those who had had the same childhood experiences, and were better able to understand beyond words" what her own childhood trauma had been. Finding fellow war children, she said, "was suddenly [like] acquiring a large family of sisters and brothers, and filled [her] with a deep sense of community."[63]

The dozens of war children who have shared their childhood narratives with me have done so, I believe, to liberate caged memories that have haunted them from childhood, to achieve peace, and to gain a deeper appreciation of who they are. Working with and learning from them, I too have come to better know myself and to admire the persistence and resourcefulness of children in peril.

My Collecting and Editing Process

Because I speak neither Finnish nor Swedish, in the beginning of my quest for war children and their stories I had to advertise my interest in American-Finnish newsletters and, later, in war child association magazines. Eventually, though, my interest spread by word of mouth and what began as a single story grew into a small but for me miraculous avalanche. Whenever I heard from a war child, it was cause for celebration. And whenever I received a new story—or usually the kernel of one—I was thrilled, though the content of developing stories often reduced me to tears.

Since 2001 I have been in contact with more than sixty Finnish war children living in Australia, Canada, England, Finland, Sweden, and the United States, and I am sorry that I can neither mention them all nor include all their stories. In most cases I have exchanged dozens or many dozens of e-mails and/or letters with each war child. With Virve Palos alone, one of my earliest correspondents, I have exchanged hundreds of e-mails, not only about her war child story but about anything regarding Finland or of general interest to us both. Initially Virve wrote to say that she had read a notice about my interest in the *Suomi-American* magazine. In May 2003 my husband and I visited Tampere where Virve lives, and in September 2005 I visited her a second time. It was through e-mails and interviews that I was able to piece Virve's war child story together—although I was the student and she the coach—and her story must stand as an example of them all.

Because Virve speaks and writes excellent English, my job was made much easier than it otherwise would have been. Even with Virve's story, however, I sometimes made slight changes to her wording so that it would be more idiomatic in English. In other instances I made changes to earlier statements Virve herself corrected in later messages. In one e-mail, for instance, she had referred to a "red tree house," which she later revised, writing, "I should have written red-painted wooden house." This going back and forth with my questions and my correspondents' answers has been typical of the process in bringing stories together. It has not been the only process I have adopted, however, because I have also interviewed several war children while visiting them in Finland, Sweden, and the United States. To compile Gertrud Rullander's story I first transcribed tape recordings she mailed to me and later visited her in Sweden to discuss and further clarify her wartime experiences.

Some of the stories required extensive explanation to my inquiries and developed in painstakingly piecemeal fashion. Others arrived in nearly complete form. What follows, of course, is material that Finnish- and/or Swedish-speaking war children have drafted in English: a language that is not their native tongue. However, many war children have informed me that writing their stories in English has actually helped them feel more "objective" about their often traumatic experiences. Others have thanked me for helping them heal and better understand the remarkable and often distressing experiences of their now-distant yet, for many, ever-present pasts. With regard to story titles, some were suggested by the narrators, but the majority I have derived from phrases, anecdotes, or images embedded in the stories themselves with the approval of the authors. In order not to privilege one story over another, I have alphabetized them according to the first letter of the last name, whether it be real or invented. Of the thirty-nine stories here, five appear under pseudonyms (and within quotation marks) to indicate anonymity.

It has been said that truth is soonest found among the very young and the very old. Here we have in every story the combined truth from the perspectives of both childhood and relative old age, and it is always spoken from the heart. What began for me as curiosity about a little-known aspect of World War II soon became something of an obsession and, later, a labor of love. I can only hope that readers will find the stories in this volume as fascinating as I do, and that the appearance of these stories in print will bring some measure of gratification and catharsis for its contributors.

Notes

1. Estimates of military losses vary. One estimate is that some 94,000 Finnish soldiers either died or went missing in action. See Tiina Kinnunen and Ville Kivimäki, eds., *Finland in World War II: History, Memory, Interpretations* (Leiden and Boston: Brill, 2012), 172.
2. Irene Virtala, "Identity Processes in Autobiographies by Finnish War Children," in *Entering Multiculturalism: Finnish Experiences Abroad*, ed. Olavi Koivukangas (Turku: Institute of Migration, 2002), 240.
3. Aura Korppi-Tommola, "War and Children in Finland during the Second World War," *Paedogogica Historica* 44, no. 4 (August 2008): 451.
4. See Pentti Andersson, "Post-Traumatic Symptoms linked to Hidden Holocaust Trauma Among adult Finnish Evacuees Separated from Their Parents as Children in World War II, 1939–1945: A Case-Control Study," *International Psychogeriatrics* [Turku, Finland] 23, no. 4 (2011): 659.
5. See, for instance, Martin Parsons, *War Child: Children Caught in Conflict* (Gloucestershire: Tempus, 2008); Kjersti Ericsson and Eva Simonsen, *Children of World War II: The Hidden Enemy Legacy* (Oxford: Berg, 2005); and Lynn Nicholas, *Cruel World: The Children of Europe in the Nazi Web* (New York: Alfred A. Knopf, 2005).
6. Annu Edvardsen, *Det får inte hända igen: Finska krigsbarn 1939-45* (Stockholm: Askild & Kärnekull, 1977).
7. See Sinikka Ortmark Almgren, *Du som haver barnen kär* (Stockholm: LT, 1989).
8. Virtala, Summary Abstract, *Finnish War Children in Literature* [Web Reports No. 5] (Turku: Migrationsinstitutet, 2004). Unpaginated.
9. Pertti Kavén, *70,000 små öden* (Stockholm: Sahlgrens, 1985).
10. Kavén, Summary Abstract, "Under the Shadow of Humanity" (dissertation: University of Helsinki, 2010).
11. Parsons. *War Child,* 158.
12. Kai Rosnell, "The Complexity of the War Child Movement from Finland to Sweden and Denmark, 1939–1946," *New World Finn* 13, no. 1 (2012): 23.
13. Veikko Inkinen to the present author in personal correspondence.
14. Ann-Maj Danielsen, *Att inte höra till: ett finskt krigsbarn berättar* (Stockholm: B. Wahlström, 2000), 8–10.
15. The Finnish government signed no treaty of alliance with Nazi Germany, but with Germany's military and material assistance Finland was able to recapture territories lost in the Winter War.
16. Before they invaded Finland, the Soviet Union offered military assistance in the event that Germany attacked Russia by way of Finnish soil. But Finland refused to

cede the Hanko Peninsula, the western part of the Karelian Isthmus, and islands in the eastern Gulf of Finland to the USSR.
17. Finland was proved right not to succumb to Soviet pressure. When the USSR signed a nonaggression pact with Germany, the so-called Molotov-Ribbentrop Pact, it included a "Secret Additional Protocol," which stated that—like Estonia, Latvia, and Lithuania—Finland was to "belong to the Soviet Union" after the war. See Martin Parsons, ed., *Children: The Invisible Victims of War—An Interdisciplinary Study* (Denton, Peterborough: DSM, 2008), 213–23.
18. Eloise Engle and Lauri Paananen, *The Winter War: The Soviet Attack on Finland, 1838–1940* (Harrisburg, PA: Stackpole, 1992), 16.
19. Winston Churchill, in a radio broadcast to the British people, January 20, 1940.
20. Philip Jowett and Brent Snodgrass, *Finland at War: 1939-45* (Oxford: Osprey, 2006), 5–10.
21. Lempi Kähönen-Wilson, *Sisu Mother* (St. Cloud, MN: North Star, 2002), 16.
22. Korppi-Tommola, "War and Children in Finland," 446.
23. Ibid.
24. Thérèse Bonney, "Children in Peril," *Collier's* no. 112 (July 3, 1943): 20.
25. Martha Gelhorn, "Death in the Present Tense," *Collier's* 105 (February 20, 1940): 15. For additional information on Finland's wars, see Max Jakobson, *Finland Survived: An Account of the Finnish-Soviet Winter War, 1939* (Helsinki: Otava, 1961); Leonard C. Lundin, *Finland in the Second World War* (Bloomington: Indiana University Press, 1957); and Kinnunen and Kivimäki, *Finland in World War II*.
26. Bowlby's work appeared in several places during 1938 and 1940, but his principal publications bear later dates. See John Bowlby et al., *Children in War-time* (London: New Educational Fellowship, 1940). See too Anna Freud and Dorothy T. Burlingham, *War and Children* (New York: Medical War Books, 1943; reprinted Westport, CT: Greenwood, 1943).
27. Engle and Paananen, *The Winter War,* 148.
28. During the Lapland War, October 1944 to April 1945, another 30,000 children were evacuated, many of them refugees from northern Finland, although most of these were relocated within Finland itself.
29. Statistics vary according to different sources, but the consensus appears to be that at least 15,000 Finnish war children were permanently lost to Sweden.
30. Rosnell. "The Complexity of the War Child Movement," 22.
31. See *Historical Statistics of Sweden, Second Edition, 1720–1967* (Stockholm: National Central Bureau of Statistics: 1969); and Rosnell, "The Complexity of the War Child Movement," 24.
32. Rosnell, "The Complexity of the War Child Movement," 22.
33. The windows of Finnish houses were also blackened to evade Soviet bomber plane detection. Some referred to the blackout curtains as "Molotov curtains" after the Russian who had cosigned the 1939 Ribbentrop-Molotov pact that would have divided Europe between Germany and Russia. "Molotov cocktails," which the Finns devised and used so effectively throughout the war, were also named after this archenemy of the Finns.
34. Kavén, *70,000 små öden,* 27–30.
35. Information provided by Tapani Rossi in communication with the present author. See too Rossi, *Räddade till livet: om en stor svensk hjälpinsats för Finlands barn*

1939–1949 [Their Lives Were Saved: The Swedish Relief Effort for Finland's Children, 1939–1949] (Höör, Sweden: self-published, 2008).
36. See Nicholas, *Cruel World,* 169ff.
37. See Rossi, *Räddade till livet.*
38. An observation made at the International War Child Conference held from September 9–11, 2009, at the University of Reading, England. The passage was provided by Ms. Brita Stenius-Aarniala in communication with the present author; it was taken from the paper she presented at the conference identified above.
39. Parsons, *War Child,* 164.
40. The quotation comes from Rosnell, "Searching for War Children": a lecture delivered at "FinnFest 2013" held in Hancock, Michigan; June 19–23, 2013. See too Kavén, *70,000 små öden,* 129–30.
41. Korppi-Tommola, "War and Children," 441.
42. For other examples of similar mistreatment, see Sue Saffle, "Children, War, and the Rhetoric of Remembrance: The Stories of Finland's War Children," *Children in War* [Reading] 1, no. 4 (November 2006): 97–103. NB: some of the stories that appear in the present volume have also appeared, albeit in different and less complete versions, in the following articles: Saffle, "Toward a Collection of Finnish War-Child Stories: The Reminiscences of Seppo Mälkki," *Children in War* 1, no. 5 (January 2008): 25–31; "Understanding Backwards: The Story of Finnish War Child Veijo (Pönniäinen) Paine," *Children in War* 1, no. 6 (February 2009): 77–84; and "The Stuff of Fairy Tales: Finnish War Child Rauni Janser Remembers," *Children in War* 1, no. 7 (February 2010): 85–92.
43. According to the *Riksförbundet Finska Krigsbarn.* Information provided to the present author.
44. For additional information about Virve's positive war child experiences in Sweden, see Saffle, "'A Happier War Child Story': One Finnish War Child's Exceptional Memories and Circumstances," in *Children: The Invisible Victims of War—An Interdisciplinary Study,* ed. Martin Parsons (Denton, Peterborough: DSM, 2008), 213–23.
45. Rosnell. "The Complexity of the War Child Movement," 25.
46. Sinikka Ortmark Almgren, *Krigsbarns erinran: snäll, lydig och tacksam* (Stockholm: SinOA, 2003), 52.
47. Kavén, in conversation with the present author.
48. Peter Heinl, *Splintered Innocence: An Intuitive Approach to Treating War Trauma* (London and New York: Routledge. 2001), 70–72.
49. Ibid, 50.
50. Ibid, 78–82.
51. See note 26 above. See too John Bowlby, *Attachment and Loss,* 2nd ed. (New York: Basic Books, 1999).
52. Virtala, *Finnish War Children in Literature.*
53. Ibid.
54. See notes 26 and 51 above.
55. Maria Tatar, "Introduction," *The Classic Fairy Tales,* ed. Tatar (New York: W.W. Norton, 1999), xi.
56. Bruno Bettelheim, *The Uses of Enchantment* (New York: Vintage, 1977), 159.
57. See Andersson, "Post-Traumatic Symptoms."
58. Ibid.

59. Mona Serenius, "The Silent Cry: A Finnish Child during World War II and 50 Years Later," *International Forum of Psychoanalysis* 4 (1995): 40–41.
60. According to https://www.barbican.org.uk/education/event-detail.asp?id=5189&pg=514 (accessed October 22, 2013) and other online sources, *Mother of Mine* won thirty awards internationally—including the Ingmar Bergman Award and recognitions of various kinds at the Cairo International Film Festival, the Lübeck Nordic Film Days, and the Palm Springs International Film Festival. *Mother of Mine* was Finland's and Sweden's nominee for a 2005 Oscar.
61. Translated from the *Svenska Dagbladet* [Stockholm] (November 7, 2005).
62. Kinnunen and Kivimäki, *Finland in World War II*, 475–76.
63. See note 59 above. Information about the speech was mailed to the present author.

1

The Work of Sorrow
Marja Hultin Barron

In the fall of 1939, when it looked like Russia was going to attack Finland, we lived in a large building in the center of Turku where my father, Heikki Hultin, worked as a superintendent or caretaker. I was four at this time, and I remember him letting me "help" him repair plumbing, elevators, and so forth. He would also take me to the top terrace of the building and show me the view all the way to the sea. He was my everything. He and mother were thirty, and my brother Jukka was born that summer.

When the bombardments began, women and children were evacuated into the countryside. Father's elderly parents knew a farmer at Parainen on the coast, and mother, Jukka, and I went there to live in a spare room in the attic of a big red house. Earlier, father had completed his armed service in the navy and now had to be retrained for land fighting. Around Christmas and before being sent to the frontier, he took off from the barracks in Turku on a bicycle, as public transportation had stopped. It was extremely cold when in heavy snow he made his way more than twenty miles to see us. I woke up when he was lifting the baby in his arms towards the light bulb hanging from the ceiling. He was admiring "Daddy's little man," and I was told to go back to sleep. In the morning he was gone.

In March my mother heard that he had been reported missing in action at Pienpero on the Karelian isthmus, and she was crushed. I remember her lying under a blanket with dark red flowers on it with her face turned to the wall, hoping that she could die to be next to Heikki. And, now, whenever I see that blanket, horrible sad thoughts come to me. Because father's body was never found, a funeral service was arranged for him in Turku, and a white sheet was to be placed in the empty grave.[1] I wondered why, when we didn't have much, a good sheet should be used. My relatives were crying, and I was given pansies, which I was told to throw into the grave. I protested, wanting to keep them, but finally I threw them in. My mother and the other women wore black veils, and to this day it still makes me shudder when I think of those times.

During the interim peace from March 1940 to June 1941, my mother, brother, and I were transported by horse and sleigh to Turku. I thought it was an exciting adventure, but mother could only cry. When we tried to return to our home, we were forbidden by the proprietress, as father was no longer providing services for the building. So we went to live in mother's childhood home. Many buildings and houses had been destroyed by Russian bombs, so mother felt her small family should be pleased to move into this house now shared by many. I remember that we chopped wood for the cooking stove and carried it up from the crawl space assigned to us by grandmother. From a well some hundred yards away, we winched water up in a bucket, then walked up steps that were icy from spills to bring it home. How unpleasant it was to live on rationed food and use the outhouse!

Mother made sacrifices, feeding her children first, though she was terribly thin and anemic. We grew potatoes, vegetables, berries, and apples in the yard and rabbits in hutches. To feed the rabbits, we collected grass from the roadside and dried it in the attic. One Christmas, mother's mother prepared a rabbit for dinner, and its fur was used in clothing. Most Christmases we spent at father's parents where his memory was maintained as that of a hero, having given his life so that we could live in a free country. When I missed father, I would cry and be told to stop because he was in heaven with Jesus. Although mother had suitors she never married, always hoping for her Heikki to return.

Father's family knew people in the country, and his sister Judith would bring us goods that we needed. Grandmother's sisters who lived in the United States also sent parcels with soap, candy, and clothing, which was taken apart and made into new garments. Through an organization in Helsinki, an older unmarried woman in Sweden got our address and sent us small sums of money as well.

When Russian hostilities resumed in June 1941, I remember not wanting to undress when going to bed in case we'd have to run to the shelter if the alarm sounded to warn Russian airplanes were approaching. Mother taught us to pile all our clothes on a chair like firemen, so as to quickly get them on. When the alarm sounded, we would run into a neighbor's cellar into which people crowded. Children slept on top of potatoes while people prayed and sang hymns in the dark or by candlelight. When we did not make it to the shelter and bombs were already falling, we sat at the bottom of the stairs with mother hugging us to her sides, and I asked, "Mother, are we going to die now?" She answered, "I do not know, but the main thing is that we are together."

Early in 1942, a Swedish women's organization invited war widows to a Swedish resort called Kungshamn. Dozens of mothers with children traveled from Turku in the hold of a ship. I was happy with our top bunk and enjoyed the excitement as ice floes beat loudly on the side. From the Stockholm harbor, we continued on a bus and were welcomed by volunteers for the organization in a large white villa on a hill where we were given nourishing food and good used clothes. Swedes wishing to take Finnish children into foster care came to pick the ones they liked, and everybody wanted my two-year-old blonde, blue-eyed brother, but mother would not part with him. At this time I was six and was asked to stay with a smiling, childless, middle-aged couple. I looked them over and, whereas I did not want to be separated from mother and Jukka, I said I'd stay because they promised me clothes and much good food. When mother and Jukka left it was bittersweet, standing on the shore watching their boat passing through a channel in the ice made by an ice-breaker. I worried about them returning to our war-torn homeland, was unhappy for being left behind, and felt guilty but also relieved to be staying in a safe place. Staying at Kungshamn until the Swedish couple came for me, I remember trying to say farewell again to mother and Jukka whose boat from Stockholm to Finland would have to pass the resort. Seeing the ship, I went on to the ice and waved like mad. The big boys chuckled at me, saying, "They won't see you from the ship!"

Finally my new foster parents, the Lindbergs, arrived to fetch me. I liked the big smiling fellow and the tidy businesswoman who took me in. My German-born foster mother, Gabriella Lindberg, whom I called "*Tant* (Aunt) Jella," was forty-two, and "*Farbror* (Uncle) August" was even older. They lived in Stockholm in a very nice apartment, where I was given a room behind the kitchen. But I was afraid of sleeping alone, so to soothe my fears, *Tant* Jella brought me toys, which she said would protect me from the boogey-men. My foster parents were good to me, and the story goes that I learned Swedish in two weeks. We shopped by streetcar. After the scarcity of things in Finland, it was wonderful to see the abundance of shoes, dresses, and bags, and to stop in a café where I got to eat a piece of wonderful cake with green marzipan on top. *Tant* Jella felt that I was too skinny and was determined to fatten me up, asking me to drink cream, which I enjoyed.

I also enjoyed our summer vacations at an old farm the couple had purchased in the countryside where I helped *Farbror* August clear the forest, swam in a lake, and was asked to sing by visitors to the country. My singing voice often entertained passengers on trains, and in the barn, I sang to animals pretending I was on a stage.

Perhaps due to the privations my family and I had experienced in Finland, I felt somewhat uncomfortable during my seventh birthday party. Kids from nearby farms brought little gifts, and I had never had that kind of attention before. Surely I was spoiled by the Lindbergs, but they also practiced German discipline and enforced strict rules. Eventually, the Lindbergs asked to adopt me, and I wanted to stay and be their own child, but mother demanded I be sent home to start first grade. I was furious and never got over it. In fact, I believe my moving to the United States in 1967 had something to do with my anger of not being allowed to stay with the Lindbergs. Mom did not want me to stay in the United States permanently, but maybe I subconsciously thought, *I'll show you.*

At the end of September 1942, I returned to Finland by plane where my mother met me in Turku. At this point, I understood no Finnish, but some of my relatives knew Swedish. I also saw my old home with different eyes. The home looked small and poor, even smelled weird. I was unhappy and explained it clearly. The food too was miserable, I thought. In addition, I didn't get along with my playmates. Because the neighborhood kids did not understand me, I kicked them. I was homesick for Stockholm and behaved badly, making my opinions known. Luckily, my first grade teacher helped me to cope by encouraging my singing talent.

I was happy to be invited back to Sweden for summer holidays. In the early summer of 1943 when I was eight, I was sent on a train with other children to Tornio, Finland, on the Swedish border. From Haaparanta (the Finnish name for Haparanda, Sweden), the train made its way to Stockholm, and for me it was a happy adventure, knowing I'd be with the Lindbergs again. I helped the smaller children and eventually climbed to sleep in the netlike hat rack. Once over the border, kind ladies fed us as much oatmeal porridge as we wanted, with sugar on top!

Tant Jella's hobbies were painting and listening to classical music on the radio. She was teaching me to be a little lady, which was not easy, as I was a tomboy. But she helped me to appreciate the arts. I was also taught to keep my clothes neat and shoes shining, though the latter was difficult, because I loved to kick—stones, balls, anything. Young boys laughed at my then still broken Swedish, but *Tant* Jella kept me company, teaching me how to bake and clean with a vacuum cleaner, which was new to me. I was also kept from bothering *Farbror* August, a politically important man who was even consulted by the king on several occasions. When Jella and August didn't want me to understand their conversations, they spoke in German, which made me hate that language.

When I returned from Stockholm in September of 1943, the bombardments accelerated, and I was sent to live with a farmer's family thirty miles from Turku. They had requested a boy to keep their nine-year-old son company but were satisfied with me, though at first they complained that I had learned to be snobbish and lazy in Sweden. I griped about the food and was quickly put in line. I also attended school, but I did not like the farm kids and the teaching, which was of a lower quality than what we had in town. After Karelia was surrendered to the Russians, I also disliked sharing the main room of the farmhouse with evacuees, but I was told that it was everybody's duty to help them.

When peace finally came, I returned to Turku, and when I was ten the Lindbergs arrived unexpectedly to visit us. Mother was shy and embarrassed that these fine people saw our simple home. When I was thirteen, I went again to Stockholm to visit the Lindbergs. Upon my return to Finland, *Farbror* August saw me off and, hugging me, he smiled and said, "When you are on board, I'll leave. No use for us to stand there and glower at each other." I must have looked sad, and he said: "You are a big girl now, chin up!" These were words of wisdom that I remembered the rest of my life: when something is final, it is of no use to glower at it. Chin up!

Back in Finland, my mother wanted me to become a seamstress or hairdresser because she could not afford an expensive higher education. She was overwhelmed by the responsibilities of taking care of two wild kids and by the cost of feeding and clothing us with her small pension, which she supplemented by sewing at home after taking dressmaking classes arranged by the government for war widows. I helped out with daily chores, such as cooking, washing, bringing in wood and water, and minding Jukka. But mother's burdens made her tired, depressed, and nervous, and she did not have the patience to guide me as *Tant* Jella had.

Despite my mother's desire that I go to vocational school, I persisted in my dream for higher education. I worked to contribute to my board and room, and, during days off school, I worked as a bicycle messenger for a florist, in an office, and later as a gardener's helper in the archipelago. Later, when I attended business school, I worked in the post office, in a bank, and as a long-distance operator. I have always worked hard, and my years of scarcity have given me a life-long aversion to waste. My grandnephew today refers to me as "Ekamarja," since I am a conscientious recycler in Turku where I have been retired for several years.

It was only a short time before my mother's death that she agreed to discuss her feelings caused by father's death. I learned that a clergyman had informed her that father had been injured in a hit on his troops' dugout shelter. When Heikki was taken away on a truck, he wrote on a cigarette box: "Goodbye, dear mother and father. I bleed for Finland. Take care of my wife and children." He also gave his watch and ring to a good friend who brought them to Heikki's parents, and today these are dear mementos that I share with my brother Jukka. Heikki apparently bled to death in a field hospital. When the corpses were transported from the frontier, the enemy, thinking there was ammunition on the train, bombarded it. Mother imagined that her one-legged husband had been lying in a ditch and had rotted there, and I imagined his bones lying under a pine with foxes carrying them around.

After *Farbror* August died, I visited *Tant* Jella in the 1970s and corresponded with her until her death. I made sure she knew how thankful I was for everything they had done for me. In retrospect, my time spent with the Lindbergs was the best in my life next to my first four years when father was still with us. I was never mom's little girl. She and Jukka were always extremely close, but I had been Dad's little girl. When he went MIA when I was four, I felt terribly alone.

As long as I can remember, I was sad and cried. As a teenager, I contemplated suicide. Many years later, I asked a psychologist, when will this crying end? She suggested that I cry hard when I felt like crying and said that "The work of sorrow must be completed.... When you have cried enough, some day you will see that it has ended." And so it happened. Gradually I studied family photographs and when I took them to heart, my eyes remained dry. now is the time for

* * * * *

Before retiring, Marja worked mostly as an executive secretary and office manager for several companies, including the National Center for Disease Control in Atlanta and the Medical School of Emory University in Atlanta in 1999. She also sang with many choirs in the United States, including five years with the Atlanta Symphony Orchestra Chorus. She married in Atlanta, though was later divorced. She has performed in Finland where she lives today and says that music has been a great comfort to her. In her apartment in Turku, her father's treasured mandolin is prominently displayed.

Notes

1. Many Finnish cemeteries have sections reserved for "hero graves." However, Marja's father was buried without military ceremony in the Turku Old Cemetery.

2

Unanswered Questions for a Finnpojke
Martti Kalervo Broström

Finnpojke is Swedish for "Finnish boy," but I consider myself to be both Finnish and Swedish. I was born in Lahti, Finland, in 1938, one year before the Winter War began. My mother Aili was then twenty-six years old, single, and working as a maid at the Kauppahotelli, a business hotel in the middle of Lahti that is still there today. We lived in a tiny room with a kitchen. When my mother, whom I called "Aili" instead of *Äiti* (mother), was working, she paid a young couple in the neighborhood, Oili and Oiva Niemi, to look after me. They were kind people, and I very much liked them. Later they told me that they had wanted to adopt me before I was sent to Sweden because they could not have children of their own. In retrospect, I think that this would have been the best life for me. But my mother refused to discuss it.

Aili had an older sister who was married and lived in the countryside south of Lahti in a small cottage near Lake Artjärvi. They had six children, and when it was possible we went there to see them. Two of the girls later moved to Sweden and married Swedish men, and I have kept in touch with this side of the family ever since.

My biological father, who was unknown to me until only recently, was a thirty-one-year-old forest technician from Hämeenlinna at this time. He worked for a logging company, directing the harvesting of trees. But during the war, he was on the northern Karelian front, fighting as a *kulspruta* (machine gunner). He fired a gun at the Russians, and he was never wounded. After the Winter War, he met a young woman, the daughter of a widow, who was five to ten years younger than he and who had inherited a small farm. They married, and he tried to take up farming, but found he didn't like it. So he went back to logging, and he and his wife moved back to his hometown of Hämeenlinna.

In the spring of 1942 when I was four years old, my mother decided to send me as a war child to Sweden. Soon after, I was put on a train towards Tornio on the Finnish border. There, with many other unhappy children from two to three years of age and up to ten and twelve years of age, I crossed to Haparanda on the Swedish side to board a Swedish train.[1] All of us were wearing name tags around our necks and carrying small bags or suitcases, containing a few clothes and maybe a toy. I don't remember anything from the journey, which lasted three to four days and ended in Jönköping in Småland. In Jönköping, we stayed at a hospital for a few days for medical examinations, haircuts, and so on. We children were often sad and frightened, not knowing what was going on, but we still had our Finnish-speaking nurses and playmates to comfort us.

My future foster parents, Albert and Selma Johansson, lived in Vetlanda, a small town about seventy kilometers from Jönköping where Albert had a furniture manufacturing factory. Albert was fifty-two and Selma fifty-eight years of age. I referred to them by their first names, and they referred to me as "Martti," just as my sons do today. They had a daughter in her thirties still living at home and three grown-up sons who had already left.

When applying for a Finnish war child, they had requested a girl that was not too young, but when they turned up in Jönköping, there were only two skinny boys left. Some mistake had been made. Later they showed me photos they had taken of me, this tiny little boy with no hair, like a skinhead. Fortunately for me, I happened to share the same birthday, August 31, as my future father, so I was chosen. But in the car driving to my new home, I realized that we could not understand each other at all. I didn't know a word of Swedish, and they didn't know any Finnish. They had a Finnish dictionary, however, and tried to find the right words for basic commands such as "Come eat," "Go pee," and "Go to bed," all pronounced in their special dialect. We must have had wonderful conversations! Luckily, in the same town there lived an old Finnish-speaking woman and, when tougher problems arose, they rang up "Aunt Ida" and asked for her help with interpretation. Also, when I received letters from Aili or I wanted to write to her, we had to see Aunt Ida who was very helpful to us. Even ten years later, when I sometimes got into mischief, my foster sister said: "Now we'd better call for Aunt Ida!"

I was very happy when we discovered that there were two other Finnish-speaking boys in the village and, according to my foster sister, we three "Finnboys" were speaking a mixture of Finnish and Swedish within six months and Swedish with a Finnish dialect in about one year.

The Continuation War in Finland ended in September 1944, when I was six years old. A letter from my mother Aili arrived, and from the contents of this letter, I understood and deeply feared that I would soon have to return to Finland, though Albert and Selma assured me that everything would soon be better there and that they would continue to help Aili and me. But I barely remembered my mother and had entirely forgotten my

Finnish. I had also become attached to my foster parents and foster sister Ingeborg, so I naturally wanted to stay with them.

For some reason I still don't understand, my return was delayed until the following year. But in the spring of 1945, we were informed that my mother was seriously ill and in hospital. When I heard about my mother, I was both sad and happy, thinking *maybe now I can remain and go to school here*. Those dreams came true, and I entered school in August.

One day in November 1945, when I came home from school, my foster parents told me that they had received a telegram, informing them that my mother Aili had died of kidney disease. Her last will was that I should stay with Albert and Selma, and they promised to examine the possibility. For the authorities in Sweden, there was no problem even though my foster parents were quite old, but the Finnish authorities were unwilling to let Finnish children remain in Sweden.

Moreover, my biological father had suddenly appeared, declaring that he wanted to adopt me because he and his wife couldn't have any children. I had never heard about my father. Though I later discovered that Aili had told the Niemi family his name, Martti Kallio, she had never said anything to me about him. Of course I would have been too young to understand.

My old grandfather and aunt and uncle in Artjärvi, however, came to my defense and wrote letters on Albert's, Selma's, and my behalf. Finally, the social authorities in Lahti decided that it was best for me to stay in Sweden. And so, in September 1946 the adoption was finalized. The next summer, my foster parents, foster sister, and I visited my relatives in Finland. After five years in Sweden I knew very little Finnish, and I also remember it being very emotional for me to meet my folks. Unfortunately, Selma became ill and died in the autumn of 1949, but at least I was lucky to have my foster sister, Ingeborg, who was at home to spoil me a little. She had always been like a mother to me.

In retrospect, I understand that Albert and Selma were very old-fashioned and authoritarian people but also honest, just, and well intentioned toward me. I don't remember ever being treated badly, though I had a well-earned beating once in a while. But what I also remember is that there was a lack of feeling or physical contact in my Swedish family. For example, Albert with four children of his own never changed a diaper or walked children in a baby carriage.

Instead of giving his children hugs, he was liberal with generous rewards when he felt satisfied with their behavior. I know this because my foster sister and three brothers had the same experiences as I and have shared them with me. Selma was a silent and kind housewife, constantly busy cooking, washing, cleaning, and sewing. But the person I could always rely on and confide in was my big sister.

After living sixty years in Sweden, where I worked and met my Finnish wife Anita, I feel more Swedish than Finnish even when visiting Finland. However, I do feel that I have my roots in Finland, and I am proud of being a *suomalainen* (Finnish person). In fact, after Albert died in 1980, I changed my name from "Johansson" to my Finnish mother's maiden name of "Broström." I had nothing against my Swedish name, but I wanted to take my own name back.

I also wanted to meet my biological father, so my wife Anita and I contacted the authorities in Lahti about how and where we could find him. Finally, it was arranged in 1995. We made a telephone call initially, but he would only say "yes" or "no." So we went to his address and pushed the doorbell. I was nervous about meeting him, and his wife who opened the door was not pleased when she discovered our business. But we spoke about Aili. He said that he remembered her, but he claimed he wasn't my father, though he had argued to adopt me when I was a child in Sweden! So his attitude was difficult to explain. His explanation was that, yes, he had known Aili, and that when he learned that Aili had died, he thought he could adopt me. But he insisted that I wasn't his child, and unfortunately at that time there were no DNA tests. But my mother Aili had *said* he was my father, and he confirmed that she worked hard and had not been a "party girl." Also, even as an old man, he physically resembled me. My wife said to him, "You shouldn't deny it. I can see that you're Martti's father with the same blue eyes, and height, and everything."

Nevertheless, when he died, he left nothing to me, no explanation. All his property he gave to his brothers. Nor did I ever ask for anything, having been adopted. Before his death my father and I corresponded for a time, but we never got well acquainted. He wrote mostly about the war and such things, and I wrote about my family and sons. I never learned to understand him.

I often wonder what would have been the best life for me. Would it have been adoption by the Niemi couple I bonded with as a very young boy in Finland? Or adoption by the Johanssons and growing up in Sweden? Or would it have been best for my biological father to adopt me? These are unanswerable questions, which perhaps many war children ask themselves. In these ways, I continue to wonder about all the different turnings my life could have taken had war not come to Finland.

* * * * *

Martti Broström worked his entire career as a salesman for a packaging industry. He and his wife, Anita, lived first in Jönköping, then moved to Örebro where their two sons and daughter were born. In 1974, they moved to Stockholm where Martti studied the Finnish language and Finnish history at the University of Stockholm. Martti died in 2012 at age 74 of a heart attack.

Notes

1. Due to disparate rail gauges at these junctures—1,524 mm for Finland and 1,435 mm for Sweden—children and their caretakers had to leave one train for another on the Finnish-Swedish border.

3

A Desire to Scream
"Emmi Eskola"

When the Winter War began in 1939, I was only a one-year-old infant. My mother was a housewife, and my father was a carpenter. I had a brother three years older than I, and during the war my mother gave birth to three more children. So, with my parents, there would be seven of us altogether. None of the children were sent to Sweden during the war because my mother wanted to keep us all near her. My father's sister who was working as a nurse in Sweden, treating sick Finnish children, wanted me to join her there, but my mother did not desire me to leave.

We lived in eastern Helsinki, very near a factory where they produced weapons. At this point in time we were living in a narrow, crowded apartment, but during the war we had to move four times, due to the heavy destruction by bombs. By the time I was four, I had already learned to read, and one of my favorite things to do at this age was to sit under our kitchen table with a favorite book. When I read a story I especially liked, I concentrated to the exclusion of everything else. Nothing else in the world existed. On one occasion, when I happened to be sitting and reading under the table, Russian bombs began dropping and sirens began yelling. I believe that the Russians were trying to destroy the nearby armaments factory. Everyone else rushed to the cellar for shelter from the shattering windows, flying stones, and exploding walls. They had not noticed me sitting under the table. Suddenly, I became conscious of the eruptions around me and a terrible roaring thunder. I was terrified and started screaming because I thought I was going to die. Then I lost consciousness.

After the bombing raid, my mother found me and took me by ambulance to the nearest hospital on the other side of the city. At the hospital I lay unconscious for three days and nights. In order to treat my wounds from the flying glass and debris, the doctors apparently had to cut the clothes from my body. After I regained consciousness, the doctors advised my mother not to mention this incident because it would add to my trauma. However, bad memories followed me throughout my childhood, and when I was older my mother finally told me about what had happened and the seriousness of my condition.

We sometimes went to the countryside during to war to be with my grandmother who lived only five kilometers from the Russian border. These visits were wonderful because the war felt distant, and there were no bombings. But sometimes we saw Karelian refugees, leading their cows and other animals toward Helsinki to be relocated after the Russians had seized their land and homes. During the war my grandmother died, which was the first death in the family for me. We all had to kiss her on the cheek as she lay in her coffin, and I remember being horrified by this.

After the war, the surviving soldiers, including my father, returned home. They sometimes related their experiences and the hardships they had suffered in the deep snows of eastern Finland. My father described many gruesome experiences. One story he told was about a time when his unit was resting, smoking, and talking, and a mine exploded near them. All his comrades in arms died except him. He said that he could see severed heads, arms, legs, and other body parts all around him from the men he had come to love as brothers. Some of their corpses had been thrown into the trees and were hanging from branches. Yet he hadn't suffered a single wound and wondered for a long time why he alone had been saved. He became religious for a while as a consequence, believing that God had saved him. Unfortunately, for a long time my father suffered from terrible nightmares and would awaken, screaming, "We have to kill them! Kill them, or we shall all be killed!" These outbursts would awaken everyone in the house and frighten us all very badly. I wanted to hide after this happened, but where could I go? Other men who returned from the war turned to the bottle and became alcoholics, which was devastating to many families. At least my father resumed his work as a carpenter after the war, but died at age forty-seven of a heart attack.

During the postwar years many veterans shared their stories, which I hated listening to because it was so difficult to forget the gruesome details of narratives that involved so much human suffering. Life returned to normal eventually, though we had little money and had to be satisfied with small things. But the most important thing was that the war was over. Finns could finally enjoy some peace. Before, life had often seemed hopeless. Now everyone hoped that life would continue to improve. Yet people still talked about their wartime privations and tragedies. When I was thirteen and went to Sweden to live with my aunt, I thought it was wonderful not to hear any more about the war and all the suffering.

Strangely, I didn't clearly remember any of these events—the bombings or listening to stories about the horror of the war—before I was thirty-five years old. Inside, I had carried my own emotional and psychological torment but had never spoken to anyone about it, thinking that this was normal. However, I had wondered why for so many years I felt an almost constant desire to scream and scream loudly for a long time. There was a dark feeling inside of me that I wanted to get rid of, which followed me throughout the years into my adult life. This feeling didn't make me physically ill but just made me very agitated and uncomfortable. My greatest desire was to go deep into the forest where I could scream as long and loudly as I wanted. Unfortunately, I never satisfied that urge, which continued to plague me. Perhaps I should have sought counseling or talked with someone about it.

Then, I happened to watch a film about a family somewhere in Europe during World War II. The mother, played by a famous actress, was sitting in her kitchen, desperately embracing her two small children on her lap. She appeared to be horrified by something, and then bombs began exploding around her house. At first she seemed frozen with disbelief. Then suddenly she began to scream very loudly and long in just the same way as I had done under our family table so many years before.

And, in a flash, a very clear memory of that day when I was four returned to me. I recognized in the actress's scream the same scream I had been hearing for my entire life, and I began to cry from somewhere deep in my heart. After I stopped crying the urge to scream had strangely vanished. I had been liberated from the desire to scream and from having to wonder about this compulsion ever again.

To this day, I am grateful to this actress for helping me to recover.

* * * * *

Wanting to learn more English, "Emmi" worked as a governess in England in her early twenties. Returning to Sweden, she married and settled in Sibbhult, working as a clerk in a municipal office for twenty-three years. She also studied several languages there, including English, French, German, and Italian, already having achieved fluency in Swedish and Russian. She has four children and eleven grandchildren.

4

Horseshoes and Licorice Drops
Juha Hankkila

Before I was born, my parents, Aaro and Anna Hankkila, moved from Pyhäjärvi, "Holy Sea," near Lake Ladoga in Karelia, to Imatra, close to the Russian border.[1] In Imatra, my father worked as a chimney sweep at the local paper mill named Tornatori. My sister Laila was born the same year my parents moved, but she died from diphtheria three years later at the local isolation hospital. This was a tragic event in my parents' lives, which my father wrote about in his war diary some years later:

> *Today it is six years since our life's first great sorrow struck. Our beloved child Laila died. Our happy home was filled with pain. The slender flower did not cope with the frost lying in wait for her. During the flourishing of the apple trees, her life was cut short… and she was taken away to the bright eternity.… A young life disappeared like dew drops in the burning sun. Then the tiny heart stopped and the large beautiful eyes closed forever.*

My brother Helge came into the world in 1934, and I was born on December 23, 1937. Surprisingly, my father enjoyed his job, though it was dirty; he also enjoyed socializing, drinking coffee, and eating buns with his clients. Every lunch he pedaled home and made lunch for us. He was an excellent chef. After he had eaten he would lie down on the kitchen sofa, placing a newspaper beneath himself since, as he put it, he was "black as a chimney sweep."

My little sister Raili was born at the end of the war in February 1940, during a bombing raid, which prevented my mother and the midwife from running to the shelter, an underground concrete cellar. Though I don't remember saying it, my mother told me that after Raili's birth, I exclaimed, "The air planes played and made a lot of tricks when Raili was born."

From the first three years of my life I do not remember a lot outside of running to air raid shelters to escape Russian bombers and how I would often fall to the ground and cry, "I cannot get away from the *Ryssä!*" (Russians). I also remember sitting on my father's lap and listening to stories about the war in which my father served as the head of a medical orderly team, taking care of wounded people. And I remember an old woman, Kaisa, who lived quite close and who often cared for us children, took in washing, and administered massages. Sitting with her in her rocking chair, I listened to hymns about God, Satan, and Hell. On one occasion, I contributed a song I had heard from older boys about *Saatana, Perkele,* and *Jumalauta* (Satan, the Devil, and a swear word based on the word "God"). The religious old woman's response was that I had better stop singing.

The Continuation War began on June 26, 1941, and in December of that year, when I was nearly four and my brother Helge was seven, we were both sent by boat to Stockholm and then by train to Copenhagen to escape the bombing. When my mother began to cry at the Imatra railway station, I apparently said to her, "Do not cry, Mummy, I will just go away and fetch a doll for Raili and a small train for myself. Then I will be back." From Imatra we traveled to Turku, then boarded a boat, the SS *Arcturus,* that took us to Stockholm from where we caught the train to Denmark. My trip, which I had thought would last only a short time, ended up lasting for five years![2]

Both in Turku and Copenhagen all the children had to hold onto a long rope, walking in a line, so we would not get lost as we walked through city streets. However, in Copenhagen my brother and I were separated immediately and met only once for a couple of days during his two and my five years away as war children. A terrible thing. Why couldn't we have been placed in the same village or in nearby cities? One can hardly imagine that this could happen today!

Furthermore, neither of us spoke any Danish. My new foster parents whom I referred to by their Christian names, father "Anfred" and mother "Valborg," were anticipating a girl refugee, since the handwritten name "Juha" had been misread as "Julia." My new home was a farm in the village Udby near Holbaek on the island of Zealand about sixty kilometers west of Copenhagen. My foster parents had a son and daughter, both older than I, and, later, a baby brother that I cared for a lot. My new siblings were nice to

Figure 4.1. *Juha Hankilla at age four, around the time he was sent to Denmark. Courtesy Juha Hankilla.*

me, but somehow I felt that they were not my real family. The youngest boy for me was an exception. I have always loved children. And on one occasion I released him from the flagpole to which his siblings had tied him, so he was very grateful, of course.

Compared with Finland, Danish winters were usually mild, but my first winter there was very cold with a lot of snow. Fortunately, in a very short time I learned Danish and eventually forgot my Finnish. I even forgot that there was a war going on in Finland. But I never ceased to think of *Äiti* and *Isä* (mother and father) as my real parents. Also *Äiti* and my foster parents exchanged letters that were translated through the Finland Aid Organization. I waited for these letters and thought of my parents very often. Sometimes I felt homesick, especially when I thought I was punished without reason.

I was also tormented by having to go to church every Sunday, especially in the beginning as I did not understand the language. On one occasion, when I was four, I urgently had to pee but was told to sit still and not speak. After a while, I wet my pants and stained the red cloth that covered the bench. I was very embarrassed when I had to shake hands with the vicar after the service, and so were my foster parents. My foster mother was a strict disciplinarian, and when I had done something unacceptable, she sent me into the bedroom to wait until she had time to come and give me a huge slap with her hand on my bare bottom.

The farm where we lived had cows, a horse, some calves, pigs, chickens, and geese. I soon learned how to attend to the cattle and to help with other things on the farm. It was no vacation, I can say. Still, I remember the best times in the evenings when we got apples or sometimes apple pie, and I enjoyed my foster mother's reading aloud from some book even if it was not a book meant for children.

I also liked many of the villagers. There lived an old carpenter across the street, and I used to visit him and his wife as often as possible. He made me some playthings, and I sat on his lap as he read H. C. Andersen fairytales to me. His wife also made wonderful pancakes. Once in awhile I asked him for a coin to buy ice cream, which I ate hiding in the bushes so my family could not see. I understood that it was forbidden—not because they were poor, but I think because of their strict Lutheran education. I did not quite fit in and chose my own way many times. It helped that a lot of good people were kind to me; maybe they felt sorry for me as a war child.

But occasionally, my ideas got me into trouble with the villagers. One day I saw the village blacksmith, Nils Henriksen, throwing old horseshoes in the backyard, and there was already a huge heap there. All the horseshoes I found in the fields and on the roads I brought to him and got a small coin for each. I needed more money for the sweets I craved, particularly cakes, which we seldom had at home, so once I picked up some of his old horse shoes from the heap and tried to sell them back to him. Unfortunately, he recognized them and got very angry and sent me away from the smithy.

I had also seen people eating small black pills, probably licorice drops, from tin boxes, and I got a new business idea: I collected dung from small lambs because their droppings were the right size, and I put them in an empty box. Then I tried to sell them to people, but they just laughed and said they were not interested....!

In order to fetch a loaf of whole wheat bread for our old aunt, I used to go every morning to Udby Bakery next door. The bakery was run by a baker called Hansen that I liked very much. He was the only one in the village who could whip your cream if you needed to bake a big cake, as he had the only electric beater in the village at that time. One day I got an idea to go to the bakery after lunch when my foster parents were taking a nap. I stood there and watched the bakers making different types of cakes, and in the end I got a delicious custard slice. This procedure went on for some months, and I gained quite a lot of weight.

One of the other neighbors I remember was the saddler, Clausen, who had never used a toothbrush in his entire life. Instead, he used a feather from some big bird to clean his teeth after every meal, and he never had a single cavity!

Another villager was Nils Hamann who had repaired and sold shoes since 1926. When television came to Udby, he started selling radios and TV sets. He was related to my foster parents, and we went often to his house to watch TV. His business grew, and he soon built a new house and abandoned the shoe business.

I also had the usual childhood accidents. The day before my younger foster brother was born, we had been out threshing, and it was my and my foster sister's job to put the bales of straw in good order in the barn loft. We then made long tunnels with the bales and hid from one another. Crawling through one of these tunnels, suddenly my older brother who had decided to join in our play, came backwards and accidentally hit me with his iron-shod shoes. I bled profusely and had a big bandage around my head when we went to fetch the baby from the hospital.

Summer came and with it the sunshine that I loved. One day I saw that the carriage with the baby stood in the sun, and I thought it was good for him. My foster sister also saw this and placed the carriage in the shade, which I could not understand. I put it back in the sun, and after awhile my foster mother came and asked if I had moved the carriage. Not understanding what she meant, I said that my sister had moved it. But I had to go to the bedroom and wait for my punishment. I was very upset as I felt I was being punished unfairly.

Another bad thing happened when I was six years old. At harvest time, I helped my foster father and elder siblings in the fields. One day we were about half a mile away from home, working close to another farm I often visited. After awhile I slipped away without anybody seeing me and went to visit the big boxer dog I liked so much. When I came into the kitchen, the dog ran forward to jump up and lick me in the face as usual. Unfortunately, this time he was tied to the stove and, as the dog jumped up against me, its collar stopped it in the air, so that its bared teeth wounded me all over my face. Then the dog slid down along my body, leaving big scratches. The dog's owners panicked and tried to wipe off the blood, but it was no one's fault, just an accident. When I saw my family's carriage load of straw pass the gate, I ran and hid in a small hollow place in the back of the load, and when the carriage reached our yard I slipped into the house through the back door, not daring to show my face. I lay down in pain for an hour in an empty room until my foster parents found me and sent for Doctor Andersen, so that I could get a tetanus injection. I still do not know why I was so afraid to tell them that I had wanted to see the dog. Maybe it was because we were working in the field and I was not supposed to play.

One of the things that I remember with great happiness was the lovely sailing boat my good friend the carpenter made for me. It was about fifty centimeters long with a compartment for small things. His wife, Herdis, sewed the sails, and the blacksmith made the helm and the keel. My best friend's father, Albert Andersen, was the village painter and painted the boat in red, white, and blue. I was mighty proud of it, especially as so many craftsmen had taken valuable time to make this masterpiece for me. Of course I brought it with me back to Finland; unfortunately, it disappeared somehow. I still think of it and how happy my sons would have been playing with it.

When the Continuation War ended, it was time for me to go back to Finland, but unfortunately I fell ill with scarlet fever and had to be isolated in the hospital for a week. Due to this, I didn't return to Finland until the next summer, 1946. Another reason for the delay was that there were not enough Finnish boats for the returning children. Also, in view of the fact that I would be beginning school in Finland, it was no good coming home without any time to relearn Finnish. I had attended grades one through three in a one-room Danish school, and while I had not forgotten my Finnish parents and longed to see them, I had forgotten the language. Nevertheless, I was quite excited to leave Denmark and return to Finland. We had spoken of it so many times.

Finally I was aboard a ship from Copenhagen to Helsinki. To my disappointment, when I arrived in Helsinki, my parents were not there, probably because Imatra is three hundred kilometers from the capital, and my father didn't have the time or money to go. At that time, it required a day's travel, but with the war child train it took almost two days and a night due to the many long stops for children to be let off in their home villages. Instead, the Lottas took care of me.[3] I was desperate, as the train journey seemed never to end, and I tried to escape several times as I believed we had already passed my station. There were two to three hundred children, and we slept on the floor and in the luggage racks of the train and got sandwiches with moldy sausage. All of us threw up, and I could not eat that kind of sandwich for many years. I remember feeling very sorry for myself. All the children were violently ill, and we felt lonely, not knowing anybody and no longer understanding our native language, though some of the Lottas spoke a little Danish.

When my father came to meet me at Lappeenranta railway station some forty kilometers from Imatra, we had a conversation in Finnish and Danish, and neither of us understood the other. Still, I was very happy; I was home at last. Being reunited with my parents was very pleasant. However, I didn't know at the time that life would be a lot more difficult in Finland than it had been in Denmark. Our small wooden house felt very out of date with no water pipes and was owned by the paper mill where other heads of families and my father worked before and after the war. We shared our house with three other families. We had to carry drinking water in a bucket from the well in our yard, as well as carry out the slops, which were thrown on the back of the firewood shelter. Our loo was in a small shelter in the yard. Older boys used to compete in throwing knives at the door of the loo, and once there was a man inside relieving himself without our knowledge. When he opened the door, he was hit with a knife in his chest. Fortunately he was not severely hurt.

I began school hardly understanding a word of Finnish, and it was quite a difficult time for me. There were many misunderstandings every day. For instance, when it was my turn to be the class monitor, my teacher emphasized that I was supposed to wipe the blackboard, clean the room, open the windows, and not leave the room to play with my schoolmates. Everything went all right for a few hours, but then I had to go to the bathroom. Because I understood I was not to leave the room, I had to find another solution. The only one I found was to piddle into the wastepaper basket. When lessons resumed, the basket started to leak, and a runnel of urine appeared on the floor. All the pupils began to laugh, and my teacher sent me out with the basket and to fetch a rag to clean up with. She explained that, of course, I could have gone to the bathroom.

At school, we sat two by two on benches, and the boy next to me was a lot bigger than I and a little mentally retarded. As with other children he often harassed me and wrestled me in the schoolyard. Once I succeeded in throwing him down, and all my playmates shouted with joy. During the next lesson, though, he got his revenge. He took his pencil and shoved it into my chest, so that the lead tip broke off. My chest muscle hurt as a consequence for several days. After this episode, the boy was transferred to a special school, and my life became a little easier.

After the war we lacked a lot of things: food, clothes, shoes, and so forth. Once a month, my teacher would deal out a so-called American parcel that was very coveted. When it was my turn, I found that among other things, the parcel contained shoes that I really needed. I received the shoes instead of another student because the teacher explained that this other student's father owned a lorry, and he could make the soles of shoes from old tires.

Due to food rationing, we also had to use coupons to buy many necessary things. I went every afternoon to a central communal kitchen to fetch soup or whatever there was for supper that day: that was our one hot meal. I carried it home in a milk pot, often thinking of the good and healthy Danish food that I had enjoyed. We had no fruit at all, although sometimes my foster parents sent large boxes of apples from their huge fruit orchard. Once, one of the local shopkeepers announced that he had gotten some oranges. They were very expensive, but I wanted to taste them, so I went with my few coins and found that I didn't have enough. Instead, I bought a few half-rotten fruits, which gave me stomach ache.

One of my friends got a job selling sweets in a shop. We put on our golf trousers and went to visit him. There we filled our trouser pockets with sweets that he gave us for free. His job lasted only a very short time, however!

Fishing interested me a great deal as a boy. I usually stood on our private bridge, casting into the Vuoksi river that flowed just ten meters from our house. But sometimes I went with my friends to the big old bridge where the trains drove on top and the cars on the street level. We climbed down and sat on concrete pillars five meters above the water without any safety net. We just sat there with our feet dangling over the edge and waited for the fish to bite. The river was torrential, and we would have had no chance to survive had any of us fallen into it. When my mother learned what I had done, she got very angry.

My father also got very angry on occasion. Chewing gum was also in short supply after the war. I had tasted it in Denmark, and like most children I liked it very much. One day there was a rumor that chewing gum was for sale in a sweets stall outside the city. All the boys and girls hurried to this place, and each child was allowed to buy one piece each. My sister and I were very happy with our gum and started walking on the railroad tracks as a shortcut home. When my father learned about it, he made us spit out our gum because no one was allowed to walk on the tracks. Every time we saw a train coming we used to hide in the bushes. Although our father was right, I will never forget this punishment.

Perhaps as a result of his years in the war, my father had a hot temper. He liked to drink, but as I can see from his wartime diary he did it during the war too, as most men did. It was a way to escape from the hard and dangerous life they lived. Even after the war, my father was frequently called in as medical assistant during wrestling, skiing, and other contests. He was also chairman of a local labor union. He had knowledge in many areas, such as geography, nature, and war literature, and he occasionally gave us quizzes on different levels to suit the age of each child. He also taught us how to play chess. Sadly, he died very young at age forty-four, in 1953, of a severe kidney illness. During the postwar years my mother worked as a secretary and, after my father died she eventually remarried and worked in a fabric shop that she and her second husband owned.

As for my siblings Helge and Raili, they had very different wartime experiences. Instead of leaving Finland, Raili was evacuated to the countryside during the war years 1941–1944. The farmers who took her in lived only thirty kilometers from Imatra in a two-story building with an outdoor lavatory, which my three-year-old sister was frightened to use alone in the morning. She once fell from the narrow board in the outhouse into human excrement and had to crawl out while crying in despair. She also lived with our grandmother and grandfather in Pyhäjärvi when they moved back to Karelia after Finnish forces had reclaimed this territory. She enjoyed her grandparents' huge farmhouse and cattle and had beautiful red stockings to wear on Sundays. But, in her words, "the rats took them into custody."

She also remembers running through deep snow to fetch the neighbors for telephone calls, as our grandfather and the village doctor were the only ones with telephones. Unfortunately, after the Soviets again seized Karelia, Raili and our grandparents had to evacuate and live with strange people who did didn't like taking Karelians into their home. Raili believed that the lady of the house hated her. On one occasion, Raili, our grandmother, and this lady took a sauna together, and as Raili left, believing that she was the last to leave, she locked the door. But the woman was still in the sauna and became so hot and thirsty that she drank a whole liter of sour milk. Raili believes she became even less popular after that.

Like me, my brother Helge was evacuated to Denmark, but two years later he returned to Finland to attend school. Unfortunately, he had a much worse experience than my sister. My brother went to three different families and apparently had an unhappy time. Perhaps as a consequence, Helge's life did not work out so well. It began in school with skipped lessons, and later on he was not able to keep on the narrow path. As he described it for one of our cousins a few years ago, "I am the family's black sheep." Fifteen years ago he changed his life as he became a Lutheran believer and got married for the third time.

When I was nine years old I made my first trip back to Denmark since leaving the country and spent my summer vacation there. I returned many times in subsequent summers to my foster parents' home. After graduating from high school I tried to find work in Finland but without success. Because of the war years and war reparations demanded by the USSR, Finland was in deep economic depression. My mother had told me about a friend's son who was a successful wireless operator, so I decided at age fifteen that I would also become a "Sparks," as they were called. But there was no money for school. I turned to my foster parents to help me find a job in a nearby mechanical workshop where my Danish friends worked. However, I was really disappointed to discover that, as farmers, they had "given me away" as a farm hand a few miles away. I loathed farming and almost hated them for that. I had looked forward to learning the job in the workshop. But I had no alternative except to sign the contract and begin working on the farm, as it was the only way to earn a little money and be able to begin radio operator training in Copenhagen later that year.

I corresponded with my foster parents and sibling for some years. My mother died in 1996 at eighty-three years of age. We never spoke much about my time in Denmark, though she visited me there in 1957 when I was waiting to begin work aboard my second ship as a radio operator. I was never bitter about twice losing both my language and friends. But my life in Finland was difficult. I had to struggle very hard to achieve my education both in Denmark and Sweden, as I had no one to ask for help. In fact, not only did I not receive any help, but I often had to send money to my mother, so that she could manage with her life and my brother's debts.

Despite my life and experiences in Denmark, I have always felt more Finnish than Danish, though Swedish has become my best language. When I watch sports I always cheer for the Finns and hope that they will win. A lingering feeling from my war child experience is that I sometimes feel rootless, but I felt this more keenly when I was younger.

* * * * *

Before his retirement, Juha worked as a radio operator on Swedish ships, as an electronic engineer, a lab engineer, and for many years as a hearing engineer at a rehabilitation center for the deaf and hard of hearing in Sweden. He was married but later divorced. For many years, he practiced sports. He is currently working on his father's wartime diary. And he travels a lot with his second wife Britt. He wonders whether his life as a war child pushed him to be "constantly the best."

Notes

1. Work was scarce in Karelia in the early 1930s when the Hankkilas moved. Young men labored in exchange for room and board. Better job opportunities existed in Imatra, famous for its raging Vuoksi River, the giant dam built in 1929, and power plant built in 1928. Unfortunately, Imatra was heavily bombed by the Soviets during the Winter War, which began in November 1939, and lasted until mid-March 1940. No return to Karelia would have been possible, since it was under nearly constant attack and was eventually lost to the Soviets.
2. Denmark had been occupied by Nazi Germany since April 9, 1940, but Finnish children were still being sent there as well as to Norway, which also came under Nazi occupation. Juha believes that this might have been due to the fact that Germany and Finland were then cobelligerents or allies in their fight against Russia. An estimated 4,000 children were sent to Denmark.
3. The Lottas were members of the Finnish women's voluntary defense service, an organization to which Juha's mother belonged and which dates back to the 1808–1809 war between Russia and Sweden. Lottas served during the War of Independence, the Winter War, and throughout the rest of World War II.

5

The Last Summer in Sweden
"Karina Heino"

I was born in 1935 in Lahti in southern Finland. My mother died when I was an infant, and my father was unable to care for me. As the only child, I was sent to live with my aunt and uncle in Viipuri in eastern Finland, which is today part of Russia. My uncle was an instructor at a military academy there. When I was four the Winter War started, and everyone had to leave Viipuri due to the bombing. We left by train for Lahti to be near the rest of my father's family, including his mother and sister and her husband. The latter had two children of their own. So, after my father and uncle were called to active duty in the war, I went to live with my grandmother, *Mummu,* who was very good to me.

Soon many Finnish children, mainly orphans, were being sent to Sweden. I was five years old when I was sent away. *Mummu* and my aunt tried to explain to me why I was going, but I don't remember much about the journey itself except that I went by ship. After we arrived at our destination I remember being in a room full of seated children and adults walking around, looking the children over. There was a middle-aged couple that seemed interested in me. The man kept circling and smiling. Maybe he liked my red hair and freckles. In any case, they chose me as their foster child, and I left with them. Though my new foster parents spoke no Finnish, I remember feeling safe in their company.

Tant and *Farbror* (Aunt and Uncle) lived just outside the small town of Falkenburg off the coast of Sweden, and though they didn't have a farm, they had a pig, some chickens, and many apple, plum, and pear trees. One of my first clear memories is how good the food was. I don't believe that I had ever in my life had such good food.

My foster father and his brothers were furniture makers. They were very good, nice people. Unfortunately, they were unable to have children of their own, but my foster father's two brothers who lived nearby had children just a little older than me. I remember having so much fun playing with them, and though I couldn't speak the language at first, this changed quickly. I was very happy for the one and a half years I was there.

I remember one early experience in Sweden very vividly. Soon after I arrived we were getting ready to go somewhere, and I cried and cried and cried. They thought I was crying because I missed my family in Finland. But the real reason I was crying is that I was afraid they were leaving me. However, I couldn't tell them this because I couldn't speak Swedish yet. It turned out that we were only going to visit *Tant*'s mother in town. And, as soon as I realized that they weren't abandoning me, I felt happy again.

I also have fond memories of Christmas in Sweden. It was a very joyful time with lots of singing and dancing, a great place to be.

In time, *Tant* and *Farbror* wanted to adopt me, and I would have been very happy to be adopted and stay in Sweden since I had spent two years with them and had come to love my life there. But my father wanted me to return. I don't know why because I didn't really know him, having lived with my aunt and *Mummu* before going to Sweden. I was very upset about having to leave Falkenburg because I had grown so attached. Also I was nervous about returning to Finland, not knowing what the future would hold. This was in the summer of 1942.

I remember being brought by *Tant* and *Farbror* to the train station but nothing else, except that there were a lot of other crying children on the train. Travel by ship had become dangerous because the gulf between Sweden and Finland was planted with mines. We first had to travel up north and around the gulf, then back down the coast of Finland. As we passed through northern Finland, I could see all the damage from the fighting.

When I returned I lived with *Mummu* and my father who like many Finns of that time was not affectionate. I had completely forgotten the language. And food was available in only very small quantities. Everyone could only receive a little at a time with their food coupons. Also the food was not good, and it would be many years before the quality improved, due to the fact that Finland was focused on paying its war debt to Russia. Nothing like fresh fruit was available for fifteen years or so.

In the fall of 1945 I began school and relearned Finnish that first year back. But it was difficult, as I missed *Tant* and *Farbror* and everything about Sweden terribly. My father then worked as a laborer in the ship-yards, and the following year he remarried. During this time I continued to stay in touch with my foster family, corresponding with them three or four times a year. They also sent many packages of clothes, including beautiful dresses that my foster cousins had outgrown. These packages were very much appreciated, since there was so little to buy in the stores in those days.

When I was thirteen my father died at age forty of heart disease. We had never become close, though I became close to my stepmother whom I called *Äiti* or "Mother." We got along well, though *Äiti* was very private and not very outgoing. After that school year ended I returned to Sweden for the summer, taking a boat to Stockholm. I was very excited about returning to Sweden, though I had forgotten most of my Swedish. One of my Swedish "uncles" met me there, and we took the train together to Falkenburg.

I was surprised to learn that while I had been away, my foster parents had adopted a little girl. But I was not too jealous because I understood that I was just there for a visit. It was a wonderful summer filled with biking and swimming in the ocean.

I stayed in touch with my foster family throughout most of my teen years, but we stopped corresponding after a time because it was to difficult finding people to translate our letters. My stepmother wanted to move to Australia or America for a better life abroad. So, when I was twenty-one, my stepmother and I moved to the United States.

I never returned to see my foster parents. Sweden was only a small part of my life, and I will always feel more Finnish than Swedish. But my last summer in Sweden remains a beautiful memory.

* * * * *

"Karina" worked in the office of the Finlayson textile factory in Finland. Her stepmother worked at a weaving machine in the same factory. Later Karina married and had two children. Today she is retired in northern Minnesota.

6

Farting in Swedish

Veijo Holopainen

I was born in 1937 in the city of Kuopio, which is about midway through the length of Finland on its eastern side. We were poor, and we lived in a big housing project built for poor people. It was supposed to be temporary housing, but it stood for over thirty years. Twelve families lived in one building, and there were three buildings in the complex. So, altogether there were 36 families living in this place, which we called the "Barracks," though it had nothing to do with the army. I can't remember too much of the war itself, but Kuopio's big sawmill and plywood mill were often bombed by the Russians. When this happened we ran into the nearby bush for protection, as we lived very close to a kind of wilderness.

Maybe because we were poor and everything was hard to get due to strict rationing by the government, our parents decided to send some of us to Sweden. My younger sister, Helli, was born in 1939, and we were the first ones to go in 1942 when the Russians intensified the bombing. It must have been February because Helli was two years and seven months old, and I was four years and four months old. Also I remember snow on the ground in Sweden when we arrived. My mother has related to me how it is she and my father tried to prepare us for the journey. My mother asked my little sister: "How do you speak Swedish?" She then told my sister that *puhua* means "to speak" in Finnish, but also "to blow" or "puff." So my sister puffed air to demonstrate that she could speak Swedish! She also sang in Finnish, *tahtoset loistaa, tietani valaisevat,* which means something like "the star blinks, showing me the way." And my father asked me if I could fart "the Swedish way," and I let go a big one!

The next thing I remember is that we were in quarantine. Many Finnish children were underfed, and we all had lice. Others like my sister were ill. For this reason she had to stay longer in quarantine, which meant that we were separated. Before our separation, though, I remember running down the hallway and the nurses and caretakers running after me.

I was placed in a family that included a grandfather and his married son and wife who took care of the farm in Medepad, a district in the village of Boltjärn. Helli was placed in Ange near Sundsvall about 25 kilometers southeast from where I lived. And, though we lived quite close to each other, we only came to discover this in 1945, three years after we were both sent to Sweden.

I can remember the horse ride through snow to come to my new home. Luckily, the son whom I came to call *Far* (Father) was married to a Finnish woman, so we didn't have any problems understanding one another. Life on the farm was different from what I was used to in Finland, but it was a learning experience. I was assigned certain chores, of course, but I also had a lot of time to myself. There were two boys and also some girls who were close to my same age living in the area, and we spent a lot of time together. There was a river and a big pond where we fished and caught crabs. This is also where *Mor* (Mother) washed the clothes. Though there was running water on the farm, the clothes needed more fresh water to get really clean. I gave a hand in walking the cows from the field to the milking place in the summer, and I can remember once walking a cow to a bull some two miles away.

Then came the time for school, which I started in 1944. I can remember the Christmas party that year during which I sang "Twinkle, twinkle, little star" in Swedish. At that same time, my older sister Eila was also sent to Sweden and to the same village where I lived. And, luckily, we attended the same school.

Before we returned to Finland, though, I remember hearing one day in school that a Finnish girl was returning to Finland. She was not in school that day, and I worried that when I went home I would be sent back to Finland too. So I took my time walking back to make sure that I would be too late to be on the same train as this classmate. In those days there was no bus transport, so we used our legs and, when the weather permitted, our bicycles. I remember being very nervous about returning to Finland since I had forgotten all my Finnish and didn't know what circumstances I would be returning to. As it turned out, Eila and I returned to Finland at the end of the war in 1945 and our sister Helli one year later in 1946. Eila remembered her Finnish since she had only been one year in Sweden, but I had forgotten my native language, so that I had to repeat the first grade. The teacher was understanding, however, and spoke some Swedish to me for my benefit.

When you are a child, you don't think like an adult. So it was curious to me that my teacher always asked about our parcels from Sweden, and that when she learned that we had received one she would send a letter through me to my mother to ask for coffee, coffee, coffee, which at that time was the same as gold. You could not get coffee in Finland, and my mother always gave her some of the coffee we received.[1]

After my return I spent many summer vacations in Sweden, which I really enjoyed. My foster parents also sent these wonderful packages, once even sending my mother a bicycle, which was very useful to her for getting back and forth from work. At this point, she was a single provider, having divorced my father in early 1945 because my father had become an alcoholic. It was very rough for us. There were four children in our family, though my older brother was then seventeen years old and living on his own, and my younger sister was still in Sweden. My mother Hilja worked in the building industry and took whatever spare jobs she could find to support us. We learned that all three Swedish families had asked to adopt us, but our mother's love wouldn't allow it, and so this is why we landed back home. This was very difficult for Helli and me who had spent some years in Sweden and had bonded with our foster families, but we had to get used to it.

As a result, though, I never got close to my mother and was never homesick for Finland even after getting married and emigrating with my wife to Canada. I think that I must have been angry with my mother for taking me from Sweden, but at that age one never understands the full story. And I wasn't alone: everyone who returned to war-torn Finland from a much better life in Sweden suffered. We were all homesick. In the "Barracks" there were many war children like Helli and me who suffered from this malady.

Helli had an especially difficult adjustment upon her return as she had been in Sweden even longer than I. She longed for her Swedish parents and the life of which she had been robbed. Like I had, she had forgotten all her Finnish. And it was a shock for both of us to go from comfortable lives in Sweden to extremely poor ones in Finland.

As for my foster parents, they continued to help our family during and after the war, so I give them my warmest thanks. My Swedish mother, Helen, and I exchanged letters until she died in 1990, and before then I visited her twice in Sweden after my move to Canada. My Swedish grandfather Eric and his son Hugo, my *Far*, passed away some years earlier than she. Of the three, I loved my grandfather best. He was a very kind man. In recent years, I have visited their graves.

Ironically, I think of Finland as my home country today, though I wasn't as happy there as in Sweden. But I have friends in Sweden with whom I am still in contact. I have begun to live through my memories, good memories in all.

* * * * *

After finishing his studies in Finland and Sweden, Veijo went to a trade school to learn to be a furniture maker but also worked in a hardware store and as a letter carrier. He was married in 1957, and he and his wife emigrated to Canada in 1960. Both his sisters later emigrated there as well. Veijo worked with Kimberly Clark of Canada and also as a logger. He and his wife are retired and live today in Thunder Bay, Ontario.

Notes

1. Ersatz coffee was made from almost anything: potato skins, tree bark, and chicory, so the real thing was especially prized. Real coffee didn't reach Finland until several years after the war had ended.

7

Sugar Beets and Spettecaka
Soile Kiema Ilvesoksa

I was born in 1935 in Harlu near Lake Ladoga in Karelia to Albert Kiema and Siiri Eronen. My father was a carpenter at the time. When Karelia came under attack and the Winter War began in 1939, everything changed for our family. In December 1940, when I was four years of age, my mother and I were hurriedly evacuated, my mother carrying everything she could, but especially warm winter clothes, as the winter of 1940 was one of the coldest on record with temperatures of –40° Celsius. She also carried food for several days' journey. My father was in the army, and my grandparents were transported with their cattle.

My mother and I didn't know where we being taken, but my mother was wise and practical: a potty was light in weight for a four-year old to carry, and she could surely have foreseen the terrible conditions of the toilets in fully packed trains that had been traveling for days. The stress and fear of the situation also made many people sick. I think that I was the only child with a potty and such a wise mother.

We were moved to the western coast of Finland to the town of Kokkola or Karleby, which is its Swedish name. During this time, at least half of the people living in this region spoke only Swedish. But we returned to Karelia in the summer of 1941, as did 70 percent of the evacuated people, and found our village as we had left it. The big sawmill began its production again and provided jobs to the inhabitants of our village. I started my first school year in 1942. But in 1943, when I was eight years old, I was sent to Sweden, due to arrangements made by the Ministry of Social Affairs and the Swedish committee for helping Finnish children.

I do not remember anything about my journey to Sweden but, like most of the war children, I traveled by train for days north to the Swedish border where we were transferred onto Swedish trains with Swedish caretakers. No Finnish-speaking adults appeared after that.

Manpower was very scarce in Finland during the war, and all women, children, and elderly people were required to work on farms, in factories, or in munitions plants, creating equipment for the army. Members of women's auxiliary services who might have traveled with the children could not be spared. Although defense during air raids was the responsibility of men, women watched for enemy planes day and night for years on end. Paperwork, nursing, communications, and the feeding and clothing of the army were also women's tasks. They followed the army to the front and did everything needed except the fighting. The army rule was: no dead or wounded could be left behind, so women also took care of the dead and sent them home.[1]

My train moved south through Sweden. In Stockholm we were taken to a hospital for physical examinations, and again there were no Finnish-speaking adults to explain things to us. I remember being very scared by my blood test, since my blood was very dark red and the other children's more brilliant bright red. I was sure that this meant I had some kind of severe illness, though it turned out that I was the healthiest and that the other children were anemic.

I was sent to the south of Sweden in Skåne County to a village called Steffanstorp near the old university town of Lund. There were nine of us Finnish children put in a Finnish children's home. We were well fed; in fact, I remember being too-constantly fed, so that I tried to hide the fattiest pieces of meat in the pockets of my apron. I have always disliked grease and fat, and I felt that I somehow had to get rid of the meat. We were sent to school, and that was easy for me because I could read and write already, and I therefore quite easily learned Swedish.

I vividly remember two festivals, the Swedish Lucia Day, December 13, with girls wearing long white gowns and Lucia with her crown of burning candles, singing "Santa Lucia." There was also a big Christmas party in the village hall. We danced around the Christmas tree, singing cheerful Christmas carols, which were so different from the melancholy Finnish songs I knew. We received lots of sweets and practical Christmas presents, but I don't remember receiving any toys. Some families brought us to their homes for short visits. One such family, the Svenssons, took me for a visit to their home, and they were very nice people. But I spoiled the visit by developing a terrible toothache that night and keeping the entire family awake.

In recent years I have read some of the letters I wrote from the children's home and learned from them that we were taken care of there by two "Aunties." We also apparently made trips to a lake for swimming and picnics. And on my ninth birthday, I had a cake and received a card from one "Auntie" and some flowers from the other. I had forgotten that I had written to my mother, asking her to send over my favorite doll, which she did. I know that she actually sent many parcels of dolls' clothes and so forth, because I have letters from me in which I thanked her for them.

By this time I had learned to date all the letters I wrote. I found in one letter that I was taken to the Larsson family on March 1945, so I was actually there for about six months, after my year in the children's home. All the children at the home had finally been placed with families living in the area. My teacher would have liked to take me, but she was single and the children were supposed to be situated with two-parent families.

My family was an old couple in their sixties—not grandmotherly or grandfatherly types, but quite remote and cool. Two of their daughters lived up north with their families and seldom visited their parents, though the single daughter occasionally took me to Lund for shopping, the cinema, and some sight-seeing. There is a very old cathedral in Lund that we also saw. The only thing I ever wrote about school was that I couldn't have a report because my Swedish wasn't good enough. I remember my teacher from this time as middle-aged and nice, but I can't recall his name. The Larssons had a big farm close to the children's home, which specialized in beet root farming. I was mostly a very lonely child and had to do a lot of weeding in the sugar beet fields. Also, while I was permitted to play with old dolls and prams in the attic, I was not allowed to touch the best dolls. The family had some parties, and I became acquainted with the loveliest cake on earth, the Spettecaka from Skåne, a high tower of meringue made with thousands of eggs and sugar and perhaps some honey too. This cake is made only for very important occasions and is usually prepared by skilled pastry chefs. One can still find it in shops and cafes in Sweden.

I was happy to return home to Finland and Kokkola where my family had been evacuated again in 1944. I now had two little sisters, born in 1942 and 1944, and because I had not totally forgotten Finnish, I easily started school and had the great advantage of speaking Swedish even if my dialect was different from that spoken in Kokkola. In secondary school we had to study Swedish and English, and many of my classmates later completed university degrees in these languages and became teachers as I did.

After the war my father worked as a carpenter in Kokkola. Though I don't remember my mother ever working in Karelia, she had many jobs after our evacuation, and for years she worked in the garment industry.

My family was never ashamed of having sent me to Sweden, and we could freely talk about the subject. We shared letters with my two Swedish families, the Larssons and the Svenssons, for many years, mostly at Christmas. But gradually the letters stopped, as the Larsson couple got too old to write.

I believe that my war child story is relatively happy for various reasons: my visit to Sweden was short, from 1943 to 1945; I could read and write, so there was regular correspondence between my Finnish mother and me; no loving family competed with my own in Finland; and I was already used to travel and dislocation when I left for Sweden.

* * * * *

Soile studied English and Swedish, receiving her language degree from Helsinki University. She taught English at the Himanka middle school, 1964–1974, and was later a school principal in Kannus. At the end of her career, she again taught school in Lapua. She was married in 1964 and had two children, Jouni and Jarna. In addition to her work, she was a painter and loved to garden. Soile died in 2005.

Notes

1. Because this army rule still exists, war veterans continue to search for fallen comrades near battle sites on what today is Russian territory. The army has a list of missing soldiers and, after identifying the remains of bodies or finding identification tags, the remains or tags are returned home to Finland. DNA technology has helped to verify the identity of many soldiers. Every summer in this way, many soldiers are brought home and laid to rest in soldiers' graves.

8
Dragons in a Handbag
Veikko Inkinen

My family is Karelian, having lived in what used to be the eastern part of Finland for many generations.[1] In old times Karelians lived in great families. For example, my family had its own village called "Inkilä," or place of Inkinen, though other families lived there, which prevented the necessity of cousins intermarrying. The reason for these great families was the land and the old form of agriculture, which demanded a lot of labor. To prevent outsiders from grabbing the land, inhabitants married inside their village. Living for generations in such close-knit big families developed a more conversational and outgoing character than the single-family life of West Finns. According to family legend, Inkinens lived there from the sixteenth century. But after the war, our family was scattered all over Finland.

My family was evacuated in the spring of 1944 from Karelia when it came under severe Soviet attack. We moved to Heinola, a little town in southern Finland approximately 100 kilometers north of Helsinki. Heinola was a center for evacuated Karelians, and my father's job was to oversee the relief stores there. Before the war my father had been a local politician, but the war destroyed his constituency and he had to look for other jobs. Also, because of his age he didn't serve in the war, but was instead a civil servant. At that time, I was four years old, my brother Heikki six, and my sister Marja eight. It was decided that we would all be sent to Sweden. I do not think that it was totally voluntary from my parents' side. There was strong political pressure on parents to send their children in response to what began as a Swedish private initiative and grew in popularity because Finnish authorities came to believe that they would receive more assistance if they agreed. One could almost say that the Finnish government was willing to sell children for butter and guns. Many Finns were also afraid that Russia would annihilate the Finnish people after conquering their country.[2]

Children older than six or seven may have understood why they were sent to Sweden, but for younger children it was deeply traumatic to be

Figure 8.1. *Veikko Inkinen at age four, around the time he was sent to Sweden. Courtesy Veikko Inkinen.*

separated from their mothers. I have read about how some mothers left their children in the trains, telling them to wait and that they would soon return. Then the mothers disappeared, often because they were too distraught to stay until the train departed. But those children who waited in vain for their mothers felt they had been abandoned. Finnish war child literature refers to that feeling as the "treachery of the mother."

I remember only one episode of my early childhood before I arrived at the home of my Swedish foster parents, the Karlssons. It is the deafening noise of Russian aircraft, flying over our home on their way to Southern Finland. My brother and I are under a table, screaming *"Ryssä tulee, Ryssä tulee!"* (Russians are coming, Russians are coming!). Because this memory is so full of terror, it alone holds the power to break through the memory block created by the shock of separation from my parents at the Heinola railway station. But this is the only part of my childhood before my arrival in Sweden that I remember today.

The shipment of children I was part of was first transported to a quarantine center and after that to collection centers in southern Sweden. From there several hundred of us were taken to another collection center named "Herrljunga" near Göteborg in Vestra Götamanland and were accommodated in a huge hall. One day a great number of adults arrived, and the women began to move around the beds and to touch us. I remember that they were stroking my hair and feeling my hands and feet. Some removed the blanket from my bed to see me more clearly, perhaps to make sure I wasn't deformed or ill. One or two even lifted me from my bed and tried to hold me on their laps. I remember that I was so afraid that I forgot to cry.

I was taken by a middle-aged farming couple, Gustaf and Thyra Karlsson, who had no children of their own, and they started very soon to think of me as their own child. They succeeded in spoiling me quite soon, and I had a very happy three years in Sweden. It helped that my brother Heikki and I lived quite close to each other, and we met regularly to play together. Unfortunately, Marja lived farther away, and I only saw her twice during her year in Sweden. Somehow, the Karlssons made me forget my Finnish past and inspire me to think about them as my proper parents. They also made me believe that my correct name should be "Bror Karlsson," "Veikko" being similar to the Swedish "Bror." You can understand my confusion after returning to Finland, when I was told that my real name was "Veikko Inkinen."

Some of my memories from this early time in Sweden include coming to a place of big houses; a ride on Gustaf's motorbike with the wind on my face to a town called Boras; a visit to a church; a mechanical toy that Gustaf gave me; a boat journey on Lake Silja; Gustaf dressed in evening tails because we were going to meet a bishop; a trip to a nearby lake where Gustaf taught me to swim; and a place with a lot of great buildings. It seems that my memories are arranged like single photographs. I also remember seeing through a window Gustaf's younger sister May making love with her boyfriend. I became very agitated, not knowing what was going on. I had long discussions with my playmates about this—we were all around five at the time—and we became dubious about the legend of storks dropping babies down chimneys.

At age seven, while I was still too young to really understand what was happening to me, I learned that I must return to Finland. This came as a great shock to my Swedish parents. It must have been equally traumatic to me because I can't remember anything about this return trip. The first clear memories are of a time from half a year later. I think that I should remember more than I do; after all, I was three years older than when I left for Sweden. But I do know that my return to Finland was a great blow to me. At that point I was a spoiled child, accustomed to having my wishes immediately fulfilled. Now I was living in a poor country where I had to fight for everything with my siblings and other children. One could say that I had come from a land of honey and butter and had been thrown into the back streets.

Also there was a lot of hostility toward the returning war children due to the belief that they had enjoyed an easy and protected way of life, while the children in Finland had suffered. War children were often better dressed, and they had toys Finnish children had never seen. Then there were problems with the language. Parents could not communicate with their returning children; other children regarded you as dumb because you didn't understand your lessons in school as well as they; and though I went to a Swedish-speaking school in Finland, I was speaking the "wrong" kind of dialect.[3]

Worst of all, though, was that I had a lot of difficulties in accepting my Finnish parents as my proper parents. I thought that I had been kidnapped from my *real* home. I dreamed a lot about Sweden until I was ten or twelve, but didn't dare to tell my mother for fear that she would think me disloyal. She struggled to convince me that I was her own child, but didn't succeed until I was over ten years old. I feel that she also manipulated my memories in some way. I think that she seemed worried about what might have happened to us in Sweden and was afraid of what we might tell her upon our return. So, for her own peace of mind, she tried to equip us with "safe" memories. How did she do it? She did it indirectly. When we had visitors at home and somebody asked about my past as a war child, she told them how kind the people in Sweden had been. She also talked about all the letters she had received from Sweden and how these letters described my happy years there. It seems that I was always listening to her stories. Later on, when I tried to find the letters, I could not locate any. Today, I believe that she was describing the way of life she had *desired* for me in Sweden. Maybe she was thinking that if you repeat a fairy story often enough, it becomes true.

As a coping mechanism, I may have invented certain stories or "memories" myself. One of my most cherished "memories," for instance, is when Mama Thyra came to the children's distributing center, swept me into a warm blanket, and carried me away to her home. I always felt peace, happiness, and joy when I "remembered" this. However, later on I concluded that this never could have happened: I would naturally have been terrified of being taken by strangers and separated from my siblings. So, probably after my return to Finland, I invented it as a comforting memory. How does one know that good memories are true and not something invented to suppress other unpleasant memories?

Also I believe that some of my more traumatic memories have been permanently erased. It is a fact that my mother left me in August 1944 at the Heinola railway station. However, I can't remember anything about it. I think that it was a very formative event in my life that influenced my later life and character. The second separation event happened three years later when my Swedish parents left me in Stockholm for my return to Finland. I can't remember anything about that separation either. I think that real childhood memories consist mainly of fear, terror, and shame. For instance, one definite memory I have from Sweden is being washed in a bathtub, having soiled myself, and being very ashamed.

Another thing is clear: the first separation from my Finnish mother forever damaged our child-mother relationship. I remember in primary school, singing a song about how grateful children should be for their mothers, but I didn't feel that way. I always had a vague feeling that I couldn't completely trust her. I remember too that I had a bad conscience for that mistrust.

My time in Sweden was not a taboo topic in my home. I could freely tell my parents about the farm where I had lived and so on. However, I do not think that my mother ever asked me about how we *felt* in Sweden, and it was forbidden to discuss *why* we had been sent there. If we children ever asked something about such matters, my mother lost her ability to speak and left the room. When she returned she changed the topic and spoke about something totally different. Thus, we learned to avoid these issues. It was like incest in the family, something you didn't speak about. Before my mother passed away when I was forty-six, none of us had ever discussed the events of August 1944. She never came to terms with these memories.

As an adult I have also found it impossible to come to terms with memories of certain events that are unrecoverable due to the early age at which I experienced them. To suddenly meet something from your childhood may be a very frightening experience. When I was thirty or so and visiting my home on Hermansö island where my family had lived since 1948, I encountered my mother's old handbag. This bag, made of paper-like material (similar to paper shoes and sheets from the period) and coated with dark paint, evoked a powerful response. According to the label, it was manufactured in 1943. There was a strange odor around the handbag. Once I opened it and put my face into it to smell the odor, to my astonishment I found that I was shaking and sobbing violently. The odor had probably awakened some forbidden memory, which tried to rise up from my subconscious.

I have sometimes thought that if I had dared to keep my face long enough in the handbag, I might have remembered something about the separation from my mother at Heinola railway station in 1944. Since then I have associated the smell in her handbag with the smell of war. To me it is the smell of fear and helplessness, of not understanding what is happening to you, and not being master of your fate. I have never touched the handbag again. I put it back on the shelf from where I found it. I still have the feeling that it is a very dangerous object to touch, like radioactive materials, doors to forbidden cellars of your mind, or areas marked by strange animals like dragons at unknown parts of the seas by ancient cartographers.

In recent years, I have thought a lot about Sweden and the alternative future that was closed to me at age seven. Today I am not sure if Sweden would have offered more opportunity than Finland has done. In 1949, when I was nine, there was a plan for me to return to Sweden. But my parents backed out at the last minute. I think that they suspected they might not get me back and became afraid of Gustaf and Thyra. Thus they deliberately cut off this vital connection. But the time in Sweden had already formed my character in some permanent way. After Sweden I was never again 100 percent Finn. I have always felt that I was something between Finnish and Swedish. For example, Swedish is a more logical language than Finnish, and when I have to make very difficult decisions I try to think in Swedish.

I sometimes also wonder how life might have been different had I been adopted by my Swedish foster parents. Though all Swedish parents had to sign contracts, agreeing to return their foster children when Finnish parents demanded them back, there was a loophole in the system. You had only to take the child to a physician and get a certificate indicating that this would damage his mental development. Then, the local court could annul the contract you had signed. I have wondered why Gustaf and Thyra didn't pursue this method. I am sure that they knew about it. But they were deeply religious people, and it might have gone against their moral convictions.

Nevertheless, I was one of the fortunate ones. As an adult, my wife Sinikka and I visited my former Swedish home. Thyra and Gustaf had preserved my old room as some kind of shrine, which amazed us. In losing me, they had in some way lost their life's meaning.

It would be nice to think that every child ended up in such a loving family, but unfortunately that is not true. The great majority of Swedes loved their foster children, but there were also farming families that were looking for cheap laborers, children in their early teens. And there have been reports about children who ended up in the hands of pedophiles and circulated from one bad family to another. Also many war children who were adopted by Swedish parents discovered that, after their deaths, they had been disinherited. After all, they had not been their "real" children. One could say that Sweden was mostly well prepared to receive some 50,000 children, but that 80,000 stretched their resources, so that many met with unfortunate fates.

Finland was also unprepared in many ways to deal with the returning war children. Finland in the late 1940s was still more or less a farming country. Very few parents had probably ever heard about child psychology at the time. A professor named Martti Kaila assisted the administration in questions concerning child psychology. But in his opinion there was no reason to worry. He believed that all children are very adaptable and would not be harmed in returning from Sweden. Therefore, nothing was done. In addition, many of the leading members of the Finnish medical faculty had close connections to Germany before and during the war. Their attitudes were influenced by Nazi ideology, and you could hardly call all of them humanists. Soft thinking was not popular. Finally, there was a lack of professional manpower. In no way could Finland have given therapy to the thousands of returning war children.

Like me and most of the war children I have known, my siblings have had difficulties in adjusting to their wartime and postwar experiences. My brother Heikki seems to refuse to admit that part of his life. And, due to our separation at the collection center, my sister Marja still has a guilty conscience about not having been able to care for her little brothers in Sweden. But the emotional challenge in revisiting the past is just one explanation for the late emergence of war child associations, such as the one I belong to. Personally, I feel there were political, commercial, and psychological reasons to explain the long silence of the war children.

The first ten years after the war were very difficult in Finland. My parents, for instance, had lost everything. Though my father had work, which involved dealing with Karelian refugees after the war, when this task was complete his office was closed and he lost his job. After that, he settled down as a farmer on a small island in southern Finland, and at one point we came close to begging. Fortunately, he had an elder brother living in America who had served in the Corps of Engineers of the U.S. Navy and who was unmarried. When he died, he left a substantial sum of money to my father, and our financial troubles were solved for a long time. I think of it as our family's Marshall Aid from America.

In addition to great and widespread economic hardship in Finland, another reason for the long silence of the war children is that there was a common understanding that one couldn't risk angering the Soviet Union in any way. For political reasons the war was a topic you had to avoid.[4] And, in addition, there were commercial reasons for not discussing the war. After Finland had paid its war reparations to the Soviet Union, Finland's commercial industries discovered to their great delight that they could sell Russians as much as they could manufacture. But also many war children, including myself, wanted to avoid thinking about their past. Most of us couldn't remember the details of our childhood experiences very well, and we were often afraid of these memories. Then there was the question whom one should hate: your Finnish parents, your Swedish parents, society, fate, or God? The safest thing was to try to forget your childhood. If one could not run away from the past, it was better to remember everything in a positive way.

But things changed in the 1990s. When the Soviet Union dissolved, so did the national consensus that the war was a forbidden topic. Also war children were reaching retirement age and had more time in which to come together and create associations where they could safely share their stories. Though my wife and I had visited Gustaf and Thyra in the late 1970s, both before and after that trip we were silent on this subject, perhaps due to my anxieties. However, after my retirement, both of us joined a war child association and started a new life with these memories. (My wife is not a war child, but one may join as a passive member.) Although the separation experiences from my Finnish and Swedish parents are not things I like to remember, sharing my story and the stories of others helps me feel I am more open, kind, and easy with people than when I was younger. I am not so suspicious and reserved anymore. I feel that I am now living the best time of my life. And in some unreligious way, I am happy and grateful for every day. At war child meetings, we can show our real feelings without fear or shame. We are finally receiving the therapeutic treatment we didn't receive in our early childhood.

* * * * *

After his retirement as a ship surveyor and his work with the European Union on a project to assist Estonia in becoming eligible for membership in the EU, Veikko became chairman of his war child association in Hämeenlinna at its inception in 2004 and has served in this capacity ever since. Because he believes that the "best and safest" way to deal with childhood trauma is to write about it, he has helped coach fellow war children in writing their memoirs and autobiographies. Though there are an estimated 30,000 to 40,000 war children still living in Finland, only some 1,500 belong to war child associations. According to Veikko, statistics on how many war children are still living Finland and Sweden are difficult to arrive at due to the constant movement of people between these two countries over the past several decades.

Notes

1. The province of Viipuri, Karelia's capital, was divided into three regions: the Karelian Isthmus, which borders the Gulf of Finland; Lake Ladoga; and North Karelia. Because the border of the Isthmus was only thirty to forty kilometers from St. Petersburg, it was a source of great tension between the two countries for many years prior to the war. As Veikko explains, "In the Tarto negotiation of 1920, Russia proposed that the Isthmus border should be moved some fifty kilometers westward. But Finland did not accept this." Veikko believes, in fact, that this is one of the greatest mistakes Finland ever made, since "We had to pay for it in 1939–1945 with nearly 100,000 casualties." Finally, Finland lost all of Karelia to Russia during the Continuation War. Tarto is the town where Finland and the USSR met to discuss the new relationship between for the former principality of Finland and its old "mother country."
2. When it appeared in 1944 that Finland could be occupied by the Soviets, there was some speculation in Swedish newspapers about whether Sweden should evacuate the Swedish-speaking population from Finland. One newspaper discussed the removal of 200,000 Finnish children and then, as Veikko puts it, "dividing the spoils between Sweden and Denmark."
3. Because of their proximity to Russia, Karelians were often viewed as Russians, even though they weren't. Thus, Karelian war children had special problems returning to Finland. Swedish-speaking Finns disapproved of the way they spoke Swedish, and Finnish-speaking Finns didn't like them because they were Karelians.
4. Urho Kaleva Kekkonen, Finland's president from 1956 to 1982, compared the Soviet-Finnish relationship to that between a crocodile and the bird that cleans the crocodile's teeth: in this way, the bird may get a good dinner, but it has to jump quickly when the crocodile closes its jaws.

9

A Good and Bad Hand

Eric Jaakkola

I was born in June 1938 as Erkki Tuomo Antero Jaakkola, but today I go by "Eric." My father was a chauffer for the government before, during, and after the war. My mother took care of my sister Airi and me until we went to Sweden, and then she had another child during the war, our younger brother, who was born in June 1944. I was one the 80,000 war children, along with my sister, Airi, who were sent to Sweden during the war. With the outbreak of the Winter War in 1939, Sweden offered Finnish children aged fourteen and under a safe haven there. Its humanitarian movement started with the slogan *Finland's Sak är vär!* (Finland's cause is ours!).

My sister Airi and I remained in Finland during the Winter War and part of the Continuation War. Some of what I remember comes from stories my mother told me about that time. She always taught us that if we were under a table, bombs couldn't hurt us, though our actual hiding place was in the underground cellar during the bombings. The cellar had tar on the walls, and I remember that, to entertain ourselves, Airi and I picked out small pieces of tar to use as chewing gum. Fortunately, our house in Tapanila, a suburb of Helsinki, was never hit by any bombs; however, our flag pole was once struck.

Once, on a day prior to a Russian bombing, I went to a store to purchase an ice cream cone, and as I was walking back home, the air raid sirens went off for some reason. According to my mother, I yelled loudly to everyone in the street to run for safety, shouting, "The Russians are coming!" But I obviously wasn't too worried, as I very casually walked home.

On another occasion, my mother had just finished cleaning the house and had gone outside for a short while. When she returned, she found that, just for fun, I had scooped up soot that was in the bottom of the stove and covered my sister, myself, and the kitchen with it. She told us to pack our bags and leave, saying, "You are not my children any more!" Airi and I took her seriously and began walking down the street hand in hand, but our mother soon came and got us, warning us never to do that again.

We also got in trouble with our dad sometimes. Once, my father caught us smoking our homemade cigarettes made out of grass and rolled up with paper. He made me promise never to smoke again, and so far I have kept that promise. Another vivid memory I have of my early childhood is of being in my bed when I heard tapping on the window. A German soldier was outside, and my mother took an axe and chased him away.

Because of the heavy bombing in Helsinki and suburbs, our parents decided to drive us to the central part of Finland to a town called Alajärvi to stay with our grandparents. As a farming community with no important targets, it was a safer area of Finland. There was also more food there since we lived on a farm.

Then, on September 4, 1944, a ceasefire was agreed upon, and Finland signed a peace treaty with Russia on September 19. But according to the peace treaty, Finland had to get the Germans out of northern Finland, which led to the Lapland War. After this, it became unsafe for us to stay in Alajärvi, which was some three hundred kilometers from the action. It was then that our parents decided that it was best that we go to Sweden to wait out the remainder of the war. So Airi and I left in the fall of 1944 on a freighter from Helsinki to Sweden. I was then six, and Airi was five.

Our baby four-month-old brother, Aarne, stayed with my mother in Finland. Many hundreds of children boarded the freighter. I remember that all of us walked in single file tied to one another with a long rope, so that none of us would be lost. The only food that I can recall from the boat was salami, and whenever I have salami today I am reminded of my early childhood voyage. Our sleeping beds were bunk beds at least three bunks high. The sea was very rough, and many kids became sea sick. Fortunately, I did not, but my sister was extremely seasick and kept vomiting. I think that she also had a premonition that bad things were to come in Sweden.

After we arrived in Stockholm, some of us were transported by train to Ronneby in southern Sweden. Around ten children, including me and Airi, were accompanied by some adult chaperones at our stop. Airi and I were taken to different families who didn't live too far from one another, but we seldom saw one another during our time in Sweden, except when Airi was able to sneak away. Unfortunately, she endured a very unhappy time there.

My future foster sister, Eva, recalls that I arrived wearing a large nametag with my name and the names of Gustaf and Sigrid Mattson, her parents and my future foster parents. I was wearing boots, breeches, and a small jacket. In one hand I held a small suitcase with some clothes and a photo of my mother. Eva was born in 1927, and I was born in 1938, so there was an eleven-year difference in our ages, but we became close nevertheless. The Mattson family lived a few miles north of Ronneby in a community called Kallinge where I ended up staying slightly more than two years from 1944 to 1946. Overall, it was a happy time for me.

From our first meeting at the station in Ronneby, I had a good relationship with Gustaf even though I did not understand Swedish. After my arrival, the Mattson family and I went by taxi from the train station to the home of Donald Berga where I had my first Swedish meal of fried eggs, bacon, potatoes, and bread. Then we traveled to the Mattsons' house, which was very large. It had three stories, and I lived on the second floor in a room with Gustaf and Sigrid.

In the beginning, I was very shy and bit reclusive, but later I often ran directly to Gustaf and hugged him. Though I had great confidence in the new family, I was afraid that I would not be allowed to stay and maybe given away to someone else. I demonstrated this for the first while I was there by not wanting to leave the house to go visiting other people like the Mattson's family and friends. So Gustaf very considerately stayed at home with me, and Sigrid and Eva would go by themselves. After a while, I became less shy and felt more comfortable at home. Later on I even thought it was fun to go on outings with the family and meet other people, and I was especially happy to go to parties. At first, I feared shopping for new clothes to wear to special occasions, but I soon liked wearing nice new clothes to parties, and I loved the delicious cakes served at the Mattsons' parties. I also enjoyed it when Sigrid played the piano, so I could sing and keep rhythm, for which I've always had a talent.

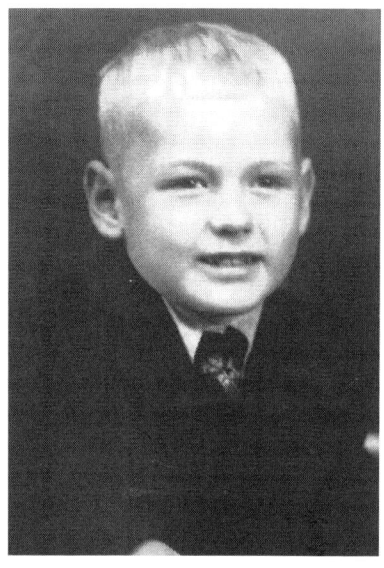

Figure 9.1. *Eric Jaakkola at age six, just before he and his sister were sent to Sweden. Courtesy Eric Jaakkola.*

During my stay in Sweden I received quite lot of new clothing, most of which I took back to Finland. Besides clothes, I also received presents on my birthdays and at Christmas. I started calling Gustaf and Sigrid *Far* and *Mor* (Father and Mother) and referring to Eva as my sister. I spent much of my time with *Far* out in the fields and visiting the animals in the stables inside the barn. I liked being with him in his workshop and in the woods. And I came to love loading hay, climbing trees, and sitting on a horse. I also enjoyed swimming in a river that was close to home. I learned to speak Swedish quickly, and this helped me to adapt to all my new and wonderful circumstances.

I remember that Swedish was taught to me by my pointing at pictures and reading the Swedish text that accompanied them. Also a lot of children lived nearby, and playing with them helped me to learn the language. My special playmate was a boy named Benny Melin. I also had a special relationship with a girl named Anita. She was older than I, but I often told people that I wanted to marry her. We danced together on a wooden dance floor that was elevated with guard rails around it. This was close to our farm and located next to a large field where there were lots of trees.

One frightening memory is of being in a field by myself and a big black bull running after me. I ran fast as I could and made it over the fence to safety. I was also really scared of the large geese that hissed at me and turkeys that were just as big as I was. Once a hornet flew into my ear and stung me. Foolishly, I put my hand over it while I was running, so that it kept stinging me. Maybe I was trying to see how much pain I could withstand!

Occasionally I played pranks with other boys. We enjoyed "packaging" cow pies to look like gifts, setting them on the road, and watching people who happened to walk by and pick them up.

Meanwhile, Airi was having a very different experience. As I learned later, her foster mother was a nurse with a daughter just one year older than Airi. Shockingly, all of Airi's nice clothes were given to this daughter, and Airi had to sleep in the attic. She was not allowed to come and visit me, and she was very often spanked. But my mother had arranged a clever way for Airi to communicate the truth about her situation. She had told Airi that when she wrote a letter to Finland, to draw a picture of a house if everything was good, but to draw a picture of a boat if things were bad. However, we don't think that her letters were ever mailed, because nothing ever came of it.

Once my sister came and visited me on a bike. She wouldn't let me ride it at first, so I ran away. She had wanted to reveal her situation to me, but she got in really big trouble from her foster parents for doing this. In addition to being spanked often and being forced to sleep in the attic, her foster parents often punished her by locking her in a bathroom and making her eat her meals inside the locked bathroom. When Airi sneaked out with the bike and found me, she was punished again the same way.

My foster parents, by contrast, were very good to me. For instance, *Far* and *Mor* kept in contact with my parents in Finland. A Swedish family in Tapanila translated these Swedish letters into Finnish, and letters that my parents wrote were then translated into Swedish. In this way, I kept contact with my biological parents. My father even came to visit me in summer of 1945 and my mother in May 1946. It was a way for them to get reacquainted with me again. If they visited Airi, she doesn't remember it. She stayed with this unkind family until the end of the war.

In the fall of 1946 I was supposed to return to Finland, but I didn't want to go. It was decided that the best thing to do was to have Eva accompany me, so that I wouldn't put up a huge fuss. I returned to Finland not only with Eva but Airi, and I remember the journey back to Helsinki was on a ferry similar to a cruise ship. Upon arriving, I was given a priority position, sitting on my father's lap as we drove to Tapanila from the cruise port.

Unfortunately, while she was in Finland, Eva became ill and had to have her appendix removed. When Eva left to go back to Sweden, I was very unhappy and asked her to tell Anita, my first crush, that I missed her. I wanted to return with Eva, and I cried a lot when she left. I felt lost upon her departure: I had forgotten all my Finnish and had lost my family in Sweden.

I attended Finnish/Swedish school to relearn Finnish, and the next year my mother and father divorced. Though I don't recall quarreling between them, my father drank and smoked, which may have been a factor. So Airi and I went to live with our grandparents in Alajärvi again.

After this, my mother decided to travel to the United States to find better opportunities, since postwar Finland was extremely difficult. She received a visitor's permit for ninety days, and within those ninety days she had to get married in order to stay in America. Luckily, she met a willing widower. Meanwhile, Airi and I waited to join her while applications for visas were being processed. During that time I played with the neighbor kids and walked to school and skied during the winter. The school was two miles away, so skiing made the journey easier. Airi told me that while skiing to school that year in Alajärvi in 1948, she had to wear a short skirt and long wool socks.

Around this time, when I was ten and Airi nine, I developed another crush on one of the neighbor girls named "Sanni." She was four years older than I. I asked her father if I could marry her, and he said yes, if I helped in their wheat fields. So I worked all summer in his fields and also worked on my grandparents' farm. I cut the wheat with a small sickle and once managed to cut my finger from which I still have a scar. But it was lucky for me that I did not cut my finger off entirely. Airi also used a small sickle to cut the wheat. Whenever possible that summer, I would sneak out of my grandparents' home to go dancing at a nearby location with Sanni.

Another memory of mine from this time is when we were staying with our grandparents, and a package our mother sent from America arrived with a large bag of popcorn inside and directions about how to prepare it. My grandmother put the popcorn in pancake batter, and when she started making the pancakes, to her great surprise the popcorn began to pop and the pancakes to fly all over the kitchen. She was very upset that my mother would have sent something like that to us!

Eventually our visas were approved, and Airi and I left for America on a DC-6, a four-engine airline propeller plane, in October of 1949. We made headline news in papers in Finland and the United States because we were two children alone: my sister, Airi, age nine, and I, age eleven.

Our new stepfather had paid for the ticket, and we were finally reunited with our mother in Nashwauk, Minnesota. On our drive from Minneapolis to Nashwauk, mother had a large bag of bananas for us to eat: these were my favorite fruit, though my favorite fruit in Sweden had been pears. When I eat a pear in the United States, it always reminds me of Sweden. And now, when we visit my cousin Hillevi in Sweden, we always have pear ice cream. It's the best!

I missed Sanni and my grandparents, but I was happy to be with our mother after such a long time. Airi and I had to learn a new language yet again, however, and for this reason I had to repeat first grade to learn how to read and speak English. But later we skipped grades to catch up with our age groups. So began our new life in America.

Finally, I enjoyed a reunion with Eva in Sweden in 1999, the first time that we were together since 1946. It had been 53 years. On our last trip to Finland and Sweden, my wife Patty and I took a ferry to an island between Sweden and Denmark. I met a woman on the ferry who had been a war child and who had chosen to stay in Sweden rather than go back to her family in Finland. It surprised me to hear that she had never taken a trip back to Finland to find her birth family even as an adult.

I have good feelings about Finland as my home country and also have good memories of Sweden. I look forward still to visiting my foster sister Eva in Sweden. I must be very adaptable because I feel at home wherever I happen to be. Unfortunately, I did not stay I touch with Gustaf and Sigrid, but my reunion with Eva in 1999 meant a lot to me. Also I never resented my mother for sending us to Sweden. I always felt very close to her and felt that she did the best she could do for us under the circumstances.

I got the luck of the draw in Sweden, ending up with a wonderful family. My sister was not so lucky because she ended up with a family who treated her in a very cruel manner. I was dealt a good hand, she a bad.

* * * * *

Eric attended Hibbing Junior College. He wanted to be an airline pilot especially since he had worn the captain's hat when photos were taken of him and Airi when they first arrived in New York. He took the training and passed all of the exams for a commercial pilot license. Unfortunately, after moving to the Twin Cities in Minnesota, he was in a car accident, resulting in severe concussion that gave him headaches for two years. As a result, he worked for 3M for thirty-seven years as a lab technician, retiring in 1999. He has been married three times and has one child. His sister Airi is a medical technologist. She does not like to discuss her experiences in Sweden and would have liked to say something about this to her foster parents, but will never have the chance as they have long since passed away.

10

The Red Shoes
Anita Jakobsson

My parents, Suoma and Gunnar Jakobsson, had been married some three years when I was born in August 1935. I was given the name Anita Linnea Jakobsson. Seventeen months later my brother Sven Olof whom we called "Nenne" was born. I couldn't pronounce his real name, so this was my nickname for him. He in turn called me "Aita," and we still use these nicknames today.

My mother spoke Finnish, and my father spoke both Finnish and Swedish. Though my parents conversed with each other in Finnish, I grew up speaking Finnish to my mother and Swedish to my father. When we were of school age, my brother and I attended Swedish-speaking schools, as did my three younger sisters who were born later.

We lived in Kokkola, Finland, in the old part of town next to the fire station. My father was a master glazier by profession, but he also worked as a volunteer fireman. For this reason there was an alarm bell installed in our home. During the war, the bell not only rang when there was a fire but to warn us that enemy planes were approaching. I was very frightened of that alarm. Even though I was too young to understand much about the war, I realized that the alarm meant danger. I also feared the news over the radio because I could see how tense my parents became while they listened to it.

I remember one particular time when we had to leave our home in the dark and head for the forest to find cover from possible enemy attack. For this reason we slept with our clothes on. Our only means of transport were Finnish kicksleds shaped like chairs on runners that one person stood on to kick the sleigh forward. Once when we rushed into the woods for cover, our father said he knew a shortcut, but he took us the wrong way, so that we had to wade through deep snow in the middle of a field, which really slowed down our progress. But eventually we found the forest, which was plunged in darkness. Even the snow didn't help to brighten the frightening dark.

As we hid, we could see in the far distance planes dropping bombs. Our parents covered us up with blankets, telling us that the enemy would think we were rocks. On that occasion, no bombs hit our city; in fact, none of the bombs hit Kokkola during the war. I have heard it explained later that there is some sort of magnetic field in Kokkola that causes instruments on planes to malfunction. But another reason the bombs misfired might be that the enemy knew that many of their soldiers were billeted in hospitals in our town. By the time the war was over Kokkola had housed some 8,000 Russian prisoners, including 649 who never made it home. They are buried outside our cemetery wall in a common grave surrounded by a fence with a monument in the middle. Their names have been documented, and many Russians have come to Kokkola to find if their missing family could be located there. Some have been fortunate in their search.

In the summer of 1939 Hitler began to demand back territories lost in World War I. According to my mother's writings it was a summer full of tension and fear and surmise about what the future would hold. Later that fall, Germany was ready to attack Poland. We were at our summer cottage at the time until the end of August. We didn't have a radio there, but we heard about Germany's attack on Poland through friends. We found this news shocking. It seemed like the beginning of the end. But we tried to live our lives as before.

Finland soon declared itself neutral along with the rest of the Scandinavian countries. However, it didn't help much. Russia began to demand certain territories in Finland for its fight against Germany. Finnish delegations were sent to meet with Stalin, as we didn't want to lose the territories we had fought so hard for. Poland collapsed in four weeks. Christmas of 1939 was gloomy for this reason. People were frightened of what the future would hold. Finnish soldiers put up a hard defense, and many more Russians were killed than Finns. But too many of our own were killed as well. The town chaplain had to bring sad news to many homes that winter.

Gunnar, my father, was called to active duty and sent close to the Russian border. We children missed our father, and we each kept a piece of his clothing like one of his shirts close to us at night when we were in bed.

The food situation was also very bad. Milk was strictly rationed, allowing only one half liter or two cups per child per day and about seven ounces for the adults.

Eventually the Winter War ended, but the peace was too brief with the new Continuation War beginning in June 1941. Again our father had to leave, and this time he was sent to the north.

At this time many children were being sent to Sweden for safety. Several of our friends and acquaintances were sending their children. So my mother started to think about this: would it be safer to send the children in case Russia conquered and occupied our country? She wrote to our father about the idea, and he felt the same: that she should at least send me, but that Nenne, my little brother, was too young. With a heavy heart, my mother looked into the idea and wrote that I sometimes seemed in favor of going and at other times not. My mother was against it from the start, but since everyone was praising the program and the good nutrition children would receive in Sweden, she began to consider the idea very seriously.

The bitter time arrived when I was to be sent to Sweden. My father was home on leave, and we stayed awake all night the night before I was to depart. According to my mother, because my little bed was next to my parents', I pushed my little hand into my father's, searching for security. But we all spent the night crying.

The next evening a children's train left for the north. According to my mother, my parents took me to the train depot where I was given a nametag to wear around my neck, and I was taken aboard the train. I apparently sat next to the window, first staring after my parents, then putting my head down and refusing to look at them. My mother says about this event that she and my father felt very guilty because they feared that I felt they were abandoning me. My mother said that she was devastated when the train left, crying bitterly along with many other mothers.

It is hard for me to read my mother's letters about this separation. Having children of my own, I can now understand how dreadful it must have been for her and for my father.

I don't remember anything about the long train ride, nor can I recall my feelings or emotions. I do remember, though, that my parents had given me a doll to take along. It had a grey dress with a pretty embroidered pocket. However, I had always wanted a doll that could close its eyes, and this one couldn't. It was a disappointment, since we did not have many toys.

Some time before my departure for Sweden, however, I actually had a blinking doll very briefly. A playmate of mine had received a new blinking doll with a blue dress from America, and this was the sort of doll I wanted. Since her old doll, one in a red dress, also blinked, I decided to make a deal with her. I happened to have a few pennies, and I took them to a nearby park where there was a kiosk to buy a few candies with my coins. My friend consented to the trade of her doll for the candies, and I became the happiest owner of a blinking doll. But I had no more brought the doll home and was sitting on the floor playing with her, when there was a knock on the door. It was my friend's mother who told me that her daughter was not allowed to make such a trade. She took the doll back, and I was broken-hearted. To this day it makes me doubt the permanence of gifts I receive. So I was never to have a blinking doll after all.

From the Finnish-Swedish border we were taken to Stockholm for a two-week quarantine. From this period, I only remember a big room with many beds. My only other memory is of all the urine samples lined up on the windowsills and my fearing that we would have to drink them.

After quarantine and medical tests, I was taken north to Ångermanland and from there to the small countryside community of Wäija. My new foster family was an older couple, Eda and Oscar Stattin, with two sons who lived nearby. The oldest of the sons lived next door with a red-headed and freckle-faced daughter named Gunbritt, and she became my only playmate.

The house in which we lived was square. I can't remember anything else about the rooms other than the kitchen because this is where I slept. I think that I might not have been allowed elsewhere. My bed was a wooden bench-style sofa that could be pulled into a bed at night. But during the day its lid was closed to provide seating by the kitchen table. There was a small pantry by the kitchen where I was given a daily dose of fish liver oil topped with a teaspoon of jam to disguise its awful taste. I was being fattened, as I too skinny when I arrived.

At least communication was not so much of a problem as it was for most war children, since I had already attended Swedish kindergarten in Finland. I called my foster parents *Tant* Eda and *Farbror* Oscar. These terms, meaning "Aunt" and "Uncle," were terms we used in both Finland and Sweden for anyone older than oneself even if they were not related to you. We also called our school teachers by these names with their surnames attached.

The Stattins were farmers, and there was a barn next to the house for animals. One incident has stayed with me about this barn, as I witnessed something there that was truly gruesome for me as a child. My playmate and I were invited to watch the slaughter of a pig. I remember that the pig calmly was led out of the barn when a person holding a giant wooden mallet hit him over the head. This was followed by a knife being stuck in the pig's throat with a dish placed beneath to catch the flow of blood, a shocking event for a child.

Tant Eda's occupation outside the home was going around the village, cleansing people's blood. I don't know how to describe the procedure, but to me as a child it was terrifying, though she took me along to watch. She heated these small shot glasses, then fastened them to people's backs. The heat made them stick to the people's skin. Then, after removing the glasses, she punctured small holes in the puffed-up pockets of skin with a knife. Dripping blood was the natural result. She never explained to me why she did this to people, but it worried me that one day I would be her victim! I later learned that this practice is called "cupping" and is supposed to relieve joint and muscle pain and to purify the blood.

Every afternoon the family assembled for coffee breaks, and alcohol was mixed with their coffee. It is hard for me to comprehend now why they always wanted me to have a taste. They kept insisting on this, so finally I had a sip and thought it tasted very bad. I told them I did not want to taste it again. It is possible that this contributed to my lifelong dislike of alcoholic drinks.

I can't recall receiving any special toys or presents from the Stattins except nice new clothes. These are my only memories since I was very young at the time, still under school age.

I have read in my mother's letters that she missed me so much that she "could hardly get a thing done for crying." In one letter, she wrote that "It helped some when the first letter came from the family where Anita lived." Unfortunately, I did not yet know how to write. In another letter my mother wrote around this time, she described taking my little brother Nenne to the same kindergarten I had attended. When she removed his outer garments and went to hang them up "it happened to be Anita's coat rack. I recognized it from the small rabbit picture next to the hook." Pictures were used because young children could recognize them better than their written names. But when my mother saw my rack, she "started to cry so hard" that she "had to run outside." Her letter continues: "Fortunately, outside I could be alone and cry very loudly." My mother also worried about Nenne, having lost his sister and best friend. She worried about him playing alone outside or on the neighbor's steps, looking lonely.

In 1941 my mother looked forward to my father coming home on leave. And several letters arrived from the Stattins, telling my mother that I was very happy and enjoying myself at their house. But my mother had decided by then that she wanted me home as soon as possible. Since she spoke no Swedish, my father had to answer the letters that came from Sweden, which was troublesome when he was away up north. She put in an application to get me home again, but it took a long time to process and apparently my foster family protested. I don't know why, since I have no remembrance of feeling loved or even liked by them. Much later I came to wonder if their primary purpose in wanting to keep me was that Swedish foster parents were reimbursed, as I have heard. Or perhaps it was for the extra ration coupons.

However, I eventually did return home, and, according to my mother's writing, "It was a day of joy and happiness. Anita hasn't changed much during her months away. Neither has she forgotten her Finnish language. But she speaks a different type of Swedish now. To begin with we had to learn to be together again, but soon everything was as before, and Nenne was happy to have his old playmate."

I am not sure of the year I returned, but I believe that it was in 1942, based on my mother's letters from this time. Also, shortly after I returned, my Aunt Anna's husband was killed in the war. She lived with us then, and when the chaplain came to break the news, I remember her screaming. It is a vivid memory to this day. I also remember that there were difficulties speaking Finnish with my mother and that our living conditions were meager.

At this point in the war Finnish troops had advanced almost to eastern Karelia. It was comparatively quiet at the front, since the Russians had other wars to attend to. We heard no air alarms, and it felt almost like peacetime. But we still had it very hard food-wise.

I began school that fall and Nenne returned to kindergarten. Women were being hired as loggers, and many of my mother's friends were among them, though most could barely hold a saw or axe in their hands. However, trees had to be felled and the wood split and chopped. Had my mother not had small children, she would have had to join in as well.

Winter passed, then spring arrived and summer. This was 1943, and it was still quiet at the front, though the whole rest of the world was fighting. The front remained on eastern Karelia. My father Gunnar became sick and was transferred home and then to a hospital in Jakobstad, a neighboring town. After awhile he was able to come home, though he would later be sent to a hospital in Helsinki. Finally, it was diagnosed that he had a bleeding ulcer. However, he was not given release from the army, just increased medications.

My mother describes visiting him at yet another hospital in Helsinki a bit later: "It was crowded on the train with no seats anywhere. I looked into several wagons, but found not a single seat. I had to remain standing. But then a military officer gave the command to one of his soldiers to give up his seat for me. He then had his men take turns, giving up their seats so that I could sit for the rest of the journey." My mother found the hospital where my father was waiting to have surgery during which they removed a hernia from his chest. Thankfully, my father was afterward released from the army because he was a very sick man.

It was around this time, perhaps owing to my father's illness, that it was decided that I would be sent to Sweden again. The war had again flared up, and the Stattins wanted me back. But because of some serious illness in the family, I did not return to the Stattin family. Instead, I was placed with Gerda and Johan Granlöf whom I referred to as *Tant* Gerda and *Farbror* Johan. They had a chicken farm, and a son Rolf, who was about fifteen, and later a daughter Mona.

I was more content with them than with my former foster family. But I remember that, at some point, the Stattin couple showed up at the Granlöf house. This surprised me. They had a pair of red shoes and said I could have them if I returned to their family. Though I wanted the red shoes, I remember saying that I did not want to go with them. It still surprises me that I refused, since I was a very obedient child and wanted to please everyone. For reasons I don't remember, my negative feelings about them must have been so strong that I just didn't want to go and hoped I wouldn't be forced to.

After peace came to Finland, my parents wanted me to come home. My father wrote the Granlöfs to this effect. However, the Granlöfs wanted to keep me longer and gave all sorts of reasons for why I should remain with them. This went back and forth, but finally my folks convinced my foster parents that they needed me to come home, despite continuing hardships in Finland.

So I finally left, meeting my parents at the train station. In a baby buggy was my new little sister, Marita Margareta. Shortly after she was born, my parents had written to me that I could name her, and this was the name I chose. I looked at the strange little baby; in her mouth was a pacifier with a huge cork at the end. I felt no connection to her, and my parents also seemed strange. I remember wondering where I truly belonged. I thought that I didn't really belong in Sweden, but I also felt the same way about Finland.

Still, we were together again as a family. Mother tried her best to converse with me in Swedish, and gradually my former knowledge of Finnish returned. Life slowly began to seem more normal, and I was a great help to my mother in taking care of my little sister Marita. It took time, but eventually I came to feel that this was where I belonged, and that this was my own true family.

I visited the Granlöfs a few times later, though my foster mother passed away at quite a young age. And some years later both my foster father and brother died of heart failure.

Maybe my years as a war child were preparation for me to learn to live one day far away from my homeland, since I would eventually move to the United States. I have no regrets. My life has been rich, and I have many fond memories. And now, instead of having only one homeland, I have two.

* * * * *

Anita worked for the post office at age sixteen and later moved to Helsinki where she continued in this work. After going to the United States for a visit, she was married there and had six children. Later she divorced, returned to Finland, and resumed work at the post office. She also accomplished her lifelong dream of earning her white graduation cap in two years. After this, she was reacquainted with her first love whose wife had passed away. They were married, visited the United States many times, and enjoyed fourteen years together until his death. Then Anita resettled in the United States permanently to be near her children.

11

Bread in a Suitcase
Rauni Janser

I was six and a half years old when the Winter War began in November 1939, at which time my family was living in Kotka, an important harbor town. Before the war, my father, Matti Leviö, worked in the harbor, and after the war he became the chief representative of Kotka's harbor workers as well as a member of the city council. Still later he became chairman over all the harbor workers in Finland and moved to Helsinki, dying in 1975. During the war, though, he was placed at the front as a lance corporal. My mother Signe stayed at home, because she was not well. Later she was diagnosed with multiple sclerosis, from which she died in 1977. Her great loves were literature and gardening. She had always hoped to study to become a professional gardener, but the war and her illness ended those dreams.

When the war situation became worse for people living in cities with industries and harbors that were subject to Russian attack, we were evacuated to the countryside and lived in my uncle's home in Anjala: my grandmother, mother, brother, and I. Our room was very small, and we slept on the floor on straw mattresses. It was terribly cold often with temperatures as low as –40° to –45° Celsius. In our room, there was a small stove on which mother prepared our meals. Our only other furniture was a small table and two chairs. During the lull in the fighting, we were allowed to return to our home in Kotka, but in the summer of 1941 when the fighting resumed we were again evacuated from Kotka to the same place in Anjala. I now had a baby sister, and my uncle himself had a very large family with his wife and five children. But, despite the fact that his house had only two rooms and a kitchen, we were again given one of the rooms. He and his wife had big hearts.

The year I came to Sweden in 1942, father was in his late thirties and my mother in her early thirties. My brother Reino was eleven, and my sister Ritva was only one. I was then eight years of age. Perhaps my mother's illness helps to explain why, when it became possible to send children to

Sweden, she desired to send one of us. I don't remember if she asked me whether I wanted to go or not, but she explained that it would help her if I did. I remember asking why Reino wasn't going, and she answered that, since he was older and bigger, she must depend on him for assistance. He was also a bed wetter, which might have made things difficult for him in a strange family. I didn't resent my mother for sending me to Sweden; in fact, I was happy whenever I returned to Finland to be able to give my family food and gifts.

When we were packing for my departure, I asked to take along one of my dolls. But my mother said that it would take up too much space in my little suitcase, and she reassured me that I would get a new one in Sweden. I left in the springtime, going by bus to the Kyminlinna railway station in the countryside. I didn't leave from Kotka, since bombing attacks on the bigger railway stations were feared. I do not remember anything of this. But sometime later my mother showed me the schoolyard from which the bus had departed.

Then I was taken by ship, the SS *Arcturus,* from Turku to Stockholm, arriving on May 26, 1942. About this I only remember sleeping two in each bed on a mattress in the cargo space and some milk I got that wasn't fresh.

After some days in quarantine in Stockholm, where we had x-rays and vaccinations against diphtheria, we went south by train to a town called Linköping. Hanging from a string around our necks were pieces of cardboard with our names on them. The cardboard also had the names of the families with which we would stay. Close to my seat on the train was another girl my age named Anja, and we became friends. She had a little brother, about three years of age, with her. Some of the ladies who took care of us during the transport told us that we would be living close to one another, and we were so happy about that. We looked forward to playing together.

When we arrived at Linköping railway station, there were many people looking around, reading the pieces of cardboard around our necks and searching for their designated child. When a lady found her name on Anja's little brother's name tag, she tried to take him, but he began to cry loudly, clinging to his sister. So someone who spoke Finnish asked if I would change to this family, so that the little boy could stay near his sister. What could I say? I followed the lady who also picked up some other children to take to their foster homes. There were three of us, all girls the same age, but we did not know one another. Later I wondered if my foster parents had been disappointed to get a "big girl" instead of a little boy. But I never asked them.[1]

My mother had told me that everything would be much better in Sweden than in Finland. So I had created a dream vision of the house and family. The house had to be white. I loved white houses. In fact, for me at that time, whiteness suggested cleanliness—white dresses got dirty easily, and I did not like dirty things—so if something was white, it was also clean. Our WC at home in Kotka was white and clean, while an outdoor loo was dirty!

In 1938, my family had moved to a modern flat, which made me very proud. The flat was in a big white blockhouse, which had been built just before the war. We had central heating, warm and cold water (though not every day during the war), big windows, which I loved, and a flush toilet. The flat was very small but modern with, for instance, an electric stove in the kitchen. The key to the flat was an Abloy.[2] Before we moved to this new apartment, my mother had explained to me how nice it would be (and it was!). So, when she told me that everything would be better in Sweden than it was in Finland, I imagined even bigger windows, a nicer WC, an elevator with more mirrors, and a bigger sauna. The shop where we bought our milk in Finland was tiled in white and operated by women in white coats. So I naturally thought that Swedish shops would be bigger and better somehow. Some time after arriving in Sweden, I wrote to my mother that my foster parents did not have a sauna, but she thought I was exaggerating or was making this up. In Finland there are saunas everywhere, but in Sweden to have a sauna one had to travel by train. Even many years later my mother could not believe this was true.

My dream house, then, had to be white with only one family living there. The furniture should be white too, and the family should be big with many children.

My future foster mother and another woman brought us from Linköping to Slätmon station where the other two girls were taken by car to their new foster families. One of them went to a family who turned out to be friends of my foster parents, so we could occasionally play and speak Finnish together later on.

I was brought to a house close to the railway station. No one was at home, and I was disappointed with the furniture, which was dark brown and glossy. But the most disappointing thing of all was that there were no other children! And when my foster mother appeared, she spoke a language I couldn't understand. I thought: *Perhaps she is a witch.*

In fairy tales, the witches spoke strange languages and lived alone like this woman. I knew only one word in that strange language, which I thought might change everything if I said it. Perhaps it was a magic formula I had to know before everything could be as I wanted it to be. These were my thoughts.

I had read many fairy tales, and I loved most those about princesses and princes. But I felt sympathy, too, for Hansel and Gretel, who are sent away by their parents because there is a famine and not enough food at home. These children wander in the forest until they come to a witch's cottage where they are fed by the witch only to get them fatter, so she can eat them. I will say the word I know in Swedish, and then everything will change, I thought. There will be a nice white bathroom, and then all the children and the husband will come home!

"WC," I said, and the witch smiled at me. She took my hand and we went out of the house. At the end of the garden was a small shed, and she opened its door. A loo! I could not believe that this was possible. I began to pee, crying at the same time because I was so afraid and disappointed. My own mother had told me a lie, or this witch had lied to her.

After, the witch took my hand and showed me something in the garden. There were boxes like small houses, and inside of them were animals, white with red eyes. Because I lived in a city in Finland, I had never seen animals like these. Now I began to cry even more! I thought that this witch took children from Finland and changed them into these animals, which she fattened and then ate.

Then it was bedtime, and the witch wanted to undress me. In Finland we had to sleep with most of our clothes on because during a bomb raid we had to go to the shelter quickly and had no time to put on our clothes. This witch tried and tried to undress me, but she succeeded only with my dress. She allowed me to keep my underwear on. Then she told me something over and over again. To me, it sounded like *suukot,* which means "kisses" in Finnish. Horrified, I thought that if she kissed me, I would become one of those white animals with red eyes! She kept repeating, "*Suukot, suukot,*" as she came closer to my bed. I had to find the password to stop her! But I couldn't think of any, so just before she came alongside the bed, I cried, "*suukot!*" Then she stood still and smiled, but I knew that even the wicked stepmother of Snow White smiled. Later on, I learned that she had merely been saying "*Sov Gott,*" which means "Sleep well" in Swedish.

When I woke the next morning, I hoped that the furniture would be white and that the house would have many children. But when I looked around the room, I saw no white furniture. Then I observed a bed on the other side of the room, and there was *a* **man** lying on it. He smiled at me and waved his hand. Suddenly I had a good feeling. I was not in a witch's house anymore!

His wife brought me a big cup of chocolate milk while I was still in bed, and because I must have been confused about the dates, I thought the milk was for my birthday. In fact, I had turned nine after arriving in Stockholm and didn't arrive at my foster parents' house until June 1, two days after my birthday. I thought that my foster parents must have known that it was my birthday, since I had been asked when I was born at the time that I was reassigned to a new family. But the wonderful thing is that the woman had changed from a frightening witch into an ordinary woman, though I was still disappointed there were no children. For several days I didn't know what to call my foster parents, but I soon learned to call them *Tant* Lisa and *Farbror* Helge (Aunt Lisa and Uncle Helge).

Tant Lisa, short for "Elisabeth," had been born in 1900, and Helge Ericson in 1896. Like my mother, *Tant* Lisa stayed at home and didn't work. *Farbror* Helge sold agricultural machines and seed to the farmers around the district. Unlike my foster mother, *Farbror* Helge was a very warm and affectionate person who eventually became my prince. We had our own special jokes, fun, and secrets. We often went out for soft drinks or pastry without telling his wife, and he bought candies for me and hid them, so that we could play hide and seek. Many years later when I was a mother, he gave both me and my daughter candies, and I continued to sit on his knee even as a grownup. In fact, Lisa and Helge became *Mormor* and *Morfar* (Grandmother and Grandfather) to my daughter and entire family. His death in a car accident in 1964 devastated me, and I became deeply depressed, which contributed to the breakup of my first marriage. Before he died, he had given me security, advice, and love, though I never realized how much he meant until his death.

Tant Lisa, was more reserved in temperament. She never showed me her feelings, but only showed them to wild birds and a cat. By contrast with my mother, she also seemed very old-fashioned to me as a child. My Finnish *Äiti* (Mother) liked nice things and had good taste. She was very interested in literature and loved nature. Both *Äiti* and *Isä* (Father) also admired innovative Finnish design, art, music, and progressive thinking. They listened to music on the radio—folksongs, national artists, Sibelius. They admired Alvar Aalto and other Finnish designers and painters. They also believed that children's play is important for the development of their imagination.

By contrast, *Tant* Lisa was a practical woman with a strong work ethic and a more simplistic and unemotional outlook who took care of the family's finances very carefully. Also, though I found two neighbor girls to play with, in the countryside play was considered more of a waste of time and even sinful. When I finally found words to ask for a swing in the back yard, my foster father made me one, but despite *Äiti's* promise that I would get a new doll in Sweden, no one ever asked if I wanted a doll.

Tant Lisa also did not have an appreciation for the finer things. In this way, she and *Äiti* were very different. For instance, in the spring of 1948 at age fifteen, I needed a long white confirmation dress. During the summer holidays in 1947, *Tant* Lisa had made a white dress for me, but I did not like the material, nor the style. I could not say anything; I had to pretend to be pleased. At that time in Finland textiles were completely unavailable, yet my confirmation was to be in March 1948. Some weeks before this, *Äiti* discovered that one shop was soon to have white material. We went there together and she bought in my eyes the most beautiful cloth—white with shining dots. She asked me which style I liked, and a neighbor lady made the dress. I was so happy and I *loved* my mother so much because she understood me and was able to make my confirmation a happy one. At the same time, I could truthfully tell *Tant* Lisa that her dress for me had grown too small in the sleeves and too short in length because I had grown. My mother loved things of quality and did not like to compromise; she preferred to go without rather than buy something she didn't like. Of course, during the war one usually had to take whatever was available. Instead, my mother took old clothes of good quality and remade them into something special. Only some years ago, my cousins told me that their parents had always admired her good taste.

My Finnish parents also prized education. *Isä* read a great deal and took an interest in politics. He impressed upon us the great importance of reading and education. *Tant* Lisa was a Baptist and believed many things to be sinful, perhaps due to the belief that to read instead of working showed laziness. She believed that even to read novels was sinful; only when my teacher asked me to read as much of everything as possible was it allowed. *Farbror* Helge, however, had read in his younger days and had a small library, mostly novels, which I enjoyed. But in Finland we had gone to the library every week, so that we always had lots of books to read.

In Sweden, the biggest difficulty for me in the beginning was the language. Not to be able to express anything in my own language was frustrating. I longed to be home with my family—*Äiti* and *Isä,* my older brother, and especially my little sister.

Another difficulty for me in the beginning was coming to terms with all the food. I wished to be able to send part of it back to Finland and felt somewhat guilty about it all. During breakfast, I was surprised by the amount of food and also by the fact that they didn't always finish the bread, cheese, and other things on the table. In Finland, mother gave us some slices of bread, and we ate all of them because we were always hungry. I remember vividly a time when we were out of bread and extremely hungry. We knew that it would be some days before we would receive our new rationing coupons. Father came home from the front during this time, and the first thing mother asked was, "Do you have bread?" But he had only this very hard stale bread in his bag. It was so hard that he had to break it against the edge of the table. We each got a piece to put in our mouths. And I will never forget that wonderful taste of the bread, which got softer after a while. Nothing could ever taste as good as that bread again! Ever!

A half year after my arrival in Sweden, my foster mother found old bread in my little suitcase, which I had taken from the breakfast table to save for my family in Finland. I don't remember having done this, and *Tant* Lisa only told me about this many years later. The abundance of food in Sweden was unbelievable to me. Each time I got an apple or something else, I wished I could share the food with my brother and sister.[3]

Little by little, I came to learn the Swedish language, though I made many mistakes, and my foster mother made jokes about it when I tried to explain something that was important to me. I often became very angry, trying to express myself when she didn't appear to want to understand. But by asking "What is this?" all the time, I learned new words every day.

School began in autumn of that year, 1942. I couldn't understand the teacher very well, of course. However, I could spend the time in class drawing, coloring, and playing. And, at the same time, I was able to slowly learn the language as it was spoken by the children in a local dialect.

However, I was very homesick for my mother and family in Finland during the following months, and *Äiti* wrote me a letter in September 1943, telling me about her poor health and encouraging me to persevere, which I excerpt from here:

Kotka 9.8.43
My Dear Child!
Did you, my child, think that your mother would be in good health, so I could come home from the hospital? As soon as mother could walk a bit with sticks, I had to go and leave a place for someone who had been wounded by the bombs. Of course, mother wished to go home. After coming home I should have gone to the hospital here in Kotka. But also here they had to make room for the war-injured, so even here there is not much space. I have been at home and I can go only to a doctor for treatment. If my situation becomes worse, I will have a place in the hospital. I have brought the milk by myself every day. One day I went to see grandmother, but as a result my legs were completely worn out. Grandmother gave me a stick and with the help of that I could go home.

Of course we will meet you with joy when you come home. If the war is not ended before the summer, the summer will be very restless. Also, now there are a great number of alarms. Mother is very pleased that you have not had to listen to the bangs of the guns and bombs for a year. Although you were not frightened, over many years, these noises can make you sick.

But perhaps my mother was concerned about my homesickness, for later that September 1943, I was sent back to Finland, though we were still at war.[4] I was so happy to see *Äiti*, my little sister, and big brother. *Isä* was still at the front, and I remember feeling very proud of him protecting our country. In fact, I loved words that expressed this pride like "mother language" and "fatherland."

Unfortunately, even after it was over, the war continued to live inside my father for the rest of his life. He had been engaged in several battles including a famous one in eastern Karelia, the battle of Rukajärvi in 1942, and he had nightmares every night until his death. The noise of his crying would often awaken us. He never shared his wartime experiences with us, however, and in those days no one spoke about treatment for post-traumatic stress syndrome among war veterans. In fact, I believe Finns were officially discouraged from discussing such things.

During this period I went to a Finnish-speaking school where I also had difficulties, since I had forgotten much of my mother tongue. Finnish students had learned material that I had not, because I hadn't covered a lot of ground in my third-grade class. Some of the students made fun of me and called me *tyhmä* (stupid). In addition, classes were disrupted nearly every day by air attacks, and the food situation was very bad. Many nights we spent in the bomb shelter, and I became much more afraid of the bombs than I had been before my travel to Sweden. Though I was happy to be home, I longed to be back in Sweden—just as in subsequent years, when I spent summer holidays in Sweden, I longed to be back in Finland. So I was never entirely happy with my dual life.

After a half year, in March 1944, *Äiti* sent me back to Sweden. *Isä* was still at the front most of the time. I was quite weak due to lack of food and nervous from lack of sleep and fear of the bombing. My foster parents wanted me to rest and calm down. I did not go to school at all that spring. But in August I was put in a fifth grade class. By that time, I had only gone through the first and second grades in Finland and only the third grade in Sweden where I learned nothing except how to speak Swedish. The few months of fourth grade I had in Finland had been a very insecure time for me, and here I was, beginning the fifth grade without knowing very much in comparison with my classmates. My teacher was very ambitious, though, and he began to teach me from the bottom. I spent every school break studying with him, and he inspired me to read more and more books. He told me that if I read a lot I would learn new words, how to spell, and the proper construction of sentences at the same time. I found Swedish and its spelling difficult to learn at first. However, I read all the books in the little village school library, and in addition I borrowed books from my teacher's private library. He was very proud of his profession and also proud of my progress.

One year later, at the end of September, I was sent back to Finland. The war was now over, but the food situation was still quite desperate. Because Finland has two official languages, Finnish and Swedish, it was possible for me to go to a Swedish-speaking school in my home town. Before the war this had been an exclusive school, catering to Swedish-speaking children from the upper classes. After the war, however, the school expanded due to the many war children returning. Most of these children came from working-class families. Their home language was Finnish, but their language in school was Swedish. Thus nobody at home could help with homework. However, the bonus for returning war children was that they learned a second language and could continue to speak it in school. Otherwise, it would have been difficult for these children to continue with their Swedish, as most families could not afford to send their children to other towns and cities, and in those days it was also difficult to get bank loans.[5] By contrast with those returning war children who gradually lost their Swedish, many of the children who stayed in Sweden lost all contact with their biological families—and, as a consequence, their native language. In the event that they were reunited with their Finnish families, they could no longer speak with parents or siblings.

I completed my education at a Finnish school for economic reasons: the Swedish school was a private institution with high tuition, whereas the Finnish school cost nothing. Like nearly all Finnish families after the war, my family faced harsh economic times, especially because of my mother's MS. For the same economic reasons, I was unable to attend Helsinki University, so I worked in an office for a year before moving to Sweden in 1952.

I can clearly remember a great deal about my time in Sweden, which holds happy memories for me. But because my sister became a war child at only two years and eight months of age, she lacks all memory of her time there. She also lost the Finnish that she had known, though I could help her upon her return to Finland since I knew Swedish. Her foster parents were younger than mine, and they had a daughter some five or six years older than my sister. She also returned for summer holidays and kept in contact with her foster parents as long as they lived. So one can say that we both had happy war child stories, despite our differences in age.

To some extent, however, I still feel somewhat rootless today, though my longing is without a face. Having lived in Sweden since I became an adult, I nevertheless long to hear Finnish. It is a great pleasure to speak Finnish and to hear the language spoken in buses and shops when I visit my native country. I also miss Finnish humor, which can make jokes of serious subjects. Like my parents, I am deeply drawn to Finnish design. And I love the sea, whether it's in Finland or Sweden: the sound is the same. It speaks the same language.

*****

Upon their return to Finland, many children had no opportunity to speak Swedish unless they returned to Sweden for their summer holidays. Rauni shares the story of another war child, Arto Vanhanen, who also lived in Kotka and attended the same Swedish-speaking school, *Svenska Samskolan,* as she. Because he could not hear or speak Swedish at home, he confused the two languages and was told by his teacher at graduation that his written Swedish was no longer correct. However, when he began his studies at Helsinki University, he took classes from Swedish-speaking faculty and lived with Swedish-speaking students, in order to perfect his Swedish. He also married a Swedish-speaking Finn. After finishing his university studies, he returned to Kotka where he became a teacher at the same Swedish school that he and Rauni attended as children. In order to keep her Swedish up to par, Rauni reads many Swedish books. And today, living in Sweden, in order to retain her Finnish, Rauni listens to the news in Finnish every day. During her school years and for many years later, to graduate from gymnasium one had to pass both Finnish and Swedish exams, as she succeeded in doing. To hold a post in a bank, post office, or any official office, both Finnish and Swedish were required, as well. Thus, war children who retained both languages found themselves at an advantage as young adults.

After moving to Sweden in 1952 when she was twenty, Rauni eventually became manager of an art gallery for fifteen years in Linköping. She also studied art history as an extension student with the University of Stockholm. Some years later she moved to southern Sweden where she studied ethnology and was a faculty member of the ethnology department at Lund University. From 1983 to 1995, she was the curator for an art gallery, *Tomelilla Konsthall,* in southern Sweden. She has one child, a practicing physician, by her first husband. Today, Rauni lives with a retired sea captain in Ystad on the southern Swedish coast.

Notes

1. When I asked Rauni about her Finnish mother worrying, due to her changed whereabouts in Sweden, Rauni replied that "In those days, you could not think about such details. Most parents knew little or nothing about where their child was placed. I have heard about parents who had to wait several months before they had so much as a note about their child's or children's location. Fortunately, my foster parents wrote quite soon to give their address to my mother. But we did not have a phone at home in Finland, and it was expensive to phone abroad. Consequently, I had no phone calls from my family. But we did write letters."
2. Still today, Abloy manufactures high-end security locks and services. Its advertisements appeal to "Security Snobs."
3. Swedes were not allowed to send food or clothing to Finland until the autumn of 1944. See Greta Littonen, *Centralized Voluntary Relief in Finland,* English summary (Helsinki: Suomen Huolto, 1949). Because Rauni and her family were from the city of Kotka, they would have had a harder time obtaining food than those living in the countryside. According to Aura Korppi-Tommola, one of the most common fears and even nightmares of children living in cities was the threat of "running out of bread" ("War and Children in Finland during the Second World War").

4. Despite the continuing danger, many Finnish authorities desired to bring war children home to continue their education in Finnish. Most of those children who returned to Finland were sent back to Sweden half a year later, due to intensified enemy bombing and severe lack of food. From this point until the end of the war and later, due to continuing difficulties and scarcities in Finland, most war children remained with foster parents in Sweden.

12

The Lucky Stain

Rauno Juntunen

I was born in 1936 in Suomussalmi, a village located in mid-eastern Finland on the Russian border. When I was two years old, my mother died. Though I had four brothers by the same mother, three of them died shortly after birth before they reached one year of age, and I can remember the funeral of one of these. Only one of my brothers lived to adulthood, dying in 2004. So today I am the last surviving child, though I have three half-brothers from my father's second marriage. My father was a shoemaker before the Winter War, but after war broke out in 1939 he served as a border guard in Suomussalmi where a famous battle took place during the first phase of the war. That same year the family was evacuated to Risitijärvi where my grandparents lived, but then returned to Suomussalmi. After the Moscow Peace Treaty in mid-March 1940, which brought the Winter War to an end, my father, stepmother, elder brother, and I were able to return home.[1]

Luckily, our home had not been destroyed because it was not close to the border where the heaviest fighting had occurred. But the Soviets launched the Continuation War in July 1941, and our troubles began anew. This is when the evacuation of children to Sweden began. Since I was only five years old, I have no memories of those times, and I don't know why I was chosen to be sent. I have never asked anybody, and now it is too late since my father passed away years ago. I have learned that I didn't get along with my stepmother, so that could be one reason. Furthermore, I have been told that I was always eager for adventure and was excited for my departure to a foreign country.

Unfortunately, I recall nothing from my travel from Kajaani to Turku, the ship voyage from Turku to Stockholm, nor the train trip from Stockholm to Kristianstad, the capital of Skåne in South Sweden, which was the end station for me and many other evacuees. There is a black hole in my memory from the very beginning of the trip to my final arrival at my foster home. My first vague memory is of my arrival on September 25 in the small village of Huaröd. Each of us had an address sign around our neck, on which was written our name and the family for which we were intended. Originally my destination was a farmer on the outskirts of the village, but when we arrived there, or so I have been told many times, the receiving family noticed a large brown splotch on my nose. Being afraid that it was some kind of disease, they rejected me and took two girls instead. Eventually we arrived at the last place, and I was alone in the car, a "leftover." The family I was brought to consisted of a country shopkeeper, his wife, and their twenty-two-year-old daughter. They had already raised an orphan boy who was grown and living on his own. Although the couple were in their fifties, they took me in, a young child. The stain on my nose turned out to be only chocolate, which vanished when I was washed. And still today, I bless this turn of events that I was placed in this family.

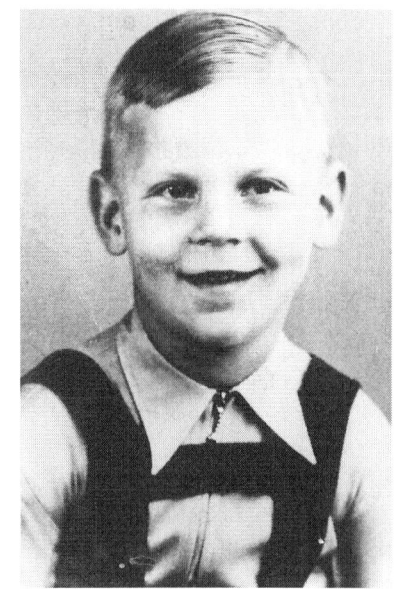

Figure 12.1. Rauno Juntunen at age five, when he was sent to Sweden. Courtesy Rauno Juntunen.

My foster parents, Gottfrid and Hildur Andersson, were kind and loving people. Gottfrid was a member of the communal council and was engaged in many communal and social activities. Hildur was a housewife and took good care of me. Their daughter, Greta, twelve years older than I, became like an elder sister to me. And then there was a shopkeeper's assistant, so we were not a big family. The orphan boy they had raised, Malte Aberg, and Greta are still living, and I have regular contact with them. When going to Sweden I always have a place to stay with my "brother." I have only bright memories from the very beginning of my time with the Anderssons.

Like all the war children I had a language problem and soon forgot my Finnish. There were over ten other Finnish war children in that small community, but I don't remember getting together with them and speaking Finnish. In any case, at a young age one can learn the new and forget the old language very quickly. For a month I was mute, so they said, and then suddenly started to talk my new language. Of course, in the beginning there were some misunderstandings. When leaving the dining table, I said, "*Var så god*" ("You are welcome") instead of "*Tack*," meaning "Thank you." In the beginning, I don't know what I called my new parents, but hearing my playmates call their parents *Mor* and *Far* ("Mom" and "Dad"), I began to call my war parents *Mor* and *Far*, which seemed natural to me. I am not sure if I quite understood the meaning. Probably I was still aware of my father back in Finland, but this memory gradually faded away, and I could no longer picture him or my older brother. I soon became Swedish.

Two years after I arrived, I was supposed to go to school. But that year there were so many Swedish children beginning school, that there was no room for me. Consequently, I had to wait until the following year, but I hardly felt bad about that. I learned to read before I started school and enjoyed such fairy tales as "Hansel and Gretel." Also I had the advantage of living only twenty meters from the school, so I had merely to jump over a stone fence that separated our shop from the school to be in the school yard and play with my friends at recess or in the afternoon. My best friend, Soini Moisio, was a boy next door who had come to Sweden at approximately at the same time as I. We often played together, and later we started school together. But after three years he left, and it was a sad moment for me. I remember crying about it for some time.

My early life in Sweden had its normal ups and downs, although I can remember no truly bad experiences. When I began school I received my first savings bank book in which *Mor* and *Far* had put five Kroner, and this book is in safekeeping to this day. After returning to Finland, my stepmother occasionally added to it, and the small pension I receive from Sweden goes into the same account.

When I was really young I wasn't of much help in the store, but as the years went by I learned to do this and that. For example, loose snuff was sold in a container, and I soon learned to weigh the snuff for clients. I could also help in moving merchandise and in weighing out kilos of sugar or flour into paper bags. During the war and for some years after, foodstuffs were rationed in Sweden as well as in Finland. People received sheets of coupons for everything, which the shopkeeper then cut out with scissors. I learned to do this as well as attach the coupons to a piece of cardboard by licking or dabbing the coupons with a wet sponge. But best of all, people subscribed to magazines, which they received from the shop, and I took every advantage of this. I read all the comics before they were sold. I also had one favorite radio program called *Barnens Brevlada* (The Children's Letter Box). Once a week I listened to it. Children wrote letters, and some were invited to the program and performed by singing a song or reciting a poem. I also devoured stories from the usual storybooks, including all the fairy tales written by the Brothers Grimm.

My foster parents' shop was located on the ground floor of a large house. Upstairs were living quarters, including a bathroom, for tenants. The ground floor also included an office, the kitchen, two guest rooms, and my foster parents' bedroom where I too slept for many years. Next to this room was another bedroom in which Greta slept, and this became my room after she moved away. Unlike the tenants upstairs, we used an outhouse. And in the village was a bathhouse, which we used weekly.

In the summers we often took trips to the seashore, because the Baltic Sea was only twenty-five kilometers away. But most exciting was to go to Sweden's largest and most famous market every summer. There was plenty to see and marvel at for a growing boy, even though there was no money to waste. My foster parents were not rich, but I got everything necessary, and, above all, their love. I never felt that I was neglected or put aside, but treated as their own son.

As far as I can remember, I enjoyed a happy time during my seven years in Sweden, but after the war ended in 1945, one by one, the war children began returning to Finland. Eventually, there weren't many remaining other than myself. Then, in November 1947, when I was twelve, came a disastrous message: all the remaining Finnish children must be returned. There were exceptions for those who had been adopted and for those who had been orphaned and had no place to return to. It was a sad moment and we all cried. After having been there for so many years, I felt that my home was in Sweden, whereas Finland was foreign and strange. This time I was not as adventurous as I had been in leaving Finland. However, no amount of crying helped. There was nothing you could do except obey the authorities, submit to fate, and prepare for the departure. I had begun the third grade, but now my school attendance would be interrupted as well.

It was the end of November, and I was taken to the same train station at which I had arrived seven years earlier. From there the train travelled first to Stockholm, where I had to wait for a day before continuing north toward Haaparanta (in Swedish, Haparanda). It was night when we crossed the border, arriving in Tornio after two days of travelling. There were three of us returning to Finland on this train, and one boy who still knew how to speak Finnish chatted with the guard who entered our car and showed us his pistol. We were allowed to handle it, and it felt very heavy. The train continued to Oulu where there was a change of train for Kajaani, which is about fifty miles south of Suomussalmi, and Kontiomäki, an important railway junction. Here my father met me, and we changed trains together for Ristijärvi where my grandfather waited with his sledge, as there was no other means of transport into the deep countryside. It was ten miles by sledge to my final destination: a small community consisting of six farming families, living in six houses on two hills. Levämäki is the name of this small village in which I stayed for two years. A couple of kilometers from our village, these houses were pointed out to me, and though I no longer spoke Finnish, I understood that this would be my new home. All of the buildings—barn, sauna, storehouses, and original house—were built of logs and had darkened over time. The interior of the house was almost empty, its walls bare logs through which daylight shone in the spaces where moss had fallen out of the cracks. Cold air blew inside.

I was given a warm welcome, but nevertheless, the culture shock was enormous. I was overwhelmed and speechless with the contrast between my home in Sweden and this new home. In Sweden I had been accustomed to electric lights, running water and sewer, central heat from the basement, and many other modern things. Here the house was a log cabin, the walls as black inside as out. There were no curtains in the windows and, instead of electric lamps, there were oil lamps. The family consisted of my paternal grandparents, my father and stepmother, and an elder brother, who had stayed behind when I left. I later on learned that he too had been willing to go to Sweden, but in 1941, at age nine, he was either considered too old or his help was badly needed at the time. Upon my arrival, I didn't recognize my father or any of these other people. Though I had seen photos of them, my memories of them had completely faded. For some time after my return, I prayed every night that I would be sent back to my warm and lovely home in Sweden. I prayed that everything could be reversed. Why must I live in such miserable conditions? However, I had to face the reality that I was now back "home" again, although the location was different from that I had left as a five-year-old boy, and now I was eleven.

From the beginning my stepmother tried to imply that she was my biological mother, but I already knew the truth. Once, when I was fishing on the lake with my grandfather, he asked me about it, and I said that I knew she was not my mother and that I'd known this even while staying in Sweden. My stepmother also suffered occasionally from mental illness, so perhaps she didn't understand reality.

The living room in the house was more like a workshop than a home, especially in the winter. There they performed all kinds of work to create the necessities of life, such as the sleigh with which grandfather had met us. Almost everything needed for the household was made from wood with the exception of some iron things. The men were very handy, and once when I had my ski broken my father made a new one that worked fine. He also made special kinds of leather boots most Finns wore at that time. During the war my father had worked as a shoemaker at the border control; thus, he was able to make shoes for us all. But after the war he returned to his parents' house to work as a farmer. He was the only one of four brothers who survived the war.

The living room also functioned as a slaughter-house. In late autumn it was common to slaughter a sheep, cow, or pig for the meat, which was either preserved in salt or smoked in our sauna. From the bones the men fabricated soap. Women had other duties, such as preparing the wool, spinning, and making knitwear. All that and many other things were new and strange but simultaneously interesting for me, and they occupied my mind during the day. In the evenings, though, there was plenty of time to long for the life I had left behind in Sweden. It took time but, as months passed, I gradually got used to my new home.

The first winter I could not go to school because I could not handle the language, so when I went to school the next fall I was two years older than my classmates. It is very common for children to tease someone who in one way or another differs from the rest. In Sweden, I was sometimes called *Finne* or "Finn" because of my origins, but I have no bad memories from that. In Finland, though, I stood out as being more different. My clothes were not like those of the other boys, and my ski equipment had been made in Sweden, so it was seen as something extraordinary. I also had my own bike, which had been sent from Sweden, and this perhaps made me envied. Sometimes in school, the children called me *Ruotsin keisari* (Emperor of Sweden). But looking back as an adult, in spite of all these disadvantages, I had one advantage: I could speak a foreign language.

In Sweden I had received great love and care from my foster parents. But in Finland it was painful to watch how my new five-year-old brother could climb and sit in our father's arms and play with him. I wondered why I couldn't be treated the same way and feel free to sit and hug my father. Perhaps I was considered too old, and I could not make the initiative myself. Although I knew that he was my real father, I never felt as close to him as to my foster father. There was some kind of conflict in my relationship with my Finnish father, and I can't recall any effort on his part to create closer contact. In a way I had become estranged during my stay abroad. I felt closer to my grandfather and grandmother (*Ukki* and *Mummo* in Finnish).

In the summertime, I was introduced to many new experiences, such as fishing on a small lake only two hundred yards away from the house. Sitting in a rowboat, fishing with *Ukki* early in the morning while the other people were still asleep, was a new experience. And this time and these moments I still remember with warmth. Another skill that I learned during summertime was how to handle a scythe, and I did many other types of work. Like all the other farmers in the area, we produced our own basic everyday foods like milk, butter, and bread. From the forest we gathered firewood for heating the house, which demanded hard labor. Fortunately, I did not have to work like adults during the haymaking season, which lasted from mid-June till September. All the work on the farm was done by hand and was very hard.

Though I adapted fairly quickly to my new home, environment, and habits, I never forgot my Swedish family and eagerly waited for letters and parcels from Sweden, which I now and then received. During my stay in Finland, everything was rationed, and you could only buy a monthly quota with the coupons that were distributed. So packages from Sweden were always welcome. Although they did not resolve any of our difficult living conditions, they showed that I was remembered and that my foster parents still cared for me. I also wrote letters myself, but can't recall what I wrote, and I don't know if any survive. Autumn approached, and I started school again. It was located three miles away, but I was lucky to have my bike, while others from the village had to walk. Now I no longer had problems with the language. And at school we received one warm meal a day, as well as the sandwiches we brought. Owing to postwar conditions, pupils contributed to the food supply by picking three liters of lingonberries in the late summer and bringing them to the school kitchen. It was not a hard task because these berries grew everywhere in abundance.

Around this time I learned to hunt for forest birds, not by shooting, but by means of different traps that had been used for generations. After school in the afternoons I made my collection rounds to see if there were any birds to bring home. Most common were black grouse, hazel grouse, and occasionally wood grouse. I remember especially one afternoon when I returned home with no fewer than eight birds. Trap hunting might not have been lawful, but it was a rather widespread way to eke out the food supply during and after the war. And, being miles away from the nearest houses and authorities, there was no fear that one would be caught. I developed a passion for this new hobby during what became my short stay in Finland.

We talked about me visiting my foster parents in Sweden the following summer, but father and stepmother came to the conclusion that I should wait until the following summer. I had received invitations and could have gone any time that my Finnish parents allowed it, so I was very disappointed.

Another winter passed much like the first. A new schoolhouse was built that was farther away than the old one, approximately five miles or seven kilometers. There were four of us schoolchildren who skied through the woods in winter to go to school. Skiing made the distance a little shorter, but many times it was a tough job to open up a track after heavy snowfall. The old schoolhouse was turned into a boarding house for pupils who lived far away, and occasionally I also stayed there during the week. Because we lived so far out in the country, the nearest shop was ten miles away. When you had to do some shopping, which didn't happen very often, you had to ski or go by horse and sleigh to the highway from which there was a bus connection to the main village. After heavy snowfall when the bus didn't arrive, you had to continue skiing or walking, which happened to me many times. The distance to the nearest town, Kajaani, was about forty miles. We had relatives there with whom we could stay overnight, and I did this sometimes. Then you could go the cinema and watch movies.

Despite primitive living conditions compared to those in Sweden, I adjusted and had no serious problems in coping with everyday life. With no electricity, we had only a battery-powered radio that was turned on very scarcely, mostly in the evenings when my grandparents listened to evening prayers and the news. On these occasions I was able to listen to the Swedish part of the news. But, though Finland was and is a bilingual country, Finnish-Swedish differed from that I was used to in the south of Sweden.

Yet another summer and winter went by, and in the following spring preparations were made for my journey to Sweden. I had my invitation, and my passport granted me three months. The intention was that I go and pay a visit there and return when the new school year began. And so I started my second exodus with the same eagerness as the first time, but with the added benefit that I now knew where I was going and what to expect. My foster-parents had sent me a one-way ticket beforehand. After school was out I excitedly waited for the day of departure. For two and a half years Finland had been my home, but I was not sorry at all leaving this house. And so, on June 3, 1950, I began my second journey to Sweden full of joy and great expectations for summer vacation: a vacation that happily stretched into fifteen years.

After traveling for two days and one night the very same but reversed route as when I returned to Finland from Sweden, I eventually arrived in Kristianstad and was met there by my foster parents. It was a sunny and warm day, that June 6, and flags were flying … not for me, but for the king of Sweden. It was his name-day. We drove through familiar districts, and I especially remember the last few miles when we traveled through beech-tree woods with light green leaves, which had just come into leaf. The family had changed a little since I left. Their daughter, Greta, had married and moved away. But the same shop assistant was there, the niece of my foster-father Gottfrid who was then sixty-two. The assistant was a few years older than I, but another big sister to me like Greta. And last but not at least there was my foster-mother, Hildur, then also sixty-two. I had no problems with the language, and after a few days of practice, I could speak as fluently as before. My reunion with old schoolmates was thrilling. Like me, they were now two years older and somewhat changed, but I still recognized them. I felt like I was home again.

Something had changed my relations and attitude toward my foster-parents, however. While I did not love them less, before I had called them *Far* and *Mor*, and now I was a little confused about how to address them. I could not call them *Tant* and *Farbror* (Aunt and Uncle) like their other foster son did, and therefore I invented many different ways to approach them, but never again called them *Mor* or *Far* as I had done for so many years. I think that they understood the change in my attitude toward them. We never talked about it. But still today when speaking with old friends in Sweden, I encounter problems in referring to my foster parents, and this contradiction bothers me.

I have many happy memories of my time in Huaröd that summer. Through the village floated a small stream, and with a neighbor boy who was a little older than I, we constructed a small pond in the stream by making a dam across it. It was broad and deep enough to enable us and a lot of other children to swim. But a couple of years later a swimming pool that took its water from the same stream was built, and so our little pond disappeared.

My nearest neighbors and closest playmates were two girls of my age. We played a lot together and, because girls by nature have interests that are different from boys, we did things like collecting wild flowers in surrounding meadows in summer. Those I gathered I gave to my foster mother, such as bouquets of lily of the valley, which we collected in May. Perhaps because of this habit, I still gather these flowers today. Another happy memory is of a great fair we used to attend about twenty miles away from my village in Kivik on the coast of the Baltic Sea. This fair in July was the biggest such event in the whole of Sweden. Masses of people, both sellers and buyers, gathered there, and because my foster mother had relatives in Kivik, this was another reason for us to go. This small town is also famous for its fruit gardens. Later in the autumn when the apples, cherries, and pears are ripe, we went there and picked fruit for the winter. There were also wild cherry trees, and a new favorite hobby of mine was to climb and eat the cherries until I almost got sick. Occasionally, especially in summertime, we also made outings to the beach where I could swim in salt water.

Quite often I had to assist in the shopkeeping as well as I could, and sometimes, when people who lived a couple of miles away ordered their groceries by telephone, I had to jump on my bike and deliver their articles. Usually I got some kind of reward, candy or cookies, but no money. Across the road was a clothing shop whose proprietor was a tailor. He was a religious man, and in his house he performed Sunday school for the children in the village. Gottfrid and Hildur went to church, although they weren't actual believers, and I too accompanied them sometimes.

My foster-parents were getting older, and they wanted to retire. Unfortunately, Greta couldn't manage the shopkeeping, the other foster-son had his own business, and I was too young, so they sold the shop in the summer when I arrived in 1950 and built a new house quite near the old. When it was finished the following year, we moved there.

I can't remember my Finnish parents opposing my staying on in Sweden. My foster parents had immediately begun the process of extending the validation of my passport. I myself was not eager to return to Finland.

And because I was in Sweden, there was one less mouth for my Finnish parents to feed. I was no longer a war child but an ordinary person, and though I was always called by my Finnish name, "Rauno," I felt that my home was in Sweden.

The spring after my arrival I got sick with mumps and had to stay in bed for some time. During this period, my friend Yngve and I played chess and card games. His family was building a new house simultaneously with my foster-parents a hundred yards away. Despite these new houses, we still lived very near, and his family and I had been very close during my first stay in Sweden. This was the only family I could visit whenever I wanted and without any particular reason, a habit I have maintained to this day, though the distance between our houses is different now.

Although my return to Finland seems sad to me now, looking back at my experiences, I feel that all of them have been blessings for me. I have learned to know my roots and feel at home in Finland. But at the same time, I have the same feeling when I visit Sweden. It is as if I have returned home and could settle down there. I am not bitter about my any of my experiences as a war child. I had two sets of parents, have two languages, and friends and relatives in both countries. All this and more enriches my life.

* * * * *

Rauno became a radio operator and worked on a ship tanker for two years. He met his wife, Sisko, some years earlier in Finland. She did not want to live in Sweden, so they settled in Finland where Rauno worked in a shop, repairing electronic devices for ten years. Then Rauno, Sisko, and his children, Merja and Timo, moved to Kajaani, a small town in mid-Finland 150 kilometers from the Russian border, where Rauno had his own shop and worked for twenty-two years until his retirement.

Notes

1. The Battle of Suomussalmi lasted from December 7, 1939, to January 8, 1940, and was a major Finnish victory, which became emblematic of the entire Winter War. It is often cited as an example of how a small force with trained fighters in familiar terrain can defeat a numerically superior army. During the war, over 400,000 people were evacuated from their homes. Those homes closest to the border were burned, so that they wouldn't fall into Soviet hands. For this reason, the return of families to this region created great hardship, but the retreating Soviet forces had left behind much valuable machinery and weaponry that would be useful during the Continuation War that followed. Due to their questionable defeat at the hands of the Russians, Finns were forced to cede 11 percent of their pre-war territory and 30 percent of their economic assets to the Soviet Union. See Jowett and Snodgrass, *Finland at War,* 7–8.

13

Paper Dolls
Sirpa Kaukinen

I was born in the fall of 1938 in Turku, Finland. The Winter War began in 1939, one year after my birth, when Russia invaded our eastern border on November 30. At the time we lived in a small flat on Hämeenkatu, one of Turku's main streets, which is now called Vanha Hämeentie, in the suburb of Nummenmäki. Life was simpler in those days. While streetcars traveled down our street, providing us with convenient transportation, water came from a well, and we used a communal outhouse. We also visited a communal sauna twice a week. Wood was used for heating and cooking. The nearest telephone was at the local grocery store, and our only sources of news were newspapers and local gossip. People did not move very often; therefore, everyone knew one's neighbors and could count on them for help.

Both my parents were young, under twenty-five at the time. Father worked at the Kupittaan Savi as a potter and an artist, a job he loved. His nickname was *kaunis Armas,* meaning "handsome Armas," and he had dark hair with blue eyes and very even features. During the war, he was located on the front, installing communications equipment once an area had been secured. My mother stayed at home. Shortly after the war broke out, my mother, her elder sister Laura, and myself as a one-year-old child went to my mother's elderly parents' home in Kuusjoki, near Salo in southern Finland. My Aunt Laura had been born with circulatory problems and was sickly, so mother had to help her out.

My only sister Sointu was born in early 1941, also in Turku. And Laura's daughter was born in September 1941. I only have two clear memories prior to my sister's birth: one of mother and I running hand in hand to the bomb shelter and another of father visiting and bringing me two small cellophane bags of hard candy, one blue and one orange. After my sister was born, mother readied us both each evening for going to the bomb shelter: my sister was completely dressed and slept in her open bunting bag, and I was fully dressed except for my shoes, hat, and overcoat, which were beside me on a chair. I later learned that Turku was bombed about 600 times during the war because of its large harbor. In those days, it was the second largest city in Finland. Perhaps I remember these events so clearly from my early youth because mother brought me up to be precocious and to remember things as well as I possibly could, since I might need to know them later. In addition, I used to discuss wartime experiences with my mother, so some memories were reinforced in this way.

Our lives became more complicated in the spring of 1941 after Aunt Laura, aged 28, had a stroke while pregnant with her first child. She was in the hospital for four months and later came to stay with us with her newborn baby girl. Though it was dangerous to remain in Turku, due to the constant bombing, my mother wanted to wait to leave because of Aunt Laura's condition, the newborn baby, and the extreme cold that winter. However, in March 1942 we left for Salo. Sointu and Laura's baby were pushed in the pram with all our clothing and other needs packed around them. There was slushy snow on the ground, and I walked behind mother, holding Aunt Laura's right hand. We took the train from Turku, then traveled by bus to where our grandparents lived another twenty-five kilometers away. Traveling was also precarious, but people on the trains and buses—mostly the elderly and women and children—helped each other out. All were leaving for the countryside to be somewhere safer. My grandparents' house was very small and the babies cried a lot, but soon Aunt Laura and mother rented their own small cottage. Life in the country was more peaceful, and it was easier to obtain food from nearby farmers.

In the spring of 1943 my aunt was pregnant again, and we moved back to Turku to be closer to doctors and the hospital. By this time there was a lot of talk of children being sent to Sweden, and mother sometimes mentioned the idea to me in passing. A girl I played with in our yard, Heli, had left for Sweden. That summer, mother, Sointu, and I went by train on a holiday to Punkaharju in eastern Finland. In the fall of 1943 Aunt Laura, whose husband was in the navy throughout the war, gave birth to a second baby girl, so now there were two adults and four small children. Father's older brother's wife who lived nearby visited us often. She seemed knowledgeable about everything and readily gave advice to mother on child-rearing and other issues. She told mother that she was going to send three of her four boys to Sweden for better food and clothing. Mother asked a lot of questions, and I could tell she was becoming interested in the idea. However, her plans were interrupted when I contracted scarlet fever in late 1943 and had to stay in the chronic care hospital, the *Kunnallissairaala,* until about March 1944.

Upon my release from the hospital, mother started planning my and Sointu's evacuation to Sweden and talking about it daily, as there was hardly any food, and Sointu was badly undernourished. With Laura's two children, mother had four small children to care for. What would Laura do if something happened to mother? Grandmother was suffering from severe heart disease, and father's parents were long dead. Mother herself had been badly injured in a fall one morning, as she rushed downtown to get some food before the lineup became too long. In addition to the practical problems of feeding and caring for us, Turku was again being heavily bombed. And many Finns feared a Soviet victory was inevitable. If Finland were destroyed in the final Russian onslaught, wouldn't it be better for the children to be living elsewhere? After the war mother used to say to Sointu and me, "I was only trying to save you and get you food." Our father also was thinking about our welfare and made me a small suitcase, which he sent during this period when it was being decided about whether or not we would go to Sweden. It is a treasure that I still have today,

So, on June 6, 1944, when I was five and Sointu was three, we traveled all night by train from Turku to Tornio, in northern Finland, and then down to southern Sweden, probably near Trosa.[1]

The train was full of crying children. Mother sat us down side by side with me near the window. I was not frightened and didn't cry. Instead, I wondered where we were going. Both Sointu and I were used to trains, but this train ride was really long. At some point, we were examined physically, and it was discovered that my sister had an ear infection and needed to stay in the quarantine hospital for about twenty days, whereas I only stayed a short time. I will always remember the hard moment of having to leave my sister at the clinic, as mother had said we should stay together.

I was taken by Mr. Carl Axelsson, whom I came to call *Pappa*. He arrived with a horse and a buggy, and together with a lady who spoke Finnish, we traveled to the Axelsson farmhouse at Nyckelby, Norrgord, in Västerljung, Sweden. Sointu eventually went to the family of Ebba Karlsson who also lived in Västerljung, not far from us. But in quarantine it had been discovered that she had ear pain, so she was first moved to Strängnäs Hospital for treatment. In fact, Sointu's eardrum had been pierced when she was six months old, and our mother never felt she could hear well as a consequence. Maybe for this reason, mother spoke a very elaborate baby talk with Sointu, something my father complained about later.

At the Axelsson home, I met my future *Mamma*, Vendela, their seventeen-year-old daughter Anne-Marie, and fourteen-year-old son Bengt. I was invited to sit at a coffee table laden with food and given a glass of milk and a small plate of cake and cookies. Later Anne-Marie took me to our room where I was given a single bed across from her bed and a dresser. During the next few days, *Pappa* and Bengt introduced all the farm animals to me: horses, cows, pigs, hens, and chickens, which, having come from the city, were thrilling for me. Anne-Marie went to school, as did Bengt, and I played in the kitchen while *Mamma* worked there. Soon, though, I met two girls who lived nearby and we played at each other's houses and yards. Everyone was very good and kind to me: *Mamma* helped me with coloring and printing cards to Finland to mother and let me bake with her. She gave me real dolls and an elaborate set of small pots and pans, spoons, and paper on which I could draw money, flour bags, and sugar, so that I could pretend to be a storekeeper. I sat on her lap as she weaved rag rugs upstairs. *Mamma* also gave me paper dolls and helped me to cut them out. Paper dolls had become my favorite playthings in the hospital in Finland, as you couldn't take anything from home, so mother had constantly brought me paper dolls. At the time I had families of them and told everyone many stories about them.

Pappa and Bengt let me help feed pigs and hens and even gave me my own small piglet to look after, which soon grew to be huge, at which point I gave it back to *Pappa*. Anne-Marie played with me and read to me, took me for walks, gave me baths, and helped me with my attempts to print letters and numbers. She also took me and my friends swimming at the nearby lake in the summer, and pulled us on a sled in the winter. I loved her with all my heart. At harvest time we prepared baskets of food for the workers in the fields. That's always my first memory of Sweden: the golden fields of wheat, swaying in the late summer breeze, and I'm lying on a picnic blanket, looking up at a huge blue sky. My days were generally very happy, full of sunshine, food, play, and peace. At night I would think of mother and see her round face, her dark, wavy hair, her big brown eyes, and her approving smile. I felt that things were well with her, Aunt Laura, and my small cousins. The only thing that bothered me was that Sointu and I were not together because my mother had wanted us to stay in one family.

I visited Sointu at another house a few times, but over the months she grew more and more distant. We ran around the yard together, but she didn't really appear to know me. Every once in awhile, she would stop and look at me for a long time and laugh. She grew taller and thinner and seemed older with her baby curls cut off. She was also quieter. She couldn't speak Swedish very well, which was the only language I spoke within two months of arriving. As an adult, Sointu believes that she stayed in more than one foster family in Sweden but cannot remember her foster parents at all. And, after the war, she never cried about her lost *Pappa* and *Mamma*.

On winter Sundays, my foster family and I went to church in the sleigh. And at Christmas, Anne-Marie was a Lucia, wearing a crown of candles, and I was dressed as her helper while we both carried cookies and sweets on trays to *Mamma* and *Pappa* and Bengt. It was a wonderful late-night party. There was a big Christmas tree in the best room, and I was even given my own little Christmas tree upstairs. I also received many little presents from everyone, which made me very happy.

Sometime in March 1945 Mamma told me very slowly and cautiously that she had received a letter. I could sense the importance of this and knew that something was changing. At the time I was sitting at the kitchen table, cutting paper dolls' clothes. *Pappa* went to stand beside Mamma, and she read to me that my mother and father in Finland wanted me to come home soon. I remember just sitting there with the scissors in my hand, which rested on the tablecloth. And then, to the amazement of myself and my family, I began cutting and cutting until the good tablecloth fell to either side of the table in two pieces. I started to cry, and *Mamma* pulled me into her lap, and everyone began crying. Then Anne-Marie took me upstairs, and I went to bed. For awhile, I was very confused and asked a lot about Sointu. Everyone assured me that she would come home with me.

Figure 13.1. *Sirpa Kaukinen at age five, with her own Christmas tree in Sweden. Courtesy Sirpa Kaukinen.*

But the day of leaving was very hard. *Mamma* and Anne-Marie helped me pack my suitcase and some boxes as well with all my paper dolls, a real doll, new clothes, a picture book, and even scissors. The whole family brought me to the train station. It was hard to experience a separation from family yet again. I loved *Mamma, Pappa,* and Bengt, and most of all Anne-Marie. We all cried, and many other children and foster parents were crying at the train station. Everyone was also crying on the train. At the next station, someone brought Sointu on the train, and tears were just streaming down her face. She didn't seem to know me, but I kept pulling her along with me until I found a seat for us. We boarded a large ship in Stockholm, I think, and settled into sleeping together in a big cabin with other children.

The next day, the ship arrived in Turku, and I helped my sister dress the best I could, but her boots ended up on the wrong feet, and that's how we ended up on deck. There we stood together, and from far away I could see mother standing on the dock. "Look, look, there is mother!" I told Sointu. She didn't appear to make any connection with this, but at least she had stopped crying. Our parents rushed up to us, and I ran to mother. But I didn't know father at all. Nor did my parents recognize Sointu. When she left Finland, at age three, she had looked like a small slightly pudgy toddler with golden curls to her shoulders. When she returned she was taller, very thin, and had her hair cut in a *polkkatukka,* a very short ear-length cut with bangs.

Sointu just stood there, and mother and father kept looking at her, reading and rereading the name tag around her neck. Finally, mother said to me in Swedish: "Is it Sointu? What happened to her? She looks so different!" And I replied in a loud voice: "Yes, it is. Just look at her." I became angry, thinking to myself, *don't they recognize her?* But, inspecting her face closely, my mother saw a small scar on her eyelid, smiled at father, and said, "Yes, it's Sointu. She has the scar on her eyelid," something she had received from a branch when she was very small.

But I was having difficulties of my own. On the streetcar ride home, I asked mother in Swedish: "Who is this man?" And mother looked at me and said: "It's your father." And I replied firmly: "No, it's not. My father is a soldier. Don't you remember? He always has a soldier's uniform on." Once mother explained the conversation to father, he looked crestfallen, I think because I didn't recognize him.

But slowly we united as a family again. It was altogether different than during the war. Father had never really stayed with us for any length of time, and now he was always with us. During the war years, the women and children also mostly stayed inside because the young children and Aunt Laura couldn't walk far. After father returned, however, we began to go outside a lot more. Father didn't talk much about his war experiences with us, but he sometimes had nightmares. He also destroyed the photos he had taken in the war. He returned to being a potter, and we bonded with him despite our previous separations. He taught us practicality, outspokenness, his love of nature—flowers, plants, animals, and cooking too.

Sointu was taken to speech therapy lessons so she could learn Finnish, and I started school that fall, soon relearning the language. We received Christmas cards and presents from Sweden for some years. But father became worried because his nephew who had been sent to Sweden for ten years had been the source of a legal dispute between his biological and foster parents. The latter wanted to keep him, and there was a tug-of-war over the boy until he very unwillingly came back home. So, after a few years, the Axelssons stopped writing and sending presents.

My sister says she had a good stay in Sweden but doesn't really remember anything. However, I often think of my *Mamma* and *Pappa,* Bengt, and especially Anne-Marie, and I miss them. They were truly good, kind, and wonderful people in every way, and I loved them.

I feel that I was purely lucky in being the age I was when I was sent. At age five, I didn't have the needs of a baby, but not that much was expected of me. I could also remember my mother and the reasons for my being sent to Sweden. Before going to Sweden, I was also lucky that my mother was so good-natured about her responsibilities, never complaining, but always looking on the bright side: "Let's sing a song. Let's read a story. Let's play a game. Isn't it a sunny day today?" Despite the chaos of war, we held onto our customs and rituals, which reminded us of better times and gave some stability and regularity to our lives.

My family was relatively lucky. My husband's family lost everything: their father in the Winter War, their home twice, and everything they possessed. His mother's only consolations were that she kept her two sons near her throughout the war and that both of them were alive and healthy when it was over.

In postwar Finland I don't remember anyone talking about the war children. But in recent years the war experiences have begun to spill out like rivulets from water long dammed. For a long time I was bothered by uncertain memories, including the dim memory of hiding in a ditch while airplanes flew overhead. They were so near and so heavy, these big grey planes, and the "drrrrr" noise they made was awful. The night my father died as an old man, I dreamed of a giant grey helicopter, sitting on top of his cottage and he, as a small boy, running away, then turning to me, laughing, and waving his hand. Along with the helicopter, he disappeared. And since that dream, so has my fear of planes.

* * * * *

Eight years after the war ended, Sirpa's family traveled across the Atlantic Ocean to Canada, where she once again learned a new language and culture. Sirpa went to business college and became an office manager in a large hospital, and later a writer. Sointu became a Special Education teacher in the public school system in Ontario. Both Sirpa and her sister have taught Finnish to children and adults in Ontario where they live, and both have received recognition from the Canadian and Finnish governments for their volunteer work in their communities.

Notes

1. Sirpa has consulted a document in the Finnish National Archives, dated 27/3/44 or 27/5/44—the script is handwritten and somewhat unclear—in which she and her sister were identified by number: "1,410" for Sirpa and "1,411" for Sointu. She also discovered that her mother had paid around 550 Marks for their passage.

14

The Woman in the Broad-Brimmed Hat
Kirsti Kettunen

I was born in January 1939 in Möhkö, near Ilomantsi, the eastern-most part of Finland known as Karelia. When the Winter War began in November, nearly one year later, my father Eino was called to the front from his work at a lumber camp. My understanding is that he was not given enough time even to say farewell to his family. Like thousands of Finns then living in Karelia, my mother and her five children, Lilja, Maire, Terttu, Juhani, and I, had to evacuate, taking whatever possessions we could with us. Because I was only an infant, I have no memory of these events, but I later learned that we were evacuated to Iisalmi, north of Kuopio, and that my three older sisters were soon thereafter sent to Sweden for various lengths of time, but that all eventually returned. For whatever reason, my brother Juhani and I were sent to a *Lastenkoti* (children's home) in Haukivuori, and this is where my earliest memories begin.[1]

One of my earliest memories is of Juhani and I lying on a long, narrow bed feet to feet. We were tied down, so that we would not fall out and also to prevent my brother from scratching scabs and irritating some skin condition. After the war, I discovered that being tied down had so greatly traumatized him that for a long time he would not speak. He was considered to be *kuuromykkäl* (deaf and dumb) and sent to a school in Kuopio for deaf children where he received very minimal care. He lasted only one semester there since he wasn't learning. He was then sent to a *Kunnalistalo* (home for the handicapped) close to Iisalmi where he was taken care of the rest of his life until his probable suicide.

I believe that he was seven when he was taken from the orphanage after spending some three years there. Many years later I visited him with my sister Terttu. Sadly, when I was living in Canada, I heard that he had drowned. The story goes that the family had just visited him and he seemed teary-eyed when they left. It seemed he understood more than he was given credit for and that he was despondent and decided just to go for a swim and have it all end. I believe that he was permanently damaged by the shock of evacuation when he was almost four and I nearly two, by being brutally restrained and neglected, and by the constant dislocations of his early years.

My next memories are of sirens going off, aerial bombings, and us kids hiding under beds and tables. Nurses were running up and down, collecting and putting us onto trucks. And off we went: where to, I still don't know. I must have fallen asleep on the truck because I don't remember getting off.

During this time I had a vision in my head of my mother, beautiful in a broad-brimmed hat. I kept that vision when daydreaming about my family, though as an infant and toddler, I did not consciously remember anything about my family or if I even had one. Other kids' mothers came to visit occasionally, but no one ever came to see me. I remember that when a mother did come to visit her child, the rest of us gathered around to look and drool and wonder why *our* mothers never came to visit. I was completely unaware as to whether I had a family or a mother until being told that another family had considered adopting me but that my *mother* had said no. I don't know what age I was when I discovered this. But this was the first time I learned that I had a *living mother*. Unfortunately I had no one to tell me about my family, no one to reinforce my memories, no pictures of my family, and no one to hug and love me. All I have from my earliest years are these vague memories, some of which might have been simply the wishful hopes of an abandoned girl, like the image of my mother in a broad-brimmed hat.

From this time I very dimly remember another incident when a kind of hushed activity was going on around one of the children's beds. I believe that a child was very sick and that he died, but I never knew for sure. Another time I was standing in the crib with woolen panties on, and I was crying. I don't know how old I was, but I must have been very little, and I don't know if I was sick or just crying for attention.

Figure 14.1. *Kirsti Kettunen as an infant in her mother's arms with her family in rural Finland, prior to being sent to a children's home or orphanage in Finland. Courtesy Kirsti Kettunen.*

The second children's home I was sent to was in Mäntyharju, which like Haukivuori was within a hundred mile radius of Mikkeli. Here I stayed until I was eleven years of age, so all my formative years were spent in these orphanages apart from my family. This second orphanage was in a very rural country setting, and the building itself was a big red farmhouse with white trimmings. Entering from the road, the main entrance was lined with nasturtiums and other flowers in summer and surrounded with lawn. On either side of the main building, there were smaller outbuildings like horse stalls, wood sheds, barns, a root cellar, and a small cottage where the custodian lived. Behind the main building were the apple trees, berry bushes, a vegetable garden, and a pathway to the sauna by the lake. In summer it was lovely to swim and lie on the grass, gazing at the clouds drifting above and imagining what animal shapes they represented or where they came from and where they went. I spent lot of time in daydreaming and wishful thinking, and whenever I felt bad or mistreated I thought if I only could be with my family things would be better. There was many a time when I cried myself to sleep, all curled up in a fetal position.

I was known to sleepwalk during the night, to cry, or do other strange things in my sleep. I had terrible nightmares. One of my recurring nightmares was that everything went wild with splashes of color and made me blind and crazy. Another was that something heavy in a big mass rolled over me, and I couldn't breathe: a giant thing that kept coming in waves and squeezed the life out of me. Another recurring dream always started out pleasantly with my believing I had made it to the pot and could just let go and pee. I felt such relief only to wake up and find that I had wetted the bed. I was also told that one night I collected all the clothes of the other girls who slept in my room and that I put them in the piss pail while sleepwalking. I don't know if that is true or not, but I do remember being told that. When I had nightmares I was sometimes forced to sleep in a kind of hallway alone, so I wouldn't disturb the other children. A few times I was so scared that the head nurse let me share her room and her bed, which is one of the few kindnesses I can remember.

One of my nightmares occurred in broad daylight. I was upstairs, and I thought some terrible man was after me with a knife. I had to get away, so I climbed through the window, went down the fire ladder, ran around the building to the other side into the kitchen, and sat on the bench there, panting with relief. Watching the people there doing their cooking, I felt safe again, but I didn't tell anyone about the man. Another time we all were treated for head lice. The nurses massaged a strong solution through our hair, but my hair was so thin that it felt like my scalp was burning. I wasn't alone: most of the children were screaming and kicking in agony.

These memories don't follow in chronological sequence. They are simply what I can remember.

We ate our meals together in one large room. Every morning we had some kind of porridge for breakfast, made from different kinds of grains. Oatmeal was one of them, but for some reason I just could not eat it. It seemed to me that there were rough husks or something that wouldn't go down my throat. When I refused to eat the porridge, my caregivers tried to force me. But I would not. One time I hid among the attic rafters in order to avoid eating that awful oatmeal. All the other children were sent to find me, but I had found such a good hiding place that no one was able to discover me. So, for a while on the oatmeal mornings, I wasn't given anything for breakfast. Lunch was thinned out porridge that Finns call *velli*. Supper was usually vegetable soup or stew with just a taste of meat or maybe a little fish. The meals were not fancy, since everything was rationed after the war. I remember once we all were given cod liver oil: one attendant held my legs, another my arms, and the third spooned the stuff into my mouth, which I promptly spat out.

Cream of wheat was a Sunday treat, and on Christmas day we all got rice porridge. I remember one Christmas being taken to church early in the morning in a horse-drawn sleigh, which was very exciting.

On a couple of occasions, "care parcels" arrived from different countries. Once, each of the children received blood oranges from Spain. We also received small toys like marbles. And we got toothpaste that we ate, since we didn't have toothbrushes and didn't know what else to do with it. Most of the food that came to the orphanage went directly to the pantry. But once, we were given some cheese that I traded for candy with one of the caregivers. The only personal possession I had, which had come in an American care parcel, was a red and green velvet belt with a big shiny brass buckle. I treasured this and hid it in my small cubbyhole until my best girlfriend had a birthday. Because I had nothing else to give her, I gave her my fancy treasure from America.

We all had small cubbyholes in which to keep our things like pen, paper, and whatnots. I had a rag doll named Pirjo Anneli that I loved and which I kept in my cubbyhole. But, in addition to loving this doll, I was quite a tomboy, since I had to defend myself against bullies. I was bit on my arm by one of the kids that left a scar of a full set of teeth for a long time into my adulthood. And, in turn, the boy who bit me was left with a scar on his scalp. I also still have a scar on my ear that was a result of a game we played called "funny poses" in which the children held hands and spun each other around and then let you go. The idea was to fall in an amusing position, but on one occasion I landed on a rock and cut my ear. We would sometimes be punished, for instance for picking apples without permission. Once we were lined up to be whipped with thin birch twigs on our bare legs because no one would tell who had committed some particular mischief. We all tried to be brave and not cry even though the whipping really smarted. One of my front teeth has a yellow spot on it, which my dentist tells me was probably either the result of malnutrition or a kick in the teeth when I was a child.

The only time we were allowed to listen to the radio and to a particular children's program was on Sunday mornings after breakfast. Otherwise, we weren't exposed to music from radio or any other media. We did sing children's songs, but without any musical accompaniment or training.

Older children were expected to do chores, such as clear the tables after our meals. I remember that most of us ran to the outhouse to avoid doing chores. My memory of the outhouse is that it had three levels of platforms with four holes on each level. There were one or two steps between levels, so that the differently aged children could use them according to their size. I think we had separate ones for boys and girls.

Every Saturday we all went to the sauna, and as far as I can remember both boys and girls used it together, at least until children began to develop. Swimming in the lake afterwards was heaven. I was pretty good at swimming, which I learned when I was around five. Before I was eleven, I completed what were called Swimming Candidate and Swimming Master degrees in Mikkeli. The first time I tried to pass the diving test from a ten-meter high platform, I was too frightened by the height. But the second time I did it, and after that it was routine. My dream in those days was to swim across the English Channel. I had often swum across the lake, and the next step, I thought, was the English Channel. In fact I daydreamed about this a lot.

We didn't have preschool or kindergarten in those days, but I began elementary school in 1946 when I was seven. I don't have too many memories of my school years, except that we walked to the nearby village school and that it always began with a Lutheran religious hour. I also remember once playing hooky. On the way to the schoolhouse there was a hay shed, and I sneaked into it. It was a nice spring day, and I remember peering through the cracks in the walls and listening to the birds sing. I spent the duration of the day, lying on hay and reading and dreaming about all the places I would see when I was grown up. After learning to read, I read all the books I could get my hands on. I loved Zane Gray's stories and dreamed about seeing the Wild West in America. I also wanted to see Death Valley, which I achieved much later. I also enjoyed reading *Gone with the Wind, The Secret Garden, Little Women,* and other novels that had been translated into Finnish. Later, in Iisalmi girl's secondary school, I learned Swedish, German, and some English, so that I had many more books to read. Reading was my great escape from reality.

I was taught to knit and crochet, and I was pretty good at that. I also liked to draw pictures, but we didn't have many of the necessary materials. Knitting socks, hats, and scarves was more practical. I was not taught to do any cooking, but we did do gardening and weeding in our little garden patches. To this day I find gardening and weeding very relaxing.

We were often spanked or put into the corner for not behaving well at school or the orphanage. I remember once the teacher asked the class who had arranged the hoops on top of the school cabinet. I knew I had done it, but I just put my head down on my desk and was afraid to look at anybody. Finally the teacher said that it was very artistically done, and I sighed with relief. Compliments were few in my childhood, but once received never to be forgotten.

In September 1950 I was sent to middle school, which was too far to walk, and in those days there were no school buses. So I was placed to live with a family while attending my new school. I believe I was the only child sent to middle school from the orphanage. It seemed that all the other orphans found work after elementary school and received no further education. I was rather terrified about my new circumstances, and strangely I don't remember the family at all, though I would have been eleven years old. But I do remember my music teacher who auditioned us all for choir. When it was my turn I sang one of my favorite Christmas songs: *Maa on niin kaunis* (The Earth Is So Beautiful). I was not allowed to finish the song but was told to sit down and never to open my mouth to sing again. I was crushed and am afraid even today to have anyone hear me sing.

My last day at middle school was September 23, 1950, because, as it states in my school report card, that is the day on which my *mother* came to pick me up and to take me to Iisalmi where she still lived. This was a great shock and surprise to me to suddenly be picked up by a strange woman who was *my mother*. She showed me pictures of my sisters and brother and told me that my father had been killed in the Winter War. She also described the family's evacuation to Iisalmi and described the family's hardships. She informed me that she had a new husband and five other children, three boys and two girls. I simply couldn't believe what was happening and felt overwhelmed. Before this, whenever I felt sorry for myself, crying myself to sleep in a fetal position, I believed that *if only I was at home with my mother and father,* everything would be good. Now I was finally going home.

We took the train to Iisalmi, and I was full of anticipation and wonder about what was happening. I had never been on a train before that I remembered, so this was very exciting to me.

My mother gave me something to eat, a *kalakukko,* which she had baked herself. It's quite a common dish in Finland—baked bread filled with fish—but I had never eaten it before, and I was not sure if I liked it. I ate it anyway, though, because *my mother had made it.*

I was very happy and curious about my new family. There were three younger boys: Jouko, Jorma, and Erkki, and two little girls, Eeva and the baby Hannele. Shortly after I arrived in 1952, another baby was born, and I'm sure that this made my mother feel more put upon and less interested in me. Maire, my second oldest sister who was born in 1931, was preparing to go to Stockholm to live with my oldest sister Lilja who was born in 1929 and who worked in a restaurant there. They and Terttu, who was born in 1934, had all been sent to Sweden during the war. Terttu, the closest to me in age, was a big help to my mother. The first year I was home, I also tried my best to be a good girl and please mother. And everyone else tried to adjust to me as well. Before being admitted to *Iisalmen tyttölyseo,* girls' secondary school, I had to return to elementary school about a mile away.

Our house was very modest and crowded, due to the number of people living there: two adults and eight children. But it was beautifully situated next to Lake Poronvesi (Reindeer Water) and, above all, my mother and stepfather owned the dwelling. We didn't have running water, so all the water had to be brought in and carried out. And our outhouse was perhaps a hundred feet away in the same building with the sauna, woodshed, and hayloft.

Although I was never given the facts, I believe that after my father died in the Winter War, my mother received a subsidy for each child and herself. I believe, too, that after our evacuation, because we were sharing a house with many other refugees, this could be why my mother sent my three older sisters to Sweden and me and Juhani to the children's home. Mother met her second husband, Reino, when she was thirty and a widow with all these children to support. This handsome soldier had lost an eye in the war and received some sort of compensation. So, perhaps with this they were able to buy the nice lot and build their home. I believe, too, that mother brought me back only after the Finnish government instructed her to, so that I could go to the same secondary school that my sister Terttu attended. But this is all speculation on my part.

The first year I was at home, everything seemed to go well, since everyone tried to adjust as best as they could. But during my second year home, it became very clear that my mother couldn't stand the sight of me. She didn't allow me to read books. I had to bring in all the drinking/cooking water from the well, which was some distance from our house and was shared by other families. And I had to split wood at the woodshed. My sister Terttu took care of the inside work and I did all the outside work, though my younger brother Jouko sometimes helped me. My stepfather delivered beer and soft drinks with a horse-drawn cart and was too tired after work to pay any attention to us.

I had to do all this work while I was going to school. But I was never allowed to have friends over or to play and visit with friends. I felt that my younger stepbrothers were allowed to have all the fun, while I had to work. My stepfather left my mother alone to deal with me, except on a few occasions when he felt she had gone too far. And I couldn't count on him. On one occasion when he was drunk and my mother was in the sauna, he came upstairs, took me in his lap, and started to fondle me. But I told him I would scream for help if he didn't stop, so he did.

One winter, after the laundry had been washed in the sauna, I was rinsing it in an ice hole in the frozen lake. My fingers got so cold that I put them between my legs to warm them up. But then I thought maybe I should just slip under the ice and end my misery. Of course I didn't, but the thought was there. On another occasion, when I tried to stand up for myself during an argument with my mother, I threatened to run away to Russia or marry a negro (I had never seen a black person before, and it would be several years before I saw one, but this just seemed to be an extreme thing to say). One time she threw something sharp at me and hit my head, which bled profusely. She must have gotten scared, because she gave me a hundred Finnish marks and sent me walking to the hospital.

I still managed to read books on the sly, even reading in bed under my blanket with a candle. But my mother caught on, and to prevent me from reading she went to the nearest two libraries and asked them not to lend any more books to me, though I still received a few from friends, which I read in the woodshed between splitting wood and resting a little. One time Jouko was helping me chop wood, and I stupidly held the wood up with my hand. He swung the ax and hit my right forefinger. I wrapped it with a rag and we never told my mother about it. I was lucky, I think, that I didn't lose it. I also didn't dare to ask my mother for any money for school supplies or anything else. When the movie *Gone with the Wind* came to Iisalmi, I desperately wanted to see it, but I didn't have the courage to ask my mother, though all my school friends went.

After completing Confirmation School, I had my first Holy Communion on March 27, 1955, when I was sixteen. One of the only photos I have of my youth is of me wearing the dress my sister Terttu helped me make for this occasion. It is a group photo. She also found an ad in an Iisalmi paper for a mother's helper. And this changed my life. I had an interview in an Iisalmi shop, and after the school year was over, I was thrilled to be able to leave my home and go to Helsinki.

I have suppressed a lot of my memories from my early childhood and youth, and I believe that had I been adopted and grown up in a family situation, I would have been happier and better adjusted socially. For many years I was very apprehensive about meeting new people and didn't feel comfortable talking or interacting with people. I don't like the spotlight on me and can't speak in public. I have also felt inferior to other people most of my life, though with age I began to feel more self-assured.

My mother never wanted to talk to me about why Juhani and I were sent to a children's home and my three sisters to Sweden. I remember her only once suggesting that she was sorry for what had happened to me. But I never received a heartfelt apology. My deprived childhood most certainly had a negative impact on me and my first marriage. I never clearly understood how a normal family works. I had no real model for this.

The last time I saw my mother was in 2002, and she passed away in 2008. I went to her funeral, and there was a wonderful family gathering. I also have in my possession some of the letters my father wrote from the front during the Winter War in which he refers to his last Christmas:

> *Christmas is now past and the new year is beginning. We don't know what fate will bring: happiness or unhappiness. Only God knows what fate he has in store for each of us ... remember to give my greetings to our children. Remind them to pray to God for shelter and protection, and also to give thanks for what they have received and will receive in the future.* [At the Front in a camp halfway dug into the earth: 31 December 1939.]

I also have some early photos of my family, including one of my mother in a broad-brimmed hat. Could this be the same hat she was wearing on the day she gave Juhani and me away? It is the image of my mother that I held onto as an infant: a beautiful woman in a broad-brimmed hat.

* * * * *

Kirsti left Finland when she was seventeen, was married at eighteen, and had three children. She was divorced in 1980 but later remarried in 1995. Her second husband died in 2012. She has lived in several locations but is today retired in Massachusetts. For a short time, she operated a B & B and was an auditor for the Bank of Boston's Freight Management Services. In fulfillment of her childhood dream, Kirsti finally saw the American West, but she writes that by then, "romantic books didn't quite compare with reality."

Notes

1. Johannes Virolainen, a Finnish politician, was in charge of deciding where Karelians would be evacuated. He tried to move families to safe areas closest to their homes. The reason that Kirsti and Juhani were sent to an orphanage is that her mother had been told by authorities to find work, so she was unable to care for her two youngest children. She had also been told that they were too young to go to Sweden.

15

Swedish Toys
Helena Nyqvist Koivisto

I was born in 1937, two years before the war began, in Kokkola in western Finland in Central Ostrobothnia. Later my family moved to the small village of Rimmi outside of Kokkola. My father was a Swedish-speaking Finn who worked in a leather factory, and we lived in a house that the factory provided. My mother was a housewife from Veteli and her mother tongue was Finnish, though she knew Swedish from school. We all spoke Swedish in the home. In November 1939, the same month that the Winter War started, my sister Nea was born, and my father was called away to join the army as a corporal, delivering ammunition to the front. He later told us how difficult it was to drive his truck on primitive roads without using his headlights at night to evade enemy detection. I don't remember much about my early childhood except Nea's birth and, later, in May 1941, the birth of my brother. Around this same time, I became seriously ill with cholera, and my father received leave to come home to see me.

The situation at home was bad because there was no shop in the village, and we had very little food. The local health nurse advised my mother that the best thing to do would be to send me to Sweden to recover. So in March 1942, when I was four, my mother saw me off at the railway station in Kokkola. I remember my mother looked very sad as she stood with my little sister and brother, waiting to see the train leave. I was completely confused about what was happening, and I began to vomit and feel very ill. The train was crowded with children who were equally confused and upset to be leaving home. Most of the children were crying. Only a few Lottas, volunteers in the women's auxiliary defense force, were there to take care of us. On the train, boards had been placed between the benches, and the children tried to sleep on these. In Turku we boarded the ship *Arcturus*, and the journey to Stockholm began. We slept in the hull of the ship on straw covered with blankets, and we could hear the ice cracking all around us, which was frightening.

In Stockholm we had medical tests that were scary and humiliating, since we had to stand naked in a long row to be examined. Those children who had lice had their hair shaved off and their clothes burned. Some children, including me, were taken to a temporary hospital. I believe that I spent several weeks there, and the days were long and boring. Finally, one morning in late spring or early summer, some of us were taken by bus to Uppsala, an old university town north of Stockholm. There, we were seated in a hall, and people began to arrive to choose a suitable child. Two ladies approached me, looked at my label or tag, and selected me to go with them. We walked to a big block of flats in the city and to a very modern apartment in the center of town where my foster family lived. My foster father came home for lunch, and the whole family seemed pleased that I spoke Swedish, due to my bilingual upbringing. Later their daughter Ulla came home from school, and very soon I began to feel like a member of the family.

The Anderssons were the best people in the world. I was asked to refer to my foster mother as *Tant* (Aunt) Maja and my foster father as *Farbror* (Uncle) Bertil. Bertil worked as a storekeeper in a paint shop. His father had a big farm outside Uppsala and also owned a butcher shop in the meat market in the city. Maja was a housewife. Their daughter Ulla was nine when I arrived, and we played together and shared a room. Ulla had lots of toys, and I received many toys and dolls as well. Every evening we said our prayers, and I always asked God to please protect my father in the war. Two years later when I was six, *Tant* Maja had a baby girl, Kristina.

Figure 15.1. *Helena Nyqvist Koivisto (left) with her foster mother and foster siblings. Courtesy Helena Nyqvist Koivisto.*

Shortly after the birth of Kristina, I was sent back to Finland for some reason. I was in much better physical condition than when I had first arrived in Sweden, because in Uppsala I had been told: you must eat; you are undernourished. But readjusting to life in Finland was challenging. Life was dull and hard. There was no running water, and the outhouse was far away from our little two-room flat. My sister Nea had also been sent to Sweden and was still there with her foster parents, so just my little brother Leo and I were at home. My father was still away at the war.

My sister's story made her eventual return to Finland even more difficult. When she was two, she was also sent to Sweden because my mother knew I had been treated well there, and our family was out of food. When mother learned that Nea had also been taken by a family named "Andersson," she assumed they must be relatives of my foster family and was pleased about this, not knowing that this is the most common surname in Sweden! I never saw my sister in Sweden, but our two foster families were sometimes in touch. Because my sister had been so little when she left home, she did not even know that she was Finnish when, four years later, she was demanded back. And getting her back was difficult. Her Swedish parents, whose six children were grown up, had become very attached to her and wanted to keep her. They owned a large farm, almost an estate. So, when Nea returned in 1947, it was a great shock to her to find herself among strangers in such impoverished surroundings. Later she insisted that it would have been better for her to have remained in Sweden. In fact, the Anderssons came to Rimmi one year later to get her back. But was impossible. I will never forget the old farmer crying at the station when they had to return home empty-handed. Nea returned to Sweden during summer holidays, though, and when she was fifteen she moved permanently back to the place where she spent her early childhood.

I too returned to Sweden one summer in July 1944 because of the dire food situation in Finland. Then, in August, I heard that my mother had given birth to a boy and that she was very ill with some brain injury contracted in childbirth. So I stayed in Uppsala with my foster family and began school at the end of summer. Everything went well that year, and I remember being very happy to be back. I received many postcards from my father, though my mother could not write in Swedish and needed translation help from a neighbor. I don't remember ever feeling homesick for Finland or my family. I did well in school in Sweden and liked my teacher very much. On the last day of school that year, I was asked to read an essay I had written called "Finland." One sentence from it that I remember read something like, "In the village where I live in Finland, the railway divides the town in two. I live on one side, and other people live on the other side."

That summer was wonderful with visits to Lake Mälaren where Ulla, her cousin Krister, and I sailed. But at the end of the war in 1945, Finland demanded its children back. For this reason, I did not begin my second year of school in Uppsala. Instead, we waited for the call, which did not come until October when the Anderssons received a letter from the Finnish government. My mother did not request that I come back; few Finnish mothers did, since there was still no food. We had lost the war, and times were very hard. I remember *Tant* Maija crying at the station when I left. She had packed lots of sandwiches and other food for me to take. After three days traveling, my Finnish family was very happy to receive all of this food. The journey should not have taken this long, but in Tornio on the Finnish-Swedish border, I and nineteen other children had been put on the wrong train and ended up in Kuopio where we stayed the night. One little boy was from Vaasa on the opposite side of Finland, so his journey was even longer.

When I returned at age eight to our very modest dwelling, it was difficult to get used to the complete absence of facilities—indoor plumbing and water—and the cramped and crowded space. In Uppsala, I had lived in a modern apartment in the center of a beautiful city, and the family had a big summerhouse in the countryside where we often stayed. My Swedish family had also bought me lots of pretty new clothes and toys. My mother thought that the toys were quite unnecessary, as we were lacking for food. So she exchanged my lovely new things for butter and other basics. Also I had been given a brooch from the Anderssons that I liked very much, and one day it just disappeared. I was upset that my mother never asked my permission to sell or trade away my things. At least my father, who was now home from the war, treated me well and had a good sense of humor. But neither he nor my mother ever hugged me. And my mother frequently said, "God sees you everywhere and will punish you for your sins." This frightened and bewildered me. I had never thought of God as angry and vindictive before. My mother also frequently had epileptic fits from her brain injury, and she frightened me.

I compared my foster parents with my Finnish parents who I thought were less loving, friendly, and affectionate. I missed Sweden and the comforts there and began to feel quite miserable and depressed. In Uppsala, the table was always set very nicely, and we ate all kinds of delicacies and cold cuts. But in Rimmi, the typical dinner was potatoes and gravy with occasionally very small pieces of ham or sausage. On Saturdays, my father went on his bicycle to buy food with our rationing coupons for the week, but we were always short of everything. Occasionally the Anderssons sent parcels, but *Tant* Maija had to get a license to do this and was under strict instructions about what she could and could not send. I have a letter in which she expresses her sorrow about not being able to get a license on a certain occasion.

My mother was still very weak from childbirth and her illness. So, as the oldest child, I was obliged to do a great deal of work. I had to fetch water and milk from a distant farm, and often late at night. I also had to walk a long distance to my old school where my classmates looked upon me as a foreign intruder, due to the fine clothes that the Anderssons and other Swedes had given me. Just to try to make friends, I gave them my few remaining toys from Sweden. The food in school was bad and difficult to swallow. And in the winter, it was hard to walk through the deep drifts of snow, though we often skied. When I was nine I went to public school, which was also some distance away from Rimmi. Following that I attended school in Kokkola for the next nine years. I had to go by train, leaving at 7 AM and returning at 4:30 PM. Earlier, I had attended only Swedish-speaking schools, but in Kokkola I had to learn Finnish, the most difficult language I know. I didn't do so well in school during this time and found the teachers very severe.

Our father worked as the storekeeper at the Kokkola leather factory, which employed many workers. Most of them took the same train as I to go to school. But father's income was very meager, and mother was completely preoccupied as a housewife and never had time for me. I felt friendless and unloved and craved affection. Also, school was not free in those days, so I had to work at a dairy, making ice cream, from the time I was twelve to pay for my schooling. I earned enough money for my first bicycle, which my mother also used. Then, when I was almost seventeen my Swedish sister Ulla got me a job in a big hospital in Uppsala, so I was at last reunited with the Anderssons in June 1954. The whole family came to the Uppsala station to meet me, and *Tant* Maija hugged me and was so happy to see me again. I lived for free in their apartment while I worked. The pay was better in Sweden, and when I returned home I was able to bring new clothes for me and my brothers.

Although the Anderssons were always loving and kind, I somehow felt that I was no longer part of that family either. Ulla was engaged to be married, and she and her husband Sven later remained great friends. Then, at the end of the summer when I had to return to Finland, my mother did not seem pleased to see me. I was able to return to Sweden again the next summer to work in a hospital outside Stockholm, and I visited Uppsala many times. But it never occurred to me to try to stay with my Swedish family. I didn't know where I belonged, although my foster sister, Ulla Wallin, wrote in a letter that "Helen has always belonged to our family."[1]

Like many war children, going back and forth between families, I always compared the two. My Finnish family lived a life of hardship, and they were not accustomed to showing their feelings. Nea and I tried to be good and to please them, but we received no response. The Anderssons, by contrast, were generous and loving. As a returning war child, I was desperate to make friends, which is why I gave away my few Swedish toys. From that time forward, I have suffered from a sense of inferiority and a distrust of other people. I never went to dances and never had a boyfriend, though I tried to be sociable. I married when I was twenty-five, but I do not think that I really loved my husband. He was a history teacher, and we had two children, but I was like a maid in the house.

I have always done what people demanded of me, and often my own children and grandchildren have treated me as a maid. My self-estimation has been very low throughout my life. After my divorce, I finished my teacher's training and began to feel more independent. But later I lived with another man for fifteen years and again started to play the role of a maid.

Many war children had worse experiences than I did. Many parents in Finland didn't want their children back and couldn't afford to feed them. Some were punished for their time in Sweden. I have even read about fathers who beat their children when they spoke Swedish, though most children after living any length of time in Sweden spoke no other language.

Despite these hardships, most of the war children I know pursued a higher education and managed to do well in life. Another thing that I share with many other war children is that I do not like people to bring me gifts. I always feel that they are showing pity for me in some way and treating me as a poor, starving war child.

* * * * *

Helena attended the University of Turku where she studied English, German, and literature. She married a history teacher and principal in her mid-twenties and taught at his school. They had two children together but were later divorced in 1977. After, Helena taught evening school in Lapua for adults. Seven years later she taught children in Ilmajoki. After she retired at age sixty-three, she received a degree in tourism and has worked as a trilingual guide in Swedish, Finnish, and English ever since. She lives today in Seinäjoki where she often gives guided tours of the city.

Notes

1. Sent by Helena's foster sister, Ulla Wallin, on September 29, 2013, to the editor of the present volume.

16
Goodbye to the Bombs
Anne-Maj Korpela

When the Winter War began in 1939, my parents, sister Clary, and I were living in the middle of Helsinki in a small flat on the second storey of a five-storey apartment building. I was then eight years old and my sister Clary fifteen. During the year ahead, my *Mor*, which is Swedish for "Mother," would have a baby boy, nine years younger than I. My *Far* (or "father"), Henrik Wiklund, was an engineer before the war, and my mother Ruth was a housewife. On the first day of the war, November 30, Clary and I went to school as usual that morning, but were sent home a few hours later during a radio announcement about approaching Russian bombers. Sirens began to blare all over the city, and everyone living in Helsinki was advised to leave the capital as soon as possible. Upon returning home, we found our parents waiting for us with our suitcases packed to go to the bus station in the center of town, and I remember being awfully shocked and frightened.

After racing to the bus station, we saw thousands of people who also wanted to get onto a bus and escape to the countryside. The driver of our bus had just stowed everyone's baggage when I happened to look into the sky and saw nine aircraft descending from a cloud and dropping bombs. Suddenly, the driver drove off with the luggage, possibly because he was afraid of being hit and wanted to avoid it, and there we were standing in middle of burning houses, shattered glass, and dead and injured people. There was an awful smell, and alarm sirens continued to fill the air. We had been drilled for a possible bombing raid, but the reality was far worse than our expectations. Then, someone yelled, "Gas!" *Far* ran with my sister to the nearest bomb shelter, which happened to be located under the Forum, a big department store then under construction. *Mor* and I tried to follow, but we were separated because of the chaos and crowds of people running in every direction. So we followed others into the bus station until the worst was over. Only later were we reunited with father and Clary. That night we stayed with my mother's elderly aunt who also lived in the city. Her home had been mostly destroyed, but she herself was ok. Our apartment building had been badly damaged and all the windows shattered, but was still mostly intact.

The next day, we went to the countryside by train to a relative of ours who lived about fifty kilometers west of Helsinki. Our luggage was eventually found, and we lived there more than two months, during which time Helsinki was bombed almost daily. But it was not safe there either because the Russians also began bombing the countryside and targeting people who had fled there from the city.

Fortunately, in January 1940, we received an invitation from my father's engineering firm for all of us to go to Sweden. Due to his age, my father did not fight in the war, but continued working for his firm, Finska Fläktfabriken, and undertook duties far from the frontlines. The date for our departure was set for sometime in February. My mother was then expecting my brother Ralf. But there were no connections between Finland and Sweden, so my father's company arranged to send a Swedish military plane to take us from Turku to Stockholm. The day before the plane was due to arrive, we left for Turku, which in normal conditions would have taken only two hours. However, because of the sirens and bombs, we often had to stop and run into the woods to take cover in the snow. And this meant that the two-hour journey turned into an eighteen-hour ordeal. At the time, this seemed disastrous since we worried about missing our plane. But once we arrived in Turku, we discovered that the hotel where we had arranged to stay the previous night had been bombed and burned to the ground. So having been late actually saved our lives!

We went by taxi to the airfield where, luckily, we found the Swedish plane still waiting for us—my mother, sister, and me, as well as two other families. The men, our fathers, weren't going because they had to assist in the war effort. Though my father continued to work as an engineer, his job would be to help fortify bomb shelters and assist civilians. Once we were in the air, I thought we would be safe, but even then we were followed by Russian bomber planes, which was terrifying.

I remember waking up the next morning at our hotel in Stockholm where we lived and ate at a small nearby restaurant for three months until the temporary peace came in mid-March 1940. It was wonderful for us to live in a country at peace. There was fresh fruit available in Stockholm, too: bananas, oranges, and sweets. We made many friends, and Stockholm became like a second home, so that, when I returned as a war child two years later, I felt very comfortable.

We returned to Helsinki in April and continued to live in the same apartment where I remained during my entire growing up until I married in 1952. I was very fortunate in that none of my friends had been killed during the bombings. On the first floor of our building were many different types of shops—a milk shop, a general grocery store, a butcher's shop, a book and paper supply shop, a children's clothing shop, a radio shop, and a barbershop. Before the war, we made our purchases from "our shops," but after we had to walk great distances and wait in long lines, sometimes for hours outside specific distribution centers. Often we would wait for hours with our ration coupons, only to learn that all the food or provisions we needed had been purchased or to find that the shop in question had been closed because it had been emptied out.

After war broke out again between Russia and Finland in July 1941, my family, including my new brother who had been born in 1940, was evacuated into the countryside, many times to Kokkola, but sometimes nearer to Helsinki. People in the bigger cities suffered more, due to bombings, sickness, and hunger. In fact, when bombs began to fall, we would say, "It's looking bad; we must prepare to leave again and go elsewhere." At least my siblings and I were continuously with my mother, though my father was mostly busy with his work strengthening shelters and helping people get to them during raids. Unfortunately, because many of the shelters were not strong enough to withstand the bombs, a lot of people died in them. During a bomb scare, he advised us to stay upstairs in the bathroom because he had seen a lot of bombed houses, and the bathrooms were usually left standing. Though bathrooms were small in those days, they had quite solid walls to accommodate the pipes. So, when we heard the sirens, we hid in the bathroom. But there were nights when we were not allowed to stay inside, and then we would go to the shelters.

I think that the worst year was 1942 when officials in government believed that the Russians would be victorious. As a consequence, it was thought that Finnish children should be sent in greater numbers to safer countries. Older children, such as myself, understood the circumstances and that we would eventually return to Finland, but very young children suffered from greater anxiety and the fear that they would never return to their fathers and mothers.

I was eleven in 1942 when my father's firm invited the children of their Finnish employees to come to Stockholm to escape the bombings, food shortages, and illnesses that followed us throughout the war. I was awfully happy to hear the news, and I looked forward to becoming a pupil at a special girls school in Stockholm. Because my family belonged to the 20 percent minority of Swedish-speaking Finns, I had gone to a Swedish school in Helsinki, and would have no difficulties with the language. The only sad thing would be to be separated from my newborn brother because I had helped my mother so much in looking after him.

In January of that year, wearing the usual name tag, I went by train with hundreds of other children to Turku. In the harbor, a big ferry, the SS *Arcturus,* waited for us. We spent the night on board, and the following morning we arrived in Stockholm. Most of the children were crying, and I tried to comfort them as best I could, but we were all very tired from our various travels, and it was difficult.

In Stockholm, an elderly woman named Greta Gavell arrived to fetch me and take me to her home, a big apartment not too far from my new school. I addressed her as *Tant* Greta and her husband as *Farbror* Uno, "Aunt" and "Uncle" in English. *Farbror* was an engineer in the same firm as my father, but worked with the Stockholm branch. They had an eighteen-year-old daughter, Gunilla, who was studying to become a nurse like her mother, and three older sons who were all studying to become engineers like their father.

I spent six months or so with this family and never experienced any difficulties. I shared a room with Gunilla who was named after a place in Dalarna (meaning "beautiful valleys"), two hundred kilometers northeast of Stockholm. The Gavells had an old house in a lovely village there where we spent the summer months and where I made many friends that I wrote to and visited for many years. Gunilla eventually became a nurse and was like a second mother to me. I was also in contact with the youngest son for a long time.

Although I was very happy living with the Gavells, I didn't become too attached to my foster parents, as they were very strict, my foster father especially. He was also rather selfish. Whereas in my Finnish family children always got the best things to eat, in my Swedish family, Uncle Uno got everything—the biggest and best cuts of meat, for instance—and the family was left with crusts. I once overheard my Swedish mother talking over the phone about me. The Gavells had apparently taken me in because they would have more rations. I was a bit taken aback when *Tant* said that I was bigger than they'd expected me to be and that I ate too much.

My foster parents were cousins and had known each other their whole lives. There were always a lot of people in the house, or when we visited relatives, Aunt Greta and Uncle Uno would say, "Oh, take your music with you," so I could play the piano for everyone. I was not such a good pianist in those days, but they liked showing me off like a little monkey! I had to be dressed in the best clothes, which they had bought for me, and perform.

I was happy in school, which was very interesting to me, and I made many new friends with whom I corresponded for many years. I did long for home and my Finnish family during this time, but all the bombings in Helsinki really frightened me.

Fortunately, my parents and I kept up a correspondence, though letters always bore the mark of the censor. If anyone ever wrote anything specific about the war, such as an "awful bombing last night," it was cut out. There could have been telephone calls, but one could wait hours and hours to get through. I was the only child in my family to be sent to Sweden, and I had chosen it. So, though I was homesick, I understood the conditions and I was comforted by the fact that I would eventually return to my family in Finland.

Also, everything was paid for in Sweden, which made my parents' lives easier. I believe that the Swedes were very much afraid of Finland losing the war and their becoming Russia's new neighbors. Perhaps they had the idea that if they helped Finland, they wouldn't have to rub shoulders with the Russians. In any case, Sweden helped Finland in other ways besides taking in their children. Unofficially, they gave weapons and some volunteer soldiers. Had they assisted us officially, they could have been subject to attack by the Soviets, too.

All in all, I am very happy that my destiny allowed me to live in a peaceful country when my own was plunged in war. Though I yearned for my family, I felt relieved to be far away from all the war and destruction back home.

* * * * *

Anne-Maj became a teacher of English, married a fellow war child, Krister, and they raised a family in Kokkola. After Krister died a few years ago, Anne-Maj retired in Mariehamn, capital of the Åland Islands, which are located in the Gulf of Bothnia and are supervised by Finland.

17

Someone's Daughter
"Leena Korpi"

I was born in Helsinki in 1942, and my family lived on the beautiful nearby island of Suomenlinna in a two-family house. I have been told by my father's sister who also lived on the island that the night I was born, there was a lot of bombing. My parents were waiting for a boat to take them to the hospital when they heard the bombs and saw fires in the city. They were afraid the hospital was hit, but luckily it was not. My Finnish family consisted of my parents, Tapio and Irma; my sister Kirsti, born 1939; and my four brothers, Kari, born 1940; Risto, born 1941; Olli, born 1944; and Mikko, born 1951.

During the war, my father was some sort of forensic scientist, determining causes of death, organizing care for wounded soldiers, and helping build field hospitals. But he never ever talked about it. After the war, if one of his four sons asked about his experiences, he refused to answer. Or, he might have shared a funny story or anecdote, but never anything serious. My mother was a nurse during the war, working in a city hospital, so my grandmother looked after us. I have no memory of my first two years in Helsinki and my home in Suomenlinna that hasn't been constructed through photographs. But my brother Risto told me that he remembers being in a cellar when Russian airplanes were bombing the city and that when the bombing was over, we returned to our two-family house. All the windows had been broken, and it was very cold.

I was only two when I was sent to Sweden, arriving with my mother in 1944. I believe that we went by boat to Stockholm and then by train to my foster family's house in a small village in southern Sweden. My mother accompanied me in part to visit my sister Kirsti who had been sent earlier by a Red Cross plane to a hospital in Stockholm to treat some illness. After she was well, she was first sent to a children's home and then to a foster family where she stayed until she was ten when she returned to Finland. But she kept in constant contact with them until her foster parents died.

My mother very much wanted to see Kirsti and to meet her foster family. But during my mother's stay, eastern parts of Finland came under attack by the Russians, and my mother decided to return, leaving me behind with this older childless couple.

I don't remember consciously missing my mother. She was soon completely gone. I couldn't hold her in my memory. I was asked to call my foster parents *Tant* (Aunt) and *Farbror* (Uncle), though I could speak no Swedish and they could speak no Finnish. Their house was in the same small village as that where Kirsti lived and was very big and very dark at night. Alone in my bedroom, I hid under the blanket. One of my earliest memories is of a big, dark, threatening figure just beside the door. Every night I saw this figure, and I used to scream and try to tell my foster parents about it. *Tant* would tell me it was an angel, but I knew that angels were white and had wings. Most nights when I screamed, though, *Farbror* came. He would bring a brown ceramic jug with white dots that was filled with water. Many nights I wet my bed, but he never got angry. He just told me to take off my wet pajama trousers to dry. Sleeping pills were prescribed to help me sleep, but once when I failed to sleep anyway, they gave me two, and I fainted. They were very scared, so they took me to a children's hospital in Lund where I was hospitalized for a short time. I had trouble sleeping for many years until I was seven or older, so I was given pills, which were big, white, and hard to swallow. I have a dim memory of the children's hospital and sitting in a bed in this foreign place where a nurse was talking. I called the nurse *Tant,* and everyone laughed. I was supposed to call her *Syster* (Sister, the Swedish term used for nurses). I was embarrassed and hid under the blanket, and when I looked up, all of the grownups were gone.

My next memories are from three years later when I was five. One day, *Tant* returned from the post office looking very irritated because a package she sent had been returned. She often sent coffee, shoes, and clothes to my mother in Helsinki, but one was not allowed to send new things, only used ones, due to the shortages that also existed in Sweden. Every package had to pass the customs officers in Stockholm, and if something like stockings looked new, they were returned. This had apparently happened before because I knew from experience that I would have to wear the itchy woolen stockings for several weeks to make them look old.

"I have got a letter from your mother," she said to me sometimes. I was not interested because I did not remember anything about my Finnish family. "Mother" was a word without meaning. What interested me instead were the apple and cherry trees in the garden, the girl in the neighboring house, and the books I read. I started to read at age four, and *Tant* was a bit proud of that. But "mother" was a dangerous word. I was supposed to react in some way that I didn't understand.

In December 1947, this mysterious person, my "mother," came to visit me. I had only one photograph of her that *Tant* sometimes showed me, saying, "This is your mother." But I just saw this foreign woman. Somehow I was supposed to feel things that I didn't feel. And when I felt other things, they were the "wrong" feelings that I wasn't supposed to feel. So, I thought, *I will have as little as possible to do with grownups.* You never knew what they were up to.[1] The only safe place was with other children in the village. For these reasons, I tried to keep away when mother visited, though I wanted to look at the four-year-old boy, my little brother Ollie, whom she had brought with her. My playmate, Rose-Marie, had a little brother who often followed us and wanted to be with us. So I was excited that I now had a brother too. But he was a disappointment. I could not speak to him, and he refused to go anywhere with me. He just hid under the table and played with his paper airplanes, though he later told me that he remembered a lot of colors and that my dress and Kirsti's were very bright. But it was awkward, and I think it must have been difficult for my mother too, looking at me and thinking, "Who is this foreign child?" However, when she left, everything returned to normal.

Another visitor to our house was Per, whom I believed was *Farbror*'s younger brother. But he wasn't really. He was *Farbror*'s eldest sister's illegitimate son. He must have been forty when I was small, but I thought he was very funny. He wasn't married, and he was always doing crazy things. For instance, once he came in a big American car and said, "You must come for a drive with me," and I said, "Oh, yes!" He was a little touched in the head, and few people in our village liked him. But my *Tant* utterly despised him, perhaps because *Farbror* helped to take care of him and employed him to do paperwork at the sawmill.

I learned not to ask too many questions, but to have big, big ears and to sit under tables, listening. That's what I did to figure things out because there were many things I couldn't ask *Tant*. I continued to be called by my Finnish name and to refer to my foster parents as *Tant* and *Farbror*. Very proper. I was somewhat envious of the fact that when my sister Kirsti lived with her Swedish family, she called her foster parents *Mor* and *Far*, old-fashioned terms for "Mother" and "Father." Apparently they were warm-hearted, nice people, but I believe that she had a very difficult experience earlier at the children's home and still becomes very tense when talking about her childhood.

Although Kirsti's foster family lived just a few kilometers away from mine, we saw each other very rarely. I don't remember her leaving Sweden, but when she came back for her summer holidays, I was stunned. She sounded completely different. While she had spoken the same southern Swedish dialect as the rest of us before she left, she had begun a Swedish-speaking girls' school in Helsinki and now sounded like the Swedish-speaking minority in Finland. I did not ask her anything about our family, but her school experience interested me very much. She told me that I could begin this school at age ten if I could pass an entrance exam and that she had passed every subject but her Swedish dictation. Her teacher understood that she, like many returning war children, had picked up a different dialect from the area in which she'd lived in Sweden, and so this wasn't really a problem. She also said that when I turned ten, I could begin attending this school. I didn't know what to think about that. The village I lived in and the house I shared with *Tant* and *Farbror* were the only places I knew.

While my Finnish parents were avid readers and spoke quite good Swedish, *Farbror* was not an intellectual and only read the local newspaper. But he was energetic and generous with his laughter, affection, and money. People usually liked him. He had always been a carpenter, but after I arrived in Sweden, he began a sawmill with around twenty employees. He married my *Tant* late, but had had a son, Folke, out of wedlock who lived in Malmö with his wife and two children. This foster brother of mine who was old enough to be my father was very wealthy, and I was impressed by his wife's modern clothes. He didn't show much affection for his father, but in those days people were more formal. I asked *Tant* if *Farbror* had been married before, but she avoided the question.

My foster mother had been a primary school teacher before they married, which now seems strange to me since she didn't naturally like children. It was probably a catastrophe for her young students. But women had only two choices at that time: they could become teachers or nurses. I don't think she wanted children of her own, and I overheard once that she believed she was too old for children when she married at age forty. *Farbror* was also old, many years older than she. I can say now that she was quite good looking, tall with good features. And I believe that *Farbror* was impressed with her looks, her education, and good manners. Her father had also been a schoolteacher, though he was deceased when I came on the scene. I met her mother and was asked to call her *Mormor* or "Grandmother." Relatives were invited for coffee, of course, and then *Tant* would make a lot of cake. But outside of relatives, she never invited anyone in for coffee and seemed to have no friends. I don't think that she knew how to socialize with other people. She was a bit odd that way. Also, though she was a woman of leisure, you always got the impression that she had a great deal to do. Her mother and two sisters frequently told me, "You must be very nice to her because she works so hard." But what on earth did she have to do? She cleaned a lot, but every second week a cleaning lady came. She made me porridge in the morning and was a good cook, but we always ate in the kitchen, never in the dining room unless there were guests.

I learned to read before I went to school from books that *Tant* had brought into the marriage. She also bought children's books for me, such as those by Astrid Lindgren. I didn't grow up with Finnish children's literature like Topelius. Instead, I grew up as a Swedish child. I had no choice.

When I was seven years old I began at a Lutheran school, the only kind of school in Sweden in those days. It was a low brick building. On the second floor, my primary teacher lived with her husband who taught the older children. There were only seven children in my classroom, and the teacher was very nice, but she didn't know what to do. We were supposed to learn the letters of the alphabet and put them together. I was asked to read with an older boy who couldn't read, and I had been reading for years. He just sat there and grunted. So, suddenly one day, I ran out of the classroom. The teacher chased me and phoned my *Tant* who later said to me, "That's not a good way to behave." But I knew that she wasn't angry because she felt that the school wasn't very good. She knew I could read and probably thought that my teacher should have made my lessons more challenging.

School began every day with the teacher playing piano and leading us in a hymn. In the winter, the classroom smelled of wet woolen clothes. And every summer when school ended, there was a special hymn that school children still sing today called "The Time of Flowers Is Approaching." When I was a school child, there was also a prayer, but nowadays this isn't recited.

One dark November day when I was nine years old and had just come home from school, *Tant* said, "I have got sad news. I had a telegram from Helsinki. Your mother died yesterday after giving birth to a little boy." I remember the event very well and the room opposite the kitchen in which there was a sewing machine. This was the room in which *Mormor* stayed when she came to visit. I remember where *Tant* stood as she delivered the news. Feeling very tense, I asked her, "Uh-huh. Well, what does it mean?" She didn't sit me down or try to prepare me for this news in any way, and yet she expected a certain reaction from me. I think she had a sort of crazy idea that I was attached to my mother whom I hadn't seen for so long. But how could I be? I had completely forgotten what my mother even looked like. My foster mother was not pleased with me. I was supposed to mourn for my mother.

Tant wasn't very religious, but she liked to observe social etiquette. A wreath was sent, and she got very angry at me when I refused to write a card for the wreath with the words *Tak, lilllemamma* (Thank you, little mother). When she became even angrier, I did not dare but write, and I remember feeling deeply humiliated by this. She also told me that my father had written, saying that I could decide whether I wanted to stay in Sweden or return to Finland. I did not answer, but just went outdoors to play with Rose-Marie who lived just behind the poplars that surrounded our orchard.

For some time afterward, I had to wear a black dress with a black ribbon on my coat. which I didn't mind. However, I found it very awkward when people asked me what had happened. I told them, "My mother died," and they responded, "Oh, poor girl" in sympathetic voices. I tried to reassure them, "Oh, no, no, no. It doesn't matter. Please don't mention it."

The next summer, my father visited Sweden. He arrived together with my sister Kirsti. He was a complete stranger to me, of course. I didn't call him anything. How do you react to someone who is your father but also a stranger to you? I answered if he spoke to me, but mostly I avoided him. He stayed at Kirsti's foster parents' home for a week or so. They were friendly and generous people and they seemed to get along well with the "foreigner." Secretly, I studied him. He was rather short and slim with dark hair. Once, he came with Kirsti and I to the beach, which stretched along the bay about sixty kilometers. We loved to go there. The Baltic is rather cold, but when the wind comes from the east it heats the water. That day, though, there were big waves. He did not swim, and I asked my sister why. She told me that he found the water too cold, which I thought was strange. Then he stayed at my foster parents' home for a time.

The atmosphere was very tense. *Tant* was angry at him, having come to the conclusion that he was not *grateful* enough for her taking care of me. He was polite but nothing more. She wanted him out of the house, so she suggested that he could borrow her bike and take me on a tour of the castle about five kilometers away. I was not a bit interested in some old castle, but I had a slight hope that he would buy me ice cream along the way. That didn't happen, but he still managed to impress me. On the way back, there was a long, steep slope. I was tired, and noticing this, he took a rope and tied my little blue bike to his, so that I could just sit while he did all the work.

Soon after he left, taking Kirsti with him. Looking back, I realize that he could have taken me as well. Legally, nothing could have stopped him.

The following Christmas I was told that I would be making a trip to Helsinki to visit my family. *Tant* brought me to Christianstad where I was put on a train to Stockholm. I had a new red coat, new shoes lined with fur, and a brown leather suitcase. I was agitated and tense because you just never knew what grownups had in mind. After an eight-hour ride on the train, I stayed overnight with some of *Farbror*'s friends, the Jonssons, who accompanied me to the airport the following day for the flight to Helsinki. It was a clear winter day, and with amazement I saw many toy cars and miniature figures skating on the ice below. After a while, a stewardess spoke to me. Because I had a Finnish passport and name, she took for granted that I spoke Finnish. But I couldn't answer and felt ashamed and nervous. How relieved I was when she came back and spoke Swedish to me and gave me some sweets. It's possible that someone told her I might be one of "those kids": a returning war child.

My father and his brother who had a car met me at the airport. I didn't really recognize my father, but I was glad to see Kirsti. She was the person I felt most comfortable with, since she spoke Swedish as well as Finnish. Helsinki was big and grey. Trams were coming and going. The apartment was crowded, compared to what I was used to. And everything smelled strangely to me, especially the water. Later I realized that it must have been chlorinated. My brothers had only begun to learn Swedish in school, and they said a few peculiar things to me in Swedish such as "I saw a bear in the forest," then laugh wildly. I thought that they were little lunatics or imbeciles. But there was a Christmas tree and presents. My father gave me a novel, *The Radetsky March*, and my sister and I went to the Swedish theater. But as I prepared to return to Sweden, my father again disappointed me. It could happen, I thought, that he would say, "Well, now that you're here, why don't you stay?" Or I hoped that my foster parents would phone from Sweden and say, "You *must* stay in Finland. We don't want you back." However, the question was never put to me by my father or *Tant* or *Farbror*: *Where would you be happiest?* And so, a week later, I was put on a plane to return to Stockholm and then a train to take me south.

After my return, I remember feeling very lonely most of the time and wondering, *Does anyone really care if I'm dead or alive?* My foster parents were nice enough, but they didn't care about me, and I always had the feeling that I didn't belong. After my elementary school years, since we lived some distance Kristanstad where the secondary school was located, I stayed in several places, going home for weekends. Other children were in the same situation. Then, when I was fifteen, a friend suggested that I could be a paying guest in her family, and so I stayed with this family for four years until I went to university.

During my years as a college student, my foster parents never contacted me, never phoned, never wrote. After finishing school, I discovered, in fact, that they had moved but hadn't bothered to send me their new address. I visited *Farbror*'s sister who gave me the address in Lund, and I wrote but was not invited to visit. Determined, I wrote again to say that I was *coming* for a visit. And I did. But I wasn't *invited*.

I was thirty when *Farbror* died and forty when *Tant* died. They left me nothing, not even a photograph, but gave everything to a niece they had seldom seen. If I had been *Tant*, I would at least have asked, "Do you want something as a memento—a teaspoon or whatever?" But no, no, no. Nothing.

Upon reflection, it would have been unthinkable for her to have written me a letter, apologizing for not being a warmer mother: I was the one who wasn't *grateful* enough, she would have thought. I think that she wanted me to grovel, so that she could feel like an important person. It is strange, too, that the subject of adoption never came up and that my foster parents never referred to me as their "daughter," but only as "our Finnish girl." When I visited my family in Helsinki at age ten, it was a bit shocking at first to be referred to as someone's "daughter." But it also felt good because I could feel like someone without having to *do* anything, without having to *say* anything. I could simply exist as *someone real,* and that was a new experience for me.

However, after returning to Sweden from Finland, I felt that there was no way back to being Finnish and someone's "daughter." It was impossible. And still today, I feel neither Finnish nor Swedish. When someone asks, "Are you Swedish?" I could say yes, but I would feel like a liar. Likewise, if I said that I am Finnish, it's not really true. I would feel like a liar.[2]

Later in life, I married a Swede and had two children by him, but changed my last name to a Finnish one after our divorce. I was eager to have children because that was the only way to finally have a family that was entirely *mine*. No one could say, "No, this is not your family," because it was and is. They are *my children*. After my children were grown, I underwent therapy for three years because for a very long time I felt that in some way I didn't touch the ground. I felt I had no history and that there was something lacking at bottom, a disconnection from some part of myself that I needed to try and understand.

If there is something I have learned from my own war child experience, the one thing I am absolutely sure of is that *parents should never send their children away like that even when times are desperate,* as they were during the war. It is terrible to feel that a central part of yourself has virtually disappeared and been replaced with a great emptiness, to feel that part of yourself is inescapably gone, which is impossible to retrieve.

* * * * *

"Leena" is a practicing psychologist living near the house in which she grew up in southern Sweden. She loves the surrounding natural beauty and nearby sea. In 1996, as a part of her postgraduate studies, she coauthored an essay about the significance of age when children are separated from parents and families. This and related studies have all suggested that the psychological health of children separated before age five is far more vulnerable and that, in their adult lives, such people will experience more difficulties with interpersonal relationships.

Notes

1. In his "Post-Traumatic Stress Symptoms" article (identified in the Introduction and Bibliography), 659, Andersson observes based on a recent evaluation of

Finnish war children that, in addition to post-traumatic shock syndrome, many display attachment disorders of various kinds. Avoidance as a survival strategy, a fourth characteristic manifested by the majority of war children interviewed, was also observed, as well as the keen desire for affectionate relationships matched by an intense fear of them, due to insufficient trust. "Owing to displacement," Andersson writes, "evacuated Finnish children had lost their primary attachment figure and been subject to the effects of privation in dysfunctional family backgrounds in Sweden. They had no survival strategy other than living with their own fear of rejection." Ultimately, he states, "The trauma of war children ... led to permanent consequences in adult life."

2. Many war children suffer not only from lifelong feelings of nonbelonging and rootlessness, but from the terrible conviction of their inner worthlessness as human beings. Mona Serenius, a former Finnish war child referred to in the Introduction to the present volume, describes these feelings in "The Silent Cry: A Finnish Child during World War II and 50 Years Later," when she writes that "Through the years I have had a depressing feeling of being an onlooker, not a participant in life, with no right to claim anything for myself." Though Serenius has "lived in many countries, worked in many places [and] met people from all over the world," she feels that she has merely "changed shape and colour like a chameleon, adjusting to the environment wherever I have happened to be but not really leaving any imprints. My compliance has almost been a compliance to death, a collusion with the effacement of my personal self." *International Forum of Psychoanalysis* (Stockholm, 2007): 46. Accessed November 2012 at http://www.tandfonline.com/loi/spsy20.

18

To the Bomb and Back
Eeva Lindgren

When the war began on November 30, 1939, I was four years old and lived with my parents, Väinö and Anja Kytölä, sister Leena, and brothers Eero and Pekka. We lived on a farm in southeastern Finland on the eastern side of the river Kymi, which was once the border between Russia and Sweden, half way between the towns of Kouvola and Kotka. These two towns were heavily bombed during the war because Kotka had an important harbor and Kouvola was a railway junction. In Kotka, there were also large sawmills and timber yards, which were constantly burning during the war years. I remember the sky from the south was always red, day and night. My father's mother and one of father's uncles also lived on the farm with us, which was owned by my grandparents. Kalle, my father's uncle, used to shake his fist at the Russian bombers and shout *Perkele!* (Devil!).

My childhood memories are fragmented and more shadowed by illness than war, but these two calamities in my early life mingle with each other in confusing ways. In the summer of 1939, I was taken to the nearest hospital in Kuusankoski where a tumor was found in my lung and I was diagnosed with actinomycosis, a sort of fungus. I was operated on for this in Helsinki and even if my survival was a minor medical miracle, my memories from this time are depressing, involving strange people in strange surroundings and being stuck with needles. Also, the general atmosphere was tense with the threat of war in the air, and bomb shelters were being built in rock formations near the hospital where I was located. The blasting through rock and tremors caused from this blasting terrified children like myself who were staying in the nearby hospital. I do not remember if anyone tried to reassure us or to explain the reason for this deafening noise. I was simply too small to understand.

Father collected me from the hospital when it was decided that patients had to be evacuated, due to the bombings. Unfortunately, my wounds were not properly healed and were purulent—still secreting pus—but there were no antibiotics at that time in Finland. I remember that I felt ashamed of the smell coming from my breast.

Shortly before the Winter War started, my father Väinö was sent to build fortifications along the Russian border. But during the war, he was a machine gunner. I remember very clearly the moment I saw my father alive for the last time. He came to the cowshed to say farewell to his mother, and I happened to be there too. I grabbed his grey mantle and cried, "You must not leave me! You will never come back from there!" And he never did come back. He was killed in 1940, only two weeks before the end of the Winter War when he was being sent home, due to his frostbitten frozen hands. As a gunner, he could not wear gloves, since he had to load the gun and pull the trigger, and this was in −40° Centigrade. Tragically, the ambulance transporting him was attacked, and he was the only one killed. His body was returned to us in a cardboard box.[1]

Due to chaotic circumstances, mother had not received any warning or message about his death, nor could the army provide a proper coffin. Mother only received an urgent message about the necessity to collect his body at the nearest railway station. In the aftermath of this, I remember nothing about my father's dead body, only the white coffin from a distance. But, according to my mother, I looked upon his body.

The winter of 1940 was very severe: −40° Centigrade.[2] All our apple trees were destroyed due to the cold. Also, due to the extremely low temperatures, electric wires tightened so that they howled all night. Both my mother and grandmother were courageous, never revealing their fear to the children. But even they could not lighten the atmosphere of despair that was often so gloomy. I was a weak and sickly child, unhappy, and withdrawn, and I often sat by myself, although after I learned to read and attended school, I discovered a new and wonderful world among books.

We children were often warned about doing certain things such as picking up leaflets of propaganda dropped from airplanes. I remember once that our yard was completely covered by such leaflets, and I was curious. But grandmother became angry at me when I tried to pick up one and read it. Later I learned that it was not the propaganda adults were afraid of,

Figure 18.1. *Eeva Lindgren's father in uniform during World War II. Courtesy Eeva Lindgren.*

but some sort of physical contamination. We were also warned not to trust strange people and not to speak with anyone we didn't know very well. There were spies, deserters, people desperate for food, soldiers, and refugees. You never knew who was your friend or who your foe. As a consequence, neither my mother nor my grandmother allowed strangers to stay overnight with us during the war, despite the ancient tradition among people living in the cold zone from Siberia to Finland to provide shelter for anyone who came to your house in the winter. Also we had no telephone or means of calling for help. The nearest telephone was at my uncle's about one kilometer from our house.

In June 1941, Russia renewed its attacks on Finland. When my father's brother (and my godfather), were killed in action in August, I was nearly six years old. I remember the beautiful harvesting day when everything mysteriously stopped on our farm and deep sorrow overshadowed us. My uncle's wife fainted and was carried from the field. But the deepest shock for me was to see my usually strong grandmother crying so bitterly. She had now lost two of her three sons. The third was only wounded, thankfully, and survived the war. But it was a terrible day, and I wanted to hide myself from the rest of the world and lay curled up under the covers of my bed.

Because we lived not too far from Kotka, we could see the fires night after night, and even my home was bombed twice. Once, we were sitting at the table eating with guests when suddenly there was a blast, and I remember how we all fell to the floor when the first and worst bomb hit the middle of the road about one hundred meters from the house. Luckily, no one was hurt and only one window was broken. But a visiting boy was terribly shocked and screamed loudly. The bombs had apparently been aimed at a unit of soldiers who were using smaller back roads to avoid detection on their way to the front. This happened in the summer, so it was the second time that we were bombed.

On another occasion, I was playing hide-and-seek with some neighbor children, and I had the idea to hide in the house. I was in the kitchen, and I began to realize that I was quite alone in the world. I wondered why no one seemed to be looking for me. Then, I heard the distant thunder. My grandmother had seen the black eggs flying in the air and she and my sister had gathered the children in a shed. But I did not hear their calls. Fortunately, this time the planes emptied the rest of their bombs before Finnish fighter planes began to pursue them, and the Russian bombs had not caused any great damage except huge holes that had to be filled. One bomb that had fallen in the middle of the road was the worst. Its imprint and damage after the explosion could be seen for many years afterwards. In fact, we children created games around it, running contests that we called *Pommille ja Takaisin!* (To the Bomb and Back!).

Once, we were playing with our cousins in their yard when a Russian plane flew over us. Suddenly, it turned back and flew towards us. My sister was clever and quick to command us to hide behind a big stone before the pilot began shooting at us. I remember the sound of the bullets, hitting against the stone. Later we dug the shrapnel out of the wall of our house. They were narrow metal sticks with beautiful red tufts on top. We collected them in matchboxes, but perhaps we were later told to throw them away because I do not remember ever seeing them again.

Due to my physical ailments, I received special treatments during the war in Helsinki. An aunt who lived there used to take care of me, and on one of my visits she took me to an exhibition of captured Russian trophies of war. I only remember how I stared at a Russian fighter plane hanging from the ceiling. But I must have been terrified because in 2000, a few short weeks before she died, my aunt told me what a mistake she had made by taking me to such an exhibition. She had had to take me out immediately because I had obviously been so shocked and traumatized. But I consoled her that I had almost forgotten the incident.

I never saw either a living or dead Russian soldier, though several Russian pilots were shot down not far from my home. My elder brother related some appalling sights that he witnessed after planes crashed whose pilots had survived but with terrible injuries. Even as an adult, I sometimes had nightmares, featuring Russian pilots with red stars on their caps. These images penetrated my dreams and haunted me.

Fortunately, we did not have to starve because we had milk and grain. Grownups were often nostalgic about real coffee, but I only dimly remembered the taste of prewar sweets. I also vaguely remembered how bananas and oranges tasted. Whatever "candy" we had we made from carrots. More important than a shortage of sugar was the absence of fruit, which caused us to suffer from deficiency diseases that caused abscesses. I developed more of these than my sister or brothers. We also had lice and hated the louse hunting my mother performed with a fine-toothed comb and white paper that was then tossed into the fire. When this did not help, our hair was soaked with kerosene and a scarf tightly bound around the head for a day. This got rid of the lice but also burned parts of the skin on our heads and ears.

A shortage of clothes and shoes was another problem. Due to wartime scarcities, shoes had to be made of cardboard and string. Once, standing at a bus stop in heavy rain, the soles of my shoes melted off. Suddenly, I had no soles to walk on, and mother had to carry me home. I inherited my sister's used clothes, but sometimes there was nothing worth inheriting, so I was always wearing clothes that were much too large or too small. One year I wore my mother's sister-in-law's garden overalls and ski boots, which were both much too big. I had to learn to take long steps and drag the boots, so that they did not drop off. Another winter, I wore cloth "boots" made of woolen strips, so that I looked like Mickey Mouse.

In the countryside the clothing situation was more dire than in cities because the shops were so far away. We would sometimes hear about clothing for sale on the "jungle telephone" when we were informed by word of mouth about the availability of some desirable item. Once, my mother's sister-in-law walked two kilometers to tell us about sneakers for sale. Because these were so coveted by young people, I rode my mother's rusty bicycle seven kilometers only to find that there was not a single pair left. It was very usual that people advertised in the paper, offering to exchange a kilo of butter for a pair of shoes.

But sometimes we received aid from abroad. A Norwegian lady sent a parcel with children's underwear, and I got the finest and warmest underwear I have ever had. On another occasion, some American aid, including tooth powder and shoe soles from U.S. Army surplus, was distributed at school. We children had never seen tooth powder before and didn't know how it was used, so some of us who liked the taste ate it in a couple of days. The shoe soles were equally useless. They were so big that not a single person living in two villages had feet large enough to use them. Everyone just laughed, and the soles lay for many years in people's attics.

Both my aunts, Matilda and Martta, were nurses and Lottas (members of the women's auxiliary unit). My mother was also a Lotta, and even my sister Leena and I belonged to the *pikkulotta* (little Lottas). Once a week in the school we would gather to do some singing, playing, and knitting for the troops. Because of the general scarcity of things, we had to be inventive. Just as mother picked apart men's clothing in our attic to make into children's clothes, we made tablecloths and curtains out of crepe paper, decorating it with potatoes cut into stamps. We sometimes had bazaars, and our products sold well.

My elder brother Eero always played a brave soldier who would one day "show" the Russians. My Aunt Matilda's wartime assignment was to take care of Russian prisoners of war in the hospital in Viipuri, the former capital of Karelia.[3] One of her patients was an artist who wanted to cheer up my auntie's militant and angry nephew. So he drew a picture of a "real" Russian soldier: a very ugly man, shaggy, unshaved, with a boil on his cheek, and a nasty look in his eyes. What an effective gesture to satisfy a small boy's expectations and imaginings of the enemy!

In June 1944, it was very critical for the Finns at the front. We were required to leave our home, providing address labels for our cows and other domestic animals. Adults prepared their children for the unhappy fact that their homes would be burned, so that no shelter or food would be available to the advancing enemy. I felt sorry for my home and for our cat, which could not be taken with us. I remember sitting with my sister on the stairs and sorting out our dolls' clothes, deciding which to take and which to leave.

Fortunately, as it turned out Stalin required his units to be moved elsewhere, and we were saved. We did not have to leave. My first school was two kilometers away, and I got there either by foot or on skis. It was sometimes really hard when there was too much snow to make tracks. The two first grades were in one room and the following four grades in another. The elementary grades were taught by a lady who always inhaled nervously in new situations. In the beginning, I found school boring because I knew how to read while my contemporaries were just learning the alphabet. But at least, when I first started, there was not too much interruption due to the war. Only once did we have to run into the nearby forest when the enemy's airplanes were heard. For my sister, it had been more difficult in 1939, since she had begun school in September, and the war broke out in November. I found her stories about running into the forest for safety very exciting. But my mother was angry that she often returned from school in the morning because she had been given a "holiday." Perhaps too much tension in the air caused her teacher to overreact.

We all grew very tired and impatient with the war. We blamed everything that went wrong on the war. I remember asking my cousin who was one year older than I how we would know when the war was finally over. After a moment's hard thinking, she enlightened me with the fact that airplanes always fly lower in peacetime. For some period of time following this conversation, I tried to detect whether the airplanes seemed to be flying high or low, though this had been a product of her imagination.

Throughout the war, our family sat in the kitchen during the evenings to keep warm, but also because we only had two windows there to cover in accordance with strict blackout orders. Every evening, blackout curtains were lowered to cover these two windows as well as any additional interior light. I often studied the army periodical, *Hakkapeliitta,* named after a cavalry hero in the Swedish Army during the Thirty Years' War. He graced the cover of this journal in which I read the names of men fallen in battle. I have to thank these men who sacrificed their lives because I learned to read through studying their names.

My Aunt Kerttu often stayed overnight with us with her two girls because their home was near vast woodlands where all sorts of spies could be seen. If she saw a *desant* (a spy dropped from an airplane), she came to us for safety, since *desants* only killed civilians nearer to the border.[4]

We always had people around: aunts, cousins, neighbors, old men, and women of all ages. The women helped each other out and because they all had one or more children, we children had many playmates, which was fun for us. Sometimes we made jokes about how popular we were due to the fact that we produced basic foodstuffs on our farm. Jokes were also made about the old maids of the village who were popular with men on the front or elsewhere. Their appeal depended on the victuals these women, especially women on farms, were able to provide, though their wooers generally disappeared from the stage when the war was over. When asked where this or that fiancé had gone to, adults would snort, "He was only a butter fiancé."

Eventually, the war was over, but we did not dance for joy. Except for a short-lived break, the war had lasted from 1939 through 1945, ending when I was nine and a half years old.

We were too devastated by all the sorrow and loss and the crushing war indemnities demanded from us by the Soviet Union. Our horse that had been conscripted for the war was returned to us from the front, but the poor creature had become extremely nervous and agitated.[5]

There is only one way out of the bottom, and it is upwards. We endured many scarce years after the war, but we Finns were all in the same boat. And, little by little, conditions improved and we even learned to laugh.

Certain benefits came with surviving the war years. I don't have to be taught to recycle waste products. It was a necessity and natural way of living long before it became fashionable in a more affluent society. Nor do I have to play survival games; my childhood was one big survival game. I also never have to ponder like many children of divorced parents what was "wrong" with me, since my father never left me. He died honorably because he had no choice.

But his death left a huge empty space that could not be filled by anything or anybody. Life dealt my grandmother and especially my mother a terrible injustice that cannot be forgotten.

As for me, when the emotional burden became too great, I chose not to remember anything sad about my father. When I am too tired to walk, he is carrying me on his shoulder. He is sitting in the rocking chair, framed by the golden dust of sunshine, or he is working in the field with the horses, and a wagtail is hopping after him. Wagtails are the first of the migrating birds to come to Finland in the spring, and I always feel that their cheerful wagging tails are father's way of greeting me from someplace else. Time does not heal all wounds, but it makes it easier to live with them.

* * * * *

Due in part to her grandmother's influence who believed that girls had no future on small farms, Eeva studied philology at Helsinki University and became a language teacher, first in an elementary school and then in a high school in Helsinki where she lives today. After retirement, she was active in sports, reading, and making traditional Finnish straw crafts. She is married with one daughter.

Notes

1. Though Finland had been economically stable in the late 1930s, the country was unprepared for war. At the beginning of the war, for instance, soldiers had no proper uniforms and wore their own civilian clothes.
2. That is: −40° Fahrenheit.
3. Viipuri, the former capital of Karelia, is now called "Vyborg." It and all of former Finnish Karelia are now part of Russia. According to Finland's Military Academy records, Finnish forces captured 64,000 POWs during the war, 18,000 of whom died of disease or famine. After the war, 43,000 POWs were returned to the USSR.
4. *Desants* or reconnaissance parachutists were often recruited from Estonia, since the Estonian language is related to Finnish, or from Finnish-speaking tribes in eastern Karelia. Eeva's Aunt Kerttu who lived next to a large forest often saw men she suspected of being *desants*. And Eeva relates that in Virolahti, a commune near the border, several civilians were killed in a hayfield by a spy and that there were other such incidents.
5. Finnish horses were used throughout the war: approximately 70,000 during the Winter War and 60,000 during the Continuation War. In recognition of their sacrifice and suffering, a monument stands in their honor in Seinäjoki, a major loading station for horses during the war. See Kinnunen and Kivimäki, *Finland at War: 1939–45*, 8.

19

A Blonde Curly-Haired Girl
Mirja Luoma

My story is different in that, although I was only six when it began, I myself went to the office where they took the names of children to be sent to Sweden. This was during the Continuation War in the early part of 1942. I was living with my mother, older sister, and brother in Äänekoski in the middle of Finland. My parents were divorced, and at that time my mother was not at home. She was with her sister in southern Finland, and my older sister looked after me. I did not ask my mother's permission to go with other children to Sweden, but I had heard that everything was better there than in Finland. There was much more food, and we were struggling to eat. When my mother returned and heard what I had done, she said she would not allow me to leave her. But later a little boy who lived in our neighborhood died under a lorry. After that occurrence, my mother said that perhaps the same God who existed in Finland also existed in Sweden. So I won her consent.

I left in late spring, March 1942, and there was still a lot of hard ice on the Baltic Sea and in the Gulf of Finland. We came by train from Äänekoski to Helsinki and from there in the steamboat *Arcturus* on March 27, 1942, to Stockholm. First, we came to a hospital. Many of us Finnish children were weak from lack of food, and some were badly ill. We lay for several days there where doctors made medical examinations. When we were deemed well enough to travel, the majority of us went by train to Brenäs near Katrineholm. Brenäs was a place where Swedish children spent their holidays in summer. But we were taken to another hospital where we stayed for several weeks. Adults began coming to select children. Fortunately, at age six I was a pretty, blonde, curly-haired girl, which Swedish couples seemed to prefer. In May a couple from nearby Katrineholm arrived at the hospital, and they chose me to be their "daughter." They had only one other child: a seventeen-year-old son, Eric.

Sigrid, John, and Eric Lindbom lived in a beautiful apartment on the second floor of a large building that they owned. "Uncle John" whom I called *Farbror* (Uncle) was a foreman at the Katrineholm factory SKF, which manufactured ball bearings. Aunt Sigrid, my *Tant*, stayed at home and was a very good housekeeper. Though I missed my mother, I felt like a princess while I was living with the Lindboms in their lovely home where I was given a lot of delicious food and beautiful clothes. My birthday in September was a great happening with many presents and cake. And Christmas was unimaginably wonderful! I received forty-three presents that year, whereas in Finland I had only ever received three or four.

Tant Sigrid and I exchanged many letters with my mother, so I never forgot her. And I had a photo of her that I cherished. At first, I wrote in Finnish, but after some months I forgot my Finnish and wrote only in Swedish, which I seemed to learn very quickly. I began my first year of school, which I loved, in Katrineholm.

After my first year in school, however, all Finnish children were required to return to our native country. We came by train on July 1, 1943, via Haparanda and Torneå, because it was very dangerous on the Baltic Sea. After my return, I quickly relearned Finnish, but I could not speak a word upon my arrival. It was very strange not to be able to speak to my mother, nor for her to be able to speak to me. However, after this, Swedish always came easily for me, which was an advantage for me in later life.

In Sweden I had missed my mother, but her photo had consoled me, and we wrote to each other the whole time I was gone. Then, in Finland, I missed my Swedish family, though we exchanged letters. Once, my mother, sister, and I even visited them. Also, some years later Eric and his wife visited Seinäjoki where I was then living. And to this day, I communicate with Eric's wife. Over the years, my family remained good friends with my foster family. When mother died in 1986, I found old letters exchanged between *Tant* Sigrid and me, which are very interesting.

After I left Sweden and throughout my years of school, I received shoes and clothes from the generous Lindboms. At Christmas, my family also received presents from them. Once she was grown, my sister moved to Stockholm to study language where she was at school for many years. And my brother also moved to Gävle, Sweden, in 1974 for his work. So I still have many close connections with Sweden.

I feel that I was very fortunate that I could live in Sweden when my own country was at war. I have many good memories of my time there. My world and circle of friends is larger because of the years 1942–1943. Many years later my mother said that it was good I lived in Sweden during the winter of 1942–1943 because at that point Finns had little to eat and were even in need of potatoes.

When the Finnish war children began to tell their sad stories, my daughter asked me to tell mine, but I said that happy stories are not interesting. Because my mother and the Lindbom family both treated me well, I can say that I have an unusually happy war child story.

20

Fishing with Ragnar
Pekka/Peter Louhimo

I was born in 1930 near the Arctic Circle in Tornio, Finland, about one mile from the Swedish border. My father, Oma Aarre Louhimo, was an engineer surveyor. In 1935 he accepted a new position in Salo, located some seventy-five miles west of Helsinki. So he, my mother, Hilde Johanna (*nee* Andersin), and family moved into a nice apartment there. And this is where my older brothers, I, and my little sister Pirkko spent our early childhood. When the Winter War began in November 1939, I was nine and Pirkko was eight. My father served as an army captain. His two brothers fought as well, and eventually my two older brothers would join the war effort.

Christmas of 1939 in Salo was a very sad one for my family. Our father was fighting somewhere in Karelia, and this was one of the coldest winters in Finnish memory. My mother woke up my sister Pirkko and me while it was still totally dark outside and mentioned something about leaving for Turku, though our home was situated at least fifty kilometers from the city. We had often visited Turku in the past to run all kinds of errands. But this time, my sister and I had no idea why were going and how this journey would change our lives. As we walked to the train station in Salo, everything seemed so oddly quiet. Only the crunch of snow under our shoes broke the silence of the frigid night. Upon our arrival, a darkened train with blackout curtains stood ready on the tracks, hissing and steaming. Once we got on board, I noticed that many other mothers and their children were sitting in the railroad car.

Everyone had the same destination as we did: the harbor of Turku. But no one had spoken to me about where we were going, so to me it just seemed a great adventure or mystery. I had no idea that my sister and I were about to be launched into a different world.

The train huffed and puffed from one station to another. My mother, sister, and I waited eagerly to arrive at the familiar train station in Turku. But peeking out of the darkened windows, we could only see steam and the bright snow through the darkness. Gradually, our speed decreased, and suddenly we found ourselves outside in the dim blue light walking toward the station square where we could see a streetcar waiting. Some of us had already climbed on board when sirens began howling. We had heard the alarms many times before, but the worry and anxiety in the voices of the grownups frightened me. Hurrying to the door of a large building, we ran down the stairs to a boiler room where we would be safe from the bombs. Enemy bomber planes were taking advantage of the clear weather conditions on this Christmas day, making numerous air raids over the home front and in the war zone.[1]

Settling down as best as we could on long benches, we removed our overcoats because of the heat from the boilers. After a couple of hours, we could smell the fragrance of Christmas goodies as many people opened their packed snacks. But time dragged on, as we were not allowed to leave the shelter. Some of us created games and other forms of entertainment for ourselves, while many older people just rested and slept the best they could.

Finally, when we left the shelter it was still dark. We began to walk in the direction where we expected to find the streetcar and were instructed by the police to move to the other side of the street, due to some dangerous electrical wires lying on the ground. A bitter smell of smoke and steam surrounded us, but nobody paid much attention to this. We boarded the streetcar, which rumbled noisily in the direction of the harbor where we arrived without incident. Though we were plunged in total darkness, I remember that everyone seemed calm and composed.

At the harbor each child was given two tags, one to be attached to his or her small suitcase and one to be worn around the neck and tucked under the coat. Suddenly I heard my mother's serious voice addressing me, "*Never get separated from each other no matter what! You must take care of your little sister and stay with her!*" Then just as suddenly, my mother disappeared into the darkness and into the crowd. There was no opportunity to say our goodbyes and no explanation of where we were going or for how long. I later learned from my mother that she thought it would be better to say goodbye abruptly rather than prolong it. She wanted to avoid a tearful and sad farewell and thought it would be less painful to get it over with quickly. But that moment was difficult for us and haunted my sister for the rest of her life. It also explains why, after her return to Finland, she never again wanted to leave our mother and the familiarity of Salo even though we both had the opportunity to go back to Sweden.

We were quickly ushered onto a waiting ship into a beautiful salon that had many soft couches and chairs. My sister began to cry, wanting to know what had become of our mother. But I comforted myself with the idea that we appeared to be in a good place. She was worried and upset, though, and kept asking me where our mother had gone. Then the engines began to turn, and everybody prepared for the night. During the trip, we had some "aunties" to look after us who did their best, showing us kindness. We were given milk and sandwiches, which were placed on a large shining table. I remember waking up a few times, due to the crashing of ice against the hull of the ship. I wanted to stay awake for this exciting adventure, but I couldn't despite trying very hard. We were allowed to go out on the deck briefly in small groups when the situation was considered safe, but even then we were chaperoned. Although we enjoyed the freedom of being outside, the cold and wind soon forced us back into the pleasant warmth of the salon.

I remember that someone suddenly mentioned that the lights of Stockholm were visible. At this announcement, almost everyone was in a hurry to go outside to see this wonder. In Finland, we lived in darkened cities with blackout curtains as a precaution against bomber planes finding us. So it was quite wonderful to see the city aglow with colorful bright lights as we approached the Stockholm harbor. It seemed like a totally different world for us after all the darkness we had left behind.

A speedy process followed as we went through customs. After, we boarded a bus to take us to Marie Prastgardsgatan in the south end of Stockholm. This was the former church minister's residence and was a very welcoming place. The big living room had been outfitted with many beds and a long table where we were served hot chocolate and fruit. At the end of the living room stood a Christmas tree with lots of tinsel and bright decorations. It was only then that it struck me that we had not been able to say goodbye to those kind "aunties" of ours on the ship, and I felt bad about this.

Gradually we made ourselves at home in our new surroundings, and we all got along well with each other. Even my sister forgot some of her sadness and played with her new friends. In the days that followed, adults began visiting to have discussions with the nurses. We did not know who they were, but we later learned that they were state officials of various sorts who were arranging appropriate foster care for the children. One by one, other children in our group began to leave for their new homes with their chosen foster parents. Then one day came when only Pirkko and I remained. After a while, we came to assume that this was to be our "home" for a long time to come. But we were treated well and didn't mind this too much, though we missed our playmates.

One evening we were called to the main hall to meet "a kind uncle and aunt." Their intention was to take my sister with them to their home but not me. Since I had strict orders from my mother not to separate from Pirkko, however, I strongly protested against her leaving without me going with her. The discussion went on for some time between the adults, and finally we were told that we would not be separated, after all. We were to be placed in the same home together, and I was deeply relieved.

The weather outside had turned warmer and the streets were wet. Light reflecting from the wet streets made the surroundings truly fascinating to me. It was a huge change from small, dark Salo to this big bright city. As we walked with our new guardians, I felt relatively safe about what was happening and observed everything around us with great curiosity. Finally, a taxi brought us to the central rail station, and rather quickly we took our seats in a brightly lit railcar. The train began to roll almost noiselessly towards our new home, and our new war parents began to converse with us with the help of a lexicon. We found it really funny to listen to them speak and could not stop laughing. It was truly hilarious for us to hear Finnish words being pronounced with a Swedish dialect. This was a good icebreaker, though, to be able to laugh. Our future foster parents seemed relieved to find us in a happy mood, though they understood nothing of what we said or why we were laughing.

After a short ride, we arrived in Rotebro where a taxi was waiting to take us to our new home, a little distance outside of Stockholm. The driver took care of our luggage, and all four of us got into the roomy car. It was only a few minutes before our ride came to an end at the gate of a big two-story house and we walked to the main door. Lights shone from every window and it even seemed rather bright outside. I felt somewhat intimidated when we stepped into the grand entrance. On the ground floor was a large living room, dining room, and a special room for entertaining. Crystal chandeliers hung from the ceilings, and there was a large white piano in the living room. A lady with grey hair in a tidy bun and wearing shiny shoes greeted us. We assumed she was the housekeeper because the house seemed huge to us and would probably require servants. We also noticed the pleasant smell of newly prepared coffee, indicating that our arrival had been expected.

After a late dinner, we attempted to carry on a conversation with always the same result: they thought that we understood them, and we thought that they understood us. The bedrooms were upstairs, and Pirkko and I were given a spacious room, into which an extra bed was brought for me. Before bedtime, we opened our little suitcases, which mother had packed for us. Only the top layer was to be used during our travel, and the rest was to be unpacked at our destination. We found a few photographs and a letter in Swedish addressed to those people who were to look after us. Handing all this over to our new mother, she read the letter out loud to her husband, wiping tears off her cheeks. I never knew what the letter contained, but I assume it explained who we were, our difficult circumstances, and the uncertainly of our family's future.

The first morning brought many new experiences for us. A neighbor came over with her daughter who was about our age and wished us well, which was the beginning of a lifelong friendship. After a few days, we also wrote letters to our parents back home. Writing was hard at first, but we were helped along with our new address and other information. One letter was to go to our mother and the other to our father at the front. My sister and I were surprised about how well our foster parents seemed to understand everything that we wanted to write.

Gradually, life assumed a new normality for us, and we lived in great comfort with our foster parents, Ragnar and Ninni Lundqvist, who were generous and caring people. They were an older childless couple, Ragnar in his mid-fifties and Ninni in her late forties. We called them *Farbror* (Uncle) and *Tant* (Aunt). Neighbors often visited to talk, but we could not really understand what they had to say. The Lundqvists were very social and seemed to have many friendly get-togethers. Soon, a lot of new clothing and equipment began to arrive for me and my sister. We were especially surprised and delighted to receive new ski boots. We made new friendships, and days began to pass rather quickly. However, despite our wonderful new circumstances as well as the abundance and good will of all those around us, my sister still missed our mother and always spoke about "going home." She never really connected with our new home in the same way that I eventually did.

Although it was hard at first, we began to understand the Swedish language a little better, so that we could more easily comprehend what was going on around us. Every evening we listened to the radio to hear the war bulletin repeated in Finnish. My sister and I patiently waited for the end of the news when we could hear how the war was going in our own language. However, it was often difficult to follow the situation. When we heard about air raids, we checked a map for those towns and cities that had been bombed and were always relieved not to hear Salo mentioned.

Our new father's job seemed to preoccupy him a good deal, and it took some time for us finally to realize the sort of work he did. In his spare time, he did a lot of reading and writing. On the envelopes we saw what he was called but did not know what it meant. However, after some months, someone translated his title for us. How lucky we were to be part of a family where the "father" was a *member of the Swedish parliament and a prominent politician!* We also discovered that he was an important person in the operation of the country's railway system. For this reason, we traveled a great deal, once all the way up to Lapland. School was put off for the duration of our stay, so it seemed like we were on holiday. We had everything we could possibly wish for.

I have photos from January 1940 taken of both Ragnar and Ninni, as well of as Pirkko and me, on skis in front of the large beautiful Lundqvist home on Norrbackavägen in Rotebro. I also have photos from a bit later that winter of the family in front of a hotel. Pirkko and I are wearing sunglasses and sitting in elegant lawn chairs, looking very pampered and cozy under blankets. And there are photos of my tenth birthday in April 1940 when the snow had finally disappeared. In honor of the event, the Swedish flag was hoisted outside our Rotebro home and several of our friends posed with Pirkko and me for photographs. I remember that hot chocolate and cake awaited us after the pictures were taken.

The Winter War ended in March, and I knew that we would soon be going home. Upon hearing this, Pirkko immediately started packing. But I felt unhappy and was not eager to return home. I liked my life in Rotebro without the constant threat of bombs, food shortages, and other hardships. I had bonded with my foster parents and made good friends. I was also concerned about my future and worried about what would happen next. What would become of all the splendid things we had received: skis, sleighs, stamp books, and so much besides? *Farbror* and *Tant* took notice of this concern and reassured me that even though we would be returning home soon, we could take our new possessions with us and that we would be welcome back anytime.

We returned to Finland by ferry from Stockholm to Turku during the second week of May 1940. Our mother met us at the dock in Turku. Luckily, we had not forgotten our Finnish but had become bilingual during our separation. I looked forward to seeing our family and friends, of course. But homecoming was a letdown for me. Everything seemed to have changed. My older brothers were not the same, and old friends seemed distant. The feelings between my mother and I had also changed somehow. She knew that I'd grown to love my foster parents and was homesick for them, but she wouldn't discuss it. It was enough for her that we had been taken good care of and spared the food shortages, rationing, curfews, air raids, and danger. No doubt having had two fewer children to worry about had been a relief for her. And because of the Lundqvists, once the school year began I was ready with new clothing, boots, and other supplies. But there was a glass wall between me and my mother that could not be removed. I don't believe that she was jealous of my foster parents and my attachment to them, but perhaps she felt left out of my life.

As soon as school let out for the Christmas holidays, I left for Sweden, my father providing me a ticket to travel by ferry. There is a 1940 photo of me visiting their holiday house on the island of Skarpö in the Stockholm archipelago where, in later years, I would come to spend many happy summers. The photo shows a snowbound wintry scene, but I look very proud and happy, wearing my new ice skates. At the end of the holidays I returned to Salo. Then for spring break, I again visited the Lundqvists. On May 1, 1940, there is a photo of me with the extended family, making preparations for the summer in the gardens surrounding their home. We all raked and cleaned away the winter debris and enjoyed our lunch outdoors. There are more photos from this time of the Skarpö shoreline and promenade with a magnificent view of the sea and shipping lanes to Stockholm.

Even when the temporary peace was over and war broke out again in Finland in June 1941, I spent as much time as possible with my new parents. There are many summer photos of me and Ragnar fishing, which was a daily event. We fished from the dock and from a boat with rods, but we also used nets. Every afternoon after Ragnar arrived from work, we checked the nets and occasionally bagged some big fish. Boating was always on my mind in Sweden, and launching the canoe that I built was a special event. Less fun was the routine of emptying the rowboat after heavy rain.

The Lundqvist's garden was extensive with apple and cherry trees. Late in the summer, we always had a good crop of potatoes. No chemicals were ever used in the garden, and the produce was always delicious. Meals were served outside whenever possible. Only when larger groups of guests arrived were meals served indoors. As guests arrived and departed, it was

Figure 20.1. *Pekka/Peter Luohimo fishing with his Swedish foster father Ragnar. Courtesy Peter Luohimo.*

all very festive. During one of my summer visits to Sweden, my mother visited Skarpö, which was located within a restricted military zone. Special permission would have been required for her to come, but I assume that Ragnar took care of everything to make it possible. I have photos of her visit with all of us sitting around a picnic table and sunning on the dock. But the summer of 1946 was my last summer on Skarpö. I have wonderful memories of my time there. As for Pirkko, she too visited the Lundqvists very briefly on a couple of occasions after the war. But she always felt more at home in Finland and is still living in Salo, her girlhood village.

My visits to Sweden were always interrupted by my compulsory return to Finland to attend school. I also volunteered in the air defense corps as a "boy soldier." Schoolwork was interrupted and became complicated after our school was bombed, but we carried on in another town. I found myself feeling lost during this time. I had become a stranger in my own country. With each year that passed, my ties to the Lundqvists and Sweden grew stronger, so that there was no doubt in my mind I would someday settle there. Never had I suffered any real trauma on the conscious level, but something had happened to me to make feel insecure in my native country. My father and I had a cordial but matter-of-fact relationship, and my mother remained distant to me.

My goal was always to return to Sweden, and that goal was finally fulfilled after I finished high school at seventeen in 1947 and left Finland, only returning to do my military service in 1954. The day after I was released from service, I left for Sweden where I continued my studies. But without the guidance and support of my foster parents, none of this would have been possible.

My memories of life with the Lundqvists are irreplaceable to me; they have enriched my life. Today, their ashes rest a few miles north of Stockholm in the Sollentuna churchyard next to the side entrance, under the gravestone marked: "The Churchwarden Ragnar Lundqvist and his wife Ninni, *nee* Karlstrand." My Finnish father died in 1972 and my mother in 1990. Both are buried in the Hietaniemi cemetery in Helsinki.

I have an indelible memory of something that occurred long before in January1940 when both Pirkko and I were living with Ragnar and Ninni. During our time with them, I participated in several organizations such as "Protect the Children," "Save the Children," "Help Finland," and others. In addition to being a member of parliament, Ragnar served as the church warden of the local Sollentuna Church.

One January night, despite the bitter cold, many war children and other local children were assembled for a special ceremony. We formed a sort of honor guard all the way from the church door to the altar, each child holding a Finnish or Swedish flag. We were all very cheerful. War children were chatting, comparing their experiences, and the atmosphere was gay. But shortly after the beginning of the ceremony, we heard a woman crying at the rear of the church: a young mother with a child in her arms who was completely lost in a bottomless and hopeless sorrow. I had never been witness to anything like it before in my life. Many kind hands supported and helped her, and I noticed tears flowing all around me. Later I was told that her young husband had been killed in action only a few days before.[2] At age nine, I couldn't fully comprehend the situation, but it brought the brutal reality of the war across the border into our community and affected me very deeply. It was good to see, however, that there was consolation in all this: she was not alone in her deepest moment of affliction.

There are dark memories from the war years, but Ragnar and Ninni forever brightened my life. As an adult, however, I eventually came to feel rootless and uncomfortable in Sweden as well. After my studies in Stockholm, I married my high school sweetheart and we moved to Canada where I finally felt myself to be at *home*. When we arrived on the Canadian border, the immigration officer noted that "Pekka" looks like "Peter" and proceeded to type "Peter" on my landing card. So I am both Pekka and Peter, although with friends and family I am still Pekka.

However my name is spelled, I would not be who I am today, nor would I have achieved what I have in life without my foster parents to whom I will always be grateful. Not one day goes by without a quiet *tack* ("thank you") to them. Sharing my story is another way to say thank you. I miss them deeply.

* * * * *

After finishing his studies in electrical engineering in Stockholm and his compulsory military service in Finland, Peter married and he and his wife emigrated to Canada in 1957. They have three children and four grandchildren and are retired today in Oakville, Ontario. Peter has contributed a longer version of his story to the Institute of Migration in Turku, Finland.

Notes

1. The "Situation Report," written by the War Command on December 26, 1939, states that "The cities targeted were Helsinki, Turku, Tampere, Hanko, Porvoo, Viipuri, and surroundings." There were also many small towns that were bombed. And, "In some places, the enemy planes have machine-gunned civilian targets." But the report also states that while the Finnish air force suffered no losses, "a total of twenty-three enemy planes ... [were] confirmed to have been shot down."
2. Although Sweden remained officially neutral throughout World War II, during the Winter War some 8,000 Swedes volunteered to serve alongside the Finnish forces, mostly contributing to Finland's defense of northern Lapland.

Photo Section

Finns rush to a bomb shelter during the Winter War. Courtesy SA-kuva.

Finns in a bomb shelter during the Winter War. Courtesy SA-kuva.

Viipuri children get ready for Sweden, May 1944. Courtesy SA-kuva.

Finnish children being led from the train in Sweden. Courtesy SA-kuva.

The *Arcturus* prepares to depart from Turku, Finland, for Stockholm. Courtesy SA-kuva.

Finnish children on board the SS *Arcturus* in 1942. Courtesy SA-kuva.

Finnish children on the train to Sweden. Courtesy SA-kuva.

Two Finnish children with a translator after their arrival in Sweden. Courtesy SA-kuva.

Finnish children waiting for their foster parents in Sweden. Courtesy SA-kuva.

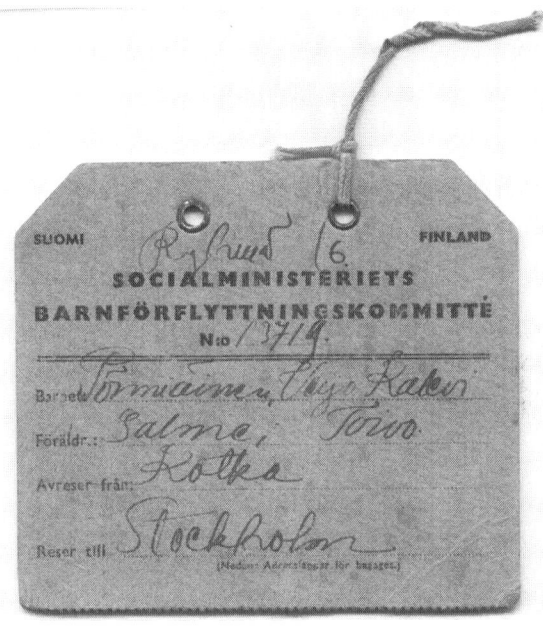

A tag worn by Veijo Paine (born Veijo Pönniäinen) during his wartime travels. Similar tags were worn by all Finnish war children during the transports. Courtesy Veijo Paine.

21

Black Birds
Seppo Mälkki

I was born in Kuopio in Savolaks, a province north of Karelia. The Mälkki family originated in Karelia in a small village called Mälkinkyla, which means "Mälkki's hamlet." This village was very close to Viipuri, the capital and largest city in Karelia before it was lost to the Russians during the war. Viipuri is now known by its Russian name, Viborg. I never knew my biological father, as I and my older brother Jorma were born out of wedlock, a shameful thing in Finland in those days. My mother's name was Eva Elisabet Mälkki, but I called her *Äiti* for "mother," of course. She was very small, kind, and intelligent. She had many brothers and was the only girl from a large family. I didn't know her parents because, during the war, the family was dispersed due to evacuation.

I was first sent to Denmark at the age of three in the spring of 1942, returning six months later at my mother's request. I believe that I was sent to a preassigned family, which I believe was a more humane system than that used in Sweden, where children were often selected at random by local families. When I was in Denmark, it was still occupied by the German forces. And though I was then a very small child, I can remember one day when my Danish "big sister" took me on her bicycle to the seashore for a swim, and we were stopped by a German soldier with a rifle. I can still remember his dark brown eyes and black hair, and many years later it struck me: *Was he really an Aryan?* Behind him I could see German soldiers building new bunkers all around the Danish shores, which the Danes had a hard time demolishing after the war.

After I returned to Finland, we were evacuees, staying with relatives in eastern Finland. But the food situation was bad, and Russian attacks and bombings were severe even in the countryside, due to its proximity to the border. In 1944, my mother and I moved to Imatra, a town near the Russian border today but which was then some distance away. It was known for its water power plant, which is still the largest in Finland. For that reason, Imatra was bombed regularly, and I remember the bombings.

Figure 21.1. *Seppo Mällki (right) at age three, with his foster sister and brother in Sweden. Courtesy Seppo Mällki.*

For me as a five-year-old kid, they were enthralling. One vivid memory is of me standing at the window, admiring the fingers of the searchlights and the anti-aircraft artillery bursts in the night sky, when my mother came and harshly snatched me away and carried me down to the cellar. She was very angry, and for reasons I didn't understand then but do today. She was simply very anxious about me. Russian fighter pilots sometimes entertained themselves by diving down and shooting civilians, so we kids were often forbidden to play outdoors, especially during the winter. War is war, and the Geneva Convention is not always respected.

In any case, my mother decided to send me to Sweden in 1944 when I was five. Her reason for sending me was unclear, but perhaps it was because of the danger and common lack of food. I was given a small piece of cardboard with a string to hang around my neck, as were all the children being evacuated. Though I have tried to remember the journey, I simply can't. All I remember is that my mother vanished as the train started, and I cried for her in the last car with my nose pressed to the window as I watched her, wearing her grey dress, growing smaller and smaller until she disappeared. I think that this was the most traumatic thing I have ever experienced in my life. Just a couple of months earlier, I had been separated from her when I was sent to Denmark. And now it was happening again. I fell into a kind of lethargy after that and don't remember anything until a week later in Stockholm where I found myself in a large room full of beds and a lot of children my same age. It may have been a hospital or the Hotel Anglais, which I later read was used to temporarily house arriving war children. Because my mother died many years ago and my older brother is senile, there is no one to ask.

Eventually I was sent to a family in Göteborg on Sweden's west coast and arrived there in June 1944. My first memory—besides their daughter, who picked me up at the railway station—is of my Swedish foster mother (German by origin), standing on the stairs. It was a large house situated in a crossing at Boogatan, Orgryte. My foster father's mother lived on the first floor, and we lived upstairs. On the first floor there was also a huge kitchen for the family. Surrounding the house was a large garden with apple trees and a big barrel that we filled with water in which I used to bathe. Orgryte was then a fashionable district in Götheborg (sometimes spelled "Göteborg" by English speakers) and still is. In those days, the neighborhood ended at the top of the hill where my foster parents' house was located. On both sides of the street were exclusive villas belonging to lawyers and doctors, and their kids were my playmates. I remember one of the boys especially because he had an uncle in the United States who had sent him a large-scale model railway with a steam engine driven by Meta tablets. The boy's father was a well-known lawyer, and his firm is still one of the largest in Götheborg. Many of the neighbors were Jews, the importance of which will be explained later.

On the other side of the top of the hill, the street continued as a dirt road. There were some farms there, and we kids used to ride on top of the loaded hay-cart after the hay had been mown. We lived in that house until the fall of 1946 when my foster grandmother sold it for 145,000 Swedish kroner, an immense sum then, probably the equivalent of several millions today. We moved to the countryside north of Göteborg where I attended a small countryside school with several grades in the same classroom, a so-called B-school. I also met a little girl whom I liked, but as she lived some kilometers away, I ran to and from her house many times that year.

At the beginning of the summer in 1947, it was decided that I would go back to Finland, and so I set out on my first return journey to Finland at the age of eight and a half. I traveled first by bus to the center of Göteborg where my foster parents, whom I called *Mamma* and *Pappa,* waved me off. Next, I got on a train to Stockholm where I boarded a ship to Turku. According to documents in the National Archive, this first return voyage was arranged by the War Child Committee.

At that time, Finnish ferries in Turku docked in the Old Town. I believe that my *Äiti* must have taken a bus from Pori to meet me there at the Turku harbor, but I can't reconstruct these events from memory. These things happened some seventy years ago, after all.

From other documents in the Swedish and Finnish National Archives, I have learned that children of my age were not allowed to travel alone, but I don't remember any other children being with me on this journey from Sweden. It must have been a highly disturbing experience for me to separate from a family and environment that I had spent almost four years in. Perhaps this is why I don't remember clearly what happened. When *Äiti* and I were reunited, I no longer recognized this woman who was my mother. Nor could we communicate, as I had forgotten all my Finnish. I quickly tried to make Finnish words from the Swedish by putting an "i" at the end of them. For instance, I took the Swedish term *hammare* ("hammer") and made it *hammari*: this was my "Finnish." *Äiti* did not understand me, as the word "hammer" is *vasara* in Finnish. I was eight and a half when I returned. My mother had written to me in Finnish, but I had no photos of her to remember her by. Nor was she able to phone me, as trunk calls were very expensive then. Also, neither she nor my foster parents had a telephone, though our landlord had a phone and conveyed messages to us.

My foster parents had not really prepared me for my return to Finland, though during a later visit to Sweden they once threatened to send me home early when I got caught reading 25-cent crime magazines that I borrowed from the landlord's son. He was not popular with my foster parents either. They never spoke about adopting me because I believe that they didn't have the necessary finances.

However, after my return to Finland, a period of moving to and fro between the two countries about once a year began.

My Swedish foster *Pappa* never played with me much. He was not too interested in children, being a big kid himself in the wrong way. Instead, he gave given me lots of war toys, which my Finnish mother threw away. She did it because she hated the war and anything that reminded her of it, but this made me quite angry and also sad. I don't remember feeling too deprived upon my return, strangely, perhaps because my mother worked many jobs, though she had no education. She was a country girl, so this was not a normal situation for her, as she was better suited to be a farmer's wife than a city girl. I entered a Swedish school in Pori on Finland's west coast in the fall of 1947. This school was very different from the one I'd attended in Göteborg where there were only ten or so students of different grades all in the same room. I was used to this and felt out of place in Finland. And because this was shortly after the war, Swedish-speaking Finns were not popular because Sweden was blamed for having let Finland down during the war, and it was partly true. I was bullied as a consequence and called a *Ruotsipukki* or "Swedish buck."[1]

As I grew older, I learned more about my foster father and his family. His father had begun a business in Latvia and St. Petersburg and married a Latvian lady with six children, eventually running his own fruit and wine import company in Sweden. As the son of an important and wealthy man, my *Pappa* was expected to complete his academic studies but didn't, and his mother (my foster grandmother) never forgave him for that. Instead, *Pappa* went to America and Canada in his twenties and traveled around. He took casual jobs to get by, once even working in a circus.

And here it is: my foster father was an active Nazi. As a young man, he had also visited Germany, and, like too many others, he was seduced by Hitler. By then, he had married my German foster mother in Leipzig, and so his happiness was complete. They had a daughter and traveled together around Germany many times during the 1930s. But even after he had settled down with his family, he was adventurous and continued to travel. For instance, in the 1930s, he worked as a press photographer, which led him to cover the Baltic Fair in Estonia when it was still a free country. He flew there privately, as no commercial airplanes were available. He once showed me a picture of a small, open biplane with two seats and he and the pilot, standing beside the plane before their journey began. They wore goggles and leather flying outfits and looked as tough as anyone could before World War II began.

When I came to Sweden in 1944, *Pappa* was an official at the German Reichs Consulate in Göteborg. As might be expected, he was strongly anti-Semitic and used negative terms when referring to Jewish people.[2] He had inherited these views from his own father who had published books on the Jewish question. Imagine all the kids my age, many of them Jewish, living along our street and playing with this little fellow from Finland who lived in the big house of the well-known and—after the war—notorious Nazi. One playmate's father was a Jewish lawyer, and a Jewish doctor lived right across the street from us.

After the war, when Nazi war crimes and concentration camps became known, public sentiment and politicians demanded that Swedish Nazis be held accountable. Thus, my foster father was sentenced to some months in prison for collaboration, and I still wonder what he did to deserve such a harsh sanction. Despite this, he remained a devoted Nazi throughout his life, and I remember old gentlemen Nazi sympathizers visited him in the beginning of the 1950s when I was about twelve. They sat in leather British club-style armchairs in the living room, had drinks, mostly fine French cognac, and smoked cigars—though my foster father always smoked a pipe—and chatted about old times. On these occasions, I would be told to go to my room.

After my foster sister grew up, she disagreed with his fascist opinions and ideas about the concentration camps, and they had many quarrels, which I was then old enough to pay attention to. I also suffered sometimes from his political views. Though my Swedish schoolmates never tormented me for living with a known Nazi, grownups often did. For instance, though I was the teacher's pet, he was a passionate opponent of the Nazis and strongly disapproved of my foster father whose fascist beliefs he tried to reform through letters, which I, the go-between, carried. Also, from 1949 to 1962, when my foster parents lived in Gråbo, a village about twenty kilometers from Göteborg, our landlord developed a violent dislike for my foster parents, which he took out on me. I still have a letter from the farmer who owned the house we lived in, which states that "no milk will be delivered and no telephone calls will be forwarded as long as Seppo is your guest." The farmer later became insane and destroyed the next-door neighbor's well by filling it up with rocks and gravel. He was eventually put in a mental hospital.[3] *Pappa's* justification of his views throughout his life was that "Hitler was a great leader and one couldn't find any complaint against him."

I was also bullied in Finland by my contemporaries, due to my having lived in the neutral and, therefore, more prosperous Sweden. Also the Fennoswedes (Swedish-speaking Finns) were by tradition the white-collar class in Finland. Because my mother belonged to the blue-collar class and lived in a working-class neighborhood, I was made fun of. I was a kind of misfit.

To return to my foster father: unfortunately, his lack of educational credentials was a disadvantage for him when he searched for a job after his six months in prison. He no longer had a German consulate to help him. He was very impractical and was best suited for paper work. So he became a writer of books. His masterpiece is a reference work about Swedish place names in the United States, and there are plenty of them, especially around Minnesota. He also wrote *Amerikabreven* (American Letters), a book dealing with the correspondence between an emigrant to America and his family left behind in Sweden.

I moved permanently to Sweden in 1953 when I was fifteen because my brother Jorma was already living there, an invalid who had contracted tuberculosis as a soldier during the 1940s. In fact, he enlisted in 1942 at the age of fourteen, claiming to be sixteen and forging our mother's signature on the form. Jorma, ten years my senior, was desperate to join up because everybody was then going to war: Finland's survival was at stake. At first, he spent many dull days in the garrison, writing letters to our mother several times a day, since the field mail was free. But later at age sixteen, he served as a bicycle orderly with the army in Petroskoya in the north of Karelia and saw a lot of action, though he never spoke with me about this.

I moved to Sweden because there were more job opportunities there than in Finland, which suffered terrible postwar poverty well into the mid-1950s, due to the tremendous war reparations demanded by Russia.

Figure 21.2. *Finnish boy soldiers of 1942. Seppo Mälkki's brother Jorma (second row center) forged his signature at age fourteen in order to join the Finnish Army. Courtesy Seppo Mälkki.*

My foster father died of a heart attack in the 1970s, and my foster mother moved to a pensioners' home where she died at age 100. I am still in contact with my foster sister with whom I bonded more than with my foster parents, though I think of them in a warmer light nowadays as victims of their own time and upbringing.

My biological mother also died from a heart attack in the 1970s. But I was not so close to her. I think that my war child experience distanced me from her and others, which is perhaps one of the reasons I never got married. I don't like to get attached to people and allow them into my sphere. It's a self-protective thing. I think that I have always felt betrayed by women, beginning with my mother, but other women to follow. It took me several years to overcome this feeling.

During my younger years, I searched for a father figure, but I never found anyone I could seriously consider. Then, some years later, I realized that I myself was a grownup and could be a father figure for other kids. They made my role very clear to myself, and some children I have helped have even called me "Pa" and asked me if I would like to become their father.

During my adult life, I have read a lot about the Finnish war children. It seems that most of us were scarred emotionally and psychologically and that we have had difficulties in our relationships with other people. Many of us have suffered from mental disorders or, as in my case, become alcoholics. I have personally suffered aftereffects from my childhood experiences that have influenced both my professional and personal life. When I first began work, for instance, I could not stand anybody giving me orders about what to do. I also had constant nightmares for many years about black birds (the Soviet bomber planes I had seen as a child), attacking me. I had many meetings with a therapist for this problem. And, as time went by, I developed a heavy alcohol abuse, consuming a quantity of alcohol enough to launch a battleship like the USS *Arizona*. Fortunately, I finally kicked the habit and haven't tasted a droplet of alcohol for many years, which feels good.

I still suffer from feelings of rootlessness and helplessness, however: the sense that I was not the one to decide my destiny and future. Perhaps to better understand these feelings, I joined the Finnish War Children's Society in Stockholm in 2006.[4]

Through my war child association, I saw a video about children sent to Sweden, which was based on monologues and concerned evacuees returning to Finland after a few years. In the film, there was a man, one of three brothers sent to Sweden, who described how his two-year-old brother had been asleep when it was time to leave Finland. He was taken while he slept, and when he awakened he was among complete strangers in Sweden. This was apparently such a great shock for him that he could never recover. Though he was eventually adopted by his Swedish family, he died at thirty-nine with no explanation, possibly through illness, alcoholism, or suicide.

I am deeply moved by such stories, which convince me that child evacuations should be avoided in the future. Though children should be protected from the dangers of war, they should *never be evacuated alone without their parents*. Too many war children have grown up to be alcoholics, mentally disordered, and damaged in various ways. Since my retirement, I have worked for many volunteer organizations that assist the mentally and physically handicapped and at-risk children. I have always liked kids from the very beginning of my life, and it's easy for me to relate to them, no matter what age they happen to be.

* * * * *

Seppo attended a technical school after completing his army service in Sweden; later he worked for ten years as head of an electronics firm, and in 1966 he opened his own electronics workshop. He was offered a co-partnership in a very successful hifi shop in Stockholm, though it closed in 1979, due to shifts in the market. Seppo then started several import companies. He also worked for many years with the Boy Scouts and was cofounder in the 1990s of a voluntary organization named *Farsor och Morsor på Stan* or "Pops and Moms in the Street," a group of some forty adults who spend weekend nights wandering Stockholm to help youngsters in distress. It has grown into a national organization called "Night Wanderers in Sweden." He also began and still hosts a radio program that addresses problems facing the mentally ill. The name of the show, *Tök-holm*, is a pun on "Stockholm," as *tok* means "crazy" in Swedish.

Notes

Another version of Seppo's story appeared under the title in Sue Saffle's "Toward a Collection of Finnish War-Child Stories: The Reminiscences of Seppo Mälkki." For additional information, see note 41 of the Introduction.

1. Although Sweden maintained its neutrality throughout the war, it allowed German troops, disguised as invalids, to travel within its borders. Sweden also delivered large quantities of iron ore to Germany. According to Seppo, in November 1945 Sweden also expelled a group of 164 Baltic refugees who had been forced to fight for the Germans during the war. Sweden sent them to almost certain death in the Soviet Union, although the soldiers went on a hunger strike in protest. Some even mutilated themselves, and seven of them committed suicide rather than return to Russia. Seppo writes, "This is another stain on wartime Sweden, which is known as the 'Baltic Deportation'." He adds that "According to International Law, there was no ground for the expulsion of these refugees."
2. According to Seppo, many Swedes, especially the officers in the armed forces, admired Nazi Germany during the war. As an example of the public sentiment in favor of the Germans, Seppo relates a story involving a Swede on the west coast who led the anti-Nazi resistance: Torgny Segerstedt, editor-in-chief of *Göteborgs Handels-och Sjöfartstidning*, the largest newspaper in western Sweden. During the war, this paper appeared often with partially whited-out pages because the censors had been at work, illustrating the fact that Swedish officials did not want publicly to go against German interests. Seppo explains Swedish pro-German attitudes at the time by saying, "After all, German had been the parent language in Swedish schools at the beginning of the last century. It was only after World War II that it changed to English."
3. Perhaps because of the political leanings of his foster father, Seppo is very interested in international politics and knows a lot about Nazi networks around the world. He says that "Due to the Internet, it's much easier to get in touch. There are a lot of underground organizations, also in Sweden. They market gloves filled with 300 grams of lead shot to protect the hands, as well as knives, Nazi and American Confederation flags, pictures of Hitler, KKK-related things, and so forth."
4. The Stockholmsföreningen Finska Krigsbarn or Stockholm Association of Finnish War Children, an affiliate of the Riksforbunde Svenska Krigsbarn or National League of Finnish War Children, was founded on February 8, 1992, and has around two hundred members, though their numbers are decreasing.

22

Terror of the Dark
Marita Merilahti

I was born in Helsinki in 1934. My mother, Kirsti Auroora (*née* Kukkonen); my father, Tauno Armas Elias Merilahti; Antero, a brother three years older than I; and I lived in a modest flat with only two rooms that we heated with wood in a metal woodstove. We had indoor water but no hot water. As children, we had to put the wood my mother brought home in the cellar cabinet, and I remember being frightened to go there alone because a neighbor had died there. But what our apartment lacked, our natural surroundings more than made up for. There were great climbing rocks around us, big trees, and lovely rose bushes. There was also good terrain for skiing and ice-skating. When I was little, I remember many winter days with –40° Celsius temperatures!

My mother had been one of eight children, living in the countryside where there wasn't much work. Life was hard, and she had to leave school and her studies after only five years in order to work as a caretaker for one of her cousin's children. She was gifted with a beautiful voice and loved the theater, dancing, and all types of music. When she was older, she came to Helsinki to work as an assistant in a hotel, cleaning and cooking. She was a wonderful cook, and her meals always melted in my mouth.

In Helsinki, she rented a room, and her landlady—my grandmother to be—had two sons. Her husband had abandoned her to find a better life in America, like many Finnish men during 1880–1910. There he remarried, leaving his two sons fatherless. My future grandmother changed her married name of "Knuters" to "Merilahti" which is how I came to have this name. Both her sons were interested in my mother, but perhaps my mother chose my father because she liked his navy uniform.

My father was a furniture maker and upholsterer by trade, but fairly early in my parents' marriage, my father contracted tuberculosis and was treated for some time in a sanatorium in Germany. For this reason, I don't remember very much of him. Because of his illness, my mother had to work very hard to support her two children. She found a job in the Auroora Hospital's carpenter-joining department five kilometers from home. She worked every day from 7 AM until 4 PM, and in winter she had to walk this distance both to and from work. In the summer, when she was able to borrow a bicycle, her life was a little easier. She always brought wood home to light our oven and to heat our small apartment. But we all bathed in cold water, something my mother continued to practice until she was eighty-five years old! We Finns are famous for our *sisu*—our ability to withstand discomfort with stoicism.

After the Winter War began, Helsinki was regularly bombed, which frightened me very much. We had to sleep with our clothes on to be ready in case of an alarm. Once, after leaving the bomb shelter, I remember seeing human body parts on the ground. Everyone lacked proper vitamins and nutritious food, due to extreme rationing. My father was a soldier in the army at the front. So, for all these reasons, I was sent to Sweden for three months in 1940 when I was nearly six years old. Along with many other children, I was placed in the bottom-most level of the ship, and I recall the deafening engine noise. The vessel was bound for the Isle of Gotland, Sweden.

When we arrived at the harbor, some Gotland horses were waiting for us, and we each received a licorice treat. I was taken to a *Mamma* Ebba and her husband whose name I do not remember. They also had a two-year-old boy named Björn, meaning "bear." Of course I understood nothing because of the language difference. But I was curious and soon learned a little Swedish. Although the dark has always frightened me, I asked my second foster parents to cover the windows, so that the Russians couldn't see us! For many years after the war and even after I was married, I used to sleep with all the lights on, due to a lingering terror of the dark. Another memory I have from this first stay in Sweden is the vision of green fields with red poppies, a wonderful memory. I also remember having animal friends to play with since my foster parents were farmers.

After I returned to Finland, I began school in August 1940 at age six. But the Continuation War interrupted my studies, and in October 1942, all children under twelve years of age were put on a train to Haaparanta just across the Swedish border, to be saved from the constant bombardments. Our group of children was put on a train in Helsinki. Though I was then nine years old, I don't remember very much about this journey because I had a high fever and bad sore throat. All I remember is that we received labels to wear around our necks and that I slept all the way on the luggage or hat shelf of the train. The train was entirely blacked out, so that Russian planes would not detect and attack us. Many trains had been bombed in this way and many people killed.

Soldiers welcomed us to Sweden, and we were taken to some sort of children's home in central Sweden where we were given nice hot baths—a luxury for me!—new clean clothes, oranges, and medical checkups. Then, most of the children were taken to their new foster homes. But I first had to spend time at a hospital in Södertälje because I had been diagnosed with diphtheria, which explained my terrible sore throat. My six weeks in this hospital were interesting. I was happy to receive so much attention and good food and snacks. But of course, I could speak no Swedish, and didn't understand what was going on around me. I do remember one day that for some reason I tore out the pages of a book and ripped them into pieces!

Then one day I was taken back to a children's home, and day by day I began to understand more. The first words in Swedish that I learned were *"Tvätta dina händer i ljumt vatten."* In English, this means "Wash your hands in lukewarm water," and I remember being pleased because I somehow understood. However, when I was sent with slightly older children to a nearby school, I sat and understood nothing. When our lessons were over, though, my teacher who was a very nice woman, read children's stories to me such as "The Three Billy Goats Gruff," and this helped me to gradually learn a little Swedish. I especially remember the following spring, playing in the brooks among the birds in beautiful surroundings.

Eventually, I was sent to an upper-class foster family in southern Sweden, a medical doctor's family. I did not like being there because I was put to work, folding handkerchiefs and towels, which I disliked. My relationship with these people was very formal. I called them "Mr. Doctor" and "Mrs. Strøbäck." Fortunately, I stayed there only a short time and was placed with a much kinder family in the countryside.

The second family consisted of *Mamma* Agnes and *Pappa* Julius Jönsson and their daughter, Inger, who was five years older than I. They were a farming family, living in Elëstorp, a little village near Båstad in southwestern Sweden opposite Denmark. Here I had a room of my own, and I was very soon more than happy, though the dark still frightened me, and I asked *Pappa* Julius to cover all the windows at night to avoid being seen by the Russians. On the farm there were two horses, pigs, many cows and calves, hens, and *Gamla Mor,* "Old Mother," the cat. I even had two calves of my own to take care of, and I enjoyed

Figure 22.1. *Marita Merilahti (right) with her Swedish foster sister in 1943. Courtesy Marita Merilahti.*

strolling with them through the fields and was never scolded for this! But here too I asked *Mamma* Agnes and *Pappa* Julius to darken all the windows at night to avoid being seen by Russians.

School began in the fall in a one-room schoolhouse that held children of all different ages. I developed a love for music and painting like my mother, and, luckily, my new family owned a piano, which was fantastic! On my tenth birthday, all the village children were invited to a party at our home. But they soon left because *Gamla Mor* was giving birth to baby kittens. My stay in this wonderful place lasted more than three and a half years, during which time I forgot all of my Finnish. Back home, my mother had to have the letters I wrote translated, so that she could read them. I did not have a photo of my Finnish mother or family, so the memory of them also began to fade.

I returned to Finland in the autumn of 1946 when it was again safe. I remember being very seasick on the return voyage since there were high winds. I vomited and a man gave me a spoon of "medicine," which was actually cognac! I don't believe that I was unhappy returning home to my friends and hobbies in Helsinki, but I could no longer speak Finnish. The first Finnish that came back to me after two weeks were the words *noita-akka,* meaning "witch" or "hag." One of our neighbor ladies thought I had a defect in speaking because I used the French "r."

I resumed my schoolwork in a Swedish-speaking school, so due to the war I mastered two languages. Also, I had the opportunity to spend my summer holidays in Sweden, which I looked forward to. And I enjoyed the voyages there as well. My war parents once drove the long distance from Skåne to Stockholm to meet me, and we then drove back home to southern Sweden together. One summer my mother and brother came to visit my foster parents and stayed for three weeks.

My time in Sweden—the three months in 1940 and the three and a half years from 1942 to 1946, as well as following summers that I visited—was mostly very happy. I have wonderful memories that still bring me joy today. My war parents sometimes visited me, for instance in 1952 during the Helsinki Olympics. We also shared many letters over the years, and I have kept up contact with my war sister. I grew up feeling equally at home in Finland and Sweden. Overall, I feel that I enjoyed a happy and privileged childhood.

My father passed away on July 14, 1947, when I was only thirteen. He had been a soldier in the army and had been hospitalized for tuberculosis for as long as I could remember. One of my most vivid memories is of him waving goodbye from the hospital gate. At the time of his death, I was visiting my foster parents, and my mother didn't have the heart to call me home for the funeral. When *Mamma* Agnes shared this information,

I ran to my calves for comfort. I remember that the sky was dark with shining stars.

I have read and heard about many very sad war child stories, especially those concerning very young children who were sent away and sometimes abused. Younger children often missed their mothers terribly. But I was accustomed at a very young age, due to my mother's work outside the home, to take care of myself, which perhaps explains why I have no traumatic memories. My mother sent me to Sweden so that I would receive medical care, good food, and a safe childhood. I don't suffer from the restlessness that many war children describe. I can be happy anywhere, but especially in the midst of beautiful natural surroundings like the lovely poppy fields that I recall from my summer visit to Sweden in 1947. My bad memories of the war have faded, and as they have faded so has my fear of the dark.

* * * * *

Marita attended a commercial night school and became a secretary in a factory that produced radios. She was married and had one daughter but was later divorced. She resumed work as a secretary in various businesses—export, shipping, confections, and a glove factory, retiring in 1990, though she worked as a tourist guide until 2007. Today she lives in Järvenpää, the city of Jean Sibelius, and is still in touch with her foster siblings.

23

Funeral Games
"Eine Miller"

Before the war, my family lived in a big town in Karelia named Suojärvi, meaning "Swamp Lake," on Finland's eastern border with Russia. Half the lake belonged to Russia and half to Finland. My paternal grandfather owned a farm with cows, pigs, and chickens, and my father worked alongside him. But he also had odd jobs. When he married my mother, who was a teacher, he went to work in a general store that he later owned. But he lost the shop in 1930 during bad financial times. And, after many children came along, my mother was unable to teach. I was born in 1935 and was the seventh child. After my younger sister was born, there were three boys and five girls in my family. We were Greek Orthodox, the religion I still practice today.

After war broke out, Russians began coming over the frozen lake in dark uniforms to shoot at Finnish soldiers in their white uniforms (to blend with the snow), often at 5 AM. One day, my family was rushed onto a sled, and my brother pulled us to the railway station, since all the horses had been taken by the army. The passenger cars were entirely full of people, so our family was put into an animal transport wagon with just a small window very high up in the car. I somehow remember this window, although I was only four and one half years old at this time. I do not know how long we traveled to our new destination. But finally we arrived in Wartsila-Patsola, a large industrial city in western Karelia, which was also under attack with bombs falling almost daily. Though the schools were operating, we spent many days in dark, cold bomb shelters. Miraculously, neither the school nor the house where we lived was ever hit. The house had formerly been a dance hall, and we shared it with men from both the Finnish and German armies, the soldiers sleeping in the hall and our family in one room with a kitchen. The armies kept horses in the field, and they always heard the Russian planes before the rest of us and became very restless. One beautiful Sunday morning, I was out walking and witnessed two planes shooting at each other. One plane was shot down and descended in flames. I heard later on the radio that the downed plane had been Russian, and I was so happy.

Also, since we still lived so close to the border, Russian deserters were always roaming around the fields and forests. When we children were sent to pick berries and mushrooms, I was not afraid of the deserters. They simply wanted to stay alive and were scared and simple men. In fact, my mother, who understood a little Russian from a teacher's seminar she had taken years before, gave them food and even cried when they told her about their wives and children in Russia. We never learned what happened to them, though one prisoner of war worked in our garden for a time. Because Russia was our enemy, however, mother warned us never to tell anyone about her speaking Russian, not even a single word![1]

Father was too old to engage in combat, so he worked as an enlisted man during the war, delivering food to the front lines. During five years of war, we saw him only a few times. But shortly before the end of the war, my mother received a letter from him, saying that he would soon be home. Then one day, she saw the village priest walking toward our house and knew that he had bad news. On one of the last days of the war, father's delivery truck had been bombed by a Russian plane, and he had been killed at age forty-three. Mother was born during the 1917–1918 war, so she was still a fairly young woman. But now she was left with eight children to raise on her own. After father's death, she never seemed to sleep, but walked and walked all day and all night. She worked so hard for us. Simply shopping and standing in line for food required the entire morning every day.

My father's funeral was very nice, though we were only able to bury his identification plate and parts of his body. Mother did not open the casket. We children cried, but we also knew that we would receive cake, which in contrast with our meager diet always tasted so good. We never had any of the ingredients to make cake, but when someone in war had died, army headquarters sent a consolation cake to the bereaved family. We had been to many funerals, due to the frequent casualties of war. At least two of my father's brothers were also killed, including a sixteen-year-old who had volunteered. As children, we loved funerals only because of the cake.

In fact, because we children had lived through five long years of war and forgotten how to play normal games, we pretended to hold funerals instead. In the kitchen, there was a wood box for the stove. We often emptied it, and I was always selected to be the dead body inside the box. I used to cry out, "Don't close the lid! Don't close the lid!" My brother Esko was the "priest," and he said the blessing. And my sisters cried and pretended to be mourners. My mother would get very angry when we did this because after the game, we never remembered to replace the wood in the box.[2]

After the war, we lived on the new Russian border, and life was very difficult. Though my mother gradually began to recover from her grief, at night she had nightmares and screamed, which terrified the children, so we pulled the covers up over our ears. We were dependent on her, and fortunately she at least received some assistance from the government for food. She also took in sewing and helped with cleaning and doing laundry for wealthier families. Neighbors occasionally helped us, too. But she never spoke about the war. No one did. It was a hard time, and I prayed a lot, which I always found helpful.

Then suddenly my life changed when some people came to the house and told my mother that her two youngest children—my pretty six-year-old sister, Anja, and myself at age nine—should be sent to Sweden to save us from hunger and diseases. My mother began making skirts and blouses for us from old mattresses and pieces of sheets left by the army. We thought we looked so lovely as we waited for the train. But then a nurse came to look us over and found lice behind our ears. So we were taken to a room where a person shaved our heads, and we received name tags to hang around our necks. We had no toys to comfort us, just one raggedy doll my mother had made for Christmas, which the two of us took turns hugging. But we didn't cry because our mother had told us to be brave.

During the long train trip, I got very sick, and the nurses tried to separate me from Anja. But mother had told me to look after her since she was younger. I put up a fight and even bit the nurse on her arm. She screamed but didn't slap me. However, my sister was taken away, and later someone explained to me that we had been separated so that she wouldn't catch my whooping cough and high fever. (I learned later that Anja was taken by a farming family with no children in Goteborg in western Sweden where she lived for two and a half years. They wanted to adopt her, but eventually my mother took the couple to court, and Anja was finally returned to Finland.)

Anja and I never saw one another again while we were in Sweden. After spending three weeks in the hospital in Uppsala, I was sent to an orphanage in Garveda, close to Kalmar in southeast Sweden. One morning at the orphanage, we were very carefully washed. Our hair was combed, and we were dressed in nicely fitting outfits. Because I was older, I understood that something special was happening. We were all playing in a big room when suddenly many adults entered and began walking around and looking at us. This continued all day until one of the nurses at the orphanage was looking sadly at the only remaining child in the room. It was me. All the other children had been chosen and had left with their new families. I felt that I had not been chosen because I was very pale, skinny, and ugly.

The nurse went to lock the door when there appeared a new family, requesting to come in. There was a mother, a father, and a little girl, and the nurse said to them, "You are late. All the children have been taken. We only have this one left." And I looked miserable. Then this small girl ran up to me and affectionately took my hand. Her parents looked at each other, then rather doubtfully at me. But this little girl kept holding my hand and pleading with them. I wanted her to be my sister!

The next thing I remember is being in a big house with a room of my own. I had never seen so many beautiful things. At first, I refused to touch anything because I was afraid of such fine furniture and decorative objects. I missed my simple things. Gradually, however, the family's kindness and love won me over. And the little girl, Carena, was so caring and attentive, always talking to me. So it was in this way that I learned Swedish. When school began, I was at first seen as stupid, but my teacher soon realized that I was very smart and learned quickly.

The two years that I spent with the Olssons were wonderful. *Tant* Ruth, my foster mother, was a very religious housewife who encouraged us to pray a lot and attend regular Lutheran meetings. I was somewhat used to this, as we had gone to church with our mother two or three times a week. But *Tant* Ruth, my foster aunt, often took us to services that seemed interminable, which neither Carena nor I liked. We often fell asleep. *Farbror* Iwar, my foster uncle, was the town judge. I grew to feel closer to *Tant* Ruth, as Iwar was usually away at work. But I became especially fond of Carena who was a true little sister to me.

Then, one day a letter arrived from the Red Cross, saying that my mother had requested that I return to Finland. The Olssons and I all cried, but Iwar, who was a judge, understood that I would have to go. So another great change occurred in my life. But this time I was confident that I would survive.

I left Sweden by train in August when I was nearly eleven. When we arrived in Haparanda on the Swedish-Finnish border, I and other returning children had to walk across the border to Tornio to board a Finnish train. About all this, I only remember a woman running toward me with a big smile, exclaiming, "Eine! Eine!" In Sweden I was called "Elli." I realized that this woman hugging me was my mother and wanted me to call her "Mamma." But she spoke no Swedish, and I had forgotten my native language. So I began to count in Finnish: "Yksi, Kaksi, Kolme, Neljä" (one, two, three, four), because these were the only words I remembered.

I knew that my life had taken another turn, and I understood and accepted it. There was nothing else a child could do. I did not resent my mother for requiring me to come home. I only felt sorry for her because she always had so much work to do. But adjusting to our new home in central Finland was difficult. We lived in a small out-building in Niemisjarvi with no indoor plumbing or heat or electricity. Later the farmer who owned the land moved us into the main building while we waited to rent a small house. When it became available, we moved, my brothers sleeping in the kitchen and my mothers, sisters, and I sharing the one bedroom. I loved that house because it was near a fast-moving river, and school was only two miles away.

Just before school began, my grandmother died, and my mother took me to her funeral. I remember thinking, *This is Finland where people die a lot more, more certainly than in Sweden.*

I was placed in fifth grade, and when I first began my teacher explained a lot to me in Swedish. But after two months, I was speaking Finnish again, and no one could make fun of me anymore! Having three brothers in the same school also helped.

The Olssons sent me letters and packages for some ten or so years, as did Anja's Swedish foster parents. But the Olssons never visited Finland, though Anja visited her Swedish family seven years later when she was fourteen. Only in 2012 did I return to Sweden to visit Carena and thank her for her goodness to me. I wish that I had visited her far sooner because when we were finally reunited after so many years, we felt just like sisters again. She had prepared for my visit by cooking and cleaning for weeks and made me feel very special and loved. We visited Ruth and Iwar's graves together. And when Carena took me back to Garveda, all my memories came back like a dream. But it was sad to see how the little village was dying. The red schoolhouse was locked, the railway station disused and rusting, and the shops and many of the great old trees vanished. But our house still stood there. Carena was surprised, though I was two years older than she, that I remembered it all so well, even the names of girls who had been in my class at school. Carena no longer lived in the big house in Garveda, but in a smaller one in a nearby village. But the table in her dining room is the same as that in the old house that had once been full of so many amazing antiques. I touched the table with love, no longer afraid of touching beautiful things.

* * * * *

"Eine" graduated from Pori Nursing College in 1959, later working as an emergency nurse in Helsinki and in Basel, Switzerland. After this she moved to New York City, where she worked as a nurse, and some time later to Chicago, where she also worked as a nurse and received her green card in 1966. She married a lawyer with whom she had one daughter and traveled the world, but they were later divorced. For thirty-four years "Eine" was head surgical nurse at an important hospital. After retirement, she moved to Lake Bluff, Illinois. She now resides in San Diego to be near her daughter and her family. Though she has come to love the United States, she writes that "inside, I am still a Finn."

Notes

1. Although Russia has been Finland's principal oppressor, Finnish attitudes toward Russians were complicated throughout World War II. According to Aura Korppi-Tommola, "On the one hand, [Finnish children] did learn to fear them, from the adults and from war propaganda.... On the other hand, this idea of Russians did not fit with their personal experiences.... The only Russians they met were prisoners of war who worked on the farms. The 'enemies' were fine people" (Korppi-Tommola, "War and Children During the Second World War," 453; see note 3 of the introduction).
2. Korppi-Tommola describes the most common fears and nightmares of Finnish children who lived through the war, particularly those who remained in Finland. In addition to bombings and starvation, "funerals were also present in children's nightmares," together with "white coffins [and] adults in black and church bells ringing" (ibid., 454).

24

The Woman in Black
Helena Nilsson

My *Isä* or "Father" was born in 1892, and my *Äiti* or "mother" in 1901. I was born in February 1940 and am the youngest of nine children, the oldest being seventeen years older than I. When the Winter War began in November 1939, *Äiti* was pregnant with me, and *Isä* decided to take us to the countryside, due to heavy bombing in Turku where we lived in a house he had built, a large house with studio apartments to let. He packed a small lorry to take us and our necessary things about fifteen kilometers away to a village where both my parents had grown up, though sometime later my two oldest sisters and *Isä* returned to Turku because of their work. *Isä* was a homeguard soldier, and sometime between 1939 and 1941, he was poisoned with gas and later contracted tuberculosis. I have very few memories of him, but I can visualize him sitting in a rocking chair, smoking a pipe with gently smiling eyes. I also remember him picking me up to sit on his knees where I felt very safe and contented. The rest of us returned to Turku when the Winter War ended in March 1940.

The year I was born was extremely cold, so cold that my brothers and sisters could not play outside together and had to wear double socks, gloves, and hats. At some point *Isä* had to go to the sanatorium, and a few of us returned to Turku, so that our mother could be near him. During night bombing raids, we had to dress quickly and run to a bomb-proof vault in a house on the other side of a field. Once, when *Äiti* was at the sanatorium late, we children didn't make it in time, and we had to seek cover in a ditch.

In 1942 two of my older sisters, Pirjo, age nine, and Maija, age four, were sent to Sweden. Pirjo was placed with a family who had a farm and one child, a son. Unfortunately, she was treated more like a housekeeper than a daughter, so her time away was not so happy. Maija was very small for her age and looked more like a two-year-old boy at that time. She was one of those children who was the last to be chosen at the last railway stop in southern Sweden. Pirjo referred to her foster parents as *Tant* and *Farbror* (Aunt and Uncle), and Maija called hers *Pappa* and *Mamma*. Two of our brothers were also sent out of the country but to Denmark.

My fourth birthday had just passed in 1944 when my parents wrote a letter to Maija's foster parents who would soon be my foster parents as well. The letter is written in rather good Swedish:

Turku, 25 February 1944.
Dear Maija's foster-parents:
Thank you very much for the beautiful card we got from you. It makes us very happy that you find that Maija is in good health and that she is a good child. You wrote that you even want to take care of our little Helena. We are so grateful.

Pirjo, Helena's sister, who will be eleven years old in May, will leave Finland and make her second journey to Sweden at the end of this month. Then we will send Helena with her. It will be nice for her to travel together with Pirjo. Of course we'll long for her and we will miss her, but here there is terrible trouble and very bad times.

We know that the children will have better times with you, and it is a good thing that Helena can stay in the same family as her sister Maija. We can imagine that she will feel sorrow at first, but we believe, on the other hand, that she will soon learn Swedish and that, in time, things will become easier for her. Helena is very happy that she will be with her sister. Because the journey will take place so soon, we haven't the time to make new dresses for Helena. [The truth is that my family had no money to buy material from the black market, the only market where cloth was available.] *We only hope that the long journey will go safely for our daughters. We are very grateful if you will write to us as soon as possible to tell us that the children have arrived. Yours truly ...*

Because I was only four on the day when I left Finland for Sweden, I don't remember a lot except that Turku was constantly being bombed. I can't remember who accompanied me and Pirjo to the railway station, perhaps the whole family except our father. But I remember waiting on the platform and someone lifting me onto to the train, a big black train that would take me, Pirjo, and many other Finnish children to the security of a country named "Sweden."

Inside the railway car were hard wooden seats. I took a place nearest the window, and my family waved goodbye. I seem to remember saying to myself very silently so that no one could hear: "This is going to be an adventure! I will be all right. I will survive." And I seem to remember stretching my back and maybe even lifting my shoulders to show that I could manage while facing an unknown future. I smiled. And then, the steam-powered train began to huff and puff and started its long journey to Tornio in the north of Finland.

There were adults on the train, mostly from the Red Cross: female volunteers who wanted to help alleviate the misery of war. All the children wore labels around their necks: grey cards with our printed names and destinations. During the journey, many of these labels became very tattered since some children chewed on them. Outside it was very cold, only the snow shining through the winter darkness, and the landscape that we passed through was lonely, isolated, and heavily forested. I have no memory of how long the journey lasted except that it was very tedious and that I slept most of the time.

Then we arrived in Tornio, a frontier town in Finland on the Swedish border. And here we had to wake up and leave the train. Later I learned that this was necessary because the tracks are wider in Finland than in Sweden. So we all changed onto a Swedish train by walking over the border where an official stamped our passports. There were a lot of people moving about, and for the first time I heard a strange new language and observed a strange new world. But I thought that this new world seemed to be wishing us welcome.

After a little time we were taken by train to the south of Sweden: to a place without war and bombs, to a new home which would be mine for some years after. A new mother and father waited for Pirjo. And a new mother and father also waited for me. My sister Maija who had arrived in Sweden two years earlier at the same age I was when I was sent to Sweden also waited. At six, she had learned to speak Swedish and had made lots of friends. I hoped that she still remembered me and wanted her little sister to be with her.

I remember observing that the winter landscape in Sweden was just like the winter landscape in Finland. I wondered about this and was relieved to think that not everything would be entirely different, then. The sound from the train, the bustle of passengers, and the uncomfortable, hard seats also seemed the same as in Finland. But the manner of speaking and even people's gestures seemed foreign.

Later, after a very long time and many hours on the train, we made a real stop, so that all the children could be examined for medical conditions and treated for lice. If a child had lice in his or her hair, then their hair was shaved off, which tormented the children. Pirjo and I were lucky and allowed to keep our hair. But I think we all felt like small prisoners. Unfortunately, Pirjo and I were separated because I had to be treated in a hospital in Gävle, I believe for tuberculosis. So Pirjo went to her foster family sooner than I did. Because my big sister Pirjo had agreed to take care of me and to accompany me to my future foster family's house, this was very difficult for us.

At the hospital I was checked again for head lice, but it was again decided I didn't have them. Some of the other children were not as lucky and had to go bald. I was put into a certain ward where I had my own bed where I would stay for about week. Most of the other children were older than I, and I couldn't understand what they were saying. I suppose that they were speaking Swedish. But they were all very kind and good to me and treated me like their little sister. They helped to take care of me and even let me play with their toys.

In the hospital there were many children from Finland but not in my particular ward. However, one day I met some other Finns. We were all in a big, long, beige corridor with very high windows along one side of the walls and doors on the other side. The ceiling was so high that I thought it must touch the sky. We were all standing in a queue, waiting to be vaccinated and wearing nothing but our trousers. At the end of the long queue was a simple wooden chair positioned so that its back faced the waiting children. When it was each child's turn, he or she had to sit on this chair backwards: facing the queue of children, legs astride the seat, with his or her back to the adults behind in white uniforms. One of these persons held a big thick syringe with a long needle in her hand. It was terrifying to see the children shot by the doctor with this needle. But the vaccine would, of course, protect us from several illnesses.

All the children were crying and hollering. I was surprised that the boys cried the hardest and most loudly. But I decided not to cry and to show that I would be strong and rise to the occasion. I remember thinking that my family would be proud of me, and that my siblings could brag that they had no cry-baby for a sister. Instead, I would be a strong little sister who could control her fears.

When it was my turn to receive the vaccine, I tried hard to think about something else. I clenched my teeth and said to myself, *It will all be over in a few seconds, and the pain will be far away.* To my own amazement and perhaps to the amazement of others, I managed not to cry. And to reward me, one of the women said something kindly, though in words I didn't understand. At the same time, she stroked my blond curly hair.

Eventually, the days in this hospital passed, and it was time to get on the train again. I remember someone lifting me up to the train, since it was impossible for my short little legs to climb from the platform up the train steps.

The sound of the train's steam pressure and the train beginning was now familiar to me. On what seemed like a very long journey, I enjoyed seeing beautiful Sweden in her winter dress. Friendly people gave me biscuits and something to drink. Red Cross volunteers also gave me food. After many hours that seemed to drag on forever, I had to change to another train. But this was the train that finally took me to the station where my new parents and my sister Maija were waiting to fetch me. Of this meeting I have no memories, however.

I do remember my first impressions of my new home, which seemed tremendously big to me. One reason that the building was so big is that it also included a flour-mill. To the rear of the house there was a big garden just like a park. In front the house was a large gravel yard and opposite this yard were more buildings. It was a very beautiful and charming place. Inside it was warm, and I remember feeling as though the house was opening its arms for me. The kitchen was spacious with a nice dinner table. But most impressive of all was my discovery that water in the kitchen came out of a tap: you only had to pump a little, and the water would come! In Finland, we had no indoor water, and the privy was in the yard. We had to fetch water from a well and, in wintertime, take snow and let it melt on the stove.

I was also impressed that there were two bedrooms: only four people were in this family, and yet there were so many bedrooms! In the room where I stayed with Maija, there was a black iron stove in the corner to give us warmth. The other bedroom was a bit colder, but I would be there very seldom. The bedrooms were located upstairs in one of the gables. And outside the kitchen in the hall was one of the greatest luxuries I could imagine: a water-closet! In Sweden I would not need to go outdoors in the cold dark night to use the loo. I began to wonder: *is* this paradise? I had been met with open arms to a warm home where there was so much food: meat, fish, bread, butter, cheese, and milk. It was made clear to me that, if I wanted it, I could even have a second glass of milk!

My new parents were always kind and loving to each other and to my sister and me. But Maija had forgotten Finnish and didn't understand me, nor could I understand her. Though it didn't require too long a time for me to learn Swedish, I could tell that Maija felt I had somehow disturbed her world. For two years, she had been the only child, pampered, with playmates her own age. So she wasn't too happy that suddenly she needed to care for me part of the time, and sometimes she ran away with her boy playmate when she was supposed to be caring for me. He was the youngest son of our neighbor, and I can still hear how they laughed when they ran away. But soon, it didn't matter so much because I liked to be alone. And I also came to know the grocer's three daughters, one of whom, Ingrid, was also four years old. Ingrid would become my very best friend. Also, we sometimes visited our sister Pirjo, and occasionally she came to us. I became friendly too with my foster parents' family: *Mamma*'s mother and sister's family and *Pappa*'s sister's family.

Mamma and *Pappa* also had friends, especially the dairyman and his wife. Because *Pappa* was the mill master, he often exchanged flour for the dairyman's milk, cream, butter, and cheese. It was a very good arrangement. Another man who visited sometimes was a musician, and he and *Pappa* were very good friend and had a lot of fun together, playing and singing. *Pappa* played the violin, and his friend played the concertina.

My new *Pappa* did crazy things like buttering a slice of cheese, making a roll of it, and serving this to me. Then he would make one for himself, laugh, and say, "*Voita pällä jousto!*" ("Butter on the cheese!") He had bought a Swedish-Finnish dictionary, so he could communicate with me, and I appreciated this helpful extravagance. *Mamma* used to smile a lot, and when she laughed she got tears in her eyes. She was a really good mother to me and my sister. We were always clean and well dressed. I grew to love her and her gentle ways.

In summertime we went to the sea and lived with *Pappa*'s sister. Holiday time! Sandy beaches, salt water, picnics, and outings. Aunt and uncle had a car in which they drove us to see new sights.

I first arrived at my foster home in March 1944, and I stayed there two springs, two summers, two autumns, and almost two winters. But I remember the two years as one long sunny summer, which was the best of my life.

In April 1945, the last of the Finnish wars, the *Lapplandskriget* (Lapland War) in the north of Finland, ended. In September 1945, my foster parents gently told me that my father in Finland had died. But I couldn't understand what this news meant.

In December of that year, an old woman from Finland first came to visit Pirjo and later, in January, she came to visit us, staying for several days. She was very thin, dressed all in black, and seemed ancient, though as I now know she was only forty-three years of age. She spoke a strange language neither I nor my sister could understand. But we were expected to sit with her for several very dull evenings for reasons we didn't understand.

Finally, the day arrived when she had to leave, and we all went together to the railway station. It was the ninth or tenth of January 1946. A very cold winter day. I longed for our warm home and wondered why we had to see this old woman off. I was impatient to return home, and after some time, I took Papa's hand and said, "*Pappa*, please let us go home now."

Then arrived the most terrible moment in my entire life. I had to enter the train and go away with that old woman! Maybe *Pappa* had tried to tell me before. Maybe both my foster parents had tried to explain that that old woman was our mother. But I just couldn't imagine that *Mamma* and *Pappa* were sending me away … and not Maija. Pirjo was staying in Sweden, too. Only I was being sent away. I was in shock. I had lost everything and felt nothing was safe anymore.

After taking the train to Stockholm, we then took a boat to Turku, the old woman and I arriving on January 11, 1946. There were a lot of my family members to meet me and my *mother*, the thin old woman in the black dress. Now began a new time in my life. The Finnish language came back to me fairly soon, after some days or weeks. I remember even asking about my father, as memories began to return. My siblings who had remained in Finland, four sisters and two brothers, were very kindly to me. But I was ALONE. In Sweden, *Mamma* was always at home with us, and *Pappa* worked in the same place where we lived. But in Finland, all the others went away in the mornings, leaving me by myself. I was given a half cup of "coffee" with a little milk, some bread and something on it for breakfast. The typical food given me for "lunch" was cold potatoes and a little slice of salted herring. In the evening when everyone had returned, there was some kind of porridge: not the heavenly food I had received in Sweden.

I was afraid during the daytime. My brother, four years older than I, took care of me after he returned from school. So I looked forward to his return as he represented security to me. We had no water-closet and no tap water inside our dwelling. It helped that every evening we were together and on Saturdays and Sundays. During the evenings and weekends, many people were always around. But my mother continued to feel like a stranger to me.

After a year of my exile from Sweden, Pirjo returned from Sweden. And after one and a half years, Maija returned. Our Finnish family invited *Mamma* and *Pappa* to Turku; however, they never came.

From old letters that were exchanged between my mother and my Swedish foster parents, I have learned that *Mamma* and *Pappa* begged my mother to let them adopt Maija and keep her permanently, and I believe that they would have liked to adopt me too. Then, in June 1949, it was arranged that Maija would return to Sweden. She was so thrilled and happy. And, as a smaller miracle, I and Pirjo would also return to Sweden but only for the summertime. I was very happy. In Finland, I had to wear old boy's pants that had been made into a skirt, and my "bicycle" had no tires, so I couldn't ride it.

On June 16, 1949, Maija and I returned to our *Mamma* and *Pappa*. They had moved and lived now in a very nice yellow house in the middle of a big garden with trees and flowers. It felt like a castle to me. The summer soon passed, and I asked with dread when I would have to go back to Finland. To my surprise, *Mamma* told me that I could stay with them and even go to school. I was very happy but also a little sad because now I missed the siblings back home. I had grown used to living in a big family and would many times in the future long for a big family.

Yet another new chapter of my life had begun. I had forgotten my Swedish, but *Mamma* was a really effective teacher, and when school started I could speak rather well.

Much later I saw letters from *Mamma* and *Pappa* about their desire and efforts to adopt both Maija and me. But our mother in Finland had promised our dead father that she would take us back to Finland. So she made a compromise, allowing us to stay in Sweden but never allowing our foster parents to adopt us. In retrospect, I have often wondered how difficult this must have been for them. They never knew for sure how long they could keep us and when we might be demanded back. And we longed to be their daughters! Our sister Pirjo returned to Finland in 1950 or 1951, and Maija and I were very sad because of it.

Meanwhile, our foster parents, Maija, and I moved from the yellow house to another, and then to another, and then to another. *Pappa* liked to buy houses, restore them, and then sell them. Finally, we left the small village I had grown to love, which was really hard for me. Our new places were always nice, but life seemed constantly to change. There was no permanence to anything. *Pappa* worked in an office and later helped his sister and her husband with their business.

When I began high school, I searched for grants but was declined because I was not a Swede. My foster parents had to pay. To help out I worked summers from my thirteenth year on, and I gave everything I earned to *Pappa*. From Finland, Maija and I occasionally received small tokens for Christmas and our birthdays. But Finland was a very poor country, and it was not easy for our mother. Around once each year, our foster parents also sent packages to Finland.

In the summer of 1954, Maija and I returned to Finland for a few weeks. But we knew now that our real home was in Sweden. I never wanted to live with my real mother: she was too old and tired, and I was too young for her. Her work in a factory and later as a cook was very hard on her. But our Swedish parents also disappointed us in some ways. After our Finnish sojourn, we both thought that *Mamma* and *Pappa* would be waiting for us at the railway station. But they weren't. So we walked home and found them in the garden. "Oh, you were coming today!" they exclaimed. And this memory still hurts me. All of the accumulated small things either done or not done by both my Swedish parents and my Finnish mother still hurt me. For instance, when our foster parents found fault with us, they blamed it on our Finnish origin, which was so insulting. This and other things made me feel that I was not considered part of their "real" family and that I was not their "real" daughter. At the same time, it is difficult to write this because I loved them so very much and so much wanted to be their daughter.

I understand that there is no guarantee that one will find absolute happiness with one's parents or in one's childhood. But at least in Sweden, I was able to attend high school, which would have been an impossibility in Finland.

In the beginning of 1960, when I was twenty years old, I moved to Stockholm. The really strange thing is that after I moved, I never received a telephone call, a letter, or a postcard from my foster parents, though I had lived with them for almost eight years altogether. Instead, I phoned them, wrote letters, and visited them several times a year. In 1970, I moved back to the south of Sweden, and some years later I received flowers from them for my birthday. After that, they visited once a year, and they seemed to enjoy themselves very much. And I often visited them. I have also enjoyed visiting with my siblings in Finland and especially with Maija. In the beginning, we were nine children, but today only five are left alive.

A few years before my foster father died, he begged me to visit him in the hospital. To my surprise, he asked my forgiveness and cried and cried. When a nurse entered the room, he said to her, "This is my daughter," not "This is my Finnish girl." It seems that, after all, we had been accepted by *Mamma* and *Pappa* as their children, which made me so very happy.

I am happy for the life I have had, because in practical terms I couldn't have had a better life in Finland. Sweden was my salvation. But both my experience in Sweden and in Finland proved to me that there is no guarantee of a completely happy life with one's parents.

* * * * *

Helena went to night school and studied two semesters at university. She is married and has a son. Most of her career was spent in office management. She enjoys mountain hiking, visiting the theater, going to concerts, reading books, and socializing with friends.

25

Understanding Backwards
Veijo Pönniäinen Paine

In the fall of 1939, when the Winter War began, I was four years old. My mother and I lived in the city of Kotka, which at that time was Finland's largest export harbor, so it was very heavily bombed by the Russians.[1] My mother had grown up in poverty, the daughter of a tenant farmer, and I remember her once saying when I was much older that being a tenant farmer's daughter was like being a lower form of life. I never knew my father. I lived with my mother during the three and one-half months of the Winter War in 1939–1940. We spent many nights in a bomb shelter whenever the weather forecast projected clear weather because this is when Russian planes typically launched their air attacks. Kotka had a small mountain with large caves that were converted into bomb shelters by building multilevel bunks. We would carry pillows and blankets to these shelters where we tried to sleep.

In Kotka my mother worked as a nursery school attendant. But when the Continuation War commenced in June 1941, she was ordered along with many other women to work in the warehouses for the war effort, and she never did go back to being a children's caretaker. That same year the city authorities ordered the evacuation of children between ages one and fourteen, and this is how I came at age six to be living in terrible and dangerous circumstances.

I was sent to a primitive farm in east-central Finland, an area called Savo. I am not sure how long I lived at this farm. It may have been six or perhaps as long as nine months. When my mother came to visit this farm and saw the low standard of living there, she made an instant decision to take me back to Kotka. Savo was a very primitive place with poor sanitary conditions. As an example, I was completely covered with lice. When she got me back to Kotka, she shaved my hair off and took all my clothes and boiled them in water to get rid of the lice. But most importantly, she knew she had to get me away from there when she saw welts all over my body from the regular whippings I had regularly been subjected to from the family's older son. This young man had suffered severe brain damage from an exploding shell in the early part of the war, and he and I shared a bedroom. I had really bad toothaches, which caused me to cry or whimper as quietly as possible at night. If the son heard me, it would send him into a rage. He would grab his soldier's belt and whip me until I stayed quiet. His parents couldn't do anything because then he would try to whip them too. I learned to curl myself into a fetal position, so that he couldn't hit my face. I also learned to tolerate pain as quietly as possible. Unfortunately, at such a young age, I wasn't always successful. I still have a hard time allowing myself to think about these experiences. After this, my mother was understandably reluctant to send me away again. Instead, she managed to smuggle me back into the city, despite the evacuation orders.

In Kotka, my mother and I lived in a small two-room flat at the rear of an old house. Every morning as my mother left for work, she would lock the outside door so I could not get out. The days seemed very long and boring. One day I managed to get the basement door open and proceeded to explore around. I noticed that a small window up close to the ceiling was cracked open. So I gathered a table, some old chairs and boxes and stacked them up under the window. I managed to climb up and open the window enough for me to crawl out. This window, which was at the ground level, was probably the way the heating coal was brought in, for my clothes got smudged with soot and dirt, and I remember thinking how mad my mother would be when she got home.

Since I now was outside, I decided to walk around. But I hadn't gone more than a couple of blocks when the air raid sirens went off. I saw people running and yelling at each other, and I could hear the bombers approaching and loud explosions. I was scared. Not knowing what to do, I just stood there and cried. Suddenly this big man was running towards me, which really frightened me. He scooped me up, tucking me under his arm and kept on running. We got to a entryway where I saw stairs going down below ground. At the bottom of the stairway I could see a number people looking up. The man yelled something to the people below and grabbed me with both hands. Just at that moment, there was a terrific explosion right behind us. I remember flying through the air towards the people at the bottom of the stairs. I don't know whether the man actually threw me or if I was hurled by the force of the blast. Luckily, the people below caught me and I was safe. My right forearm was bleeding from two shrapnel cuts, but otherwise I was OK. I never learned who my savior was, but I have always wondered what happened to him. He had been standing at the top of the steps with his back facing the blast. If I had received two minor wounds, how badly must he have gotten hurt?

It was this incident that decided my mother to send me away again—this time to Sweden. In May 1942, I was six and a half years old. Like all the other children being transported, I wore a tag around my neck with my registration number. Each child was assigned a number that appeared on the nametags that hung around our necks. My number was "13719," which means that 13,718 children had preceded me. Swedish families were also given documents when they were preparing to send the child or children back to Finland. Thanks to one of my Swedish foster sisters who kept my nametag and other documents, I have these today. There was a lot of pushing and shoving among the children after we were loaded into the train cars. Everybody wanted to catch a glimpse of his or her mother and older siblings. All the children were crying, and so were the mothers standing outside the train. I had to elbow my way to a train window in order to wave to my mother who I could see outside crying.

We were packed into a special train that transported hundreds of children to the city of Turku in the southwest corner of Finland. There, we were transferred onto a specially modified cargo ship for an overnight trip to Stockholm. It was specially modified, in that the cargo areas below the decks had been converted into huge sleeping areas with hundreds of children just separated from their families and heading into the unknown forever. At least, that's how I felt. I had no way of knowing if or when I would see my mother again.

It was no vacation cruise. Although the older children were prohibited from crying, no matter what our caretakers said or did, we all cried. It was an experience that none of us who lived through it will ever forget: you cried until you couldn't cry any more. Then, after a while, somebody near you began to cry, so you started again. And so it went, on and on. What made this trip even worse was that during the night the ship started to rock. Apparently, we were experiencing some heavy seas, and many, many children got seasick. It was impossible to sleep that night with so much crying, kids throwing up, and nurses and caretakers running around with pails and towels. But the smell from the vomiting and messy pants was overpowering. It must also have been difficult and unpleasant for our caretakers.[2] Thankfully, the boat trip lasted less than 24 hours, which nevertheless felt like an eternity.

Once we landed in Stockholm, we were loaded onto a train, which proceeded southwest from Stockholm. It seemed that the train stopped at every station along the way, and at each station a group of children got off. The Swedish organization called "Help Committee for Finland's Children," who had arranged this evacuation had also received commitments from families in those communities. Thus, they knew exactly how many children to leave at each station. This same committee also provided instructions to the Swedish families on what to do once they received the child.[3] The same document goes on to thank the foster parents and to provide them with advice regarding several things: how to obtain a ration card for the child, how they might contact a local representative for any necessary information, and what to do in the event that the family moved or the child should be injured or require health care. It also instructs the foster parents to "notify the child's immediate family about their arrival in your home and to provide updates about how the child is doing from time to time" and warns them to "maintain the greatest caution with food since Finnish children are not used to nutritious food." According to several war children, they remember having become very ill shortly after their arrival in Sweden, due to the rich food they were given.

I ended up sitting on this train for at least two days and maybe three. It seemed like a very long time. But finally we arrived at the small village station of Horred near the southwestern coast of Sweden where I and a dozen other children were taken off the train and led to the small old-fashioned railway station. It was completely empty. We were seated somewhat apart on wooden benches lining the walls of the station, and the doors were opened and throngs of people poured in. They began to walk around us, checking us over, which was quite intimidating.

I was selected to live with Johan and Agda Wester, a reasonably well to do farming family in nearby Kålleberg. *Pappa,* as I came to call him, was a tall lanky fellow with huge hands, and *Mamma* was a pleasantly plump woman. The Westers had five children of their own, all of them older than I. Their youngest daughter was seven years my senior, so I became the junior of the family. One of my early memories from this time was that one day the family spoke of "Stina" coming. Terrified that "Stina" was someone or something to drag me away again, I ran away to hide in the fields until my Swedish father strode after me and took my hands in his. He made me feel safe, and I followed. I was very fortunate to have been chosen by such a wonderful and caring family.

My first stay with the Westers lasted only eleven months when, at the request of my mother, I returned to Finland in April 1943. This first departure wasn't so difficult, as I hadn't formed the strong emotional bonds that I would develop during my later stays in Sweden. Strangely, though, I have no recollection about my return trip to Finland. Certainly, it was not as traumatic as my first trip to Sweden. I do not know why my mother asked for me back, but at that point in time, the war was going reasonably well for Finland, and I believe that she wanted me to be educated there. My mother's older sister was a grade school teacher in farming country in west-central Finland near the village of Jokipii about fifty kilometers south of Seinäjoki. She had offered to have me live with her family and to go to school there, so after some time visiting with my mother, she brought me to Jokipii, which is where I lived until the spring of 1944. Because I had lived in Sweden for less than a year, I could still speak Finnish fluently.

Unfortunately, by the spring of 1944 the outlook of the war had completely changed. Russians had intensified their bombing of cities, and the Finnish troops were retreating on the eastern front. My Swedish family wrote to my mother several times, saying that they would more than welcome me back, and in the spring of 1944 my mother relented. After the school year ended, she brought me from my aunt's home to Riihimäki in south-central Finland. There we intercepted a train full of children headed to Sweden. Though most of the children were in the same situation I had been in when I first departed in 1942, I was all excited for I knew where I was going. In fact, I counseled some of the other kids about what to expect once they got to Sweden. I probably felt somewhat smug, because I didn't have to wear a nametag around my neck, since I was not part of the organized evacuation.

However, things didn't go quite as planned for me. The second day on the train I started to feel very strange and dizzy. By evening I had completely lost my sense of balance. If I tried to open my eyes, everything spun around, and I was sick to my stomach. After that, I don't remember anything for a week. I was supposed to have arrived at my Swedish family's place on the fourth day after I got on the train. But when the train arrived, there was no Veijo aboard. My Swedish family sent a telegram to my mother who replied, confirming that she had put me on the train four days earlier. Both my mother and Swedish family made urgent inquiries to authorities responsible for child transports in both countries. They discovered that I had indeed been brought aboard the train at Riihimäki, and the Finnish caregivers even remembered that I had gotten sick the following day. People were sent to search on both sides of the railroad track because the authorities feared that I had fallen off the train, perhaps because of my illness.

It was explained later that I had contracted a severe inner ear infection in both ears, which had caused a very high fever. In effect, I was delirious for approximately a week. It was also learned that the train had crossed the border during the middle of the night and that in the confusion of train crews and nurses being changed on the Tornio/Haparanda border, someone had made the decision that I should be hospitalized immediately. So I was taken off the train and sent to a hospital in Haparanda in Sweden. Unfortunately, someone had forgotten to document the transfer. So there I was in a small hospital in northern Sweden, incoherent. As far as the rest of the world was concerned, I had disappeared from the face of the earth.

The way in which my mother discovered what had happened to me is, in itself, an interesting story. To my recollection, I started to feel better after about a week. One day, a Finnish-speaking nurse stopped by my bedside. I was so glad to talk to her since my Swedish was quite poor after not having spoken Swedish for over a year. She asked where I was from and about my family. As we talked, I suddenly had the desire to write to my mother. The nurse volunteered to get an envelope and mail the letter. I didn't have any writing paper, so I grabbed a sheet of toilet paper and wrote a very short note. I didn't have the sense to tell my mother where I was, but the nurse also included a note, explaining where I was, what had happened to me, and how I was doing. It is hard to imagine how my mother felt when after two weeks she found out that I was still alive.

I would see that note again many years later and many miles away in the United States. After my mother died in 1974, as I sorted through her belongings, I picked up my mother's well-worn Bible. Between its pages were several papers with their corners sticking out. As I pulled out these papers, there was the little letter I had written to her from the hospital, which she had saved for all those years. Translated into English it reads:

> *A Letter to my Dear Mother. How are you, Mother. I long for my mother. I cry as I write this letter to my dear mother but this is a very short letter not much! And now I'm too tired to continue. I have to go to sleep. God bless my Mother.*
> *Best wishes. Veijo.*

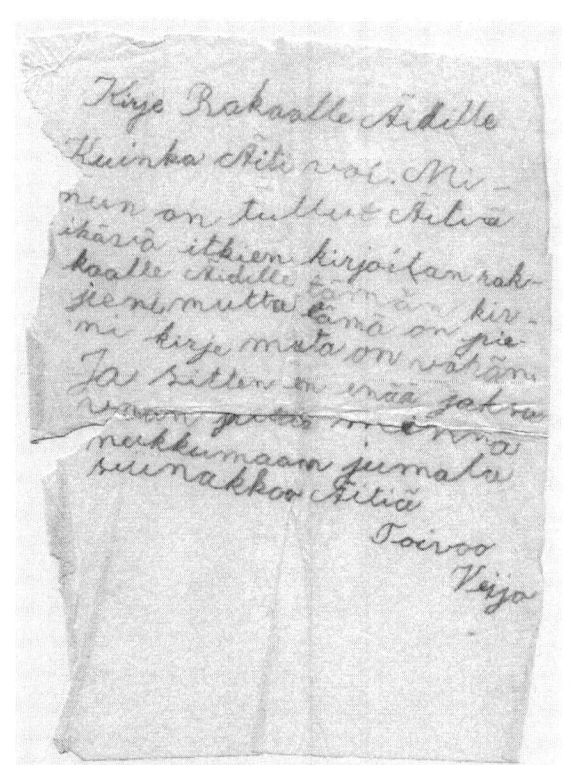

Figure 25.1. *Facsimile of a letter written on toilet paper by Veijo Paine to his mother from Haparanda, Sweden, where he was receiving medical care. Courtesy Veijo Paine.*

Upon my return to Horred I remember crying myself to sleep because I missed my mother. But I soon relearned Swedish and bonded with the Westers with whom I lived until the fall of 1945. After the war ended, I lived with my aunt's family in Jokipii during the 1946 and 1947 school years, returning to Sweden during the summers. In the fall of 1947 I began middle school in Kotka, living with my mother, but again returning to Sweden in the summer of 1948. My foster parents would send a ticket for me to travel to my second home country, and I would leave Finland with very little except the clothes on my back, returning in the fall with a suitcase full of new clothes. Over this time, I had become fluent in Swedish, attended Swedish school, and most importantly had developed a son-parent relationship with *Pappa* and *Mamma*. The postwar years in Finland were very difficult for my mother and me, and I had no hope of attending high school, let alone college, because of the stiff tuition fees. We simply didn't have the money for me to get an education, though my mother's sister, the teacher, told her, "This kid may have more than sawdust between his ears."

I loved my family and my life in Sweden, and every time I had to return to Finland, I was angry at my mother. Then, in March 1950, my mother and I left Finland together so that she would have the opportunity to meet the Westers for the first time. After this meeting, my mother planned for us to sail on the SS *Stockholm* in Göteborg for the United States to begin a new life. But I didn't want to go: I wanted to remain with my loving Swedish family. I was over fourteen at the time and had spent much of the past eight years with them, visiting them six times prior to our coming to the United States. My first visit was in 1942–1943; my second stay was for about eighteen months in 1944–1945. And, after the war, I spent three summers in Sweden over the years of 1946 to 1948. This visit in 1950 would be my last. Separating from them was the toughest thing I've ever had to do: a trauma that has stayed with me for my entire life.

The night before my mother and I were due to depart, *Pappa* and *Mamma* begged my mother to leave me with them, promising that one day I would inherit the family farm. Their oldest son Sven didn't care for farming and was in the automotive trade, and two of the four daughters were married and lived elsewhere. I served as the interpreter between the Westers and my mother, hoping that their arguments would win out. But my mother held firm. The following morning, *Pappa* vanished twice while goodbyes were being said. Then, Stina told me that *Pappa* wanted to see me in the barn. Usually fairly undemonstrative, *Pappa* dropped the broom he held when he heard me enter the barn. Then with great force, he crushed me to his chest, weeping, and with equal force pushed me toward the door.

This was my sixth and last childhood trip to Sweden. From the spring of 1942 when I first lived with the Westers until the spring of 1950 when my mother and I departed for the United States, I moved fifteen times. The longest time I had spent in any one place was the one and a half years I stayed with the Westers. My happiest years growing up were spent in their loving company, and I still think of them as my family.

Beginning in 1945, I had hateful feelings toward my mother, which intensified after our departure for the United States where I once again had to learn a new language and adapt to a new culture. I blamed her for taking me away from the Westers, but especially *Pappa,* the only father I had ever known. At the same time, I felt guilty for all of the hardship and anguish she had experienced. Today I acknowledge that she meant well; as a parent myself, I understand how difficult it would be to lose a child, but particularly for my mother since she had no other intimate family.

In 1956, when I applied for U.S. citizenship, I was offered the chance to change my name. Over my mother's objections, I chose "Paine." Upon our arrival, the umlauts over the "a" and "o" in "Pönniäinen" had to be dropped, so we ended up with "Ponniainen." I simply dropped the "o," "n," "n," "i," and the last "n," producing "Paine." I chose this, too, because *paine* is a Finnish word that means "pressure." Thus, all my Finnish relatives were able to recognize and pronounce my name. My mother never changed her last name nor did she ever become an American citizen.

For many years, I had terribly conflicting feelings toward my mother. But one day, watching her play with my own young children, I finally forgave her.

After the war, nobody wanted to talk about the child transports. Neither Finnish nor Swedish media addressed this issue. Government remained silent about it. Even academia avoided it. The war children themselves were reluctant to talk about their experiences. I myself maintained public silence until after I retired because the memories were simply too traumatic to confront. My story was under lock and key until the events of 9/11 and the televised horrors of that day. Strangely, it was this event that compelled me to face my past and gradually to put it into words. In looking back, my going to Sweden turned out to be a very good experience because of the love and respect I received from Westers. I recognize that not all war children had such good experiences; however, I think that the Finnish government made a correct decision to send the children to Sweden. Many children were saved. And many children were spared suffering from famine or wounds from bombings. Unfortunately, I don't think Finnish society, or any society for that matter, really understood the mental/emotional impact on the children back then. I believe that society today is much better prepared to handle this kind of tragedy and, hopefully we will apply our knowledge to helping current and future generations of children in emotional jeopardy.

* * * * *

Veijo received his electrical engineering degree in 1960 at the University of Minnesota and earned a second degree in business management in 1968. He worked most of his career for Honeywell and Alliant Techsystems, a large defense contractor. Though he officially retired in 1994, he continued to work on special assignments. His final position at Alliant was director of Program Management. He has been married for over five decades to his "lovely wife Margaret," with whom he had four children. He writes that, though he "endured tough times as a child, I have been really blessed, I have had a good, productive career and a wonderful family." He credits his mother for the sacrifices that enabled him to have a "better life than I could have had in Finland or Sweden."

Notes

Another version of Veijo's story, edited by Sue Saffle, appeared under the same title in *Children and War*. For additional information, see note 41 of the Introduction.

1. Kotka also marked the beginning of the Kymi Valley, in 1939 the most heavily industrial region in the country; thus, it was a natural target for enemy planes.
2. Many of the women who accompanied the children on these transports were Lotti: members of the Lotta Svärd, a Finnish women's voluntary national defense force that undertook many wartime duties: operating canteens, caring for wounded soldiers, preparing bodies of the dead for funerals, and caring for children on child transports.
3. Veijo had the document recording his own transport translated into English. Headed with his registration number of 13,719, it reads: "Into your care has been entrusted the Finnish subject Pönniänen, Veijo Kalevi: Kotka, Museokatu 9 (Ronkainen)."

26

A Happier War Child Story
Virve Kaisu Kyllikki Palos

I was born in March 1942 in Tampere, the first child of parents who were both telegraphers. Soon after I was born, my mother became ill as a result of general poisoning as a complication of tonsillitis. Her recovery took months, but we had a wonderful helper who left only when I was sent to Sweden to escape the dangers of war.

My father, Jaakko Klaus Wilhelm Palmroos, later "Palos," was born in 1895 in Tampere where he was taught Russian, which he could both speak and write. After completing school, he went to work in the local telegraph office, and was later transferred to Swedish-speaking Vaasa where he had to learn Swedish in earnest, though he had learned some Swedish in school. He wanted to return to Tampere, so he wrote his resignation in Russian to the last czar![1]

After two weeks, he received his old job back in Tampere, and when civil war broke out in 1917, my father and his colleagues secretly conveyed messages to the Whites between Vaasa and southern Finland. In the end, the Red Guards found out and imprisoned them in a school.[2] After the war, he continued in the telegraph office and was married. But his first wife died soon after, and he was later married to my mother, another telegrapher, before the Winter War began in 1939. Around this time, they managed with great difficulty to rent a flat from my father's former schoolmate who had a construction firm. Throughout the war, my father worked at the front as a telegrapher, and my mother continued her work at the telegraph office.

My mother, Greta Maria (*nee* Sjöholm) Palos, was born in Turku in 1905 to Swedish-speaking Finns. Her father worked in ships as chief engineer. Unfortunately, he lost this job due to a drinking problem or so my aunt, his daughter, told me. So he moved to Stockholm to find work. There, he made friends with the family of one of his fellow workers on the railroad whose name was Henning Nyström. Ashamed of his real reason for leaving Finland, he told the Nyströms that he'd had to flee Finland because he'd participated in the murder of the Russian general Bobrikov.[3]

In 1912 my maternal grandfather managed to sign on a ship in Norrköping. Unfortunately, his cabin was unheated and he was taken ill and died. Before this, he had routinely sent magazines to his family in Finland, and Henning Nyström continued to do this for many years. Later Inga, Henning's daughter, began to correspond with my mother's family and send them magazines. This is relevant to my story because when, in the autumn of 1944, my father feared a Russian invasion, he wanted to save me, and the Nyströms in Sweden offered to take me in. My family suffered from too little food, and for some reason I wasn't eating even what I was offered. There were serious problems with my health, apparently.

The first letter from my future foster parents that referred to the plan to transport me to Stockholm was dated September 11, which happens to be the day on which my sister was born one year later. First, there were some necessary formalities like obtaining a certificate of the Nyströms' suitability to take care of me. Luckily, my mother's brother-in-law worked as a lawyer in the provincial government in Turku, and he was able to arrange my passport at once. He dated it October 14, 1944. I left for Sweden on November 7, 1944, and the first pages of my passport are crisscrossed with stamps.

On November 14 my passport indicates that I was graciously allowed to get 106 grams of Christmas candles for the Christmas tree in Sweden, which happened again the following year. The crisis committee in Stockholm had also granted me shoes and clothes and several purchasing or rationing cards. I didn't know that there was any rationing in Sweden. The bombing of Sweden was news to me, too. Maybe it was only meant as a warning as luckily nobody died.[4]

I don't remember a thing about the voyage to Sweden, nor my few days in quarantine. My parents' understanding was that I wouldn't be quarantined at all because they had made private arrangements for my transfer. However, though I was not part of an organized group of children going to Sweden, I ended up traveling with such a group. There were Lottas taking care of us all. And when we arrived in Stockholm, we were all put in quarantine in a town called Strängnäs, two hours from Stockholm. I believe that I had with me some of my dearest toys, including my favorite doll Molla-Maija. I have been told that, although I had rubber boots in my baggage, the nurses let me go outside in my summer shoes, so no wonder that I caught a very bad cold.

Figure 26.1. *Virve Palos at age three. Courtesy Virve Palos.*

My mother learned that I had not been immediately taken to the Nyströms but had been placed in quarantine from a friendly postcard written by nurse to inform her of my whereabouts. But she was greatly offended when the nurse referred to me as "Virva." My mother thought that she had given me such a beautiful name and detested distortions like "Virpi" and "Virva," which were far more common Finnish girls' names. "Virve" means something like "ripple on the water," and of course it is close in sound as well as spelling to the French *vivre*, meaning "life." In the offending card, the nurse, named "Mirjam," writes that I am a sweet and obedient child, that I eat well, and that my cough is getting better. After the Nyströms finally got me home, however, it was clear that I was still very ill and they took me to a doctor who angrily asked, "What has been done to this child?" During the almost two years I spent in Sweden, apparently the Nyströms continuously worried about me repeatedly catching colds and developing bronchial conditions.

The Nyströms lived a short distance from central Stockholm in Gäddviken in a red wooden house with one big room, a big kitchen, and a big bathroom. They heated the house and cooked with wood. I don't remember electric light, but I believe they had it. There was *Pappa* Henning (born 1893), *Mamma* Ruth (born 1894), and the children Inga (born 1917) and Arne (born 1925).

The Nyströms were perhaps somewhat better off than my Finnish parents, at least during the 1940s. *Pappa* Henning worked on the railway, in spite of leg problems and frequent sick leaves. Inga would have liked to become a primary school teacher, but her parents didn't believe in paying money for a girl's education. So she learned typing, shorthand, and languages, and worked in an office as secretary all her life. When the Nyströms needed extra money, it was always Inga who paid. Arne was dating a girl named Ulla whom the family believed to be unsuitable, but who was a great favorite with me, according to one of the many letters the Nyströms sent my parents. Arne and Ulla had to get married too early in the opinion of the family. They had two children, Margareta and Lars.

There was a temporary difficulty with me not knowing any Swedish. At the time I was born, parents were generally warned against confusing children with more than one language, so my Swedish-speaking parents had only spoken Finnish around me, although I called them *Pappa* and *Mamma* instead of the Finnish *Isä* and *Äiti*. My foster sister, Inga, began our communication by telling me that her name was "Inga Harriet." After hearing this, I apparently went to the bathroom and brought her a brush: referred to as *harja* in Finnish. This was considered very funny by my parents back home. I'm told that after two months I spoke like any Swedish child of my age. The Nyströms thought that I understood my parents when they sometimes telephoned me. According to letters, I listened keenly but didn't say anything. After these calls I used to phone *Mamma* with my toy phone. The Nyströms always told me that I had my own parents in Finland and that one day I would return to them. They even had photographs of my parents to show me. Inga and my mother had a lively correspondence, and I was always asked for a contribution.

Although *Pappa* Henning had long sick leaves, Inga regularly sent parcels to my parents with food and clothes, like so many Swedes did. She also sent magazines just as her parents had done.

My mother especially liked to get coffee when it could be sent. In addition, Inga's colleagues and all the Nyström relatives often sent packages. My mother was so grateful for an old cardigan and some mended stockings. Once, Inga's *Tant* (Aunt) Hilda even sent several kilos of sugar, a great luxury.

During my first few weeks in Sweden, I had a few crying fits because I missed my mother, according to a letter. I also had some difficulties eating the new food. One of my earliest recollections may be of sitting in the Nyströms' kitchen with a plate of porridge. The others had eaten, but somehow I couldn't bring myself to swallow the food. Then there was the shameful occurrence of soiling my knickers just before we returned home after a visit in the city center. I also remember that I loved the rolling stairs or escalators in the department stores. Every day when Inga came from work she gave me a brightly wrapped chocolate sweet. I still remember what they looked like. And in exchange, I offered her several cups of "coffee" with my toy service. Saturdays were also workdays for Inga, but she spent as much time as possible with me. *Mamma* Ruth was a housewife and was mostly occupied in this way, but she also kept an eye on me when I was out playing. Inga cared for me after work, and the men took care of me too. Arne played with me, and *Pappa* Henning entertained me with funny stories. I can't believe that I was such a sunny, obedient, and loveable child as the Nyströms described in their letters. But I also remember the Nyströms as very loving and generous.

In our neighborhood, there were other families with children in my age group, and we got along fine. One little boy often let me use his tricycle, and I still remember what it looked like. Then, when I turned four years old, I received one myself that was bigger and bright red. Once I left it outside in the rain, and I remember being rebuked for that. After my return to Finland, we continued to use the tricycle for many years. I was told that when I played outside I must always stay near the house, so *Mamma* Ruth could keep an eye on me. Sometimes, I played with Inga's cousin, Inger Nystrand, who was one year younger than I.

In spite of rationing, the Nyströms and their relatives arranged real Christmas feasts with heaps of presents for me and Inger. The Swedes also celebrate St. Lucia day on December 13, and I vividly remember the morning when Inga woke us up with a coffee tray and candles on her head. It was a wonderful vision! I also enjoyed the splendid Lucia train in the center of Stockholm.[5]

In the kitchen I had a corner for my large toy collection. One of my Christmas presents was a sleeping doll that was problematical for me. I kept trying to open her eyes when I put her down and trying to close her eyes when holding her upright. But her eyes kept falling into her head. *Pappa* Henning saw that this puzzled me, so he did "surgery" on the doll, opening its head, lifting its eyes back into place, and closing the head up again with a band aid. The adults couldn't understand why I kept breaking the doll: it was a child's scientific experiment.

I invented a friend whom I called *Ungen,* which is Swedish for "brat." I blamed *Ungen* for every misbehavior, for instance when I was scolded for mimicking Arne, who in turn blamed *me* for his own offences, though he was usually kind and played nicely with me. When traveling, *Ungen* had to have a seat beside me and so forth. I have since heard that lonely children invent companions, but how could I have felt lonely with this family and other children living nearby?

When my father celebrated his fiftieth birthday in January 1945, I was duly informed and we sent him a birthday card. When in March I turned three, I insisted on also being fifty years old, since I believed that this was the age a birthday was about.

The Nyströms had a beautiful summer place with lots of flowers. Sometimes we went there on a tandem bicycle, but they also had a black Morris car. To reach the nearest lake, we had to walk some distance and then cross over some train tracks. I remember being afraid to crawl under a train, which sometimes was parked across our way. We took this shortcut when we should have gone around the train.

Because of the two families' relationship going back some decades, the Nyströms were eager to get to know my mother, so they invited her to visit Sweden during her vacation in the summer of 1945. They also thought that it would be good for me to see my mother again. She accepted, although it was difficult because she wasn't allowed to take any money out of Finland. In addition, she was heavily pregnant with my little sister. But she missed me and wanted to be with me and the friendly Nyströms. She must also have been keen to speak of her father whom she barely remembered. Upon her arrival, I was at first very shy, but I soon clung to *Mamma* Greta all the time. After a nice three-week holiday, she left for home on August 2. The Nyströms had given her so many presents that she feared difficulties with the Finnish customs people. The Nyströms later invited some of my maternal relatives from Turku and took everyone in our family to their hearts.

I have always been charmed by babies, and as a little girl I loved children smaller than myself. So in September 1945 I was delighted when told that I now had a little sister of my own. Inga was asked to be one of my sister's godmothers. The baby was called "Tuulikki Inga Margareta," and from then on I distinguished between my foster sister and my real sister by referring to them as "Big Inga" and "Little Inga."

In October 1945 all the children living in Sweden were allowed three bananas each. They were the first in my life, and I liked them very much. Some children didn't like them, though, and one poor child protested, crying, "I don't want any cucumbers." Later the authorities actually had to sell leftover bananas free of rationing because they threatened to go bad, and as a result the Nyströms managed to get 1.5 kilograms more! Arne and I had a feast as the others didn't much care for them.

My return to Finland occurred on August 20, 1946, and Inga and *Pappa* Henning accompanied me on the ship voyage. We all shared a cabin, and I remember that it was filled with things the Nyströms had given me. There were dolls, stuffed animals, doll furniture, Christmas decorations, balls, a grand doll's carriage, a tricycle, and a lot of clothes. (Later, to accommodate all my new possessions, my father made a play-case, in which I was allowed to neatly arrange all my playthings.)

When we arrived in Turku, I saw my mother among the waiting people behind a rope, and I ran into her arms! My new little sister was there, of course, and Aunt Carin and her daughter-in-law Valma were there, too. We later met my father at the railway station in Tampere.

After I left Sweden for home, I don't remember crying for my Swedish *Mamma*, nor any particular trauma associated with my departure. But I remember *Pappa* Henning was very sad the evening before. I was still sleeping on the morning he and Inga left and that evening I cried, begging my mother, "*Mamma*, don't you leave me too." Some months after I returned to Finland, the Nyströms wrote to say that *Pappa* Henning was ill and that he missed "his little lass." I suggested brightly to my mother that we could travel to Stockholm to care for him and that *Pappa* and Inga would manage splendidly with the help of our daily maid Rauha. But it was impractical at the time, unfortunately.

During these difficult years, Inga sent us many parcels of food and other necessary things, sometimes two to four parcels a month. They were very welcome additions to our meager household. For Christmas, Inga hid forbidden things in packages of food. And, luckily, the customs officers never discovered the leather mittens and other delightful presents she had hidden. Big Inga also sent my father's first mother-in-law, whom we called "Mummi," a package of real coffee once. It overwhelmed Mummi who wondered, "How can there be such good people that they send COFFEE to other people they don't even know?" With a shaking hand, she wrote a letter of thanks to Inga, which my mother translated into Swedish for her.

Because I was only two to four years old when I lived with the Nyströms, I have had to reconstruct my time in Sweden through old letters and stories that I have been told. My old passport has also enabled me to learn more about what happened and when. One example involves the precise dates of my arrival in Sweden and return to Finland: November 7, 1944 and August 20, 1946, respectively. I've also consulted literature on the war children. And, in addition to the more vivid memories I've described above, occasionally other less vivid memories come to me, such as going to Gröna Lund, an amusement park in Stockholm, and enjoying a carousel ride there.

After returning to Finland, there was the difficulty of speaking a "foreign" language, of course. A funny thing happened before I had relearned any Finnish. When the children in the yard called "*Äiti! Tuu ikkunaa!*" (Mother! Come to the window!), I began to shout the same thing without knowing what it really meant—or so I have been told. Anyway, I never called my Finnish *Mamma* "*Äiti*," so I obviously didn't know what it meant. Before I learned to speak Finnish, the girl who lived on the same floor opposite our apartment thought that I was stupid when I couldn't answer her questions. After, we became friends for life. Later, when I spoke some Finnish, a girl living above us wanted to know how to say "*Kom hit!*" (Come here! in Swedish). And this is how she called to me when we were playing together.

After the war, my family struggled to maintain itself. The country was busy with reconstruction and times were challenging. War-disabled men sang in the yards, and people threw coins to them throughout the 1940s. Lacking legs and even arms, some of these men weren't able to participate in the rebuilding of the country. And many of those outwardly whole veterans who had mental problems and suffered from nightmares were just as pitiable. I don't believe that there was any psychiatric help for them. In many people's eyes, the war veterans were crazy. No wonder that the men who had fought ceased to talk about their war experiences. And, some of them simply wanted to forget everything connected to the war. Many children didn't want to listen to "those endless old stories" either. My father used to reminiscence with his best friend, but I don't know whether they swapped stories with others. Ironically, when I was growing up I devoured historical novels and didn't realize that I had all these living heroes around me.

We Finns are good at being silent. Like other Finns, I used to think that big emotions were a luxury I couldn't afford and that one should just soldier on against difficulties.

Eventually we acknowledged our veteran soldiers with parades. It was not until very recently, however, that the war children were discussed. The authorities came to be ashamed of the war child transports, and it was something people just didn't talk about. Also, most of the war child stories I have read are terribly sad: many war children themselves probably don't want to reflect on their early childhood. Today, though I have never been a crybaby, I have only to see books about the war children to feel like crying.

A friend of mine, another girl, was also sent to Sweden as a war child but stayed there after 1945 for medical reasons. When she returned home, she was so angry that she didn't speak to her mother for months. She wanted to be left there.

In 1959 my mother, Little Inga, and I visited Sweden and the Nyströms for two weeks, and I remained there for almost two months. Big Inga also visited us, sometimes with one of her parents several times before her death in 1971. I also received many postcards from her during the years she traveled around Europe. My mother died in 1960 when I was eighteen and Inga was fourteen. Our father died in 1964 after I had finished my education and had full-time work. Inga and I moved to a flat of our own and struggled to survive. But we never actually starved. I'm rather proud of the way we managed on our own. We both learned to economize. Today, reading some of the letters my mother sent to Inga Nyström between 1945 and 1951, I better understand how hurried and worried my mother often was. And so very often ill. It is difficult to read these letters. On the other hand, Inga and I shouldn't forget those times and how kind and hopeful our parents were for their daughters' happiness.

It has been said that the war children just like war veterans were war-disabled. I'm sure that most of the Swedes who took us in did all they could and more to compensate for the child's loss of his or her parents and culture. But little children, even if adaptable, can be easily hurt. I now realize how important it was that my Swedish family regularly reminded me that my "real" family was in Finland and that one day I would go back there. My parents also phoned me every now and then from Tampere, so that I learned to recognize and remember their voices. And we wrote letters. Best of all, though, was my mother's visit in August 1945. That's why I recognized her when I returned the next summer.

In later years, I was often told that I would have died if I hadn't been sent to Sweden for better food and medical care, which I received and benefited from. I was truly a happier war child than most. Having read many war child stories and watched documentaries on the war children, I have come to deplore what happened to Finland's war children, and I firmly believe that such things should never happen again, to *any* children *anywhere*.

* * * * *

Virve worked for many years in the cotton, advertising, and electricity industries in diverse capacities, first in Tampere and later in Helsinki. She was married to a business schoolmate but later divorced and had no children. She has always read voraciously and currently she reads in four different languages. Swimming contests with people of the same relative age give her and her sister "reason to keep in shape," and both have won hundreds of swimming medals. Today she lives with her cat Nici in her hometown of Tampere, Finland.

Notes

Another article about Virve's story, written by Sue Saffle, appeared under the same title in *Children and War.* For additional information, see note 39 of the Introduction.

1. Finland was a Grand Duchy of Russia from 1809 to 1917 and at first enjoyed liberal treatment by Czar Alexander I who allowed Swedish law, the Lutheran religion, and the Finnish constitution to continue unchanged. Under Nicholas II at the turn of the last century, however, a period of Russification began, which required that Russian be adopted as one of the principal subjects in the Finnish school curriculum, which explains Virve's father's fluency in the language.

2. The Finnish Civil War was caused in part by the social turmoil of World War I, the collapse of the Russian Empire, and the undemocratic class system that had originated with the Swedish regime of the seventeenth century, which had divided the Finnish people. The civil war was fought between the Social Democrats or "Reds" and the Conservatives or "Whites" from January 27 to May 15, 1918. The city of Tampere where Virve's father's family lived was traditionally a "Red" city; therefore, Virve's father was taking a chance in conveying messages to the enemy "White" forces.

3. In 1898, during the oppressive Russification period when Finland was still part of the Russian Empire, Nicholas Bobrikov was appointed governor general of Finland. An "ultranationalist," Bobrikov "had no patience with Finnish claims to constitutional government." See Eino Jutikkala and Kauko Pirinen, *A History of Finland,* rev. ed., trans. Paul Sjöblom (New York: Dorset, 1988), 203–4. When Bobrikov was assassinated on June 16, 1904, his murderer Eugen Schauman who took his own life became a national hero.

4. Although Sweden was not directly attacked during World War II, some bombs were accidentally dropped by the Soviets on certain cities near the Finnish border. The rationing of food and other supplies in Sweden came about because of British and German naval blockades, which led to problems with the supply of food and fuels. After Germany invaded Denmark and Norway in April 1940, every shipment had to be negotiated through both British and German authorities, radically reducing the volume of trade.

5. The Lucia procession and parade also take place in Finland on December 13. Though electric candles have replaced real ones, it is a spectacular event with a Cinderella-like carriage and enthusiastic cheering crowds. My husband and I witnessed this event in 2000 in Helsinki after a ceremony in the Lutheran Cathedral where special carols were sung to St. Lucia.

27

No Easy Choices
Ossi Rahkonen

When I was born in May 1940, my family lived with my grandparents outside of Turku in a farmhouse located directly beneath the flight path of Russian planes that were bombing the city. My parents, Paul Erik and Hellin Rahkonen, had been to a Bible and Missionary School in the 1930s with the intention of becoming missionaries as some of their close friends already had. But the war interfered with those plans.

Because of where we lived, we were given priority as children to be sent to Sweden for safety.[1] It was a very difficult decision for my mother who had been only twenty-two when the war began in 1939. Both she and my grandmother were strong-willed and determined women and didn't want to give me up. But in the end, I was in Sweden from the beginning of 1944 to the summer of 1947, a length of time nearly equal to my age of three years and nine months when I first left. To an adult, four years might not seem very long, but from the point of view of a child those years are much longer.

I left Finland by train with my older brother Jarkko sometime in February 1944. We arrived at a children's distribution center north of Stockholm in March 1944, where we spent at least two weeks, having medical checkups and being treated for lice, which was spread easily during the child transports. I do not remember much of my time at this distribution center, except that I ate my first orange and banana there, since there were no imported fruits in Finland during the war.

Swedish families came to the distribution center to choose their foster child or children. My older brother Jarkko was taken by a couple with one daughter in Nyköping, about seventy-five miles south of Stockholm. They owned a soft drink plant located close to the city and were quite well-to-do. But for some reason, Jarkko did not like his stay there and desired to return to Finland as soon as possible. In addition, my older sister Pirkko came to Sweden at age seven, but I don't know exactly when. She was first placed with a farming family outside Nyköping and had some real adjustment problems. After being assigned to a different family in Nyköping itself, however, her experience improved.

My foster parents, Ulla and Fritz Johansson, whom I called *"Mamma"* and *"Pappa,"* were a childless couple in their forties who wanted a Finnish child, perhaps in the hopes that they could eventually adopt him or her, although they never mentioned this to me. At the time, I don't think I wanted to go to a strange home, though I knew I could not stay at the distribution center. I remember arriving at my foster parents' apartment in Nyköping and getting some candy for the first time in my life. They did not know a word of Finnish, nor I any Swedish, so our early communication was very limited and difficult. But gradually I became used to Swedish city life, and *Mamma* and *Pappa*—who referred to me as "Jussi"—tried their best, I believe, to help me adjust.

I was accustomed to life in the countryside where we did not have tap water or an indoor toilet. I did not even know how to ask for water. But I believe that the ice-breaker came when I saw a horse outdoors, the first familiar thing to me from my earlier life in Hirvensalo, my grandparents' farm outside Turku where I had lived. Luckily, Ulla recognized the Finnish word *hevonen* (or "horse").

Pappa worked in a sort of tobacconist's shop, a typical Swedish business, where newspapers, magazines, candy, tobacco, and other things were sold. He was always elegantly dressed, and he brought home a lot of children's serial and picture magazines about Donald Duck, Asterix, Wild West stories, and so forth. I was very interested in these and waited eagerly every day for him to return home with a new stack of magazines, which also helped me to learn Swedish more quickly.

Mamma was a very good cook and baked a lot for the family, as well as for a wide circle of lady friends. I was often the center of attention at their social gatherings, since none of them had ever seen a small boy from Finland before.

There were many children living in the neighborhood, both in our apartment building and in other buildings nearby. I must have played with them a lot because in August 1944, after only six months in Sweden, I had become quite fluent in Swedish. Unfortunately, because there was no one with whom I could speak Finnish, I began to forget my native language.

We played many children's games, mostly in the nearby woods. At first, the boys and girls played together, but when I was nearly six in 1946, I played more cowboys and Indians with other boys in the woods. We also went fishing a lot at the nearby seaside and also from a bridge near an ancient castle where we caught eels. These were sometimes difficult to get off the hook, as they were large and slimy and writhed like snakes. The city, too, often organized supervised camping and swimming excursions to popular beaches. Girls and boys went together on these trips, which were very popular with hundreds of us being transported by buses. I remember these occasions as being very enjoyable. Other highlights of my early life in Sweden include a circus coming to town when, occasionally, in exchange for helping set it up, we received free tickets.

There were also bicycle trips to the countryside with *Mamma* and *Pappa,* to visit their cabin in the woods, relatives and friends, or to pick forest berries, especially blueberries, lingonberries, and wild raspberries. We also visited *Mamma's* relatives on the island of Gotland where she born, as well as *Pappa's* relatives near Nyköping and in Stockholm.

Though my brother Jarkko and sister Pirkko were living close to me for part or all of this time, we were not allowed to meet for complex reasons. Many people believed that if Finland were engulfed by the Soviet Union, it would be best for the Finnish war children to be adopted. And, if this should transpire, it would be best if old attachments were severed. I do not even know when Jarkko and Pirkko returned to Finland, but I believe that it was when the war ended in 1945. Their experience was not as good as mine, perhaps because they were older when they were sent to Sweden. It is possible that Jarkko failed to learn Swedish because he didn't want to be there. In my experience, older children often had more adjustment problems, because they remembered their life in Finland. In my case, I adjusted to life in Sweden quite quickly due to my young age and soon forgot my past in Finland. I think the most important factor in war children's happiness was how they were treated by their foster parents. From the very beginning, I felt like *Mamma's* and *Pappa's* own child, the child they never had on their own.

After my mother's fourth child, Riitta, was born, she came to work at a children's care center in Nyköping in the spring of 1944. She supposedly came to visit me when I was five, but I don't remember the visit. I believe that like my older siblings, she and Riitta returned to Finland sometime after the Continuation War concluded in September of that year. Unfortunately, though she had come to Nyköping to be near her children, her work took all her time and imposed certain restrictions that made seeing us difficult. She could not even be with her infant Riitta more than once a day. But, despite the fact that we saw each other only once, it is interesting to note that my whole family, except for my father (my brother Esa was not yet born), lived in or near Nyköping for some time in 1944.

My father, born in 1913, was twenty-six when the war began and served in the 14th Infantry Regiment, which was composed of men from Turku and surrounding areas. At first, they were sent to defend Ahvenanmaa, the islands between Finland and Sweden. Later they were sent far north to the Arctic Sea to defend areas which then belonged to Finland but which were lost after the war. After that they were sent southeast to fight battles in Karelia both north and south of Lake Ladoga. For more than two years they stayed at the northeastern front, some one hundred miles inside Russia along the railway line running from the Arctic Sea to St. Petersburg. My father worked on medical evacuation teams, transporting the wounded and dead to field hospitals to be sent back home. He also worked as a cook and was a member of one of the army choirs, as he had a fine baritone voice. The choir visited various military bases along the front to entertain and encourage the soldiers. (In fact, mother often said that one of the reasons she had married him was that he was a good singer—something that unfortunately didn't carry over in the children!) He was twice wounded, once with shrapnel that entered his heart muscle and which remained in his body until he died in Turku in 1995. He was decorated with various medals for his contributions and bravery in wartime.

I returned to Finland some three years later in 1947 when I was nearly seven years old, as according to both Finnish and Swedish law, I had to begin school that September. My mother had received a letter from Ulla and Fritz about wanting to adopt me, but my mother did not accept this idea, and she arrived in Sweden shortly thereafter. One reason that she did not demand me back earlier, I later learned, was that my grandparents' farmhouse had become very crowded. Not only did our family of seven live there, but also my mother's niece and four children for at least one year, as well as ten Karelians, a refugee family. I was apparently told by my Swedish parents that my mother was coming to collect me, but I do not remember this.

I was not eager to return to Finland—was dead set against it, in fact—as I enjoyed my life in Sweden and had bonded with my Swedish parents. Also, I did not know or remember anything about my life in Finland and had forgotten all my Finnish. I do not recall any discussion about my Finnish parents while I was in Sweden, nor any letters or phone calls from them. It had, of course, been hard for my mother to send me away, but it was equally difficult for my foster mother to give me up several years later in 1947 because, in her own mind, she had already adopted me. After my mother arrived, Ulla and Fritz tried to persuade her to let me stay, promising that they would provide me with a

Figure 27.1. *Ossi Rahkonen at age three, sitting in his father's lap during his father's leave from the front. Courtesy Ossi Rahkonen.*

good home and education. But my mother would not relent. I sometimes wonder if my foster parents had not sent that letter if I would have remained in Sweden longer or even permanently. I did not recognize my mother when she came to pick me up, and of course I resented her forcing me to return to Finland. But, looking back, I do not regret returning to Finland. I was a Finn, after all. And, from 1948 onwards for about five years, I returned to Sweden every summer.

My family still lived in Hirvensalo outside Turku, all seven of us sharing the upstairs, except my oldest sister Pirkko who lived downstairs with my grandparents. It was quite cramped, but I liked my life there and apparently adjusted quite quickly, although I did not forget my time in Sweden. I do not remember much about my first couple of years in the Swedish primary school, *Cygneus Folkskola,* in Turku, which was located at the market place next to the Orthodox Church. We had a nice teacher, though, and I learned to read and write fairly quickly. I also remember enjoying woodworking sessions that I had already had some experience with in primary school. We used birch wood from the outside woodpile for our various projects. Just getting to school, though, was quite difficult. First, I had to walk for almost a mile to the bus, which took them another half hour to reach the school due to fuel shortages. Frequently, we had to stop for the bus to fill up with charcoal. Pirkko and Jarkko attended the nearby Finnish school, only about one-half mile away, so they had a much easier time.

When I wasn't in school, as a seven-year-old I enjoyed being outdoors in the fields, farm buildings, and garden surrounding the house. I also went with my grandfather to the forest parcel he owned alongside a lake where there were hay and wheat fields. There was a lot to do and experience. Increasingly, too, I spent time with my brother Jarkko in the nearby forests where we built tree houses and enjoyed the surroundings. I also started skiing in the winter, and this widened our area of play. (Later on, when I was twelve or thirteen, we made really long ski trips during the weekends, sometimes fifteen miles away where we created small ski jumping hills and enjoyed ski jumping.)

In 1948, my Swedish parents came to Finland to visit me and my parents. There are photos from this period of both sets of my parents traveling together to see the sights. Surprisingly, there seemed to be no awkwardness or anxiousness in this meeting. Ulla and Fritz fitted in very well with my Finnish life. (My Swedish parents also came to my high school graduation in 1959 and to my wedding in 1961.)

The whole family moved to Turku in the spring of 1949 to an apartment building reserved for large families like ours. Our apartment had all the modern conveniences. We even had a housekeeper as my mother was working full time as an accountant, and my father was working at a bakery as master baker not too far from where we lived. The building was also not too far from Hirvensalo, where we continued to spend a lot of time—not only Jarkko and I, but all of us. Much of our food supply—potatoes, milk, vegetables, apples, berries, and so on—came from there.

Yet, despite our improved circumstances, I still yearned for my life in Sweden and the much higher living standard, which existed there after the war. I also missed the freedom I had enjoyed as an only "pampered" child. And I missed small-town Swedish life, which was very organized and pleasantly predictable.

By contrast, there was terrible hardship in Finland after the war, a lack of basic goods, so that people had to go to Sweden for all sorts of things like kitchen sinks. The physical hardship in Finland added to the emotional hardship of being separated from my foster parents. I wanted to go back to Sweden. However, I now understand how challenging it was for all parties. Added to these challenges, my family did not always get along with one another, since my grandparents, Anna Vilhelmina, August Emil, and my father were all quite hot-tempered by nature.

One new development in our lives was that father had received a three-acre lot in Hirvensalo at very low cost as compensation for his wartime services as a frontline soldier. He was among many such soldiers compensated in this way. But there was a requirement that a house had to be built on the property within five years, which was difficult for us since we were all living in Turku and the children attended school in Turku. However, my parents began in 1950–1951 to build a rather small but still adequate house. In addition, a log house was built in 1954 on the lake property my mother inherited, using timber from our own forest. Another summerhouse was completed on the lake property in 1959 and is still there. All this activity was directed mainly by my mother who was constantly planning and on the move, although our financial means were quite limited.

But while all this was going on in Hirvensalo, we continued to live in Turku where there were hundreds if not thousands of children in the apartment building where we lived. As a result, there were whole armies of boys roaming around the surrounding area, which consisted of big rocks, bombed-out city blocks, and the Aura River: ideal locations for large-scale war games, since the war was still very fresh in everyone's minds. These games, involving opposing armies, never got very serious but were just a lot of fun.

In 1950 when I was in fourth grade, my parents decided that I should attend a Finnish school, *Martin Kansakoulu,* not too far from where we lived, to further my integration into the Finnish community. I had been in the Swedish-speaking school for three years, and upon hearing our plan, the Finnish instructor, Mr. Korpijarvi, said, "But you don't even know Finnish." The first time I took the entrance exams in June 1951, he was proved right and I didn't succeed. The next day, I left for Sweden and Nyköping, which I had done every summer after returning from Sweden in 1947. But upon my return at the end of August, I was able to pass the exams. Though I had no one to practice my Finnish with in Sweden, I had a Finnish Old Testament, which I studied every day. In retrospect, this must have been a requirement of my parents that they discussed with my foster parents. In this way my Finnish improved.

After I turned twelve, I had jobs in the summer, which prevented me from returning to Sweden, though I returned with a group of young men in 1956 to work in a large department store in Göteborg on the west coast of Sweden. Around age twelve, my affections began to change, and I became much more attached to Finland. Though my boyhood friends and I in Sweden had been a close-knit group, they dispersed as they grew older, and my foster parents rented a summer house in which we lived when I visited, which further separated me from my earlier surroundings.

Looking back, I can say that I had a happy war child experience, which helped me in later life to have an international career, due to my being totally bilingual. But I am aware that many war children had less fortunate experiences, such as my own siblings. And our parents probably endured far greater difficulties than we can imagine.

My father spent nearly six years at the front, first building fortifications on the eastern border in the spring of 1939, followed by his involvement in the Winter War, beginning in November 1939; the Continuation War from 1941 to 1944; and the Lapland War to drive the Germans out of northern Finland from September 1944 to the spring of 1945. No one spoke about post-traumatic stress in those days, but I believe that he was affected, as were many others. We saw many veterans who eventually died of alcoholism, mental disorders, and homelessness when I was young.[2]

My mother too faced great challenges: she was tormented until the end of her life by her decision to send her three young children to Sweden and often wondered if she'd done the right thing. She was a deeply religious woman, having gone to Bible school before the war and her marriage. In her youth, she had even planned to be a missionary. But at the end of her life, she suffered from self-doubt, which I tried to relieve, telling her that I fully understood her decision and that it was "old history" by then. I reminded her that all her children had done well in life, all had received higher degrees and, despite their wartime hardships, had succeeded.

Difficulties faced during the war and postwar years were things you didn't speak about after the war. Only now, in the war-child associations, are we discussing these experiences. But many of us gained strength of character due to our early challenges: perhaps one reason many of us worked so hard in school and beyond is because of the stupendous challenges faced in Finland during and after the war. Other war children had substantial adjustment problems in returning to Finland that were greater than when being sent to Sweden, however, and often they had serious problems succeeding in school.

After my Swedish foster parents died, I inherited precious photos and the medal they received from the Finnish Government for taking care of me. Though I might have resented my mother shortly after returning to Finland, today I harbor no hard feelings toward her for sending me to Sweden. I came to understand that she did what she had to do under terrible circumstances: there were no easy choices in wartime Finland.

I do feel more Finnish than Swedish now but have no problems in assimilating within the Swedish community. Just as I went back and forth between the two countries as a boy, I am able today to go back and forth and feel at home in both places.

* * * * *

Now retired, Ossi worked as an economist for the Finnish government and in several different countries before moving to the United States to work for the World Bank. He has had his own consulting firm and worked as project manager for many international firms. He was elected president of the Finlandia Foundation National in 2013. Every five years, this organization sponsors a ski march in remembrance of the some 8,000 Swedish volunteers who contributed to Finland's defense in the northern sector in Lapland.

Notes

1. As stated in the Introduction, many Finns, including the Conservative and Agrarian parties, were opposed to sending children to Sweden, preferring to relocate them in the Finnish countryside. But discussion of the child transports was not permitted in parliament after 1942. According to Ossi, "There is a lot of documentation in Finland and Sweden about the discussions which took place for and against sending the children. It was not a free choice for every mother or family to send their children even if they wanted to. The first priority was given to those who had lost their fathers in the war, the second priority to those who had to be evacuated from lost territories, i.e. Karelia, and children who lived in specific danger zones, which was the case with my family."
2. Wounded soldiers were treated in field hospitals. The more serious cases, however, received care away from the front. Many went to convalescent homes if their wounds, such as serious head injuries, resulted in total incapacitation. Most of the other returning injured veterans had to manage on their own, as there were insufficient resources to care for them all. The recognition of need arrived much later, but those still surviving today are compensated with free transportation from wherever they happen to live to rehabilitation facilities in Finland.

28

God natt, sov Gott
Lea Rehula

I was born in Seinäjoki in Ostrobothnia in 1928 and was eleven years old when the Winter War began. Before the war my father worked as a supervisor at the post office in Seinäjoki where the employees were mostly women and young boys. My mother did not work outside the home, as she was busy caring for four children. Eila, my little sister, was born in 1929 and was one year younger than I. We had two little brothers. After the war, another sister was born.

My mother was skilled in sewing clothes, and she also had a garden with berries and vegetables, which were important to us during the war when food was scarce. She took good care of our small home, which was located near to the railway station. Like a lot of women during the war, she also knitted socks and mittens for the soldiers. Wool was regularly brought to women for this purpose. When the men were at the front, women also helped each other out, caring for each other's families. When the war began, my father was already forty-six years old, so he did not fight at the front but continued his work at the post office where he was needed.

Before the war my life was very stable. I went to school and played with friends and siblings. But everything changed on November 30, 1939. Air raid warnings sounded and school closed, so that all the children could run to bomb shelters. The nearest shelter for my family was a cellar in our neighbor's back yard, which accommodated three families. The cellar had been strengthened, and there were candles and seats because sometimes the alarms lasted a very long time. Every evening after the first alarms sounded, we arranged our clothing very carefully beside our beds, so that it could be found quickly in case of an attack.

Soon after the war began, it was decided that children should be sent to Sweden for their safety. Due to the war, schools had been closed, but our former teacher was the one to suggest that we should leave for Sweden, and authorities arranged for our flight. On February 3, 1940, when I was twelve and Eila was ten, we traveled by airplane from Vaasa to Sweden. Tragically, on the same day we left, twenty-seven Russian planes dropped bombs on Seinäjoki and ten people died. I remember being excited to leave, not worried.

In Sweden, we were taken care of by the Swedish authorities. For the first full day, we stayed in a schoolhouse, but I don't remember the name of the town. Then we were taken to the Finnish Aid Center to select things we needed or wanted. I picked out some dolls, which I still have. And for the second night, we were taken to Vasteras, a town near Stockholm, where we stayed at the local hospital for medical exams. I remember that Eila and I were eating a meal at a restaurant when we first met Carl Andersson, our future foster father. I never learned how much he knew about us beforehand, nor why he and his wife had volunteered to take us. They didn't know our parents. But luckily, we were the same age as the Anderssons' own children.

Mr. Andersson drove us to his manor house, "Häggesta," in Odensvi, which was some hours away. He could not speak any Finnish, nor we Swedish. But once we arrived, we were warmheartedly welcomed by his wife Elin, her sister, and the Anderssons' three young sons. We were also given our own room. At bedtime, *Tant* (Aunt) Elin, her sister Greta who lived with the family, and sometimes Edla—who lived in nearby Vasteras and also cared for a war child—came to say goodnight to us with the words *god natt, sov gott*.[1] As we did not understand Swedish at the time, we thought that *sov gott* ("sleep tight") meant *suukot* ("kisses" in Finnish).

I had only studied Swedish for one year at school, but I learned very quickly, as I spent most of my days helping my "aunts" around the house, dusting, setting the table, and cleaning up after meals. We also baked often, for instance cookies for charity fairs to help Finland. The baking table had a big round surface made of marble. And every Sunday when we dined in the parlor, we made a layer cake for dessert. The older sons were at school, but Eila played a lot with the youngest son, who was not yet attending. Eila and I went there sometimes for handicraft lessons, as one of the aunts was a handicraft teacher. We crocheted many blue and white potholders shaped like the Finnish flag that always sold very well at the fairs. The proceeds were sent to Finland to help with the war effort. A common slogan in Sweden at the time was *Finland's sak ar var* ("Finland's cause is our cause").

Mr. Andersson whom we called *Farbror* or "Uncle," was a farmer by profession, and on their large estate there was a wonderful garden that Aunt Elin cared for with great love. There was also a big barn for the cows where Uncle Carl worked with another man. They had many animals, but the aunts did not work around them. That was a man's job. When Uncle Carl came in for lunch, he always smiled in a friendly way and inquired about what we, the girls and women, had been doing. We ate very well at the Anderssons, sometimes even caviar.

There was a lot of snow that winter, and we were allowed to drive with the plow when clearing snowy roads, which was fun. Also, after the boys came home from school, we often went skiing. And in the evenings, we entertained ourselves with fairy plays by Finnish author Zachris Topelius. Uncle Carl recited poems by another Finnish author, J. L. Runeberg, who is the national author of Finland but who also wrote in Swedish. Uncle Carl had been taught these poems by his own uncle, and in his old age when visiting us in Finland we continued to recite them together. We also visited our foster parents' friends' homes. It was a full, rich life that was very enjoyable and comfortable.

When the Winter War was over on March 13, 1940, the plan was to send Finnish children back home if their families' living conditions were adequate. Because my and Eila's home still existed, it was decided that we should return. *Farbror* Carl drove us to Västeras on May 1, 1940, for the train journey home via Haparanda opposite Tornio in Finland. On this return trip, we older children helped to take care of the younger children. From Tornio we continued by train to Seinäjoki, traveling a distance of around 1,000 kilometers altogether. We actually arrived on our mother's birthday and we were very happy to be home, though we had had a wonderful time with the Anderssons. Our entire family was together again, and our home had avoided the bombing.

Because my sister and I had only been away for three months, we had not forgotten our native language, so the adjustment was quite easy for us. When we arrived in Sweden we had good clothes and didn't need new clothes during our stay there, though we must have received new rubber boots since Eila remembers accidentally kicking one of her boots into the river. But after we left, we received packages from the Anderssons, including fabric for dresses. We also received Christmas parcels with clothes. Because Swedes were not allowed to send new clothes, those we received were second-hand clothes from our foster cousins. When I had my high school matriculation in 1946, though, the Anderssons were somehow able to send me a new dress, which was wonderful. The first time my sister and I returned to Sweden to visit the Anderssons was in 1949 when one of our foster cousins got married. But in later years, both families visited one another, so our contact remained close over the ensuing decades. *Farbror* Carl died at the age of ninety-four in 1977, and *Tant* Elin died ten years later.

Because we were older when we left for Sweden, we understood the reasons for our going. We also always knew that we would return to Finland one day. Because our stay was comparatively short, we didn't have the language problems so many war children encountered upon their return. In later years, we were excited to visit the Anderssons but also pleased to return home. So I am able to say that both Eila and I enjoyed safe and happy childhoods, thanks to our good parents both in Finland and Sweden.

* * * * *

Lea worked for some years as a school teacher. Later she stayed at home with her and her husband's three children.

Notes

1. "Good Night, Sleep Tight!" in Swedish.

29

A Lifelong Exile
Kai Rosnell

June 4, 1942 was an historic day for me. That morning I stepped out of the ship *Heimdall* and took my first steps on Swedish soil, in Stockholm. It was a bright summer day, and I was surrounded by many other children like myself coming from Finland to find new homes away from the dangers of war. I remember nothing of the journey, nothing of how I got into the ship the previous evening. But I remember we were taken to some sort of hospital for examination to make sure we were healthy enough to be placed in private homes. Those who were found to have any disease were taken to a hospital or orphanages for further examination and care.

Of this day's happenings, no reports appeared in the Finnish newspapers. Instead, the big news in the *Helsingin Sanomat* and the Swedish newspaper *Hufvudstadsbladet* was that Marshal Mannerheim, Commander in Chief of Finland's defense forces during World War II, had received an unexpected guest to celebrate his seventy-fifth birthday. It was Adolf Hitler who greatly admired Mannerheim and had come to pay his respects to his companion in the war against the Soviet Union.[1]

I was nearly seven years old, born in Eurajoki in western Finland, close to Rauma and Pori. I was selected by my parents as the second of five sons to go to Sweden, to help relieve our family's relative poverty. My father worked different jobs, mostly manual labor, as he was very strong, but he also fished and hunted to help feed his family. My mother tended the house and children, but often helped the farmer who owned the land on which our cottage stood. We lived there in exchange for work, and often we children worked too, for instance in digging up potatoes. I understood why I was being sent and that I was to stay in Sweden for half a year and then come back.

In the hospital I lost my new long brown stockings, which had been sent to be laundered. Although our clothes were not burned, as many war children's were as a precaution against lice, ours got all mixed up so that none of us could find anything. Worse, I also lost contact with my neighbors from Eurajoki, Anneli and her younger brother Ilmo. The loss of Anneli affected me most because she was my secret love, the girl I fancied and had decided to marry. Nobody, however, knew about these plans, not even Anneli.

After a couple of days I was taken on a train accompanied by an elderly lady. According to the Register Lists, located in the National Archives in Stockholm where all the information about the Finnish war children is kept, I was one of a large group of children traveling that day on the same train – and that Anneli and her brother were there, too. However, that is incorrect; I trust my own memory more!

In Göteborg, the second biggest city in Sweden, I was handed over to another elderly lady, Gunhild Johansson, who took me to her home some ten miles away, where I was mostly taken care of by her daughter Gudrun, who was sixteen years my senior. There was also a son, Berndt, who was eight years my senior, and her husband, Erik, a tall, dark man who owned a grocery store in the village. I was asked to call my foster mother *Mamma* and my foster father *Pappa*. They had agreed to care for a Finnish child, and they had chosen a boy because they had lost a son some years before from appendicitis that had not been treated in time.

I did not know a word of Swedish, so I did not understand anything they said to me.

I remember my first night there: the woman took off all my clothes and put me in the bath where I stood stark naked in front of this stranger. I cried for my clothes: *Vaatteet! Vaatteet!* "Do you want some water?" she asked.

Though the son and daughter were very kind to me and helped me in every way, their mother was no good with children. Thankfully, the family had a small booklet with useful phrases in both Swedish and Finnish, such as *Onkho sinulla hauskha thällä* or *Onkho sinulla nälkhä*? ("Do you have fun here?" and "Are you hungry"? I have misspelled the Finnish intentionally to indicate that they could not pronounce the words properly). Thus, I learned Swedish fairly quickly.

I had been in Sweden for perhaps two weeks when I got a letter from home. Mother told me that I now had a new sibling named "Sisko," which means "sister." She was born just a few days after I had left. What a surprise! I knew where babies came from, but no one had told me that my mother was expecting. That was the first time I felt something like homesickness.

After three months, I began school. For the first few days, I just sat there and tried to understand what it was all about. My teacher, a charming old spinster, Cecilia Johansson, had the reputation of being quite severe and stern, but to me she was very kind, understanding, and helpful. She soon found out that I could already read, write, and count, so I was moved from first to second grade.

By Christmas, after half a year in Sweden, I spoke Swedish in the same way as all the other kids: nobody could say that I was not a native, because I had even learned the local accent.

Overall, I had a good time in Sweden. I was lucky in that my foster family was kind; they did not beat or abuse me in any way, though of course I had to help with chores, such as weeding the vegetable garden, drying the dishes, and so forth, like most children. I was also fortunate in that my destination and the family I would live with had been decided beforehand. Unlike many war children who traveled by train from station to station where adults arrived to choose their favorites—pretty little blonde girls were especially popular—I did not suffer this humiliation. Many children were overlooked at every stop, going all the way to the end station without being chosen. What message did this send to such children? "You are no good. You are worthless."

Figure 29.1. *Kai Rosnell (right) at age nine, standing next to his Swedish foster brother Berndt, who holds an accordion. Fall 1944. Courtesy Kai Rosnell.*

I was even treated kindly by the old man, my foster father, who let me watch him play chess with the neighbor. So in this way, I learned how to play chess.

Unfortunately, I got enough religion to last for a lifetime. Nowadays, I never go to church unless it is for a wedding or funeral. But I still like the old hymns, which are beautiful. One doesn't have to believe in the words.

There were two other Finnish children in the village. One was a girl my age, Raija-Liisa Nieminen from Pori, who lived with my foster father's chess mate. Later I found out that she had come on the same ship as I from Finland. The second was a boy, Pertti Korhonen from Hyvinkää, who lived with my foster father's brother. We spoke Finnish with each other to begin with, but were encouraged to speak Swedish in order to learn the language faster. So, gradually, all three of us forgot our Finnish.

When I returned one year later to Finland—by train all the way around the Gulf of Bothnia—I was happy to meet my parents at Pori railway station and recognized them immediately, but they seemed to have grown so small. I remembered them as being much taller. What really came as a shock, however, was that I could not understand them! I had forgotten my Finnish completely. It was hard to return home, feeling like a stranger in my own family and not being able to speak with my brothers and lovely little sister whom I was now seeing for the first time.

Evidently, though, my Finnish was not that far away. It must have been just beneath the surface because after a week, I could understand my family again and soon learned to speak with them too. When I started school later that fall, I had no problems at all.

If I had remained in Finland from the summer of 1943, I am sure that I should look back upon my time in Sweden in much the same way as most former war children: as the happiest time in their lives. Only pleasant memories.

But the war went on, and my mother had another little girl in October 1943, so that there were now seven children. Perhaps for this reason, when in the summer of 1944 I received an invitation to return to the same family in Sweden, my parents thought it would be a good idea. Not just for me, but for the whole family. So I agreed to go, thinking that I would again return to Finland after one year. My parents apparently sent me this second time because they felt that my Swedish foster parents truly liked me and would again treat me well. But many years later I learned that my mother also sent me in particular because she knew I "would manage."

My parents may also have considered the danger of Russian invasion and occupation, which Finns generally feared at this time: what would happen then, and wouldn't it be better to save at least one member of the family?[2] The end result of their decision, however, is that seven years passed before I saw my family again. I did not return until the summer of 1951.

Of my second journey to Sweden on September 1–2, 1944, I have very few but distinct memories. There were perhaps forty or fifty children on the ship, and I shared a cabin with five or six older boys. I became very seasick and vomited into some sort of vessel or pot. Evidently, my cabin mates didn't like the sound of my vomiting, and one of them took the vessel and poured its contents over me.

Back in Sweden, I fortunately did well in school and was considered clever and bright. Among all the students, in fact, I was the best at Swedish spelling. And this was one of the reasons for my extended stay: I recently discovered a letter from my mother written during this period to the Finnish authorities, asking for permission to allow me to stay in Sweden to finish my studies. In addition, there was tuberculosis in my family back home, which affected my father and three of the children. Two more children had been born in my absence. And my father probably suffered from post-traumatic symptoms, due to his wartime experience. He returned home in January 1940, after having been in the Winter War only one month, due to some serious illness that was never diagnosed. Even the ticking of a clock sounded like a hammer in his head. He had fought in the famous battle of Suomussalmi, which ended in Finnish victory, and he had witnessed terrible things.

Later, when his children asked about his war experiences and put the question to him about whether or not he had killed any Russians, he replied, "I didn't have to." But he related one story about how he'd come upon a circle of Russians, sitting in the deep snow around some dying embers and how they were very nearly frozen to death. One Russian was leaning against a tree with a rifle cross his knees who apparently could only move his eyes and soon died. My father and some other soldiers loaded the dead Russians onto a truck to bury them.

At age sixteen, I wanted to relearn Finnish, and upon my eventual return to Finland, one of my new siblings, my five-year-old sister Hento, became my best teacher—and went on to become a very competent and popular school teacher as an adult. I bought a dictionary and a grammar guide to study the structure of the language, and during those summer months I learned enough of everyday Finnish to get along.

I returned to Sweden and finished school, studying languages at the university with the intention of becoming a professor of language. During this time, I was not living with my elderly foster parents. Instead, I moved into their daughter's house when she married in 1953. To help out with the cost of keeping me, I had a job on the side, proofreading for a newspaper, which later offered me full-time work as a journalist. After, I worked at a Swedish news agency, then returned to work as a sports writer. My foster parents died in the late 1950s, but I kept in contact with my foster siblings as long as they were alive, and we shared many fine memories. I have also maintained contact with my Finnish siblings and visit our old home at least twice each year.

I married a Finnish girl in the mid-sixties, and we planned to move back to Finland and settle there. Though I searched for work as a journalist with the Swedish newspapers in Finland, no one was interested. My Swedish was impeccable but my Finnish was not. Thinking that the Finnish authorities would want their lost children back, I sought their help. But they refused any support. The war children were forgotten.

There is a lot of bitterness left among many war children who remained in Sweden, though for different reasons. During our long years in Sweden, war children lost all contact with the Finnish language and culture. We became strangers in our own country. Many are bitter towards their mothers who sent them and find it difficult to understand the reasons for their forced separations. Some 80,000 fates, all unique, ranged in degrees of happiness from Heaven to Hell. To me, the most tragic effect of the war child movement is that it separated and cracked families and family bonds, which in many cases were damaged beyond repair and could never be the same again. So, although some stories such as my own are relatively happier, taken altogether the war child operation was not a happy one.

For me, having been rejected by my native country when I wanted to resettle permanently in Finland, has made me feel like a life-long exile. This event left a thorn deep in my heart, and every time I touch the thorn, it hurts even more.

* * * * *

Kai worked for many years as a journalist in Sweden. Since his retirement, he has contributed a great deal of time to his war child association quarterly magazine, *Finska Krigsbarn,* which he has edited for thirteen years since 1999 and to which he has contributed innumerable articles. In the early 1990s, Kai visited the Swedish National archives in Stockholm to discover when and how he first came to Sweden, which led to his investigations on behalf of dozens of other war children who desired to find lost relatives and rediscover their roots. In doing this, he has reunited hundreds of people with lost family members in Finland and also Swedes who wanted to be reunited with former Finnish foster children.

Notes

1. Finland and the Third Reich have been described as "co-belligerents" in their war against the USSR. Mannerheim arranged for the meeting to occur in Imatra rather than Helsinki to avoid the appearance of an official state visit. And, though Hitler's purpose was ostensibly to pay tribute to Mannerheim, he had also come to ask the Finnish commander to intensify operations against the Soviets. For additional information about Mannerheim, see Sakari Virkkunen, *Suomen presidentit* [Presidents of Finland] (Helsinki: Otava, 1994).
2. Kai points out that this raises an interesting hypothetical question: had there been a full-scale invasion, would Russia have demanded that Sweden return all Finnish children, and how would Sweden have responded to this?

30

Take the Bed Down!

Gertrud Rullander

Those who have made a journey always have something to tell. My journey began when I was born in 1938, one year before the war started. I was the fourth child of my parents, Helmi and Toivo Auvinen. He was not the typical Finn in appearance, but more of a gypsy with black curly hair and dark eyes. My mother was also unusual with one blue eye and one brown, and I remember that I could gaze at her eyes forever. My two oldest siblings were my brother Unto and sister Anya. Urhu, my second brother, was only one year older than I. Finnish names often have interesting associations. My mother's name, "Helmi," means "pearl," and my father's name, "Toivo," means "wish." I was named "Terttu," which means "cluster" or "bunch."

My parents originally lived in Lahti but, during difficult times there, they moved to the nearby countryside where they had a farm, growing potatoes and so forth. Father also had some cows and a horse. We lived in an old house, and conditions there were very primitive. My father was a wonderful singer, and one of his many brothers, Pauli, sang in the opera. They often sang beautifully together.

Unfortunately, both were sent to the front after the war began. My father's job was to drive to the front with bombs, bullets, grenades, and other military equipment. Upon his return trips to Lahti or Helsinki, he transported dead soldiers to their home cities. His brother, Pauli, lost one of his legs, and my father was also seriously injured. Our house was small, so the children slept all together in one bed. When father was able to visit us during the war, my brother and I slept on the floor to make space for him.

My very early childhood was clouded by the war. I hated the bombing. I also hated the Russians for starting the war and for taking my father whom I dearly loved away to the front. Sometimes father was allowed to visit us, and I remember being so disappointed one Christmas when father couldn't come! In the middle of the night, though, we were awakened by the sound of his stomping to knock the snow off his feet. I remember another Christmas when we were all in the kitchen together and were so happy. Father was home from the front, and he brought me a wooden doll's bed that was painted green. My doll, which my mother had made out of cloth, was too long, so we bent her legs so that she would fit. Father also brought two candles and we celebrated together that night.

As a child I was ill with pleurisy, and there were no medicines available in Finland then. Once when I was very sick, the candles were lit just for me, and my siblings were jealous. Looking at the candles burn helped me to be still, which was difficult for me. Because I fidgeted all the time, my mother said that I had quicksilver in my legs! Like medicines, food was very scarce during the war, and on many days we went without food altogether. Mother worked during the day at a factory making uniforms for the soldiers, and my older sister Anya took me and my brother Urhu to kindergarten where we stayed until our sister picked us up. Urhu and I were very close because we spent so much time together. Sometimes when we were little, we'd go to a nearby military camp where young men were trained for a year before being shipped out of town to fight on the front. Sometimes we'd sing for them, and occasionally they'd give us a penny. When this happened we were so proud to take home extra milk money to mother.

Every day we heard bombs and had to run to a special cavern in mountain where there was some sort of mining operation. It wasn't a real room, but it was safer than the kindergarten school building. One by one, we ran across the schoolyard, not all together but one by one while our teachers yelled, "Run, run, as fast as you can!" Our teachers didn't run with us because if the airplanes saw too many people on the ground, they might assume that it was a military camp. This is why we ran one by one. I never liked that mountain slope where we ran for protection. It was dark and wet. And, after the bombs had fallen, it was very smoky. We screamed at the Russians, *Jättäkää meidät rauhaan, ryssät!* ("Leave us in peace, Russians!").

At some point during the war, my father returned home with pneumonia. His arms and fingers had been destroyed from cannon fire and were twisted from frostbite and rheumatism. It was a frigid winter, and his army clothes had not sufficiently protected him from the elements. He could no longer clutch things with his hands and was in constant pain for which he took all sorts of pills and powder in paper packets.

On weekends mother worked on Lahti Square at the *tori* ("market") where our grandparents sold fish. Early in the morning, grandpa bought fish from a fisherman's ship, then cycled to the square where mother and grandma sold them. Sometimes there was leftover fish, which mother brought home to us. In addition, we raised rabbits, and we played with them. I didn't know at that time they were also our food. I'd ask mother, what happened to a certain rabbit, and she would say, "Oh, he was so fast, he ran away!"

Because my mother worked all of the time, it was Anya's job to take care of me. When we were at the *tori* with mother in Lahti and the sirens began, mother told us to run home. But Lahti was more than two or three kilometers from home. So, once when the alarm sounded, we ran to the railroad station and to a nearby bridge. Beneath this bridge, there was a tunnel where people collected during a bomb attack. It was dark and we all stood very close to one another. Someone, a man, lifted my up onto his shoulders to make room for others. And when the second alarm signaled the end of the bombing, he said to us, "Have a nice day, girls!" Anya said he was an angel.

In the summer, it was Anya's and my job to find rabbit food called "worm roses." We must have picked thousands of these to feed our rabbits. Another job of ours was to go to the shop and fetch milk with a milk can. One day, some schoolmates of Anya's began to argue with her, so she said to me, "Go sit by the side of the road. I have to beat up these boys." I was so affected watching them fight that I accidentally kicked the milk can, and the precious milk ran out onto the road. Anya and I were worried about what to tell mother, so we told her a white lie and blamed it on the boys: it was they who kicked the milk can! In response, our mother went to the boys' mother and asked for a portion of their milk.

We also planted potatoes to harvest in the fall. One autumn day when my brother Urhu and I were digging up potatoes, he became angry and impatient with me because he thought I was working too slowly. But I wanted to find ALL the potatoes and was just being thorough. Urhu grew so irritable that he took his hoe and hit me over the head with it, making a gash in my head. Even today, I have no hair on that part of my head, due to this incident. Sometimes I'd show Urhu the spot, and he would feel bad.

One morning I awakened to an awful smell in the air and asked mother about it. She said that I should go to the window and look out. I was shocked to see that my playmate Lisa's house was gone. I asked, "Where is Lisa's house?" and mother replied, "The Russians wanted it." "But where is Lisa?" I asked. And my mother said, "She's gone to heaven." Then I hated the Russians more than ever. Lisa had had a doll, which I liked better than mine. One day I found it in a ditch and I asked mother, "Why didn't Lisa take her doll with her?" And mother replied, "She doesn't need it in heaven." So I asked her if Lisa would want me to have it, and my mother answered, "Of course."

The winter of 1944 was a bad time. We could never take our clothes off because of the constant night bombing raids. One night when we didn't have time to go to the shelter, we sat in our *kuisti,* the cold porch in front of our living room where we took off our shoes and boots before entering the house. It was very cold, and I began to cry because I wanted to go back to bed. But father said, "Don't cry today; cry tomorrow. If the Russians hear you, they will come in and shoot us." After the bombing, we discovered a hole one-half meter across. It was shining red and molten, and it was only three or four meters away from our house. I was distressed to see that father was crying and asked, "Why are you crying, father?" He responded by saying, "We're allowed to cry now because that bomb could have hit us, and then we'd be in heaven with Lisa."

Due to these events, my parents began to discuss sending Urhu and me away to a safer place. Everybody was talking about *Ruotsi* or "Sweden." I didn't want to go, although my sister Anya and brother Unta were jealous; they understood that in Sweden there would be meat and food to eat. But I was afraid until Unta asked if I would prefer to be bomb *ruokka* ("food" for the bombs).

In the early spring of 1944, when I was five and a half years old and Urhu was six and a half, we were awakened one morning by our mother to go to the railroad station in Lahti, where Anya and I had earlier hidden from bombs. All the children there were weeping, and when Urhu's and my names were called, mother put us in the long line of children. The steam train was spouting black smoke. I was very miserable with pneumonia and was very sensitive to the fumes. Someone lifted me up onto the train. A second bell then sounded, and the train began to move. I wanted to say something to mother and looked for her, but she was nowhere to be found. I started to scream, "*Äiti! Äiti!*" ("Mother! Mother!") and to run through the train, but a lady in a gray uniform with Red Cross insignia on her sleeves took me back to my wagon. I complained to her that my mother wasn't there! And in a cruel icy voice she said, "Your mother is not *supposed* to be here."

I felt abandoned and cheated because I believed mother would be coming with us. I apparently screamed for three days until my brother Urhu warned me that the Russians might hear me and come after us. Father had made wooden name tags for Urhu and me, and I tried to discard mine and was scolded by our caretakers who said that without my tag, no one would know who I was. I remember saying in return, "I know who I am. I know my name, so I don't need this!" (Today, I would give anything to get my name tags back, but after I was placed with a Swedish family, my foster mother one day asked me if I wanted to keep my few belongings from Finland, including my name tags, some trousers, and other old clothes. She had stored them in a little shed outside and seemed to imply that they were rubbish. In order to make her happy, I put them in the stove, and they were irretrievably gone.)

The train began to smell very bad because many children messed their pants. The women taking care of us had to wash our bottoms and give us new trousers. I happened to be wearing a dress made by my mother with red buttons on my shoulders. Even though my mother had made it from an old man's trousers, it was the most beautiful dress I had ever seen, and I was worried about it getting dirty and spoiled.

We came to Vasa, where we had to wash up in the bathing house and be treated for lice in our hair. All the kids were washed except me because somehow my foot had become stuck between two wooden boards on the floor. Though I was only five and very thin, the ladies shouted at me, "You're the biggest one here, so you must wash yourself. March away and make yourself clean." I tried to explain that I was stuck and that my foot hurt very badly. And their response was, "Well, then, you'll have to go to Sweden dirty as you are." So I arrived in Haparanta, the Swedish border town, dirty and smelling awful in my new ruined dress.

In Haparanta we changed trains and boarded Swedish wagons in which we could look out of the windows, because they hadn't been painted black like those in Finnish trains. From there, we traveled south with many children getting off along the way. In Sunswaal in the middle of Sweden, Urhu and I were taken off the train, and a bus took us to a school in the city where we stayed for three weeks. I was in very bad condition, suffering from malnutrition and pneumonia. Also, I had screamed so loudly on the train that my throat had become inflamed and I couldn't speak.

After I was cured, Urhu and I again boarded a train in Sunswaal and travelled about one hundred kilometers west to Ange. At the railroad station there, people came and looked and read our labels. There were Red Cross women and others helping out. After reading my label, a lady named Birgit Sarbeck took my hand, and pulled me up off the floor where Urhu and I were sitting. She said, "This is my girl." At this, Urhu began jumping up and down and screaming at the woman, "You go to Hell! If you touch my sister again, I'll hit you. You go to Hell as fast as you can!"

Urhu at that time was very cute. While I had dark skin and hair, he had white-blonde hair like a little angel. It must have been bizarre to see my brother, this little angel, screaming swear words in Finnish, but he had been told by mother never to leave me. The woman read his label and suddenly understood: he was only watching over me, per our mother's instructions.

We all sat down together, and my future foster mother held one of my hands and smiled at me. Urhu held onto my other hand. Another woman, Anna Karlsson, said that she would take Urhu. They tried to make us understand, but Urhu wouldn't listen. So I said to him, "They don't look like bad people. See how kindly their expressions are." But he was distrustful: "They look nice, but how do you know they don't have Russian bombs?"

"No, no," I said. "They don't look Russian, and they aren't wearing uniforms." Some discussion ensued, which we couldn't understand. Nor were there any translators on hand to help us. It was now April. A month had passed since I'd seen my mother, and I no longer screamed and cried for her.

It was a beautiful day, and I remember walking outside with our future foster mothers who both looked very nice to me. When we had to go our separate ways, the women tried very gently to explain to us that we would see each other soon. So Urhu and I parted, though we kept looking back at one another as we were led away. I tried to memorize the road he and his new mother walked down. In the days following, I often asked, "Urhu?" And my foster mother understood. Luckily, the Carlsons lived less than five hundred meters away, so we saw each other frequently.

Edith's husband, my future foster father, was named Gustave. Their house had nice furniture and a big kitchen. And the food! It was amazing to see so much food and such variety of food. I was used to eating potatoes and berries when they were in season. And rabbits. Unfortunately, I became very ill that first night at the Solviks. When I pointed to a sandwich, Edith said "*Ja*" and gave it to me to eat. Then I pointed to an egg, and she said "*Ja*," and gave it to me to eat, and so on. During the night I got very sick with a fever and suffered throughout the following day. After this, I wasn't given so much to eat. A doctor advised my new parents not to overfeed me because Finnish children had been underfed for so long and couldn't handle normal meals.

Gradually I learned a little Swedish by asking, "What's that?" And *Mamma,* as I soon came to call her, would answer, "stool," "wood," "table." My brother didn't learn as quickly, so I often translated Swedish into Finnish for him.

One year later, when the war ended in 1945, Finnish children were supposed to return to their families. One day Urhu went away. I can't remember when exactly when, but suddenly he was just gone. Before he left, he had begun school in Onge. But I hadn't because of my age. I adapted to my life in Sweden and don't remember thinking much about Finland at this point. I had everything I desired: food, dolls, and the freedom to play. My foster parents had a son who was thirteen years older than I and living elsewhere. Occasionally he came to visit, and I would wonder, "Who's he? What is he doing in our house?" So within a year I had come to feel like *Mamma*'s and *Pappa*'s daughter.

My Swedish *Pappa* worked for a co-op that assisted people in need. There were many such co-ops where poorer people could buy goods for less, and Gustave was the supervisor for several such shops in and around Onge, while *Mamma* was at home, cooking and so on. People used to say at the time that taking in a Finnish war child was mostly an upper-class thing to do and referred to the practice disparagingly as a "hobby." Though war children were sent to poor families, too, it was often wealthier Swedes who took in foster children.

Pappa was more affectionate toward me than *Mamma* Edith, who couldn't have any more children after her son was born. She was thirty-nine at this time and *Pappa* was forty-four. Both of them wanted a girl and wanted to keep me. So they contacted the Red Cross to inquire about adopting me. I was also very attached to them, though *Mamma* was rather strict. But my Finnish parents wanted me back. Discussion over this issue continued for three years. Finally, at age eight and one half, and after finishing the first and second grade, I was told that I would have to return to Finland, the prospect of which I found very exciting.

Edith and Gustave accompanied me home to our old 1800s farmhouse. We brought many parcels with us: my bicycle, toys, clothes, and all the things they had given to me. *Pappa* and *Mamma* cried a lot throughout our journey. They also repeatedly asked me if I wanted to stay with them or return to my Finnish family. I felt divided, torn in half by these two families. I think that I longed to stay with my Swedish parents, but for some reason I said that I would stay here in Finland. My old Finnish home looked awful. There was only one road, nothing more, and two other farmhouses in the vicinity. But I thought, ok, I *have* to stay here, because this had been the reason for the long journey with my foster parents. When we first arrived at the farmhouse, I had clearly forgotten what my mother looked like and hugged a woman whom I thought was my mother. But Urho said, "No, no, that's not our mother. The woman you're hugging is just a neighbor." Edith and Gustave stayed for a week in our crude house as our guests. Knowing my parents wanted me back, they didn't try to talk my parents into letting me be adopted because they knew it would be futile.

After a week my foster parents were due to return to Sweden by way of Lahti where they would get a train to Turku and from there a boat to Stockholm. When they left, they cried copiously, but I tried not to cry because I wanted to be tough. I remember that I ran into the forest and sat there for hours, crying. But as it began to get dark, I knew I had to go return home. Urho came looking for me and sought to reassure me. But I felt that I had made a bad decision when I saw my Swedish parents off. I had forgotten my Finnish, so Urho was the only one I could talk to, and he tried to explain that everything would be fine, that I would like my new school, and that I would get used to being back home.

When school began I went with Anja and Urho to the sea, where there was a boat. Then we rowed to another island where another boat took us to the coast of a third island where the school was located. We were in the same class with students of all different ages, and the same teacher taught this mixed group. I had forgotten my Finnish, and I couldn't understand a word. I could only understand figures and count. I was sent back to the first class to learn to read and write, which upset me very much at the time.

None of the other children talked to me at school. Instead, they spat on me and resented the fancy clothes and shoes from Sweden that I wore. My schoolfellows had nothing to compare with my clothes, so they were angry at me almost every day. That winter when I received new skiing equipment from my Swedish parents, one of the students broke my ski poles and skiis and put them in the tiled stove to burn them up.

I also argued with my teacher who reported back to my parents. Eventually, they began to think that I had become "too Swedish" to adapt, and they began to wonder if they should send me back. In addition, my parents in Sweden repeatedly asked if there was a possibility of this. Meanwhile, I dreamed of returning to my family and friends in Sweden. I had only Urho to talk to. And, though I tried to talk in Finnish, my teacher would say, "That is not the correct pronunciation. Don't talk like that."

Sometime during this difficult adjustment, my Swedish parents phoned. The connection was bad and very crackly, but when they asked me if I wanted to return to Sweden, I said, "Yes, yes, I want to come back to you." Then one day my father asked me if I wanted to go back to Sweden, and I replied, "Yes, yes, yes, yes!" I was taken to the doctor to see if I was healthy enough, and to prove I was healthy, I climbed all over the office furniture! So, finally, my parents relented, and I flew from Helsinki to Stockholm. My Finnish parents were clearly attached to me and didn't want me to leave, but they were so poor. They hadn't any money. There was little food for us. On the day I was due to return to Sweden, I jumped and screamed, "Hurray," and both of my parents cried. I said to them, "Don't cry. Not now! Now we should be happy," which made them cry even more. I couldn't understand why they were crying when I was so happy. But of course they were crying because they had officially given their permission to let me be adopted and to lose me forever.

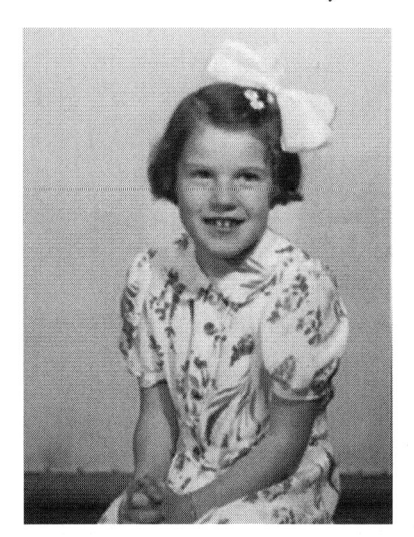

Figure 30.1. *Gertrud Rullander at age seven. Courtesy Gertrud Rullander.*

My father brought me to Helsinki where we stayed for a night with one of his brothers, probably Pauli with the lost leg. Then my father brought me to the airport where an official for the Red Cross said, "I will look after her." So I sat with this lady, and I was so happy because she could talk Swedish. I can't remember whether I kissed my father goodbye. But this was the first time I had flown, and I was so excited. My parents in Sweden had been informed that I was coming. But *Mamma* was still very anxious that something would prevent my return and had refused to take my old bed from the attic until she knew for certain that I was back. I was the last one to depart the plane, and there stood *Pappa* Gustave, waiting for me. When I finally reached *Pappa,* he took me in his arms and said, "We have to run!" I didn't know why. But he found a telephone box and made the shortest call in his life to Edith, saying, "Take the bed down. She's back."

It was a long journey to Onge of several hours, but I was so very happy! And now that *Mamma* knew I was with Gustave, she phoned everyone: all my old school friends and even friends of friends. To my delight, when we got in Onge very late that night, perhaps at 10 or 11 PM, there was a crowd of people, at least twenty-five or more, to welcome me back: "Welcome back, welcome back!" I felt like a movie star.

Some time after this, the adoption was finalized. I didn't see my Finnish parents again as a small child. But when I was in the fifth or sixth grade, my Swedish parents bought a Volvo, and we drove from Onge up to Haparanda and down to the farm outside Lahti. It wasn't the same place I had left. They were doing a little better at that point in time. At age thirteen or so I also understood better that I somehow belonged to both of these families. I spent the rest of my life growing up in Sweden, and there was only one more time that I visited my Finnish family as a young girl. Later, after I had children of my own, my new family visited Finland almost every summer. Both my Finnish and Swedish fathers died in 1982.

Long before my Swedish parents died, they left me their summerhouse where I had so often fished with Gustave. In later life, when I phoned my mother in Finland, she would always ask, "When are you coming? Are you coming this summer?" And when I phoned my Swedish parents from Finland, they asked, "When are you coming?" All four parents wanted to have me: there were arms to hold me in both Sweden and in Finland.

I was very happy and proud to have my name changed to the Swedish "Gertrud," because before that everyone always asked why I had the curious name of "Terttu."

Many war children were saved by going to Sweden where we received life-sustaining food and a good education. But in the process, many of us lost our souls. We feel neither genuinely Swedish nor Finnish, and many of us have suffered from a lifelong emotional division as a consequence of our war experience.

* * * * *

A celebrated natural healer, Gertrud is still living in Sweden. Her homeopathic approach to medicine has been much discussed in the media, and she has appeared on numerous television and radio programs. She also produces clothes from labels, for instance a blouse made from 250 manufacturing labels, and has had her clothing exhibited in Stockholm. She married for the first time in 1957 and had three children, but divorced in 1975. She remarried in 1979 to Lorentz Rullander who is now deceased. Gertrud is retired in Nora, Sweden.

31
Waiting for the Time to Pass
Irma Saarinen

I was born in 1939 in southern Finland in a town called Hämeenlinna. Though it was small, Hämeenlinna was a center for military depots—weapons and so forth—so it was often bombed. When the Winter War began, my father was twenty-seven and a humanist and pacifist. He worked at a leather factory, and was not inclined to be a hero. But in the middle of one night, there was knocking on our door and he was told to dress and join the artillery. He was stationed on Karjalan kannas, a neck of land south of Lake Laatokka in south-eastern Finland, and was wounded twice but survived. After the war, he sometimes talked about the war and how he and his comrades shared everything they had and how terrified he was that he would die.

My mother stayed at home throughout the war to care for the children since my older brother Seppo, younger brother Pekka, and I were very little. We didn't have much to eat, and I was very thin and often sick. To earn a little income during the war, my mother worked packing pipe tobacco, which she did in the potato cellar of the house that we rented. The cellar also functioned as a bomb shelter during bombing raids, or sometimes we ran into the woods. My mother was a very calm and balanced person, which is perhaps why I don't remember the bombing attacks as very frightening.

I was five years old in the spring of 1944 when my mother was contacted by authorities who instructed her that it would be better for her to send her children to Sweden. She tried to explain to Seppo and me that we would be better off living in Sweden while the war continued. Seppo was seven years old at the time and thought this prospect sounded very exciting, but I didn't really understand that we would leave without our mother and that we would be separated from her while we were away.

I will never forget the day Seppo and I left Hämeenlinna by train. When I realized that my mother and little brother Pekka wouldn't be coming with us, I fell into a panic and cried and screamed. My mother cried too. I was crushed and crestfallen on the journey that took us to northern Finland and from there to Sweden. When we left home, I had been wearing a white blouse and a red skirt, but somewhere along the journey, my clothes had been replaced with new ones, which I didn't like. In Sweden, I believe that we were first accommodated in a schoolhouse. My mother had told Seppo that he should never separate from me, but I didn't see him at all for several days, perhaps because the boys and girls had separate dormitories where we were given medical examinations.

After pausing in this place, what followed was a series of train trips from one location to another. We seemed constantly to be on the move until finally I became numb to what was happening. I do not remember whether Seppo and I were reunited on the train, but I remember seeing him at one of the stations.

After some weeks of travel, a woman met me at the last station. I don't remember being selected at random out of a group, so I believe that my foster parents had previously committed to taking care of me. I was brought to Karlskoga, a small town in the district of Värmland in southwestern Sweden, where I met my new foster parents: a middle-aged, childless couple named Maj and Robert Gummesson, who took me to their home. Since I spoke no Swedish and they spoke no Finnish, I didn't understand that I was there to stay. Instead, I thought that I would soon be moved to the next place, wherever that might be. For this reason, I resisted going to sleep that night and for several nights to follow, worried that I would be traveling again to yet another place. But eventually I came to realize that I would be living here for at least some weeks or months. Meanwhile, my brother had gone to live with an elderly pair in Villingsberg, a couple of miles from Karlskoga.

Everything was very different from what I was used to. My foster parents, *Tant* (Aunt) Maj and *Farbror* (Uncle) Robert lived in a very big house, the finest in the whole town. Robert was an engineer, working at Bofors, a factory that produced bombs and all kinds of weaponry. He was also something of a self-made man with many hobbies. Maj was a housewife who was helped by a housemaid, Greta, who came to clean the house once a week and who talked to me and let me help her. Maj had a very different personality from Robert and was often sick and depressed. I believe that she had suffered some nervous collapse because she was so often sad. Her family was very wealthy and sometimes visited. She had a brother whom Robert didn't like and an Aunt Olga, a retired teacher who was very strict and frightened me.

I came to like my *Tant* who sometimes played the piano and sang to me. But I don't remember she or *Farbror* ever reading to me, playing with me, or tucking me into bed. Instead, I was given lots of fine toys and nice clothes. I had no photos of my own family and missed my mother and especially Pekka. Nor did I make many friends. When I met other children, I felt that they were not very nice to me. So I was a very lonely child during my time in Sweden. I had nothing much to do and remember just waiting for the time to pass.

Occasionally, I received letters from home because my mother had a friend whose language was Swedish. I don't remember how long it took, but it seems that I learned Swedish and forgot my Finnish fairly soon. Seppo's foster parents occasionally came to visit, since they thought I was unhappy and sad. They also brought me to visit them so that Seppo and I could be together sometimes. Unfortunately, my Finnish mother had no telephone, so I didn't receive phone calls from home. But even without photos of my mother, I never forgot what she looked like. I even remembered my father's face, though I hadn't seen him all that much when I was little.

I later learned both that my foster parents wanted to adopt me and that my parents wanted me back. Shortly before I left to return to Finland, they adopted a baby boy named Lennart.

After one and one half years of life in Sweden, my brother Seppo and I returned to Finland together, first by boat and then by train from Turku to Hämeenlinna. Neither of us was sad to leave Sweden and looked forward to being with our family again. I still remember the night we were reunited. It was very late in the evening and very dark. Mother and father were at the railway station and were terribly glad to see us, and I felt the same. At this point, I couldn't speak a word of Finnish, but my mother's Swedish-speaking friend helped out until Seppo and I relearned our native language. My brother had attended school for one year in Sweden, and his teacher there had said he was an intelligent boy. But in Finland, he was regarded as stupid in school because he didn't understand what his teacher was saying, though we both relearned Finnish fairly quickly.

Besides the language difference, there was a huge contrast in our standard of living with what we had experienced in Sweden. Our parents belonged to the working class and were very poor, like nearly all Finns after the war. Even when we had money, we couldn't buy anything because nothing was available. Despite this, most people were simply relieved that the war was over and believed in a better future. Our father was grateful merely to be alive. He often played with us and helped us with our hobbies. He also joined us in sports. I especially liked skiing and skating very much. I don't remember missing the toys or fine clothes that I'd had in Sweden, nor the big house and its luxuries. In Finland, I had friends to play with, which I had yearned for in Sweden. I think that the only thing I really missed was the good coffee. In Finland, there was no coffee for several years.

After the war, my mother had two more sons, Jukka and Eero. Unfortunately, Jukka died when he was little in an accident. I was eight years old at the time, and it was a fine summer morning. My father and Seppo were visiting our grandparents and my aunt in eastern Finland. In those days, most people didn't have phones, so it took some days before our father learned of Jukka's death. That morning, I had awakened early and was making some tea when my mother asked if I would go buy some milk for breakfast. As she was helping me to unlock the door, somehow little Jukka had come into the kitchen and reached for the pan with boiling water. I ran to my uncle's house as fast as I could. Although I didn't have any shoes on, I remember that I didn't feel the rough ground under my feet. My mother and aunt took Jukka to the hospital, and Pekka and I were simply in shock. We didn't see our mother again for many days while she stayed with Jukka. One morning, however, I awoke to see her and understood by her expression that Jukka had died. He is now buried in my hometown, and every Christmas Eve we went to the beautiful cemetery and lit candles for his grave. We never spoke of our loss, though, and life went on.

I visited Robert and Maj during the summer when I was eleven, and they often sent small gifts. Because I had studied Swedish for two years in school, I could still speak to them, and we had a nice visit.

This is what I remember of those years. Most Finns were grateful that the Swedish took care of Finnish children during the war. For a long time, however, no one talked about how shocking and traumatic it was for us to be sent away. Only when my generation became middle-aged did we begin to discuss our experiences, and finally some books came to be written by the *krigsbarn* or former war children.

* * * * *

Irma was a teacher by profession, teaching Finnish, Swedish, and English in high school and in junior high school. In the seventies, many Finns moved to Sweden due to high unemployment in Finland. Often, their children did poorly in school since they did not understand Swedish. To solve this problem, many teachers like Irma moved to Sweden. In Stockholm, Irma taught children aged six to nineteen. Irma was married and had one daughter, but was later divorced. Today she is retired and is a member of the Stockholm Finnish war child association that meets regularly and publishers a paper called *Medlems Nytt,* Member News.

32
Children's Prayers
Kaarina Siilasto

The war between the Soviet Union and Finland broke out in 1939 when I was three years old. My father was in the war, so when the area in southern Karelia came under Soviet occupation, my mother and three siblings had to leave our home. We were transported with many others on the cattle cars of a train that journeyed through the night with no light for fear that Russian bombers would see the train and attack it. Now and then, the train stopped so that people could answer nature's call.

Once we had arrived in a safer territory, our family had to move from place to place before we were able to settle down in the small village of Pälkäne in western Finland in the Pirkanmaa region. At first we lived in a small rented house with one room and a kitchen. Other evacuees often stayed in the house as well, so there could be up to ten persons living in this tiny crowded place. Later, though, we were able to get a house of our own with a little more space. After functionaries discovered our whereabouts, some of our furniture finally arrived.

The situation in Finland was critical, since the Soviet army was aggressively trying to occupy our country. For this reason, my parents decided to send my brother and me to Sweden. They wanted at least two of their children to survive in the event of a Russian victory. And Sweden had offered to care for as many war children as Finland could send.

Thus, in 1943, when I was seven, my brother and I with many other war children left on a ship bound for Sweden. To avoid Russian attack, the ship sailed during the night, using as little light as possible. It was very dark, and we were all terribly afraid. But none of us cried because we thought that Russian planes could hear us if we made any sound. Ever since that long journey on the dark and silent ship, I have been afraid of darkness.

Finally we arrived in Stockholm where we were in quarantine in a school for a few days. While we were there, we were all washed with powerful disinfectant, the smell of which I will never forget. Our hair was also cut very short for fear of lice. I had brought my dear doll with me, but it somehow vanished during this time. So did my clothes.[1] I soon received clean, new clothes, but I never saw my dear darling doll again, which was distressing to me.

From Stockholm we were sent to a city in southern Sweden called Jönköping where we all stayed in a schoolhouse for some time. A fence surrounded the schoolyard, and when the children were outdoors playing, strangers stared at us from behind the fence. I almost felt that I was an ape. After having gotten the necessary information about us, Swedish families came to select those children they thought they could cope with most easily. One childless couple chose me, but they didn't want my brother. Another family who lived in the countryside chose him, and so we were separated. I only met him once during my stay in Sweden, and this made me feel very sad.

My foster parents, Aunt Berta and Uncle Sven, had a very nice house situated somewhat outside of Jönköping. It had four rooms downstairs and two rooms upstairs that were rented by Aunt Berta's sister. Everything was very well kept in Berta's and Sven's home, unlike my own home in Finland. They had a small garden full of flowers and all kinds of vegetables that bloomed and grew in the summer. And there was never a single weed in their garden and yard. I could have helped with the weeding, but I didn't like it so much and nobody forced me to do it. Every Saturday, I raked the paths and made different patterns on the gravel, which I did enjoy. Sometimes I sat in the garden in a big tub filled with water and imagined myself swimming. Jönköping is located near Sweden's second largest lake, Vättern, in addition to two other lakes. I had learned to swim in Finland and wanted to swim in the lake. But Aunt Berta and Uncle Sven would not allow me to do this because the lake is very deep and its water extremely cold.

Uncle Sven worked in a paper mill, and Aunt Berta was a housewife. And though they belonged to the working class, they seemed to have enough money to lead a comfortable life. They were very religious people and kneeled every evening beside the bed and prayed.[2] I found it very odd because my parents at home never did this But I also learned to pray. First, I said aloud some children's prayers for the benefit of Sven and Berta, but then I silently prayed my own prayer: *Gode Gud, hjälp mig att jag inte kissar ner mig* ("Dear God, help me that I don't wet the bed"). I had done it the first night I was there but never afterwards, so maybe God heard me.

My foster parents were very loving and caring people, but I liked Uncle Sven more than Aunt Berta because she wanted to be my mother, and I knew that my real mother was in Finland. Berta was a very good cook, though, so I came to appreciate good cooking after the very poor food

I had been used to eating in Finland. Every week she baked lovely bread and buns and the most delicious cookies. All her baked products were kept in beautiful tins, and I sometimes took a cookie when Berta was outside. This hurt my conscience, but I prayed to God to forgive me, and I think He did.

In the winter I went to school. By this time I had spent all of one summer in Sweden, so I had learned enough Swedish to get along in school. I could hold my own ground, and the other pupils never teased me. Soon, I made many new friends there, and I also had a very nice teacher called Lilly who once invited the whole class to her home for a party. I had no difficulties with the assigned school subjects either. So, overall, I enjoyed my school days in Sweden. In addition to my school friends, I made friends with Aunt Berta's brother's many children of about my age. This family lived quite near my family, and we played together nearly every day.

When peace was established between Finland and the USSR, my parents learned that they could never return to Karelia because part of the peace agreement was that the Soviet Union now owned that territory. My parents had lost their old home forever.

I was now nine and had been in Sweden one and a half years. Aunt Berta and Uncle Sven wrote to my parents and asked if they could adopt me, and when I learned this I again prayed to God that my parents would take me back. Luckily, they answered that they wanted me and my brother to come home, which made me very, very happy.

Some time later, then, I returned to Finland. Unfortunately, I had forgotten much of my Finnish, so I experienced some language problems. Also, everything was quite different from what I had experienced and grown accustomed to in Sweden. After the war, there were terrible shortages of everything, food in particular. At the time, I just thought that my own mother couldn't cook as well as Aunt Berta! We also had little clothing and lacked building materials for our new house. Needless to say, no one had any money. I often compared my life in Finland with my life in Sweden and came to the conclusion that I had had it much better in Sweden. But, after all, I had prayed to return home and to my family. And at heart, I was happy to be home again.

When I was seven years old, I had to adapt to a new language, a new culture, new parents and friends, and to a religious way of living. When I was nine, I had to adjust to the Finnish way of living, another "new" language, new schoolmates, the prevailing poverty in Finland, and my family's poor circumstances. Perhaps the time in Sweden taught me something important: that you mustn't be afraid of new countries, new languages, new cultures, new families, and new friends. One should take them as a challenge.

* * * * *

Kaarina died in 2006. Additional information about her post–World War II life proved unavailable.

Notes

1. War children routinely describe the disappearance and burning of their Finnish toys and clothes, a customary precaution against lice and potentially contagious diseases. War trauma experts today realize that the destruction of these last tangible tokens from home contributed to the emotional and social pain endured by war children, as Veikko Inkinen states earlier in the Introduction to the present volume.
2. Jönköping is referred to by Swedes as the "Jerusalem of Sweden" due to its many churches.

33

"Send the Little Ones!"
Bodil Nordman Söderberg

I was born in 1939 in Helsinki. My first name, "Bodil," is originally Danish but is now a fairly common Swedish name. My family is Swedish speaking, so we belonged to the 6 percent minority of the Finnish population for whom Swedish was and remains their first language. Before and during the war, we lived in an apartment building in the center of the city on Bulevarden 10 where many of our relatives also had apartments. Because it had been built in the 1880s, it had high ceilings and large tile stoves with which to heat the rooms. The building—today mostly offices and an embassy—is located just across from the "Old Church," and I remember the church park being a nice place to play.

Our block was never directly hit by bombs, though most of the blocks around us were damaged to some degree. I remember one morning when everybody was happy because the Russians had bombed their own embassy by mistake, although Finns had to pay to rebuild it for them after the war![1] Many of the windows in our apartment house had been broken in the blasts, and my father marked on a map where the bombs had fallen everywhere around us. Somehow, though, our building remained intact. My older brother turned nineteen in January 1944 and was drafted into the army. The reason that my mother was reluctant to leave the city was in case he could ever visit us on furlough. My father was rather deaf and could not serve in the military, but was active in the civil defense. Before and throughout the war until his retirement, he worked for an insurance company with a degree in engineering.

Also in January my younger sister, Carin, was born, and for a couple of months after this we remained in the city. But there were so many bombardments in Helsinki that we finally had to leave and go to the countryside to our summerhouse west of Helsinki on an inlet of the Gulf of Finland, near the small town of Tammisaari. Many of our relatives did the same, though my uncle was head of the National Museum and had to stay in Helsinki with his wife. Otherwise, most of the women and children left the city.

In July 1944 my brother was on the Karelian front when things started looking really bad. He sent a message home: *"Send the little ones to Sweden!"* My mother took his advice seriously and took me and my sister Carin by boat from Turku to Stockholm that same month. Many children were sent in big groups without a parent to Sweden, but since my sister only was six months old, my mother was allowed to accompany us. Friends of friends had found me a place with an elderly widow in Uddevalla on the western coast. I was lucky that I traveled by private arrangement, since many children were picked at random by prospective foster parents. No one wanted to take a six-month old baby, however. My parents hoped to send my older sister, Inger, along to take care of Carin and also get her out of harm's way. But Inger was sixteen and, due to her age, had to work, filling in for the men who had been sent to the front. It was not unusual for farmers, too, to have to give up their horses, which were needed in the war. She worked on a couple of farms, at one point working alongside a Russian prisoner of war. They would have worked in the same general region as our summerhouse where grain, sugar beets, cabbage, potatoes, and hay were grown. As for my sister Carin, she was eventually placed in an orphanage in Uppsala.

I remember the boat trip from Turku to Stockholm, which was a safer and shorter route than that from Helsinki to Stockholm. I had my favorite rag doll "Tötterman" with me, and my mother had made her a nametag like mine, which we both wore around our necks. I had had the doll for at least a year by then and was very attached to her. She was called "Tötterman" because my brother and older sister had friends by that last name, and I had often heard it spoken. Unfortunately, one of these friends was killed in the war.

The cabins were very crowded, and when news was broadcast over the radio, there was a sudden hush, as every adult concentrated on listening. At that time, the situation at the Karelian front was extremely serious. My mother must have been beside herself with worry, but I don't remember feeling such apprehension. In fact, I don't remember having been afraid even during the bombings in Helsinki, though I can vividly remember sitting in the bomb shelter in our apartment building many times at night when the raids usually occurred. When we heard the sirens warning us to take cover, I always complained that we had to walk down to the cellar instead of taking the elevator! One older cousin who lived in the same apartment building always brought a tin of hardtack with her, and my mother always brought the same book to read to me, an old one that had belonged to her mother.

After arriving in Stockholm we went first to Uddevalla by train, then to a house on the coast where the lady who had agreed to take me in spent summer months. It was in the countryside, and I remember it as a beautiful place with interesting seashells. I think my mother probably spent a day or so with me there before she and Carin went to Uppsala and the orphanage. In retrospect, I can't understand how she could handle it, leaving her two little girls with strangers, having her eldest at the front, her husband in Helsinki where the terrible bombing continued, and her teenage daughter working on a strange farm somewhere in the countryside. Returning to Finland, she would not have known whether she would ever see me and my sister again. I remember her standing at the railing of the little steamboat that took her back to Uddevalla. I noticed she was crying, and I thought that was strange because it was supposed to be just "a little while" until we would be united. Originally I was only supposed to spend the summer with Mrs. Sanne and then be transferred to another family who had a little girl a bit older than I. Nobody warned me beforehand about this planned transfer, however.

I was quite close to my mother at age five, and I remember missing her a lot in the beginning, though the woman caring for me, Mrs. Sanne, was very kind. I called her *Tant* (Aunt) Greta. She had an adult son who was away studying, but she had a most wonderful kitchen helper, Gladys, with whom I spent a lot of time. I also spent some time with another war child, a Finnish-speaking boy, who lived at a neighbor's house. His foster parents could speak no Finnish and so were having difficulties. But because my family in Helsinki had a kitchen helper who only spoke Finnish, I was able to do some interpreting. My first translation job!

I spent about two months with *Tant* Greta when, towards the end of the summer, we took the steamboat in to Uddevalla one day. At the boat dock was a strange lady and a little girl whom I had never met. This was how they had planned to transfer me to the other family! I had just gotten used to my situation at Mrs. Sanne's and was somewhat over my homesickness. But upon realizing that I was being given away yet again, I completely lost it. I don't remember too much of what happened, but I apparently had sort of a "meltdown" and screamed and howled so hard that Mrs. Sanne changed her mind and said I could stay with her, after all.

My mother later told me that Mrs. Sanne had sounded quite pleased in her letter, describing the failed transfer. She was obviously flattered that I wanted to stay with her and she described with relish how miffed the other lady had become. But can you imagine not preparing a child for something like that? I was too young to understand the reasons behind the arrangement, of course, but this experience clearly traumatized me.

In September we moved to Mrs. Sanne's apartment in Uddevalla where I stayed until January or February 1945. My mother was able to call me on the phone about Christmastime, and I was so happy to hear her voice. But I had such a lump in my throat that I couldn't say a word. I remember my mother repeating, "Please say something!" She wanted to hear me speak, but I was too completely overcome with emotion to utter a single word. My mother and Mrs. Sanne corresponded regularly, and I have a collection of postcards that were sent from Uddevalla on which I wrote my name. I also liked to draw, and when I was reunited with my mother, she was amazed to see that my suitcase was full of drawings I had made over the months. She had been hoping, of course, for new clothes for me. However, Mrs. Sanne had taken good care of me. For instance, noticing that I was fond of cheese, we often shopped together at a delicatessen where the owner let me try various cheeses and I was allowed at age five to choose my favorite!

Although she was quite well-to-do, *Tant* Greta was quite eccentric in many ways. For instance, when my mother returned to collect me in early 1945, my foster aunt put me in the same paper shoes I had arrived in, which I outgrew in six months. But what I remember was the plane trip: this was my first, and it was so very bumpy that I became quite airsick.

Later in the spring my mother returned to Sweden to pick up my sister, Carin; however, Carin did not recognize her at that point, and my mother said that she screamed all the way back to Finland, as though she were being kidnapped! Carin had been at the orphanage for about ten months and was only one and one-half years old upon her return, so she has no memories of this time she was away. However, we believe that she had been taken very well cared for: the nurse who was her primary caretaker had a son of Carin's age and was very sympathetic. She and my mother stayed in contact for some time, and the nurse and son visited us in Finland one summer. She told my mother that if anything had happened to our parents, she herself would have adopted Carin.

Because our family spoke Swedish at home, I had no problems either in Sweden or upon my return. I merely acquired a somewhat different Swedish accent. Many of the children sent to Sweden had a very difficult time with the language difference both arriving there and returning to Finland, however. In the event that they stayed long enough, they completely forgot their native language. In my high school graduating class were many girls who, like me, had spent time in Sweden during the war. But those from Finnish-speaking homes experienced far greater difficulties, so that their parents often placed them in Swedish schools. I've admired the fact that they became completely bilingual, whereas I had to learn Finnish, a very challenging language, from scratch.

Although one of my first cousins was killed in the war and my brother was slightly wounded, our family came through. I'm glad that I was old enough during the war years to have some memories from that time. For instance, I remember what it felt and sounded like to walk on shattered glass, which covered the sidewalk after a bombardment. And I remember some of the foods and the almost constant *lack* of food. Back in Finland, I noticed that my mother cut the bread thick but put very little butter on it due to food shortages, whereas at Mrs. Sanne's, I had gotten used to just the opposite: thin slices of bread with lots of butter! After the war she stayed in touch with my mother and me.

I also received many postcards from Gladys, Mrs. Sanne's wonderful kitchen helper. I don't remember if Mrs. Sanne sent us packages, but I remember that in advance of one of my birthdays she wrote to ask what I would like her to send. It must have been shortly after my return to Finland because I actually asked for a box of sugar cubes, which I received and hid on the shelf of my closet, so that Carin wouldn't find them and eat them all!

Gladys introduced me to the Swedish custom of celebrating St. Lucia Day on December 13. She played Lucia, and I played her attendant. After returning home, I apparently wanted to continue this practice because my mother wrote to Gladys, asking her for details. In response, Gladys sent us the lyrics to the song we should sing and described the crown of candles that Lucia should wear. So my mother had a crown made for me, and we started the St. Lucia Day tradition in our apartment that year, which we have continued to this day. I practiced it with my children when they were little, and now my daughter observes the tradition with my granddaughter.

In the summer of 1952, returning from a trip to southern Europe, my parents and I went to Uddevalla to visit Mrs. Sanne. We saw her at her lovely summer place, and she seemed very happy to see us. It was a good thing that my parents sent the endangered "little ones" to a happier place during the war. I have nothing but happy memories of my time in Sweden.

* * * * *

Bodil graduated from nursing school in Helsinki in 1961 and came to the United States to work as an RN in Ann Arbor, Michigan, where her brother had settled earlier. She met her future husband in Michigan, and today they live in Marquette, Michigan, where Bodil owned and operated a gift shop for many years that specialized in Scandinavian imports. She and her husband are retired in Marquette and enjoy visiting with their three children and six grandchildren.

Notes

1. On the first day of the Winter War, November 30, 1939, Soviet bomber planes accidentally dropped bombs on the Soviet embassy in Helsinki at the corner of Bulevardi and Albertinkatu. The fire brigade was busy putting out fires all over

the city and only one bucket hose could be sent for this purpose. There is a story about an old lady passing at the time who asked the fireman hopefully, "Are you pumping gasoline on the fire?" This was an embarrassing mistake by the Soviets, but one that the Finns had to pay for at the end of the war. See "Axis History Forum," http://forum.axishistory.com/ (accessed October 25, 2013).

34

A Tale of Two Sisters
Marja Tähtinen

In 1939, when the Winter War broke out, I was four years old, and we lived in a house built on a hill outside Helsinki. I don't remember so much of that time except hearing the alarm and seeing lights in the clear sky, seeking Russian bomber planes. Ours was a working-class family. My father, Paul Särömaa, was a metal worker, and my mother Aili worked in a printing factory. When the war began, she was called to work in the government's printing factory, and my father was sent to the front, so he became a stranger to me until after the war had ended.

In 1942, during the Continuation War, my mother who had a full-time job in Helsinki decided to move with me and my younger sister Sirpa, then five years old, to one of the big wooden houses that my grandfather had built and where all our relatives lived near the center of Helsinki and where my grandmother could take care of us. We had only one room and no conveniences, so it was very primitive. The house was on a rocky hill, and there was a bomb shelter built into the rock.

In February of that year, the bombing in Helsinki was very heavy. Because of our mother's full-time work, she decided to send Sirpa and me to Sweden when I was eight and my sister was six. I thought it would be an exciting adventure, for in those days we knew nothing outside of home and school. On a cold February day, we all went to the train station where many children and mothers were crying, and my mother's last words to me were: "Take care of Sirpa." The conditions on the train were not comfortable, as we had to sleep on the floor or on the baggage shelves. Finally we came to Tornio in northern Finland, where we crossed the river on foot to the Swedish train in Haparanda; then the journey continued. What a difference between trains! The seats were soft, and the food we were given was good. We were then taken to a garrison in Umeå in northern Sweden, where we were examined by doctors and given shots against diphtheria. Our clothes were burned and we were bathed. Unfortunately, I had a rash on my legs, so I was taken to a hospital where they scrubbed them very harshly. My little sister was very unhappy when I disappeared, but she was relieved to see me come back.

We waited together for Swedish families to pick us up, and it was not very long before this happened. Sirpa's "family" and mine were friends, but we saw each other very little during our time in Umeå. I can't remember separating from her, but it must have been difficult since our mother had told me to look out for her. My family lived in the center of the city, and Sirpa's on the other side of the river. Her foster family had no children, but mine had a daughter one year older than I named Berith who had many toys and colorful books. Unfortunately, she got scarlet fever shortly after I arrived and was taken to the hospital. Even though I could not understand Swedish at that time and had never had the disease myself, I remember thinking that it was somehow my fault. Once, when we went to the hospital together to visit her, my foster parents brought grapes, something I had never seen before in my life and was not allowed to taste.

My Swedish parents asked me to call them *Mamma* and *Pappa*. There were so many strange new things to assimilate: the foreign language, which I did not understand a word of, is just one example. Many children had brought small Finnish-Swedish dictionaries, but I didn't have one. Also, my new family lived in a house with many rooms, beautiful furniture, a bathroom, a French bulldog, and a housemaid. The family also had a car and a summerhouse. My biggest problem was that I did not eat butter. As a small child, I had eaten so much butter that I developed a serious reaction to it and couldn't eat it. But my foster parents, trying to give me nourishment, put a great deal of butter on my bread. However, this problem was nothing next to my homesickness.

I was a shy and sensitive child, but I possessed Finnish *sisu* or determination. I remember being ashamed to be Finnish and to speak the Finnish language, though my foster parents often asked me to say something in Finnish. I refused. Why did they need to hear me speak my native language? Swedish sounded like music to me, and they wanted me to translate Swedish words into Finnish, which didn't make sense. Once, *Mamma* asked me to sing a song in Swedish and when I refused, she almost slapped me. My foster mother didn't like my stubbornness and said, "We shall take the Finnish *sisu* out of you!" However, they never beat me. I liked *Pappa* better because he was always kind to me. The family owned a store where they sold radios and beautiful crystal chandeliers.

Because I was so homesick, one winter day I took the kick-sled and fled, determined to find my way back to Finland. After that I had to wear the carbon label around my neck during the journey to Sweden, although I cannot remember how long the trip took.

Because of my terrible homesickness, I also wrote letters to my mother to come and fetch me. I even wrote to my father at the front to please come take me home. And he replied, but due to the censors, there was not so much in his letter that I could still read. Unfortunately, there are no such letters left. I know that my Swedish foster parents had one of them translated into Swedish, and perhaps they destroyed them after that. Not very fair!

Summer came, and we moved into the summerhouse where I had to do many chores I was not used to doing in Finland. For instance, I had to ride a bicycle to buy milk at the store, and it was a long distance away. I also had to carry fresh water from a spring and clean the rooms and do the dishes. *Mamma* called me her little "cellar maid" because the food she told me to fetch was stored in the cellar.

In September I started school and did not have any difficulties. In fact, I once read a Swedish poem before an audience, and it was a great success. Some time later my school teacher in Umeå even told *Mamma* that "the Finnish girl is my best pupil!"

Meanwhile, Sirpa was having a very sad time. Her memories are vague, but she remembers the day we were separated quite vividly. First, she was very upset when I was taken away because it was believed that I had a communicable disease, though it turned out to be eczema from my allergies, and I was brought back. Families had been asked if one would be willing to take two children, since we would be happier staying together. But this didn't occur. Instead, two families who knew one another and lived in the same town of Umeå arrived. Sirpa was disappointed because she would have preferred to go with my future foster mother.

Although Sirpa has chosen to forget most of what happened to her in Sweden at age five and six, she remembers being sent to the store to buy milk and slipping on the ice on the way back and losing the few pennies of change she had in her mitten. Her "mother" sent her back in the freezing cold to find the few pennies in the snow. Another memory she has is of the time when she was chosen to be one of St. Lucia's attendants, a very big honor for a six-year-old war child! Mothers had been asked to sew simple white gowns made from sheets for the attendants to wear. But Sirpa's "mother" just sat and cursed and pricked herself with the needle, then threw the sheet across the room and started screaming and cursing at my sister.

Sirpa and I stayed in Sweden for fifteen months, and in May 1945, after the war had ended, we left our foster families. I cannot remember anything about this separation. Nor do I remember the return journey to Finland, first by train to Stockholm, then by boat to Turku, and finally by train to Helsinki. I was so happy to see my mother at the railway station in Helsinki and to return to our one-room apartment. It was small, but it was *home*. Sirpa no longer remembered any Finnish, so we spoke Swedish together and regarded this as our shared secret thing. Knowing Swedish was very useful later when we attended a Swedish-speaking school in Helsinki. Sirpa, however, remembers how very frustrating it was not to be able to speak to her own mother upon our return and also how we were discriminated against by other children who called us *hurri,* a bad name for Swedish-speaking Finns. To a certain extent, we didn't feel comfortable either with Swedish-speaking Finns or regular Finnish children.

I often wonder how my experience in Sweden affected my character. I was very shy in school and had a strong inferiority complex after returning to Finland, and sometimes wonder if this was due to my war child experience.

The war also dramatically changed my father, who became an alcoholic. The government gave veterans sites outside of Helsinki where new homes could be built. So in 1948, we moved to a new home, but it was unfinished because there were no building materials available after the war. In 1952, my parents divorced, and my father eventually remarried.

Sirpa and I returned to Sweden in the summer of 1946, and I alone in the summer of 1947. I have been in touch with my foster sister, and we still write to each other at Christmas.

* * * * *

Marja studied languages at the University of Helsinki. She was married and had three children, but was later divorced. After this, she moved from Turku to Helsinki where she worked at an employment office, retiring in 1998 at age sixty-three. She was remarried in 1990 and saw much of the world with her second husband. In 2010, they moved to Turku to be near Marja's children, but her husband died shortly thereafter. Marja further pursued her studies and received a higher degree. Her sister Sirpa was married in 1962, and she and her husband moved to Los Angeles and later to San Francisco where they are retired today. She has two sons.

35

Swedish Fish
Rolf J. E. Tarvala

My father, Jarl Viking Tarvala, born in 1911, was a serviceman at an ESSO gasoline station when he received his military mobilization order in 1939. After training, he was transported to the eastern front near Viborg (then "Vipuri"), his birthplace. The Winter War began in November 1939, and my father's job was to bring food to Finnish troops closest to the enemy. To do this he used horse-drawn wagons. A standing order required soldiers always to carry their rifles with them. My father felt that carrying the rifle on his back was very awkward while he transferred food from the wagons to the soldiers, so he asked if he could carry a pistol instead and leave his rifle in the wagon. He was allowed to do this, but he had to buy the pistol himself, because the Finnish Army was too poor to provide him with an additional weapon.

At the end of January 1940 my father was given a three-day leave. He was extremely tired when he arrived home and spent most of his leave sleeping. One day, however, I went out shopping with him. The winter of 1940 was extremely cold; temperatures dropped to –40 C or even lower, so he wanted to purchase some warm clothing. He also found a suitable pistol, and the local police station gave him a license to carry it. These were thrilling moments in my life. But I could not guess that they were the last moments I would ever spend with him.

After returning to the front and during a bombing raid on March 11, 1940, my father was severely wounded near Vipuri. After receiving first aid, he was transferred to a military hospital in Luumäki-Taavetti, where he died two days later at noon. My mother was tremendously sorrowful and depressed. On April 1, 1940, my father was buried in Hämeenlinna, our hometown.

After my father's death, our family received a small pension from the state, and ESSO Oil, my father's former employer, paid his salary to the end of 1940. Our grandparents could help us only occasionally, but I was able to visit them for short periods of time in Tampere.

My mother Aino kept a clothing store. When the Continuation War began in June 1941, food and supplies almost disappeared in Finland. Wholesale merchants stopped selling notions such as socks and underwear altogether, so my mother could only find odds and ends to sell, which didn't provide enough income for us. We began to feel desperate. It seemed like the end. I had quit going to school, as all the schools were closed due to the war.

As a neutral nation, Sweden could not officially offer military help to Finland during World War II, but the Swedish government organized a war child exchange program modeled on a similar program used during World War I. Their offer to Finland was that it could send up to 100,000 children to Sweden. My mother decided to send me in advance of any conflict, and possibly my other siblings (a younger brother and sister) later. Because I had been orphaned, my passage to Sweden was assured. I was nine years old when I left Finland and had only a little previous experience of traveling by train: once to Helsinki, a trip of about sixty miles, and once to Tampere, a trip of about forty miles. The trip by train to Turku, then by ship to Stockholm, therefore became one of the great adventures of my life.

On November 11, 1941, an elderly lady who was a friend of my mother's brought me to the railway station and train. I had no friends to travel with, and I do not remember very much about my journey to Turku, but I remember the excitement in boarding the big ship to Sweden. It was night and very dark and cold when we reached the harbor. We had to cautiously jump on board from the dock. I could hardly grasp how big the ship was, and I couldn't see its name. Was it "Oihonna" or something else? The personnel helping us said: "Children, down to the room!" This wasn't a passenger ship, but a cargo vessel with room for war children only in its "stomach," a big room filled with bunk beds. The room was warm, and I sank into a deep sleep quickly, although many children were crying their hearts out. I slept so soundly that I never learned first-hand whether the ship encountered mines or bomber planes, always a danger. Later, however, I heard that there had been no unusual events during our trip.

The next day, November 12, we came to Stockholm. It must have been dark because I have no bright memories of our arrival. We were taken from the ship to the Stockholm train station where I observed that Swedish trains were mostly electric-powered, while Finnish trains were steam-powered.

Our train full of war children started off and paused in Gävle, a town famous for its factories. That was the only stop until we reached Härnosand, which took a long time. There, we were boarded in a local school for medical check-ups, vaccinations, and other examinations. I have very faint memories of the school except that it was a very dark November time with snow on the ground and no sun. I do not remember if we stopped a few hours or a few days. Finally, our trip (now under steam power) began again. Sollefteå was the next and final stopping place for me where I was told by the service personnel that I had to leave the train. The actual distance from Härnösand to Sollefteå isn't very great, but I had the feeling that our steam-powered train took an enormously long time before arriving at our destination.

When we finally arrived, it was after 9 PM before we were allowed to walk out of Sollefteå's station. This was a small town with fewer than 10,000 inhabitants; at least that was my impression. I remember standing in the big station hall with my identifying emblem around my neck so everyone could see my name on the card. At around 10 PM, two or three ladies came closer and said, "This is the our war child!" They took me and my luggage, and we walked into the frigid night with a temperature of about −20° Centigrade: very cold!

We walked to a big black Volvo taxi, and to my surprise a six-year-old boy named Aarne entered the same taxi. Mr. Lögdberg, the taxi driver, started the engine and we left the river-valley town of Sollefteå. The Volvo's headlights showed us a real winter scene with lots of snow on woodland trees and along the roadsides. Everything was so scenic!

I remember it well: the old road from Sollefteå toward Graningebruk, about twenty miles long, was narrow and contained several curves. Slowly I became more and more nauseated and finally could not bear it any more. I had to throw up. But, thankfully, the ladies had some paper bags with them, so I vomited into one of those bags. I was the only one in the car to suffer from motion sickness. Fortunately I didn't vomit on the car or any of its passengers.

The car stopped in Graningebruk, and for the first time I saw the single-family house, belonging to Emil Lantz, the village shopkeeper. Emil and Mimmi Lantz were to become my war parents for the next ten months. The other boy, Aarne, was taken to the next house, on the opposite side of the road. I later saw Aarne only occasionally, as his interests and mine were different since I was three years older than he. "Mr. Emil," as I thought of him, welcomed me when we came into the kitchen. I was tired but also hungry, so they gave me milk and sandwiches. My motion sickness had passed. They made several attempts at conversation, but I didn't understand what they said. Finally, it was time to go up to bed. The bedrooms were in the attic, two floors above ground level.

The Lantzes had placed an old crib in a bedroom intended for adults. I was nine years old and about 120 centimeters or just under four feet tall, and the bed was shorter than I was. I found it difficult to jump into that kind of crib-bed. But I learned how to manage. These things didn't bother me very much. Later I believe they found a better bed for me. That first night I was so tired that I fell asleep at once. However, during the night I awoke to complete blackness. I had no idea where the toilet was, but Mr. Emil heard me and, guessing my problem, he advised me to use the chamber pot. At home in Hämeenlinna, we had an indoor toilet, so it wasn't easy for me to use a new system and in total darkness! But Mr. Emil also provided light to help me. Later I learned that their privy was an outdoor one near their cellar about 150 feet from their house.

The next morning we had breakfast in the kitchen. Mr. Emil was already there and eating when I came downstairs. He had a small booklet, a dictionary made especially for talking with Finnish war children. He asked me some pre-made questions and I was able to answer him, so he could understand me. He and I were both very happy about this development! Mrs. Mimmi asked me if I wanted to have coffee or tea. I tried both, and my final selection was tea. Mr. Emil then began working in his shop, so Mrs. Mimmi showed me their house. Within a few days and weeks I had learned enough of their language and local dialect to be able to ask and give simple answers to questions. An interesting experience!

The Lantzes' son, Martin Lantz (born in 1928), was attending high school in Sollefteå. During the school week, Martin boarded at his grandmother's, Mimmi's mother's home, and returned to Graninge on weekends. *Tant* (Aunt) Mimmi said to me, "So next weekend you'll see Martin. He wears a special school cap if the weather allows." *Tant* Mimmi also told me that the Lantz family usually traveled during the Christmas holidays to Sollefteå to celebrate the festival at her childhood home. And so it happened for Christmas 1941. I was unhappy, though, when I heard that we had to travel by bus into town because I always suffered from motion sickness. Bus travel was a disaster for me and not pleasant as it was for some. Unfortunately, anti-nausea drugs usually didn't help.

Tant Mimi and I planned to send a Christmas parcel to my mother, brother, and sister in Finland. The Lantz family would donate the gifts. During the war, however, there were strict regulations concerning what one could and could not send abroad. Apparently, we put some food, clothes, and other goodies in the package. *Tant* Mimmi understood the regulations, but I had no idea about them. When everything was ready we brought the parcel to the post office, and later my mother wrote to tell us that the parcel had arrived undamaged in Finland.

On December 24 we traveled to Sollefteå to walk around town and buy some Christmas gifts. I didn't have any money of my own, so I made my purchases only in my imagination.

When I saw some toy horns in a shop-window display, I was enthralled. I did not then know why I was interested in toy horns, and I have no explanation to this day, but *Tant* Mimmi must have observed my interest and bought one for me. It was the use-once-then-discard kind. *Tant*

Mimmi also told me that they had a nearly new accordion at home in the attic, so I became interested in that instrument as well and later tried it out, though my attempts didn't produce any real results. We visited several shops that day, and *Tant* Mimmi had her hands full of various gifts. I am not certain whether I helped her carry some of the packages. We had to hurry to reach her childhood home in time to see Martin's grandmother and to begin our Christmas Eve celebration.

For some reason, Christmas in Sollefteå, 1941, at Mimmi's mother's house was depressing for me. The house was located on a hillside, and we could see quite a distance by looking down toward town from the house. But I remember being very sad as I looked at the landscape. There had been some sunshine on December 24, but now the sun was setting and twilight was coming closer. I was thinking of my mother, brother, and sister back in Hämeenlinna. I was worried about whether they had enough food to eat while I had so much. Entering the house, I noticed that the ceilings were low and that tall people had difficulty moving about. I didn't hit my head on the ceiling, but I nevertheless have very scanty memories of those Christmas days, though we had a lot of good food to eat several times during the holidays.

Another one of my memories is that at around 6 PM on Christmas Eve, the Swedish Santa Claus arrived. He was called *Jultomten,* "Jul" meaning "Christmas," and "Tomte" referring to Santa's helpers. He gave me several gifts, including winter clothes, skis, and other equipment, and I was able to begin skiing the following day in the yard of Martin's grandmother's house. There was a real winter that year in Sollefteå with lots of snow that nearly covered the house. Afterwards, I learned that fourteen-year-old Martin Lantz had himself played Santa Claus that year, and I remember guessing that it had been he.

Helge and Emma Thor were close friends of the Lantzes. My foster family didn't have their own car, so Helge organized transportation for everyone. That winter we took a drive, stopping at a fairly new log cabin where there was skiing, and I was happy to use my new skis. Apparently Helge and Emil also had hunting or fishing on their minds, though I don't remember seeing any animals killed during that trip. I remember best those outings documented in photographs taken by Martin Lantz. We also did some winter fishing on Lake Grove (Hultsjön), a large lake where the Lantz and Thor families often fished through the ice. On these occasions, I had nothing to do except look at the different fishing maneuvers executed by Helge or Emil and at Martin who was skillful at drilling holes in the ice. In late spring, everyone on fishing expeditions wore rubber boots because of the wet snow. And spring ice was surprisingly fragile. Usually, they didn't catch much. For me, the most enjoyable part of these trips were those moments when we drank coffee or juice and ate sandwiches.

Aarne was the nearest war child to me in Sweden, and sometimes he came to the Lantz family's yard to talk or play with me. He learned Swedish much more slowly than I did, but we could still talk in Finnish with each other. Sometimes I rode a toboggan or small sled I found in the attic of the Lantz's storehouse. And sometimes Aarne and I went up to "Lantz Hill" for this purpose.

Over Easter, April 5, 1942, we could really feel spring approaching. The snow was melting. Martin came home from town. He was on vacation from school, and we had a good time. He told me many interesting things he had learned at school, though at the time I was not interested in reading books. That enthusiasm came later, when I was one or two years older or even a little older than that.

At Easter, however, I fell ill with the mumps, also known as "parotitis." I have no idea where I contracted the illness, but I remember that I suffered from fever and swollen salivary glands under my jaw line and that I was very tired. *Tant* Mimmi brought me water and other liquids and later on some food. She also introduced me to a special Easter dish: brown beans. If I couldn't eat the beans, though, she said that she would save them until later. I did not like brown beans, so what could I do? I was very hungry because I had avoided those beans: this was perhaps the most dismal single experience of my entire time as a war child.

In the spring of 1942 my birth mother Aino wrote the Lantz family from my hometown in Finland and said that she would be very happy "if Rolf could attend the local folk-school" (or public school). The result was that I began attending the school in Graninge and went there from January through May 1942, when the spring term ended. I even received a report card. The school building wasn't far from the Lantz's home, but reading and writing were taught differently in Sweden than they were in Finland, and I sometimes became confused. In Finland, we write down words as they are pronounced, and we say words as they are written. In other words, our language is phonetically consistent. I could not understand, especially in the beginning, why the Swedes did so many simple things differently from the way we did them in Finland, including phonetics. I was also unfamiliar with the school grading system. Finnish schools used a 10-9-8-7 system, without pluses or minuses. The Swedes used an A-B-C system, with pluses and minuses added. In any case, I received "A's in deportment (*Uppforande*) and in discipline (*Ordning*), a "B+" in singing, and so on. Hugo Nilsson was the schoolteacher as well as the local music teacher, and he signed my report card on May 28, 1942.

Later my mother wrote again and sent another wish: that she would be very happy "if Rolf could have some instruction in playing the piano"! Mr. Nilsson gave me piano lessons for two months, and I was able to use the piano at Näslund's house, next door to the Lantz's, to practice.

During the summer of 1942, we made trips to pick berries, so that *Tant* Mimmi could make jellies. I sometimes played with Åke Lögdberg and his sister, the children of Lögdberg, the taxi-driver, who attended the same school (*brukets skola*) as I did. Åke and I had some similar interests and got along well together.

During that same summer, Graningeverket, the forestry and energy company, decided to make some repairs in the area where I was living. They drained almost all of the water from Hultsjön and Graningesjö lakes. Seen from Thor's windows, the river and the rapids in it appeared to be dry or almost dry.

The landscape with these empty lakes was now a miserable sight, but we boys loved the situation. We were eight, nine, and ten years old, and we loved exploring the lake beds, looking at the fish between stones at the bottom of the lakes. We tried fishing from stones or from pontoon bridges the timber company had built, though the bridges were now quite low since there was so little water for them to float on. We didn't actually catch any fish, but it was fun trying. For one thing, we didn't have good fishing gear, and our plans were too grand for our equipment. But we were happy.

One morning Åke and I were walking to the emptied Lake Graninge. One fisherman had caught a fish that was unusually long. Åke knew what it was: an eel! I was surprised; I didn't know much about fish at that time. But I learned a lot in Graninge and made many new discoveries.

Graningeverket, the same company, built a new dam and other things, including a drain pipe used to float timber to their lumber mills. I was fascinated to see what they did and how they built all these things. For one thing, they needed a lot of gravel, so they built a special funnel in a gravel pit. When the funnel had been filled with gravel it was emptied, and the gravel fell down into a truck. The amount of gravel was just enough for one truckload. Several times each day trucks carried their loads of gravel from the pit to the dam. In 1943, the dam was finished and the lakes were returned to normal—that is, again filled with water.

Sometimes Emil and Mimmi Lantz visited their friends, and I was allowed to accompany them and see how other Swedish people lived during those days of World War II. Janne and Aina Näslund, the closest neighbors to the Lantzes, were teachers. They had a daughter, younger than I was. Like Helge Thor and Emil, Janne and Emil were enthusiastic hunting and fishing partners.

The Lantz family didn't have a sauna. Nor did they have a shower. They used to take baths in a wooden tub that was placed on the kitchen floor and then filled with warm water that had been boiled on the kitchen stove. It was almost as if we were bathing with the Vikings! We also brushed our teeth in the kitchen.

The Thors enjoyed a higher standard of living and had a bathroom in their house, but no sauna. They also had hot and cold running water and a modern toilet. Because Helge was the local chief of the Graningeverket company, I imagine they lived in company housing and that the car that he drove was a company car. Their house was close to the village center and, before the rapids were drained, you could see the water running down river to the old iron foundry from this house.

The Thors' son, Ingemar, then eighteen years old, was a cheerful person who enjoyed a joke. He taught me some of his favorite tricks: how he could move his ears or his scalp by using his scalp muscles. He also showed me how to blow into his finger and make his hat rise on his head. The explanation was this: he moved his head and hat backwards against a wall as he blew onto (not actually into) his finger, and the bill of the hat rubbed against the wall and made it rise on his head. Finally, Ingemar taught me a new way of attracting attention at school by beating his index finger against his other fingers. I thought at the time that this wouldn't be acceptable in Finnish schools!

On the side of the river opposite the Thors' house was the main street of the village, a kind of boulevard. Along it were several houses very similar in style, probably the houses in which the factory workers had once lived. In one of these old houses was the post office, which organized its mail in an interesting way. There were lots of pigeonholes on one wall, apparently one for each family. Letters, magazines, and other mail were placed in the proper holes, and people came to the office to collect the mail from the slot assigned to them. Perhaps seven to nine years later I was working one summer at the post office in Hämeenlinna where I saw a similar system except that mailmen emptied the holes themselves and brought the mail directly to the customers' homes.

In August 1942 the Lantz family informed me that my return trip to Finland would take place the following month. Emil and Mimmi Lantz had already decided that they would buy me some clothes before I left in September, and they said: "Let's travel to Sollefteå again! They have good clothes for you there." Aunt Mimmi and I traveled by bus to town where we walked around and looked for suitable purchases. I received a cap, a suit, a shirt, and a sweater, similar to one Martin had. I was very happy to receive these new clothes as gifts.

One day, a few days after receiving these clothes, we decided to walk to the Sound, the narrow river connecting the Hultsjön to the Graningesjön. Because of repair work on the dam, the Sound was still almost without water. The old floating bridges placed there by the timber company were partially on the water itself and partially stuck on dry stones, so we could easily walk on them. Suddenly, Martin saw an interesting culvert and jumped on it. Then I took my turn. When I jumped, however, everything started breaking up. Stones started rolling down to the remaining water, and I began rolling with them. I got wet and so did my new clothes, which I was wearing for the first time. The wooden parts of the old culvert had simply been too rotten to withstand the strain of several boys jumping onto them!

My new sweater was spoiled in the water, and the colors in it ran together. Also, a few falling stones from the culvert hit me as I fell, and I was bruised and unhappy. The goal of visiting the Sound had been to have fun, not to drop into the water and ruin my new clothes. As we walked home through the pine trees, I moped and felt sorry for myself.

Finally, it was time to leave Sweden. *Tant* Mimmi and Martin took me to the nearest large railway station in Långsele because Emil had to work. A special train for many returning war children arrived, and I jumped on board. I was unhappy to be leaving; and as I waved my hand to say "farewell" to Mimmi and Martin, I had tears in my eyes.

I had all my things with me; however, I wasn't allowed to take them. Instead, my various packages had to travel via a different route. Our train ran to Haparanda on the border across from Torneå in Finland because the earlier route, from Stockholm to Turku, had become too dangerous. At the border we had to switch to the Finnish train.

I arrived in Hämeenlinna on Tuesday, September 29, 1942. I was home again, but I could not explain my adventures in Finnish. I could no longer understand my own language! School in Hämeenlinna had already begun on September 1, but my mother was anxious that I go to school as soon as possible. During one class, the teacher asked the pupils to write an essay about our summer experiences. I wrote about my miraculous summer of 1942 in Graninge, when I encountered so many new things. At the time I didn't know the Finnish names of the fish I had seen. And for that reason, my composition, full of the Swedish words for fish, caused a lot of fun for the other pupils! Eventually, though, I relearned my mother tongue.

When I think about my time as a war child or see old photos, I feel happy. Yet I also easily become sad when I remember my loving war parents, Emil and Mimmi, and their son Martin. I also remember Jenne and Aina Näslund and Helge and Emma Thor fondly, though all of them and others I remember have long since died.

* * * * *

Rolf completed his university studies, was married in 1961, and had three children. He belongs to a war child association in Tawastland. Now retired, he enjoys many hobbies, including research on tombstone architecture.

36
Horses in the Kitchen
Jorma Törmänen

I was born in 1936 in the town of Soivio about 30 kilometers from the center of Kuusamo in eastern Finland. Kuusamo, which today is an international winter sports center, is in the province of Oulu and Lapland whose surface comprises more than half of the whole of Finland. There are spruce, pine, birch, and European aspen forests there, as well as primeval forests in conservation areas today. Kuusamo also abounds in lakes, ponds, rivers, creeks, marshes, and mountains. This is where my family lived during and after the war. In the 1930s, Soivio had only around 150 inhabitants. It was a farming community in which people raised reindeer, cows, sheep, and pigs. The men also hunted grouse, wood grouse, and other creatures for food. I was the third oldest son among five children, and I would later have two more siblings, my youngest brother and sister.

My mother both taught in and was principal of a small elementary school where my family was also housed. It was a reduced elementary school in which the upper levels were combined in the winter, and in the fall and spring two elementary classes were combined. Its rooms had to be heated every day, and the students were offered free lunches. My father was a building contractor, and because my mother also worked we had two maids to care for our cattle and other animals, the children, and the household. It was common at that time to have a girl from a neighboring family to help with the chores. Like other maids, they slept either in the kitchen or in a little room next to it. For our family the maids were a necessity; like most maids, they had finished their obligatory schooling and were basically waiting to get married. I liked one of the maids very much and remember her reading and singing to me, though she later married and left our home.

Another happy memory from my very early life is of mother taking all of us children to pick blueberries, lingonberries, and cloudberries. I also remember the lake where my brothers and I went fishing in the evening and sometimes stayed all night. We were living in the middle of nature with lots of mosquitoes.

Twice we were evacuated from our home. I was four years old when my family was evacuated for the first time after the Winter War began on November 30, 1939. We were told to leave because everyone feared Russian occupation. I do not remember very much from it, except that it was very frightening and threatening and that I cried after the maid who had been caring for me.

A few months later, after the Winter War and during the temporary peace, we returned home. During this time, Finland was looking for an ally against Russia, and cooperation between Finland and Germany began. Germans were accommodated near us, and they often visited my family wanting to listen to our radio since there was no electricity then. They also brought cognac and took photos to become better acquainted.

I remember Soviet intelligence planes and children waving at them. Parents sometimes told their children that if they didn't behave, the partisans—groups of Russians who were dropped from enemy planes—would come and burn down the whole house with everyone in it, which they actually sometimes did. Everyone was worried and scared, and I remember that when I went to bed, I pulled the blanket over my head, so that I would be safe. Like all the other children I had nightmares about enemy planes and bombs, which I remember exploding in the neighboring village. After the second evacuation, we also found ammunition left behind from the Germans who had lived in our village during the war. We found rifles and all kinds of guns, and some boys got injured while handling them. We Törmänen boys, however, were skillful with guns and didn't hurt ourselves.

The second evacuation occurred after the Continuation War started, June 25, 1941, when I was seven years old. Thus, I remember being cold during the first evacuation, but not the second one because it was fall. Word of the impending move was spread by a person who was assigned this task. There were also newspapers and big posters that announced these wartime movements beside the road, and neighbors helped spread the word. I was at school when the news came, and my mother asked me to go into the schoolyard and tell the students not to come in but to go home because of the evacuation. I remember that the girls began crying.

But from my point of view, I thought that the second evacuation was exciting. Unlike the previous experience, we had time to prepare. A pig was killed, and we hid our things up in the barn and in the attic of the sauna building. My oldest brother, Antti, took a bike and walked with the maid and our two cows. But the rest of us left on my father's boat to cross Soiviojärvi (Soivio Lake) because we had so many goods and luggage to carry. In fact, the boat was so loaded down that it was probably only five centimeters or maybe two inches above the surface of the water. Father was not with us, since he was working as a pioneer and often in charge of building roads, bridges, and trenches. So the rest of us rowed to cross the lake.

After the boat ride, we went by truck. It was a brisk fall day in late August, and our mother who was six months' pregnant rode inside with the driver, while the rest of the family sat on the bed of the truck without the protection of a roof. Some currants were all we had to eat. During our travel, we saw lots of cattle being led along the roads and calves struggling to free themselves. There were both Finnish and German forces in Kuusamo, and we saw German soldiers going in the opposite direction from us with their artillery covered to prevent wetness, driving in motorcycles with sidecars toward battles farther to the east and the Soviet border.

Finally we met Antti (who had loaned his bicycle to a strange man) with the maid and the cows in Utajärvi near the River Oulu. In Utajärvi, there was a railway for people to be sent farther. My mother asked to be able to leave for Ruovesi about 80 kilometers from Tampere because her parents lived there. Fortunately, my mother received permission to do this, though refugees from Karelia had been placed in my grandparents' home and had to be assigned another one upon our arrival. Like many thousands of other Karelians who had lost their homes to the Soviets, these people had to be given shelter, which put out many Finns. Some resented the imposition of having to share their property and meager supplies, but mostly these unfortunate people were treated in a friendly and polite way, and everybody tried to help one another.

Some time after we arrived at my grandparents, my family eventually received back not only the bicycle Antti had loaned to the man, but our cows and pig, which is surprising considering the scarcity of everything and people's desperation for food in Finland at the time. There must have been thieves during the war, but it was common for people's goods to reach them.

In Ruovesi, we children were able to return to school. And this is where our mother bore her sixth child. All five of her previous children had been born at home, but my youngest brother, Eero, was born in the hospital in Ruovesi.

Our father was busy with his work building trenches and roads, but he came to visit us every now and then. It was said that there were Russian war prisoners working in the big farmhouse near our grandfather's house. Everybody called them "*Ryssä*" (Russians). I don't remember seeing these war prisoners. But I remember that at school the children had to take turns fetching milk from a farmhouse and that there were lots of people from Karelia in the village.

When the war was over our father came home and we prepared to return home. The trip from Ruovesi to Oulu was long and arduous. We had to change trains several times. And because we took our cattle with us, we had to travel in a cattle train with no seats and only hay on the floor with the animals at one end and people at the other. The combined train travel, which lasted twelve or more hours, was very bumpy and uncomfortable, and though we had food with us, it was difficult to get any water. We were also not allowed to step out of the train at the stations because it was dangerous. Finally, in Oulu, we went on toward home by truck and were stopped many times by police asking who we were, when we were born, where we were going, and so forth. Unfortunately, our father had difficulties in remembering all the birthdays of his children. And he was also annoyed with the police, so that he intentionally wrote down the same birthdays for many of his children. Then, closer to home, we saw that not only had all the houses been destroyed, but the bridges had been blown up as well. The route was so badly demolished, in fact, that the truck could go no farther. We were ordered to walk straight about 15 kilometers and watch for markers that indicated the presence of mines along the route.

We were horrified to see all the damage done to our village and its houses, many of which were gone with only the chimneys standing. There was great bitterness towards the retreating Germans who had also burnt so many houses on their transit out of the country. Having been forced to leave Finland as part of the peace terms with Russia, they had burnt everything in their path. Moreover, some girls were expecting babies by Germans, which was a great disgrace after the war. Finns mostly have blue eyes, but these children often had brown, which set them apart.

Despite our dispiritedness, though, as a big family we had to start cleaning and renovating right away. People lived where they could—with relatives or friends until they were able to build new homes. Many people rebuilt with the help of others whom they repaid by helping them out in some other way later.

Luckily, the schoolhouse where we lived was still standing, but it was filthy. The Russians had used the kitchen as a stable. Of course all the furniture made by our father had been stolen not once, but twice. The locks on our home had been broken during the Winter War, and during the Continuation War anyone could have gone in and stolen whatever they liked. Later my family actually saw pieces of my father's furniture in a house in another village. But eventually village horses came back, though they were in a very bad condition and angry after having been conscripted for the army.

There was a serious shortage of everything. The Office of the United Nations High Commissioner for Refugees, or UNCHR, began sending all kinds of odd surplus such as army caps, boots, big trucks, canned fruit, and sugar. But mostly they sent things that were unsuitable like high-heeled shoes. And many of the men in charge of the deliveries stole much of what was donated. We received sweet toothpaste, which we kids ate not knowing its real purpose. And sweet milk in big wooden barrels was sent to lumberjacks to distribute. I remember the man in charge of the distribution making the children lie down and pouring the milk into our mouths, which was fun. I also remember a big sack of sugar and another of flour in the school kitchen where meals were prepared for the children. Later our American relatives—my mother's uncle and family living in California—began to send packages of sweets, clothes, and other useful things, which came to the center of the village.

Most of the stories from the war are sad. But there is one funny story I heard from my boss years later when I was working in Lapland. It was about a train wagon full of spirits that the fleeing Germans had to leave on the station tracks. According to the treaty with Russia, Finland had to drive out the Germans as quickly and efficiently as possible. So, because there were many Germans in the northern part of Finland, our army traveled north. When the pursuing Finnish army found the deserted alcohol tank wagon somewhere near the eastern border, they were thrilled and couldn't resist drinking this unexpected bounty. All the soldiers and officers were very drunk for the next couple of days after which they continued until the alcohol was gone. Luckily for them, the Russians never learned about this unintended detour in their pursuit of the Germans!

There are not very many veterans left. They have a choir of their own where I live in Espoo, and it is always very touching to hear them sing. For a long time after the war, people were very quiet about the veterans. But finally they are honored and given credit for what they did in the war and for having kept Finland a free country.

We all paid a high price for that freedom, but generations of children have benefited for those sacrifices.

* * * * *

Jorma, a registered land surveyor, received his degree in engineering from the University of Technology in Espoo, Finland. He married Anna-Liisa, his wife, in 1964. They have had three children together and are today retired in Espoo.

37
Rita, not Rauha
"Rita Trent"

I was born in 1940 and raised on a small farm in the village of Kinnala in southern Finland. Our lives were simple, but basically we could sustain ourselves from what we grew until the war when we barely survived due to lack of food. One year, our potato crop froze in the root cellar, and we ate frozen potatoes. Freezing causes the starch to turn into sugar, and to this day I dislike anything too sweet that reminds me of these. From the war years, I also remember the black-out curtains that had to be installed, so that no light crept out. And even during the most bitter cold of winter, we could not use our woodstove to heat because the smoke, like light from the house, could attract enemy planes in the night.

As we children grew up, like all children do, life became a bit more difficult. We were all a bit timid and told to be good, but there was little trouble to be found in our small corner of the big world. The Winter War had just ended, but was still ever near and on everyone's mind. Our home still had the black-out curtains, and we were still ordered not to use the wood stove to heat during the night because of the fear that enemy planes would fire upon our village. As children, we knew little of the details of war, but we knew enough to be cautious and very quiet in the presence of adults when serious discussions were going on.

It was during this period of time that our mother told us one day that a little girl would be coming to live with us. She cautioned us that if anyone in the village asked who she was, we were to say she was our "sister." Indeed, this small, frail girl with very long, thin braids hanging down to her waist came to live with us. She was extremely quiet and sad. In fact, I do not ever recall her speaking out loud. She went to school with us and stayed at our home, but she really did not participate in our family life. I believe that she was not Finnish and was unable to understand our language or we her language.

One day, she did not come to school with us, and when we arrived home from school, she had disappeared. *Äiti* (Mother) never mentioned the topic again, and I have wondered for sixty or more years what became of her. I now suspect she may have been a Jewish child smuggled out of Russia to save her life and passed on to be safe in another country. I questioned my mother about her, but she just smiled and said that she didn't recall anyone like that and that I must have "dreamed it." But I did not dream it; that is for certain.

Despite the fact that my earliest years coincided with the war, I have many happy memories from this time. *Äiti* kept a garden with flowers and veggies where I loved to dig up new potatoes when they were small and delicious. We children also loved swinging on the garden gate, though we did it when *Äiti* wasn't looking. Our home was painted the typical red of farmhouses in Finland with white trim around the windows, and the entryway had a small open porch where it was lovely to sit in the spring and fall, enjoying a small treat such as coffee with *nisu* (coffee bread) that we commonly ate. My mother warned me that if I drank coffee my hair would turn black, however! Perhaps she told me this because real coffee was almost nonexistent during the war, but since I did not know anyone with black hair, I was a bit afraid of the little coffee she gave me. I also loved our front yard and the clump of white birch trees, which we could see from our kitchen window. There was another type of tree that I cherished: the *pihlaja* (rowan tree). This tree has fragrant flowers in the spring and bright red berries in the fall that many birds eat and which can be used for making jelly. I still love birch trees and have several on my property today far away from Finland.

I also remember with fondness helping my mother on baking day, although at a very young age, I couldn't have really helped much. She would bake enough bread on baking day to last for weeks or even a month. The bread was baked round with a hole in the middle, so that it could hang on a pole attached to the wall near to the kitchen ceiling. In this way, it could be stored in the air and not take up too much space. *Äiti* also made donuts that were so delicious hot out of the frying pan and rolled in sugar: yum, yum!

In early summer we all headed into the woods near our home to look for mushrooms. *Äiti* took us children along, though we mostly chased rabbits, squirrels, and the like. Playing hide and seek in the beautiful clean forest was great fun. Blueberry season was always something to look forward to as well. We had a favorite patch where we picked most of the day, pausing for our favorite snack of coffee and *nisu*. *Äiti* preserved the blueberries in jars, and they were wonderful over rice pudding during the winter months. I still pick blueberries to this day and freeze them to enjoy in oatmeal and muffins and cakes. And in the marshy area near our home grew another wonderful berry called cloudberry. It resembles a raspberry, but is soft orange in color and grows in abundance on the low ground.

It's delicious to eat, and of course jam and soups were made from it to have as another treat over rice pudding. It was always an adventure to trek off with *Äiti* for the day with some of the neighbors to pick berries and enjoy a picnic lunch in the beautiful forest. The birch trees were looking for summer sunshine and storing food for the long, cold winter ahead. A small world for a small girl, but I was perfectly content in it, picking buttercups and clover blossoms to bring to my mother.

Finland is a beautiful country of many lakes, waterways, and forests. Fir, beech, and white birch trees grow in abundance everywhere. It would truly not be summer if you could not jump into a crystal clear lake and swim until you were blue in the cold water and then run to the sauna, an everyday part of life. Our sauna stove was a metal box which had a firebox at the bottom that you filled with wood. Beach rocks were placed on the top of stove, which became very hot from the fire underneath. To test the temperature, you would throw a small amount of water on top of the rocks, and if a generous steam arose, you were ready for a really relaxing experience. Then, when you thought your skin was on fire, you ran and jumped into the refreshing lake. After many runs into the lake and back into the sauna, you were truly squeaky clean and felt wonderful. Later, it would be time to grill the sausages that you brought along and, of course, a cup of Finnish coffee would end the meal. There is nothing better than this pastime for a neverending summer day. Such fun! When floating on my back and feeling the warmth of the sun on my face, I felt perfectly at peace with the world, and that was the only thing that mattered. It was difficult on such days to believe that the war had scarred so many lives, some of which would never heal.

Äiti was a good cook, and though it was difficult during the war years to get certain ingredients such as sugar, spices, and coffee, somehow there was always something sweet and delicious to share when friends and neighbors dropped by to visit.

Juhannus or Midsummer was wonderful. Everyone in the neighborhood decorated their entry with freshly cut birch saplings and made a row of these on either side of their walkways. The saplings swayed in the breeze, which was a lovely sight. We had races and all sorts of games that the whole family enjoyed, and there was a dance at an outdoor pavilion. To crown the festivities, a giant *koko* (bonfire) was lit at midnight and was a thrilling sight. The only bad part about *Juhannus* was that it was hard to fall asleep with the continuous daylight.

I also enjoyed winter and especially those years when we received lots of snow. Finnish winters are long and hard, but it is still my favorite season. By about the beginning of April, I would sometimes heat some water on our wood stove and take it outside to pour on some snow just to marvel at the suddenly appearing patch of bare ground. We also used the sauna in winter, which was especially enjoyable because one got a chance to cool off, walking from the sauna into the warm house. Today in my own home, I have a sauna, which I enjoy tremendously.

Christmas was also a very happy time. Neighbors came in for coffee and treats, and that meant that we children had more friends to play with. On Christmas Eve, we spent the day in the forest selecting and cutting down a tree, which our horse pulled back to the house. That evening, we would decorate the tree and, later, just before our meal, light candles on the tree. Sometimes, we heard bells ringing out or a knock on the door to announce that *Joulu Puukki* (Santa Claus or, literally, "Christmas goat") was visiting to leave us a basket of goodies, mostly consisting of home-made dolls for the girls, carved wooden trucks for the boys, and maybe some apples. The one Christmas in particular that I remember is when we heard bells and looked out the window to see a *real reindeer* pulling Santa in his sled. This was an unbelievable sight even for Finnish children (since everyone knows that *Joulu Puukki* comes from nowhere else but Finland!).

Another beautiful Christmas custom in Finland that is still observed today is to visit the parish cemetery on Christmas Eve. Candles are lit by the gravestones and left to burn throughout Christmas night. The war dead are honored in this way, and in summer beautiful begonias are planted on each grave in bright red colors to show that the living have not forgotten those who gave so much. This is an important part of Finnish life: to respect the sacrifices made in the name of freedom for our country.

The war years were very difficult, but the postwar years were difficult as well. A deep quiet and sadness clung to everything, and the rationing of goods continued for many years after. I recall my mother going to the local store after hearing that they had received a shipment of mustard. She stood in line for a long time only to be told that the mustard was all sold. We were all very disappointed. In addition, school supplies were difficult to get, so I learned to write my ABC's on the borders of old newspapers. Each family saved their newspapers, and we carried them to school for our writing practice and math problems. We were issued only one pencil per school year, and that was to last the whole year, or you would have to find your own replacement. It would have been an unacceptable excuse to go home and explain why you no longer had a pencil. Hence, very few, if any, replacements were necessary.

I had both an older and younger brother and two younger twin siblings, a boy and a girl. Unfortunately, for reasons I can't explain, my father took his own life on May 1, 1945, perhaps due to war trauma. May Day is a holiday in Finland to welcome spring and freedom from the long, hard winter. It is usually celebrated with athletic contests, races, and other outdoor activities. University students wear their special caps to picnics and social activities. *Äiti* had gone to the village center, and we children were at home waiting for her, so that we too could participate in the excitement of the day. But my father, who was then thirty years old, had decided for whatever dreadful reason to end his life on what should have been a wonderful day. How he could have left all of us with so little consideration, I still cannot comprehend, but I did not walk in his shoes. In recent years, I have learned from one of my siblings that he did some sort of espionage work during the war. He loathed Communists and spied for the Finnish government, helping to arrest Finnish turncoats. At least, that is what I've heard. However, this tragedy that left our family to fend for itself was indescribable. My mother, a widow with five small children, did not know where to turn. She had never worked outside the home, and in the rural area where we lived, there was no opportunity for work.

After his death, *Äiti* would never speak of my father, and I doubt that my siblings know any more than I do about this sad turn of affairs. But it was catastrophic for us as children, as I explain below.

My mother remarried a strong and powerful man named Juhani who ran our small farm and whom we called "Papa." This new stepfather was very strong-minded and one-sided: his side. And my mother was not one to argue. After their marriage, my siblings and I were all sent away, shipped here, there, and everywhere one by one. I believe that he simply did not want us around and that that is why we were shipped out. My older brother was the first to be ejected and, while I was too young to understand the circumstances, I wondered about this when I saw him sometimes, living and sleeping in the neighbor's barn. Another brother was taken by a military officer and was schooled and taught to play the French horn for the Finnish army. My twin siblings were also sent away. My sister had a really sad life, living on city streets at the age of eleven or twelve, though she finally found work in a coffee shop and was taken in by the people she worked for. She has never recovered and is bitter to this day about her childhood experience.

Then it was my turn to be banished from home. On November 9, 1948, when I was three months into second grade, my stepfather said to me, "I am going to Helsinki. Would you like to go with me to see my sister, Aunt Riika?" This sounded good to an eight-year-old—a trip to the big city where I had never been. The next morning as we prepared to leave, I was excited but also a bit puzzled about not seeing *Äiti* who was nowhere in sight. We took a bus, a new adventure for me, and we spent the night at Aunt Riika's, Juhani's sister's apartment. But in the morning, no one was there—no stepfather and no Aunt Riika. Finally, a woman I had never seen before arrived to announce, "We will be leaving now." I had absolutely no idea who she was or where we were going.

The strange woman took me by streetcar to the Helsinki airport where another complete stranger took charge of me. I had no idea what was going on and was too afraid to ask. At age eight, I had never seen a city before. Nor had I ever seen so many automobiles, to say nothing of trains or airplanes. I found myself seated in the plane, and when we took off, I truly believed that it was the end of the world. I became violently ill, and when the plane landed many hours later in Boston (I discovered some time after that New York City had been its original destination, but a storm had caused the plane to be diverted), a Danish couple sitting opposite to me on the plane saw my plight and took me to the Boston Copley Plaza Hotel, where I spent another night with total strangers. It was very cold in Boston, but by this point I was beyond thinking about creature comforts. I still have my coat from that time. My mother made it by cutting down her only winter coat to make into a coat for my journey. But I had nothing else with me: no doll or toy to comfort me and to remind me of the home I had left. The Danes spoke no Finnish, but somehow the American couple that had been waiting for me in New York arrived at the hotel the next day and took me to what became my lifetime home, which no one had told me anything about or prepared me for in any way. These Americans also spoke no Finnish, and I desperately wanted to speak to someone who could send me back to my mother and family. But that did not happen. And here I am in America some sixty-four years later.

To be wrenched away from a familiar life and set down in a matter of hours in a land where not even words had meaning was traumatic, if not a catastrophic experience such as a life-threatening illness or accident. From a close-knit, small village to a city and family that did not speak my language left me in total despair. The effects of such a change quickly resulted in complete withdrawal. I was not able to express even hysteria. The shock was so great that even a new doll would not arouse any response. I merely withdrew from participating in my surroundings and did not utter a word for days at a time. I never felt that I belonged to anything, as though I was in limbo without identity. I would wonder—what am I doing here, where should I be, and who am I? It seemed like I was living in two separate worlds and not belonging to either, but was totally isolated from both.

Although I waited for an explanation and news of my mother and siblings, I never heard from anyone in my family—no letter, no communication of any kind. I sometimes tried to ask my new "mother," "Why doesn't *Äiti* write to me?" And she would say, "Your mother wants you be an American now," adding, "Don't bother me with silly questions." I couldn't imagine what had happened to explain my coming to America, and I sometimes wondered if my entire Finnish family had somehow died. This at least would explain the bewildering silence. Many years later, *Äiti* assured me that she had written to me many times. I too wrote letters, but I doubt they were ever mailed. Clearly, my stepmother Sylvia had hidden or destroyed my mother's letters as well as mine. But as a trusting eight-year-old, I couldn't have imagined that one's caretakers would lie!

My new foster parents were an older childless couple in their mid-fifties who had no experience with children and didn't appear to like them. Sylvia worked in an insurance office, and Magnus worked as a mechanic in a local machine shop. I do not remember calling them anything: it was distasteful to me to refer to them as "Mom" and "Dad," as I was instructed. So I avoided calling them anything. Magnus was a first-generation American from Swedish parents born in Vassa, Finland. But I doubt that his being Finnish-Swedish had anything to do with my adoption. I was told years later that their marriage was on the rocks and that they thought a child would save it. Since Sylvia was unable to have children, they had to look elsewhere. But I believe to this day that I was taken in to be nothing more than their maid. So my sad and demanding life commenced on the third anniversary of Armistice Day 1948, when I was just eight years old.

When I arrived in the United States I was very, very sick, due to malnutrition. Though I was tall for my age, I weighed only 47 pounds, and the teeth in my gums were loose. I was taken to a wonderful Jewish doctor who agreed to see me immediately, despite it being Armistice Day and a holiday. I was severely dehydrated and unable to keep anything down, so he prescribed ginger ale and lollipops, neither of which I'd heard of or seen before! The only good thing my adoptive parents did for me was to take me to a dentist right away, and every Monday for a year I had to visit the dentist for treatment. I also had to have a tonsillectomy shortly after I arrived.

I had never had a doll of my own, other than the rag dolls my mother made. I had never seen a doll carriage or other children's toys. But in my new home I was given a beautiful doll complete with carriage that was so pretty that I couldn't believe that it was real. The doll was an infant size and so lovely. The beautiful blue eyes would close when you laid her down and opened when you sat her up. She had blonde, curly hair and a pretty blue and white dress. I was not sure how to play with her. I knew no children that I could communicate with, so I did not learn by seeing how American children played with their toys. It seemed that I spent most of my time just looking at the doll and the beautiful blue carriage. The carriage was a high-styled model, such as an English pram, with a canopy top that was movable. It was medium blue, trimmed in cream pin-striping, and was ever so lovely. I had never seen anything like this, and of course I was fearful of breaking it or having some accident with it. But because I did not play with it as my step-mother expected that I should, they misunderstood my fear and thought that I did not like it. One day I came home from school and found that my beautiful doll and carriage were gone from my room. They had been given to another child who had just come to the United States from Finland with her parents. I knew then that if I was ever going live in the real world here, I would have to become tough and not cry or show any emotion. No matter how hurt and broken I felt inside, no one would ever see it on my outside. I was starting to learn survival skills that would never allow anyone in who could hurt me again. Soon I began a game of being invisible. When I was in a stressful situation that I did not understand, I would pretend that no one could see me, and I shut out everything around me. The loss of my carriage and doll was devastating, and that necessitated my "being invisible" for the first time. Soon I realized that it helped, and this trick became my friend. My little pride would not allow anyone to see me cry, though certainly it must have happened sometimes, but not often. It seems impossible to me now to have been able to hold all that emotion in my small body, but I did.

Soon after the American couple took me, they also did some other very damaging and humiliating things to me. First they changed my Finnish name "Rauha" to "Rita" and made me write out the word "Rita" many times, although I couldn't say it correctly and didn't even know what it meant. They cut off my hair so that I looked like a boy and tried to Americanize me in humiliating ways. For instance, like all Europeans, I had been taught to hold my silverware differently. My new "parents" didn't approve and made me learn the new way by tying my left hand behind my back at the dinner table. As a consequence, I developed debilitating issues with eating and didn't care if I ever saw food. In addition, I was very seldom allowed to go outdoors to play; instead, I was expected to do endless chores at home, although nothing I ever did, even as an adult, passed my "mother" Sylvia's tests. When she came home from work, she put on a white glove to see if I had gotten all the dust off the top of the dresser. It would tie my stomach in knots just to hear her opening the door.

Yet this same woman who was so oppressive and demeaning toward me at home put on a happy family act for the public and especially at church. Magnus sometimes defended me, saying that he thought I should be outdoors with the other kids playing instead of being cooped up in the house doing chores. I don't think he had any real idea of what his wife expected of me. She gave me no instruction, yet expected me at age eight and nine to be able to clean the house perfectly. I have since wondered why she must have felt so out of control that she had to subject me to a life of guaranteed failure. As a mother today, I want nothing more than to see my children succeed, and I believe that most parents feel this way. I wonder, too, if it is more common for adopted children to feel they must prove they are good and deserving of love and approval.

As a child, I was not able to recognize that these things were not my fault and that I was actually a victim of Sylvia's control. But I suffered for many years from extremely low self-esteem, though my teachers at school and people at church often befriended me.

Initially I was terrified of going to school, which I began only two or three days after my arrival. I was frozen with terror, because I understood nothing of what was expected of me and knew absolutely no English. However, I came to love school because of the kindness of my teachers who often gave up their coffee breaks to read to me—not because I could understand what they read, but so that if I heard English spoken out loud, I would learn to speak without an accent. And it certainly worked: no one can detect that I am not American-born today. Neither Sylvia nor Magnus ever read to me. Nor did they try to teach me English. It was all done by my elementary school teachers and, for this reason, I love them to this day. Many years later, I began to dream of continuing my education at a state teacher's college. But when I asked my adoptive parents about this, I was told that it was totally out of the question, though tuition at that time was only $100/year, and they could easily have afforded it. I myself could have earned enough at my part-time job, flipping hamburgers and scooping ice cream. But Sylvia forbade this, and I believe the reason is that she really wanted me *not* to succeed. Unfortunately, not having an education beyond high school has blighted my life and has left a hole in my heart that has never mended.

For all these reasons, I never thought about my foster parents as being anything like family or close connections, and I still feel that way today some sixty-four years later. A long time ago, I froze out that part of my life, so I would not be hindered by the emotion of it. In the same way, as I was growing up during those long lonely years in America, I don't think that I spent time thinking about Finland because I really could not wrap my mind around what had happened to me. I could not understand how one day I had been in Kinnala, looking forward to a new adventure in Helsinki, and that on the next day I had been transported to such an alien and strange place. In some way, I feel that God shielded me from the nightmare, so I would not kill myself or go berserk. Had I chosen to feel bitter, I believe that bitterness would have eaten me up alive.

Later, as a young woman, I began to remember my early childhood home in loving and vivid detail. I began to fantasize about being back in Finland and lived for the day when I could earn enough money to buy a one-way ticket to Finland and return home, even if my family did not want me. Finally I achieved my dream. I did return to Finland: unannounced, in 1961, and for the first time. I could no longer speak Finnish, of course, but amazingly I found my way back to the countryside where I had lived. I arrived at 2 AM just after my younger brother Pentti had returned from a dance under the midnight sun. I saw a light in the kitchen window, and knew right away that this was *home*. It was quite a bizarre reunion. My brother opened the door and had no idea who I was. No one recognized me. But finally they woke *Äiti*, and she started to cry and shout. Since then, I have gone back nearly every year and have developed relationships with my siblings and step-brothers and step-sisters. I also made the discovery that, like me and my older brother, my other three siblings had also been ejected from home during their early lives.

Only lately have I pondered my mother's decision to send me and her other children away. I can't understand how she could have let us all go like that even if Juhani was strong willed and domineering. As a mother myself, I can't comprehend or even think of a situation that would make me give up my children. Despite this, I do not blame my mother for anything. On one of my last visits home, *Äiti* said to me that she was amazed I never once spoke badly about what had happened or criticized her for it. But I have tried to think that what she did or perhaps agreed to do under pressure was done with my best interest in mind.

Perhaps I can't face the truth, but I feel that if I dwell on the negative, I will become nothing. So, long ago I chose to forgive and get past it as best I could. It is important to remember, too, that I was given away during the desperately difficult postwar years and that, at that time, everyone in Europe believed that the streets in America were paved in gold. Perhaps my mother thought that she was doing me a favor.

After the deaths of Sylvia and Magnus, I found some of their old documents including the airline ticket they bought to bring me to America. Apparently the process had begun in 1947, immediately after my mother remarried. I also discovered that I had been placed on a U.S. immigration list that required a wait of one year; nevertheless, I had been moved up, due to my frail health as a child in need of medical relief.

As for my Finnish stepfather, Juhani, each year that I have gone home to Finland, he has found a quiet moment to ask for my forgiveness. He never explains to me what he's referring to, but it finally dawned on me during a recent visit. I finally connected the dots. Still, I have never complained or blamed *Äiti* or Papa. Despite what he did to his stepchildren, it would never occur to me to treat him without respect. It is in a Finnish child's genes to be polite no matter what, even now.

Today I am extremely wistful when I remember scenes from my early childhood: *Äiti*'s garden and home, the special foods that she prepared, the saunas we shared as a young family, Midsummer festivities, mushroom and blueberry seasons, and the appearance of *Joulu Puukki* at our home at Christmas.

For years after I became an adult, I sought acceptance for who I was. The past can be buried for just so long, but it comes crawling back when you least expect it. I have often wondered: is there a way to be whole again? I have always chosen to be quiet, but "quiet" is different from "silent." Quiet is peace and tranquility by choosing to turn the volume button of one's emotions down. Silence, on the other hand, is pushing the OFF button: shutting down all of it, which I did for years, making myself invisible.

It has only been recently that I have actually thought about how awful my childhood and young adulthood were and how out of balance my life really was for so long. I still have not been able to comprehend why my life turned out the way it did. There is a part of me that remains "in flight," meaning that I try not to think about my childhood and young adulthood. Strangely, I took care of my adoptive parents in their old age and even paid for their funerals, though I was not left anything by them. The photos of my childhood from that period were thrown into a landfill. Only because the keeper of the landfill recognized me was I able to retrieve any of these images from an unhappy time.

A few years ago when I was home for *Juhannus,* I experienced a heart-stopping moment during the festivities while I was watching the bonfire. It brought back such memories that I could hardly contain myself.

There is a poem that perhaps best describes the loss of my childhood in Finland: "To the house and garden, field and lawn / To the meadow gate we swung upon / To pump and stable, tree and swing / Goodbye, goodbye to everything."[1]

* * * * *

Currently, after working for thirty-two years, Rauha is "happy to be a homemaker and grandmother and married to a wonderful and supportive husband. I enjoy a good life in spite of my unhappy beginnings."

Notes

1. The quotation represents the second stanza from "Goodbye to the Farm" from *A Child's Garden of Verses* by Robert Louis Stevenson.

38

Repairing the Clock
Kaj Wanne

I was born in Helsinki on December 5, 1940, shortly after the Continuation War with the Soviet Union began. My father was a soldier in the army, and though my mother tried to take care of me, it was not easy. The building in which we lived on Jungfrustigen in the center of Helsinki was destroyed by Russian bombs, and food was very short.

My mother Helmi was born in 1911 on Pargas, an island outside Turku in the southwest part of Finland. Her parents, Carl and Matilda Grönberg, were farmers and had three other daughters. Perhaps to find better opportunities for work, my mother moved to Helsinki where she worked as a hairdresser. She was a very sensitive person with weak nerves and, for this reason and because she had trouble with her stomach, she frequently stayed in the hospital, though I don't know what type of hospital it was. I remember taking her flowers there with Ilmari, my father, after the war.

Ilmari was born in 1907 in Nådendal, a small village outside Turku. His parents' surname was Lindblad, and they were also farmers. They had three sons, including my father, and one daughter. After Finland won independence from the USSR, there was a strong will to make everything more Finnish, so many Finns with Swedish names changed them to Finnish ones. All three sons changed their surname from the Swedish Lindblad to the Finnish Vanne, but I later changed my last name to Wanne to separate myself somewhat from the Finnish. My father studied music as a young man to become a church musician, but for some reason he didn't finish his music studies, perhaps due to the war when he was drafted as an officer into the army. My parents weren't actually religious and didn't go to church on Sundays. But I remember that when I was older, my father took me to some sort of meeting where there was a projector, showing very beautiful pictures of Jesus with a lot of gold in them, which I later understood to be icons. So perhaps he was religious in his own way.

In 1942, when I was about eighteen months old, the Finnish government decided to send me together with many other children to Sweden literally to save our lives. Like many of these children I was very ill from undernourishment. It was summertime when my mother had to hand me over to total strangers, which may have been terrible for her. Like many infants and very small children I was sent by plane instead of by rail or boat. After the flight from Helsinki to Stockholm, I was taken to a children's home governed by the Swedish Red Cross in Södertälje. I was apparently extremely weak and almost didn't survive. But after some two months, when I was around two, I was put on a train that was traveling through Sweden from east to west. At every station the train stopped, and people entered to select the children they wanted to care for. The healthiest and strongest looking were picked first. Brothers and sisters who had grown to depend on each other and who were each other's only security were often divided. Because I was so young and unhealthy, it seemed that no one wanted me. In fact, it wasn't until the last train stop that a couple agreed to take me. All this was explained to me later by this couple who became my foster parents.

Einar and Hanna Olsson were really wonderful people. They had no children of their own, although they clearly loved children. Hanna was born in 1895, the youngest of eleven children. And, until her parents died, she had to take care of them. In those days it was usually the youngest girl responsible for taking care of parents in their old age. There were few social institutions then to care for seniors outside of the *Fattighuset* (or poorhouse), and it was considered shameful to commit your parents to such a place. As a consequence, Hanna didn't marry until later in life, which could explain why she and Einar had no children.

My foster father was born in 1900 and was raised by his single mother and grandmother. He began work at thirteen in a glass factory, making art glass. Then, at eighteen, he started a taxi business and later owned buses as well. At the time I arrived he had a gasoline station in Arvika, a small town in Värmland in western Sweden near Norway and only 28 kilometers or so north of Göteborg. Arvika had only about 20,000 inhabitants at that time. We lived in a small suburb called Västra Sund in a house near a lake called Värmeln. I of course had no memory of my Finnish parents at this time and called my foster parents *Mamma* and *Pappa*. Later they took another Finnish war child named Paula Annelie Helenius, who was a couple of years older than I. She came to Sweden in March 1944 and left in January 1945. I have few memories of her except that she and I played together.

When I first arrived I could only speak a few Finnish words, but I soon learned to speak Swedish. Because *Mamma* and *Pappa* had trouble pronouncing my Finnish name Kauko, they called me Kaj, which I later made official. With my own children today, I refer to my deceased foster parents as my grandparents, *Farmor* (Grandmother) and *Farfar* (Grandfather). It is now ironic to think of my Finnish name Kauko, which means something that is "far away," because for my Finnish parents I was far away in Sweden, and later, after I had to return to Finland, I was far away from my Swedish parents, whom I continued to think of as *Mamma* and *Pappa*, while I called my Finnish parents by their first names, Helmi and Ilmari.

Einar was very attentive to me and took me with him everywhere he could. He was an outdoors person, and we did a lot of fishing together, catching bass and pike in the lakes and small salmon called *öring* in the rivers. He was very technical, and when I was older he taught me how to repair motorcycles and other vehicles. When I was about five, I remember that *Pappa* gave me an old alarm clock and some tools and told me to repair the clock before he came home that day. It was broken into small parts, but this was a good learning experience for me. He was very loving, and when I was upset or angry, he sat me gently in his lap and tried to distract me until I was calm and happy, a practice I continued with my own children. But he also had strict rules that he followed. Though I had a lot of independence, when it was time for dinner I had to come in immediately from playing. He was also very humorous and liked telling stories for which he became popular and widely known in the area around Arvika.

Many years later, in 1998, when I was working at the Volvo car corporation as a consultant, I met someone who remembered my foster father by his nickname "BussEinar," and some of his jokes came back to me. For instance, in Arvika in Värmland, where we lived, there was a very eccentric person named Elis Taserud. My foster father enjoyed inventing stories about him. In one story it was dark, and Elis was looking for something under a street lamp. A local policeman asked Elis if he had dropped something, and Elis said that he had dropped the keys to his motorcycle. The policeman asked, are you sure you dropped them here? No, said Elis, it was over there, but it is too dark to look there. Another story BussEinar told was a fishing story. Two men were arguing about which had caught the biggest pike. One said, "My fish was so big that my arms were too short to measure it." The other man said, "When I was out fishing, a big pike pulled my boat over the lake, but I managed to fasten it with my grappling iron on the beach. We had meals from it for an entire week, and then it managed to set itself free and disappeared!"

I was very fond of BussEinar, and I was equally fond of *Mamma* who was always there to care for me and who never raised her voice against me. I truly loved her. And I loved their spitz-dog, "Bussie"—a word that combines the word "bus" and the Swedish "bussig," which means to be fair and helpful. Bussig was with me everywhere I went. I also had several playmates, though my memory of them is weak. I do remember playing with my foster sister, Annelie, however. I was always playing outdoors in every sort of weather. One Christmas, I received a toy motorcycle, which I really loved. And I loved skiing and ice skating on the nearby lake. I also remember visiting an old scrap yard with old vehicles and obsolete farming machines. The man who owned this yard was very friendly, and he always invited me to "help" him. I called him *Skrot-Emil* ("Scrap-Emil").

I stayed with my foster parents until I was six, so I was with them for four wonderful years. But in 1946, one year after the war ended, the Finnish government demanded all the war children back. I didn't want to return because I had no memory of Finland or my Finnish parents. Naturally I had come to think of *Mamma* and *Pappa* as my true parents. Even my Finnish mother did not want me back because conditions in Finland were still very hard, and she had a new baby, my brother Pertti, to care for. My Finnish father had survived the war, but he was wounded in one leg from a piece of shell. My Swedish parents tried to adopt me but were denied by the Finnish government. I remember *Mamma* bravely trying to prepare me by talking about how exciting it would be for me to meet my newborn baby brother. She and I often lay on her bed, talking about various things and then, finally, about my going back to Finland.

I remember saying farewell to *Mamma* at the train station in Arvika, but I can't remember how I felt on that day. I must have shut down or repressed those feelings. *Pappa* and I went by train to Stockholm and then by boat to Helsinki, but the journey is a blank in my mind. I don't believe that my foster father tried to get me back, realizing that it was hopeless.

The day on which *Pappa* brought me to Helsinki to meet my Finnish parents was shocking. They were complete strangers to me. My Finnish mother Helmi could speak both Swedish and Finnish, so I could at least communicate with her. But all communication with my father, Ilmari, had to be translated by Helmi. It was equally shocking suddenly to be living in a small one-room apartment compared to the spacious house in Arvika. The food supply was still very short, and we ate a lot of cabbage soup. But my problem wasn't with the food. I used to eat everything, and I still do. I understand that my Finnish parents did the best they could under the circumstances, and luckily my foster parents regularly sent food and clothes to me.

After the war my Finnish father worked as a welder at a shipyard, perhaps the Wärtsilä shipyard, which was within walking distance of their apartment, a different one from that in which I had been born. I remember carrying food to him when he worked overtime. The building in which we lived was situated at the top of a hill with a steep street leading down to the harbor. He was a very active man, although he walked with a limp, and he seemed to be proud of me and spent a lot of time with me. He also played violin and piano. He never complained about anything, but when he was sad he took his violin and played. He also arranged for me to have piano lessons. Unfortunately, they didn't take; I was not interested.

As a young boy, however, I *was* interested in his war stories. One experience he shared was about him and several of his men, sitting in a cart driven by horses. They were sitting opposite to each other with their machine guns that pointed upward on the floor between their legs. One of the soldiers had forgotten to secure his weapon, and the road was very bumpy. The cart shook so much that the machine gun fired a couple of shots. Unfortunately, the shots hit this soldier in his jaw, passed through his head, and killed him immediately. Another story my father shared was about him resting against a tree in the woods. He was very tired and fell half asleep. But suddenly he heard a voice, urging him to move away. Luckily he heard the warning and moved just before a Russian shell hit the tree and created a crater where moments before he had been sitting. He felt that he had been saved by a guardian angel. This made a big impression on me. I remember, too, that he never spoke hatefully about the Russian people but that he hated Josef Stalin and his Communist cronies. He described how badly Russian soldiers had been equipped, especially those sent to the front during the Winter War. Many of them didn't even have proper boots but boots made of cardboard.

Sometimes my father was very hard on me. I was punished once when I accidentally broke a big window in a toy store. I had been fighting with a couple of boys who pushed me into the window, and the shop owner caught me, while the other boys disappeared. Some of these boys spoke Swedish and called me *svikare* ("traitor") because I had left Finland during the war. My father was working at the time, so the shop owner told my mother who didn't believe my story about being pushed by other boys. She told my father that it was my fault.

After I was put in school, I learned Finnish fluently. But

Figure 38.1. *Kaj Wanne's father Ilmari Vanna, an officer in the Finnish Army during World War II. Courtesy Kaj Wanne.*

discipline in Finnish schools was quite severe at this time. On one occasion the teacher had to leave the classroom for some reason, and she chose me to sit in her chair to superintend my classmates. It was strongly forbidden for students to talk or move, and it was my assignment to write the name of anyone who misbehaved on the blackboard. When the teacher returned, she punished the pupils whose names I had recorded. And that got me into trouble with some of them. I was often fighting with boys in the schoolyard, and before I learned Finnish I was teased because of my strange accent. One boy in particular who was very strong followed me around the schoolyard. Although I wasn't big, I could run very fast. Sometimes I managed to get away, but he often caught me and wrestled me on the ground. Also I was often punished in school because I was a lively child, and it was difficult for me to stay still. Once I was punished by having to stand in a corner, facing the wall with all the other students watching, which was humiliating for me.

From the few letters I have that I wrote to my Swedish parents there is one in which I make the remark that I had received the highest marks in my first class, shortly after I returned to Finland. At that point I was eager to please. But in a letter I sent later, I wrote that I had been bad. My teacher had informed Ilmari and Helmi about my low grades on tests, especially in math, and that I had not attended school for a few days. In fact, I had played hooky with some other boys, and for this I was punished. I was also spanked when I took some money from my small savings (sent to me from *Mamma* and *Pappa*) and bought a ballpoint pen, a new thing that had just arrived in the biggest Helsinki department store, Stockmann's. I couldn't resist the temptation, but Ilmari and Helmi did not approve. Another time I misbehaved was when a classmate and I played hooky from school. We were then living in a new apartment in Kampgatan, which my parents managed to buy and where they lived until they died. Though I was not allowed to have friends over, my friend and I were in our apartment and took a book, maybe a schoolbook, tore all of its pages out, and made paper airplanes from the leaves, which we threw out of the apartment window onto the street. We thought that this was very creative, but the landlord informed my parents and I was punished. The street name, Kampgatan, no longer exists; it was renamed Urho Kekkonengatan, after Finland's president from 1956 to 1982. The building in which I lived—I lived in three different apartments during my four years with Ilmari and Helmi, and this was the last—still exists, but because of the change in name, you cannot find Kampgatan on the map.

Helmi was mostly working as a hairdresser, and I was quite often alone, wandering the streets and looking in shop windows, dreaming. I can't remember who took care of my younger brother Pertti, but it must have been some relative. During my four years in Finland my Swedish foster parents sent gifts, even to my brother Pertti, clothes and toys. I missed the frequent celebrations with friends that they used to have, since my Finnish parents never had friends over or seemed to celebrate anything.

I now realize that I became a pain in school and at home because I didn't like living with Ilmari and Helmi in Finland, and this resulted in spankings and rough punishment. But the reason I misbehaved is because I thought such misbehavior would hasten my return to Sweden. It was my strategy to go back as soon as possible, and I prayed to God that this would happen.

Fortunately, every summer *Mamma* and *Pappa* provided me with a boat ticket between Helsinki and Stockholm, so that I could spend my summer holidays with them. I hated going back to Finland at the end of the summer, but this was something that I had to do and I dreaded it. Also, because my father was bald, my mother took precautions against my going bald by shaving my head just before I left for Sweden each summer. She thought that this would stimulate my hair growth, but I hated it because I felt that I looked terrible and worried that my Swedish parents would find me repulsive and reject me.

I can't say that I ever loved my Finnish parents, though I liked Ilmari better than Helmi because he paid some attention to me. Helmi only nagged me all the time, telling me in Swedish—the language she usually used to speak to me—how bad I was. She would never let me talk about my time in Sweden. And she was very dishonest, blaming me for things I hadn't done. She was also a perfectionist and made very difficult demands on me regarding my performance in school, nagging me incessantly to get better grades. In one way I am grateful for this today, however, because it made me more ambitious in my later life. I became quite ambitious in my late teens, and when I attended university I remember thinking, *I'll show her.* But I can still hear her voice, teasing me about how worthless I was, whereas my Swedish mother always put me on a pedestal. I remember Helmi telling me that the only thing I was fit for was picking up rubbish off the streets or being a shoe shiner. But the worst thing about her was that she wasn't sincere. She could be nice one day and cruel the next. And she didn't trust me. I remember that when we saw a lorry with a name written on its door, I read the name out loud and said it was the name of a company. She opposed me, saying it was the brand of the lorry. But I protested because I knew I was right, which ended with her hitting me. I believe that my Finnish mother wanted me to stay in Sweden at the end of each summer holiday and perhaps treated me meanly to make the final break easier. She also wanted to show my foster parents what a nice and clever boy she had raised. She was very concerned when I fell ill and contacted the doctors immediately, for instance when I had tonsillitis and had my tonsils out. I believe that she wanted to keep me healthy, so that my foster parents would still be willing to take me back. This is a dark picture of my mother, but that is how I understood her. I just didn't like her, I am sorry to say.

One of the few happy memories I have of Helmi is of our walking together on Saturdays to the *Saluhallarna* or market hall to buy fresh bread and real butter, which tasted delicious. She and I also occasionally visited family members in Åbo, the Swedish name for Turku. I remember my Aunt Lydia and a girl cousin. She was very nice and took me to my first movie, a cartoon with Donald Duck. I still love this cartoon. When we went to Åbo, we went by train, and I remember that the curtains had to be drawn when the train passed Hangö, which was occupied by the Russians at that time. This excited me because it was like going through a tunnel. But I continued to pray that I could one day stay in Sweden permanently.

Finally my prayers were answered in 1950 when I was ten. *Mamma* and *Pappa* consulted the Swedish authorities and our parish minister when it became clear to them how unhappy I was with my life in Finland with Ilmari and Helmi. Although the Finnish authorities refused to approve my adoption, I was granted leave to stay in Sweden. So I began school there that year, and it went very well. My Finnish parents did not try to get me back to my knowledge, and I was extremely happy when I finally understood that I could stay. It was my Swedish father who told me this. I made new playmates around this time, and we fished for cod and mackerel in the sea. Also *Pappa* had a friend with a big motorboat, and we often rode quite far out to sea, almost to Denmark. I was very lucky to have been loved and taken care of by my Swedish parents Einar and Hanna. They saved me, and I will be forever grateful for them.

Soon after I returned to Sweden, I completely forgot my Finnish and can't speak a word of it now. I had little contact with my Finnish parents after 1950, though I received a congratulation card every birthday, and Helmi came to Sweden in 1955 when I had my confirmation. She gave me a very beautiful gold ring from her and Ilmari, a custom in Finland. On this occasion, my Swedish parents also gave me my first suit and a Bible, though they never went to church and were not religious.

A big influence in my life after returning to Sweden was my best friend. I knew him when I was living in Mölndal with my foster parents between 1950 and 1960. His name was Ain Ala and he was from Estonia. He and his parents had fled from Estonia during World War II when the Russians occupied that nation. The family escaped in a small fishing boat together with some other people. They managed to reach the coast of southern Sweden where they were rescued. Ain's parents were very highly educated people, but in Sweden his father could only get factory work. My foster parents and Ain's parents became friends, although only

Ain's father could speak good Swedish while his mother had a hard time. However, I was able to talk to her because I still remembered some Finnish, and the Estonian language is quite similar. Ain and I became really good friends, though he was a couple of years older than I. We went to the same school and lived in the same apartment house at Sörgårdsgatan. He was a very clever boy and taught me to play chess, though I was never able to beat him. We also spent many hours at the local library, borrowing books about aircraft and boy books about the English hero Bigglesworth, a war pilot. We dreamed of being pilots, and we built a lot of model airplanes. Ain later studied civil engineering at Chalmers University. Instead of working with aircraft, he worked with computers, which was very new at that time in 1962. His connections helped me to work in the same business, and I began programming this enormous computer, Alwac 2, which took up a whole room. It didn't have transistors but thousands of vacuum tubes. You could never cut off the electricity because that created problems in restarting the system. But one night, a cleaning lady unplugged the computer to plug in her vacuum cleaner. As a consequence, it took more than a week to restart the computer and get correct results again. This was a new and fascinating world for me. So Ain led to the beginning of my career and was a very important person in my life.

After I married, Helmi and Ilmari visited me and my wife Rona in 1969, but it was very formal. I couldn't speak to Ilmari, so everything had to be translated by Helmi. My wife Rona tried to make the best of this meeting, but she was instead insulted by Helmi who said that she was lazy and that I should have married a Finnish woman. My brother Pertti has a different opinion of Helmi and Ilmari from mine, and he defended them when I complained about them in my letters to him. I suppose he had a very different experience with them growing up. It is true that they gave him a good education, which enabled him to become a lawyer in Helsinki's city government.

It took more than twenty years before I visited my old country in 1974, and I have only been back three or four times since then. My only relatives in Finland are a few cousins and my brother. Unfortunately we have had very little contact. Though he has two children, I have never met them. My feelings toward Finland are still very mixed. Sometimes I feel Swedish and sometimes Finnish. I am proud of having been born in Finland, and when there's a sports contest between Sweden and Finland, for instance in ice hockey, I usually side with Finland. I also *feel* Finnish in that I have a strong will, what the Finns call *sisu,* and I never give up. And I have physical courage. I like to drive a motorcycle and parachute from planes. Though I don't speak very much and never brag, I am a good listener. And I am also Finnish in my enjoyment of the sauna. I have a sauna in my house, and a friend of mine has a sauna built close to Lake

Mjörn (only a couple of kilometers from me); there we can do the proper sauna, jumping in the lake afterwards. In the wintertime we also ice-fish together. Finnish humor is very dry and sarcastic, and many Finns suffer from sadness and melancholy, which you can hear in their music such as Sibelius. In Scandinavia, Finns are called the "Scandinavian Japanese" in a positive way.

But because I spent only four years and eighteen months in Finland, of course I feel more Swedish. The first language I learned was Swedish, and I regard it as my mother tongue. I am also very proud of the technical achievements of this small country. And I feel Swedish in that I am honest and have tolerance, humor, and optimism.

Ilmari died in 1973, though I don't know the cause of death, and Helmi died in 1985 of cancer. My foster parents are also deceased. *Pappa* Einar died in 1978 at age 78, and *Mamma* Hanna died in 1977 at age 82. They were wonderful grandparents to my children, and they continue to live in my heart.

Because I am now retired, I have time to think. It is an important for me to process old memories and to try to reconcile my experience with Helmi especially. Though I am not religious, I believe that my foster parents were my guardian angels. My religion if I have one is a mixture of Christianity and Buddhism. The supreme God I believe in is Love. I think all people have their own karma and create their own hell or heaven, depending upon their actions and thoughts. I have been thinking about what has influenced me most, inheritance or milieu? It is definitely milieu. Most of my values, ideas, and interests come from my foster father and foster mother. The fact that I had to learn two languages has been stimulating. I don't believe in the theory that you have to learn your mother tongue perfectly before you learn a new language. I am not bitter, nor do I feel that I was victimized by my bad start in life. Instead, I believe that it brought me many opportunities, and I will always be very thankful for my foster parents.

*****

Kaj studied computer science and economics at Göteborg University. Until he turned twenty-one he was a Finnish citizen; then he applied for Swedish citizenship and completed his obligatory military service in Sweden. In 1964 he married Rona, a "wonderful and understanding Swedish woman." They had three sons, and later four grandsons. They also became foster parents for two children—siblings who came from a dysfunctional family. Kaj says that having been a foster child himself inspired him to help these children who received good educations, later married, and today have children of their own. Until his retirement, Kaj worked as a systems analyst and IT consultant and had his own business for a short time. He is a widower today, living in Lerum, a small suburb of Göteborg.

39

Soldier Boy
Norman Westerberg

The first time Russian bombers visited Turku, we were standing on the frozen lake near the sauna building. Suddenly we heard loud bangs from anti-aircraft artillery, and saw small dark clouds forming about three kilometers to the north. The sky was clear, and since the danger seemed far enough away, we did not hurry into the woods. In a few seconds, however, we had ten three-engine Russian airplanes on top of us, and we sure ran quickly for cover. On this particular day they came twice.... We climbed up on a high hill and saw three huge fires in the distance.

This is a letter I wrote on December 25, 1939, to my Aunt Edith, who lived as a widow in Helsinki.[1] I have translated it into English, along with several other letters I quote from in my story. Aunt Edith collected all the letters and postcards I wrote to her until she came to live with my family in 1961 in a different place in Helsinki. That is when she presented me with the huge box that contained all my letters to her. It is through these letters and ones my parents saved that I am able to reconstruct my years of growing up during the war.

When the Soviet Union attacked Finland on November 30, 1939, I was ten years old. My father Eric was then forty-seven, and my mother Hellin was thirty-nine. I had two brothers, nine-year-old Sven and four-year-old Finn. I was actually born in the United States, but my parents returned to live in Helsinki in 1930 when I was only one. Then, in 1937 we moved to Turku, where I attended *kansakoulu* (elementary school). Out of twenty boys in my class, three, including myself, were allowed to skip grade four and transfer directly to the *lyseo* (with eight grades leading to the high-school diploma) in the fall of 1939.

In July of that year, Sven and I spent a few weeks at a summer camp held on an island in Nauvo, reached by ship from Turku. "Norman" is an unusual name in Finland, though sometimes appearing as a surname.

We still laugh when we recall one of the camp leaders asking "Sven Norman" to say grace before a meal. Later that summer, the two of us spent a month with a pastor's family near Lempaala south of Tampere. They had two girls our age, and we had lots of fun taking care of farm animals, helping with the haymaking, and swimming. Above all, we improved our Finnish, which was the main purpose of our stay there. This was common practice for kids growing up in Swedish-speaking families like mine.

Everywhere we went we heard about men and women who had worked as volunteers in Karelia since 1938, strengthening defense lines, as war with Russia seemed imminent. I am not sure if we kids understood the implications. But in October our father was ordered to attend reserve officer's training. He had become a second lieutenant (*vanrikki*) in 1918, though he was not a very military type and battled severe diabetes. The rest of the family visited him for a few days when he was still stationed in Kerava (near Helsinki). In another letter to Aunt Edith from Kerava, dated October 24, 1939, I wrote:

When relatives from Loviisa, east of Helsinki, wrote us that we should visit them, we first debated whether to take the bus or the train. It turned out differently. When a man we knew, who had just returned from taking his family to safety in Denmark, offered to take us to Helsinki in his car, we accepted. The first part of the trip was fine, but then I started to vomit. From Helsinki to Loviisa we had to change bus once. There was standing room only, and again I did not feel well. After a few days in Loviisa, we learned that our father would soon be sent from Kerava to an unknown destination east, so we took a bus to Porvoo, and then a train to Kerava. Everywhere it was crowded with soldiers in the reserve. I did not recognize my father when he met us at the station in his military uniform.

This was my first ride in a passenger car. There were few cars in Turku before the war, and even fewer during the war years when all cars had to be turned over to the military. Secondly, even main highways were gravel roads and very curvy. Easy to become a pale face!

We returned to school for about a month before the bombings started. We were then living in a six-story apartment building at a street corner near the Auran silta (the central bridge over Aura River). The square building had a small central courtyard, and we lived on the third floor with a view of the courtyard. Every apartment had a small storage room in the basement with shelving for preserves and a bin for potatoes. In the fall of 1939 these spaces were strengthened with logs and two-by fours, and the potato bin was often removed to provide room for sleeping cots. We later spent many a night in these air shelters, which sometimes shook but never crumbled.

One day I noticed our janitor affixing something to a lamppost in the inner yard. It was a triangle, with about two-feet long sides, made of one-inch diameter iron rods. Hitting it with another iron rod, he proudly demonstrated it to me. This became our first air attack warning system until much later, when we received electrically operated alarm sirens. In the parks, holes were dug for additional air shelters. They were not very deep, but fortunately in the early stages of the war the Russians dropped mainly incendiary bombs. Due to Turku's predominantly wooden houses, these too could be devastating, however.

The letter that is quoted at the beginning of my story was written at a mansion (*kartano*) named Brinkhall that was located ten or so kilometers south of Turku. The owner of this mansion kindly opened her house to families with children who needed to be evacuated from the city. From Brinkhall I wrote to my father on December 13:

Dear Pappa! It is now 7 PM and very dark outside. Finn and Sven are drawing pictures, mother is knitting, and I am writing this letter to you. Last Monday at 11 AM, just when the milk truck was about to pick up our luggage to take it here to Brinkhall, an air-raid warning was given, and we rushed to our basement shelter. The warning lasted only half an hour this time, so we were able to bring down our luggage to the truck. But when we returned to the apartment, mother noticed that our clock had stopped and sent me outside to check the big clock at the street corner. We feared we would never make it to the bus station, but we all ran and made it to the first bus stop near our home. We pushed ourselves into the last standing room in the smoking area in the rear, but later even got to sit up front, as other passengers reached their destinations. Since we had had no breakfast, we enjoyed the coffee upon arrival at Brinkhall and then went down to start heating our assigned quarter, the sauna building by the lake.

That winter was very cold, often around −30° Celsius, which is comparable to −20° Fahrenheit. It was difficult for us to keep the space warm, and soon we moved into a room in another building near the mansion. Overall, there must have been at least thirty children evacuated there. We all were assigned duties. I particularly liked to chop firewood, and lots of it was needed. I also made the fifteen-minute walk to the bus stop many winter evenings to pick up everyone's mail. It was frigid but very dry, so I wore three pairs of woolen socks on my feet instead of boots. Later I received my first real felt boots, which were Finnish army model.

Air attacks became a daily routine. I believe Turku had half a dozen fighter planes that bravely met the many squadrons of Russian bombers, and we often saw Russian airmen parachuting to the ground. One day someone who had visited the city brought back terrible news. The main post office had two entrances to its bomb shelter. One entrance had remained locked by mistake after the siren sounded, and while people hurried around the corner to the other entrance a big bomb exploded next to them. Many people died on the spot, and one can still see the marks made by flying shrapnel on the granite walls.

We had not heard from our father for a long time when he suddenly appeared on our doorstep at Brinkhall. He looked dead tired and told us his story. He was a platoon leader in the ErP18 (18th Separate Infantry Battalion). The battalion had been held in reserve most of December near Loviisa, from where they fortified the archipelago and operated anti-aircraft guns. At midnight on New Year's Eve, the entire battalion was moved in open trucks in chilling cold weather to Kouvola, where the men were loaded on a train that took them via Tainionkoski and Sordavala to Suistamo. From there they started their foot march at 4 AM on January 2, 1940, toward their first destination: the village of Kokkoselka. Our father Eric's sugar levels had risen catastrophically, and he had a very bad cold. The army doctor ordered him to get home as quickly as he could. So he started walking back to Suistamo by himself, and fortunately about halfway here, he got a lift on a returning horse-drawn army supply sled. After many train changes and stoppages due to Russian air attacks, he finally arrived at Brinkhall on January 6.

During a short visit to Turku, I wrote to Aunt Edith on January 7:

We are planning to leave for Sweden next week, possibly as soon as Sunday. Father will follow along us to Tornio, the border crossing.... Our apartment is still as before, but many windows in the building are broken.

My father was anxious to get back to the action at the front, and my mother was looking for a chance to serve as a full-time Lotta (i.e., a member of the women's corps). All schools in Turku had been closed since the start of the war, and would remain closed until it ended. The decision had been made that we three Westerberg boys should join the many thousands of Finnish children who were being sent to Sweden. When my father received a short assignment to the troops in northern Finland and could thus join us on part of the journey, the departure date was quickly set for February 11, one day after my eleventh birthday. We stopped for one hour at the city apartment, and then took the train leaving at 7 PM to Toijala. Our connecting train from Helsinki going north was very late, because it had to wait to get through the key railroad station in Riihimaki, where the railroad tracks had to be frequently repaired following constant bombing by the Russians. The Toijala station was completely dark and crowded with soldiers in gray. Finally our train arrived, and in the dimly lit wagons were hundreds of children, each wearing a large nametag. A few women were there too, supervising this mass exodus. We were very lucky because our parents were on the same train, and they were asked to be in charge of our wagon.

Contrary to many other child transport trains north, when children often had to take refuge in the forest during air raids, I think our journey went smoothly. We arrived at Tornio at 5 PM the next day and stayed overnight with one of the local families who had volunteered to house people like us. The next morning, February 13, we said goodbye to our father and walked over the Tornio River bridge to the neighboring Swedish city of Haparanda. After customs formalities and medical examinations, we proceeded to the railroad station where friendly Swedish women volunteers met us and provided free train tickets for us to Stockholm. The train going south left at 5 PM.

Finn, Sven, and I were also lucky because, unlike most of the children sent to Sweden, we spoke Swedish fluently. We admired the calm and patience of the hundreds of other children who only spoke Finnish and could not communicate with volunteer workers. My mother Hellin offered to help with interpreting and was asked to travel with us the 1,200 kilometers to Stockholm.

Soon after we left Haparanda, Finn charmed a Swedish officer into giving him a ten kronor bill, which was enough for our family to upgrade to a sleeping cabin where we could take turns resting. Next morning, the Centralstationen, or main railroad station, in Stockholm looked like a holiday bazaar. There were tables heaped with clothing for the arriving Finnish war children, and busy volunteers were handing out instructions. Finn was to stay in Stockholm with a younger Swedish couple, while Sven and I would stay together with a family in Råda in Varmland. Then came time to say goodbye to our mother Hellin, who had to return to Finland to rejoin the Lotta Svärd (Women's Auxiliary Service). Someone asked Finn why he wasn't crying like almost all of the other small children, and he replied, "No, I am from Finland."

Råda is a small town near the city of Hagfors, west of Stockholm, near the Norwegian border. It is situated on the river Klaralven (Clear River), which runs south from Finnskogama (Finnish Forests). The name of our host family was Lunden. They had seven children, but only the youngest, Lennart, was still at home. The head of the family was the chief forester in his district, which included the Finnskogama. Little did I know then, that in the sixteenth century, Sweden had moved many Finns, especially from the Savo province, to that area. And hundreds of them in 1638 had been shipped to the New Sweden colony in North America.

Both Sven and I attended *folkskola* (elementary school). I still have a small silver cup awarded to the best foreigner in a cross-country ski competition there. It is my only sports trophy ever, and I have a suspicion that I was the only contender in that category. Shortly after March 13 the Lundens received a telephone call from Finland that the Winter War had ended. On April 7 I wrote my parents in Turku:

Just home from Sunday school. It is fun now that spring has arrived, and we can play with marbles outdoors. I bought 26 marbles for 13 ores (one Swedish crown is 100 ores), and have lost all but one. That is because I am a beginner. Tomorrow at school I must try to win some back.

Very soon after this, space was found for us on the famous Finnish steamship, *Oihonna*. Sven and I picked up little brother Finn in Stockholm, and we all sailed to Turku, sharing a small cabin below and aft and close to the propeller. It was very noisy as the ship made its way through the ice on the Sea of Bothnia. In the morning, Finn was missing, but we soon found him eating a boiled egg in the ship cafeteria. We must have reunited with our parents before April 15 because on that date I passed my first tests for Third Class Boy Scout.

After our separation from our father in Tornio, and after he had completed his temporary duty in the north and left for the Karelian front, he was given the task to organize a *Kenttapostikontori* 27 (similar to an APO address in the U.S. Army), which censored and distributed mail to soldiers via thirteen sub-offices at the front. By the time the Winter War ended on March 13, the staff of his military post office near Imatra numbered 100 people. The infantry battalion ErP18, which he had left on January 3, experienced its first combat with the enemy at Lemetti on January 9, when eighteen of its soldiers were killed, including one company commander. Several officers and many men had also been severely wounded. In all, the battalion had recorded 120 killed, 170 wounded, and 140 injured by frostbite. This represented half of those who had served with the battalion.

During the so-called Interim Peace, March 1940 to June 1941, schools returned to normal. I attended the Svenska Klassiska Lyceum, Finland's oldest school whose history goes back to the fourteenth century when clergy were educated there. The discipline I experienced was still fairly medieval. It really hurt when a teacher hit your knuckles with his wooden pointer.

In addition to scouting, I also rejoined the Suojeluskunta (Civil Guard). In 1938 the Suojeluskunta numbered 100,000 members and a trainee Boys' Department of 30,000. In the 1920s, my father had bought a small accordion or squeeze box, which I had learned to play. I often found myself playing patriotic music to accompany the singing at gatherings of the Civil Guard.

The food shortage continued, and Finland was very poor. Great effort and resources were devoted to relocate 400,000 Karelians who had lost their homes. Finland also became more isolated from the rest of the world. On April 9 Germany occupied Denmark and Norway. On June 14 the Russians shot down a Finnair (then "Aero") plane on its regular route between Tallinn and Helsinki over the Gulf of Finland.

In May 1941 a great event occurred: a competition among ordinary people in Sweden and Finland to promote walking as a way to better health. You could choose how far you wanted to walk, and I remember receiving the ten-kilometer badge. Over 100,000 Finns walked that day and beat the Swedes. In a letter dated May 22 I wrote to my Aunt Edith:

> *School is over, and I received a scholarship of 100 marks. Thank you for the money you sent me for my name's day.*

(My first name is actually "Eric," and the name day for Eric in Finland is May 18.)

My mother was born in Loviisa (Lovisa in Swedish), and most of her family still lived there. Her older brother, my uncle Hugo, was especially dear to me. He owned an auto repair shop. There were always old cars in the yard used for spare parts, and I just loved to play in them. I used to sit in one with only a steering wheel for hours and pretend to be a good driver. Hugo also employed a blacksmith who made various auto parts and equipped horses with shoes. Sometimes I wondered why the horses did not cry when he hammered on their horseshoes.

On June 19, 1941 my father was ordered to travel to Oulu to report to the Finnish army northern command. There he met his former classmate, Hjalmar Stromberg, who had changed his family name to Siilasvuo and was soon to be Lt. General Hjalmar Siilasvuo. My father in his younger years had worked for Finnish companies in Hamburg, Germany, and St Petersburg, Russia. His language skills were very valuable. At this time the presence of German troops in Finland was primarily in the north, and he was often asked to serve as an interpreter for the high command. When the Continuation War between the Soviet Union and Finland started in June 1941, he was present at Raate when Finnish and German troops crossed the border on June 30. In August he was in charge of a camp near Kuusamo for three hundred Russian prisoners of war. He was promoted to First Lieutenant on August 6.

As soon as the war started, it was no longer safe to stay in the city of Loviisa as it was only a short hop from Soviet-held Estonia and was frequently bombed without advance warning. We three Westerberg boys and half a dozen of our cousins were moved about seven kilometers west of the city to a small farmhouse owned by a distant older relative, Aunt Agda. From there I wrote to Aunt Edith on July 7:

The sun is shining so my arms are burning. Thank you for the money you sent. Unfortunately, our country store no longer has any candy, but I will bike there and buy some juice. We have raised a tent in a nearby meadow and sleep in it when the weather is nice. We are fine here, though we hear airplanes buzzing all the time.

My mother, who visited us, added her own comments to my letter:

Tried to telephone you, Edith, from the post office, but by the time the air raid warnings were over, it was already too late. Today we saw our own soldiers thoroughly search the forests for Russian spies, which are believed to have been dropped nearby us.

Many spies were parachuted during the nights. Later we learned that some of them were young Estonians forced to make the jump. I was too young to participate in the searches for them, but older boys and girls helped our soldiers and members of the Civil Guard to form human chains that combed the area. Russian airplanes also liked to shoot at anything that moved. One afternoon, when we were hiding near our tent, one pilot decided to practice on cows in our field and managed to kill one.

Time had come to move back home. In a short note to Aunt Edith, dated August 9, I wrote:

We are now in Turku again. Our apartment looks so empty, as a lady has moved some of our furniture and household items to a safer place. We have not had any air raid warnings yet.

School did not start until November 3 and then only the five lower grades. The three highest grades, corresponding to senior high school in the United States, remained closed as most of the students were serving the military in some function. There was not much scouting activity either as all our leaders were at the front. I received my Third Class Scout badge in November 1940, and the subsequent notations in my scout report card are dated towards the end of year 1942, when I also received my Second Class Scout badge. I therefore intensified my involvement with the Boys' Department of the Civil Guard in Turku.

In October 1941 I was working full time as *Sotilaspoika* (soldier boy) for an anti-aircraft artillery unit, stationed on top of Vartiovuori, a hill near downtown Turku. My duties were to run errands and take messages to and from the military headquarters located in the basement of a downtown high rise. I also had to chop firewood, and keep the *kaakeliuunit* (tiled stoves) warm as well as tidy the commander's office. I was especially proud of a certificate I carried, reading *"Sotilaspoika Norman Westerberg on oikeutettu liikkumaan Turun kaupingilla polkupyortillti ilmahtilytyksenkin aikana"* (Soldier boy Norman Westerberg is authorized to bicycle the streets of Turku during air raid warnings).

As we approached the end of 1941, war activities shifted to regions east of the Russian border, to positions the Finnish troops had reached and which they were to hold for the next two years. For my father Eric, active military duties at the front came to an end due to his poor health. (In subsequent years, he struggled to hold jobs in the hotel and restaurant industries but passed away in 1949.) Schools in Turku had returned to normal, and schooling was only interrupted once for about a month in early 1942 when my school building was used to lodge German troops on their way to the war front.

Closed trading channels and the loss of agricultural areas in Karelia drastically decreased food supplies in Finland after the Winter War. In May 1940, bread and milk were rationed. Soon followed butter and, by November, meat. And there was a serious shortage of potatoes. Real coffee had disappeared from the stores, and all kinds of *korvike* (substitutes) were invented, many based on roasted rye. Tobacco products were strictly rationed in an effort to keep sufficient supplies for the fighting men and women. I remember my mother giving up a portion of her small sugar ration in exchange for extra cigarettes for my father.

All free hands participated in maximizing the utilization of the natural resources in our forests. School kids, scouts, and other groups picked berries, mushrooms, and waste wood like fallen branches and cones. Bigger boys felled trees marked for that purpose by foresters and cut them into firewood. Different sizes, shapes, and colors of lapel pins were given as awards for these activities. I remember cherishing a green ax-shaped pin I received for chopping one cord of wood, the only source of fuel for heating in Finland. We also raided attics and other storage places to collect any metal items not in use, which were then transferred to the steel mills as raw material.

There was no gasoline available for civilian cars and buses. But with amazing speed all buses and the remaining few passenger trains were equipped with generators for producer-gas.[2] Paper sacks containing wood chips were placed at strategic locations along the roads. When needed, and that was often, the bus stopped and the driver climbed on top of the roof and dumped the content of a few sacks into the feeder of the generator. The horsepower of the engines was naturally much reduced, and on steeper grades all able hands were asked to get off the bus and help push it up the hill.

I believe our family received a total of three packages, *Amerikanpaketti,* from kind Finns living in America. They usually contained some coffee and cigarettes in addition to clothing. From one man's used suit my mother made suits for both me and Sven. Once we received a pair of men's shoes that did not fit anyone in our family. When one of my school mates visited us, my mother showed the shoes to him, asking, "What size shoes do you wear?" He answered, "It depends," and later we saw his father, a distinguished university professor, wearing them.

In October 1941 my brother Sven, then eleven, had a chance to visit Sweden again and remained there for over half a year, due to his breaking a leg while he was there.

In summer 1942 we had an extra long school break, which allowed me to work from mid-May until the end of September as a *Sotilaspoika* for the Finnish defense forces. I was assigned to the *Vapaehtoiskeskus* in Turku, a center to which all volunteers from foreign countries reported for duty in the Finnish military service. Here they stayed until they received their clothing and further directions. Most of the volunteers arrived from Estonia and Sweden. I worked from 8 AM until 5 PM six days a week. One of my jobs was to serve as a messenger on my army bike between various military units in the city. I also helped clean the facilities, usually school buildings converted to temporary barracks. One of the toughest jobs was to sort incoming recycled clothing, such as used uniforms, boots, and so forth. All had to be sent to the laundry and sometimes out for repair by seamstresses or shoemakers. We then tried to find the right sizes for each volunteer. It was an odd-looking bunch that left our center for unknown adventures.

At one point we were located for several weeks at a vacated school on Luostarinkatu across the street from German troops who were lodged in another school. From our windows we could observe German soldiers exercising and were impressed by their rhythmical singing. In the summer of 1943 I served in a similar position for another two months. Many years later, mostly during the last ten years, I started receiving military decorations for my boyhood services. The Finnish Defense Forces have been very generous in expressing their appreciation for something we all took as a natural duty to our country in crisis.

In January 1944 the Soviet Army began to assemble a massive force—approximately 500,000 men, 10,000 artillery pieces, 2,000 aircraft, and 1,000 tanks—for a final offensive to defeat Finland. On January 14 I wrote in a letter to my Aunt Edith,

> *Schools have again closed in Turku. But we received lots of homework, since we will have to pass exams in the spring in order to advance to the next grade.*

Children were asked to leave the city, and I, then fifteen, my thirteen-year-old brother Sven, and eight-year-old Finn found a temporary home with a kind family in the village of Dragsfjärd, a community in the Turku archipelago, some fifty kilometers south of Turku. Finn attended the local elementary school there, while Sven and I tried to study on our own.

There were interesting distractions. In February the Soviet Air Force struck Helsinki repeatedly with hundreds of bombers. These air attacks were intended to force Finland to capitulate, but since only a small percentage of the bombs hit population centers of the city, it had little impact on public opinion. The reason for the misses was that Finns lit bonfires in surrounding nonpopulated areas, and the bombers mistook them for legitimate targets. We played similar tricks in our area, so that Russian aircraft making nighttime raids on Turku often dropped their bombs in our neighborhood as they were passing over Dragsfjärd because they had failed to locate Turku. In the mornings, we kids took our *potkukelkka* (kicksleds) and ice picks and went out on the frozen lakes or seas in a hunt for pieces of exploded bombs. In this way, we collected big amounts of scrap metal for the steel mills.

In early March my brother Sven left for his third stay in Sweden, this time back to the Lunden family in Råda, where we had visited in the spring of 1940. As for me, I had a lucky break from my self-studies. One of the girls' schools in Turku decided to open an "evacuation" school on March 13 in the village of Kemio (Kimito in Swedish), only fifteen kilometers from Dragsfjärd. The facility was a vacant Civil Guard building, and the school became known as the Kimito Samskola (*Samskola* meaning "co-educational"). Fifty girls lived in the school building, and many more were placed in private homes in the area. I believe we were about a dozen boys attending the school. Two of my classmates from Turku joined me in the highest ninth grade and were the only boys sharing the classroom with twenty girls. Actually there were no classrooms as such, since lectures were held in the main assembly hall, or wherever space could be found.

Two Henriks and I shared a small attic room in a home near the school. We ate our meals at the school where the girl students took turns doing the cooking. Teachers wondered how their discipline would work with the taller boys, but they didn't need to worry. One of the boys from Helsinki suffered from a superiority complex, but it disappeared very soon when he noticed how hard everybody worked in class and how the girls were our equals in snowball fights during school breaks.

In the evenings, we had many educational programs for anyone interested. Students rehearsed and performed plays, and those who could sing or play musical instruments contributed to the programs. Public dancing was not allowed during the war in Finland, but we used every opportunity to dance in smaller groups. I was one of two boys who played an accordion. Some weekends I visited with little brother Finn in Dragsfjärd. The three-hour walk each way was good exercise and often fun in company with schoolmates from nearby villages. At the end of May I received my report card from an "all-girl" school, and returned to Turku.

Part of the summer I spent in Kokkola, where my father was working at the time, and I participated in all kinds of sports activities, especially in track and field events, there. At this time the news from the war front was not good. The Russian offensive was in full swing and casualties were high. Despite miraculous efforts by the Finnish troops, it became necessary to arrange for a ceasefire on September 3, 1944. One of the demands by the Soviet Union was the disarming and internment of all German troops still in Finland. Thus, the Lapland War began that month and ended in April 1945.

Finally, the war was over. We faced extremely tough Soviet demands but had avoided being fully occupied by Russia. Schools in Turku opened in November 1944. After years of irregular school sessions, we were eager to do well in school, thereby also honoring our parents, teachers returning from military service, and our country that had made such sacrifices to safeguard our freedom. It was not an immediate return to normal, however, and the four years to follow have often been referred to as the "Years of Danger." I am not sure how much of the danger I grasped, but some of the conditions must have affected my life decisions.[3]

In a letter to Aunt Edith in April 1945, I wrote that

Sven received candy today from Sweden. Each student in classes I to IV (corresponding to grades five through eight in the USA), received one bag. When we get some Russian karkki [candy], we will send some to you older folks to taste also.

We had not seen any candy for almost five years. And in 1946, Finns still needed over fifty kinds of ration cards. It wasn't until two years later that half of the basic food items were free from rationing. And it wasn't until the end of 1949 that the ration regime was over (except for coffee, which was not available until 1954). Coca Cola first arrived in 1952, likely a must for the American athletes to survive the Helsinki Olympics.

During the summer of 1945, high school kids had to volunteer for work, often at farms where manpower was short due to war casualties. I was sent to a farm in Iitti, some 150 kilometers northeast of Helsinki near Finland's eastern border. To get there, I boarded the train from Turku to Helsinki, and as we approached the Porkkala region the train stopped. Here, the Finnish locomotive was replaced with a Russian one, and outside shutters were pulled over the passenger car windows. After the ride through the Russian naval base, shutters were removed and another Finnish locomotive pulled the train into the famous Helsinki railroad station designed by Eliel Saarinen.

In Helsinki, I stowed my bike and suitcases on a train bound for Kausala, and the next morning I biked the seven kilometers on a curvy and hilly dirt road to my destination to my host family, the tenant farmer of lands owned by the local parish. The Oksanen couple had two daughters in their early twenties and two sons who were eighteen and six years of age. A male cousin to the kids, a seasoned war veteran, also worked on the farm. On June 8 I wrote to my mother Hellin:

Kauko (the eighteen-year-old), his cousin, and I sleep in an iso tupa [large room], *where there is a loom and a huge baking oven. For now I keep my clothing in a suitcase, as there is no closet or chest of drawers. Today was my first day of work. We put up barbed-wire fences to contain the cattle. These fences are moved periodically to new grazing areas. It was really hard work to move the heavy rolls of wire through scrubby and marshy terrain. At noon we all ate lunch. Lots of food to eat, and I liked the taste. I do not think they will need any of my ration cards, but I will ask before I send them to you. They found some old torn rubber boots that I can use for now, but I hope you can arrange to mail me aunt Elsa's boots. My socks are all wet, but should dry up by the morning.*

On August 10 I wrote Aunt Edith:

I have enjoyed my stay here in Iitti, and I have not been sick one day. The people are just wonderful. In the beginning, the job was tough, but I have learned it well.

While moving barbed wiring was the heaviest work and removing weeds from the vegetable fields the dullest, haymaking was the most fun task because I was allowed to take the horse-drawn hay wagon to the barn. Working days were long, but after the Saturday evening sauna, my body felt strong and clean. Sunday was truly a day of rest with swimming and rowing on beautiful lakes. A fine relationship developed between me, a city boy, and this farming family.

Scouting was my main extracurricular activity for the rest of my high school years. In September 1945 I was named Scout Master for Troop II in my organization. I was in charge of over thirty boys of ages ten to fifteen organized in four patrols, with my brother Sven as one of my patrol leaders. In addition to lots of outdoor activities, we developed a new event we called "City Orienteering," in which the patrols competed in activities aimed at strengthening their powers of observation. Planning was time consuming but rewarding, as the boys really liked it.

In the fall of 1945 my school received an invitation from the a high school in Strängnäs, Sweden, hoping for an exchange of student representatives at the time of their annual celebration of Gustav II Adolf Day on November 6, which in Finland we celebrate as "Swedish Day." We were eager to accept and decided to send one senior and one junior student to this special event. I was elected to represent the junior class, and as vice-president of the *Konventti* (student body), I served as spokesman. I was granted my first Finnish passport, valid for the one-week visit to Sweden. As Finland was extremely short of foreign funds, I was allowed to buy only ten kronors in Swedish currency. My father, who always had a sweet tooth, asked me to spend half of it on some marzipan for him.

A student from Strängnäs met us when we arrived in Stockholm on the ship *Heimdall* and served as our guide during the stay. We were treated to a fine program. In Stockholm the stops included the Royal Castle, Skansen's open-air museum, and the 1912 Olympic Stadium. The festival in Strängnäs was a unique experience. In the school's main auditorium and with over five hundred people in attendance, I had the honor of reciting my school's proud 600-year-old history, as it is inscribed on a plaque in its entrance. In the evening we marched with thousands of people carrying torches and led by a large military band from the local armored regiment. We walked through the city streets to the market place, where speeches were given and patriotic songs sung. As it turned out, we did not need any money on the trip and even returned home with suitcases filled with gifts of clothing and food items.

One evening in Stockholm we enjoyed a Strauss operetta at Oscar's Theater. The Finnish actor Gerda Ryselin appeared in one the bigger roles; this reminded me of my short stint as a child actor in Turku a few years earlier, when Ms. Ryselin had played the title role in a musical called *100,000 Dollars for a Wife*.[4] In that show I played a black bellboy at the resort hotel where the main action took place and appeared for a few minutes at the start of the play and again for a few minutes at its end. During the two hours between my acts I remember sitting in an attic room backstage, my face itching from its drying black paint. The musical was showing a dozen evenings. On both occasions, I carried the star's suitcases and sang a few verses.

On New Year's Eve, December 31, 1945, Finland's Minister of Finance announced on the radio that half of the value of all outstanding Finnish *markka* bills would be withheld as a compulsory loan to the government. In practice this would happen by cutting in half all bills 500 marks or higher in value. The left halves would serve as valid means of payment (at half original value) until February 16, 1946, when they had to be exchanged for intact bills of new design. The right halves would become temporary receipts for the loan. In addition to forcing the Finnish people to save, the hope was to catch black marketeers and others assumed to have stacks of money hidden in mattresses and elsewhere. The operation was criticized as unsuccessful, partly because rumors of such an event had long before been circulated, and many had taken precautionary action.

In any event, this happening made my 1946 summer job more exciting. My father, then working in the city of Kotka, had arranged for me to work three months as a teller at the Kotka branch of the Union Bank of Finland. It was a time when many of the bank's clients were still confused about what had happened to their money, but it was also a time when part of the loan repayments began. Our family had rented a summer cabin outside the city. In a letter written on July 18, I wrote to aunt Edith,

> *Every morning I take our rowboat for a ten-minute trip to a nearby boat landing, from where at 8 AM a motor boat takes me to downtown Kotka in forty minutes. I work from 9:30 AM to 4 PM and make it back by boat to the cabin by six o'clock.*

Late in 1946, my parents, like many other Finns, decided that there would likely be a safer future for the family in Sweden. Since I was a senior in high school, I decided to remain in Finland, and graduated as class valedictorian. In my graduation speech I noted that our eight years in the *lyseo* had started with the Winter War in 1939 and ended at the time of the Paris Peace Treaty 1947: an exciting, challenging, and monumental time in our nation's history, and a fascinating time to have grown up and to have served as a "soldier boy."

* * * * *

In 1950 Norman married another former war child, and they had three children together. Norman himself earned graduate degrees in chemical engineering from the Universities of Turku and Helsinki and later worked in several capacities as a laboratory chemist, project engineer, and company president. From 1985 to 2000 he was an Honorary Consul of Finland in Washington State, where he and his wife live in retirement today.

Notes

A longer and quite different version of Norman's war-child story appeared in several installments in *New World Finn* from April to July 2001. The present version is published in the present volume with his approval as well as that of *New World Finn*'s editorial staff. Unfortunately, the photographs that illustrated Norman's story in its original version were unavailable to the present editor.

1. All letter quotations in this story appear in italic type.
2. Also known as "wood gas" and produced in a gasifier to power vehicles of various kinds, especially internal-combustion engines.

3. Norman has also written: "Due to the continuing fear of a possible Russian occupation of the country, an effort was made by demobilized Finnish officers to hide weapons and ammunition throughout the country in order to arm a guerilla force if needed. Unfortunately, this was discovered by the Soviets, and the 'guilty' were punished. Later Finland was forced, in conflict with Finnish law, to bring its 'war criminals' to trial. In 1946 former president Risto Ryti was sentenced to ten years in prison, and a dozen other leaders also received prison terms. As late as spring 1948, then president J. K. Paasikivi suspected a Communist-led coup-d'etat, and commanded the Finnish Army to disarm the state police. The parliamentary elections in July 1948 finally brought a change, leaving the Communists out of any key cabinet posts. War reparations to the Soviet Union cost Finland 15 percent of its national budget for several years, and it should be remembered that, fearing Soviet opposition, Finland did not accept any Marshall aid offered by the USA."
4. Lyricist(s) and/or composer(s) unknown. Performances of *100,000 Dollars for a Wife* also took place in the United States during the 1940s: for example, on March 5, 1945 at Northwestern University. See the "Mailbox" column of *Northwestern,* the university's alumni magazine, http://www.northwestern.edu/magazine/northwestern/winter2004/mailbox/ (accessed October 25, 2013).

Appendix

A Swedish War Child Administration Form

Swedish authorities employed documents to keep track of Finnish war children. The translation below is of a document issued by the Hjälpkommittéen för Finlands Barn (Help Committee for Finland's [War] Children) on May 4, 1942 on behalf of Veijo Paine, one of the contributors to the present volume.

HELP COMMITTEE FOR
FINLAND'S [War] CHILDREN   Registration number   13719
Formerly Finnish Summer Children
Herkulesgatan 26
TELEPHONE: Say "Finland's Children"
POSTAL CODE: 19 03 03

Into your care has been entrusted the Finnish subject [named]   *Pönniäinen, Veijo Kalevi*
[of]   *Kotka, Museokato 9 (Ronkainen)*

In Finland, who through the Help Committee for Finland's Children, has been transported to Sweden to stay as a guest in your home until further notice.

The committee wishes to herewith convey its warm thanks for your hospitality in opening your home to this child. This measure is of the greatest importance to the child himself and for a strengthening of ties between Finland and Sweden.

The committee advises you to take good care of the child's identification documents.

A ration card for the child can be obtained by turning to the area's war-time board and showing the identification documents. If identification documents for the child are lacking, a ration card can still be issued upon the presentation of this proof of receipt (according to the Provision commission's letter of 10 October 1941).

In the event that you need advice or instructions regarding care of the child or other similar matters, you are instructed to contact your committee's representative:

Mrs. Maja Sundström, Even Ericssongatan 17, Borás

The representative or other certified person will, to the extent that is possible, pay a visit to your home in order to hear your or the child's wishes.

Should the child's address change for any reason—i.e., through a move, hospital visit, etc.—*this shall be reported to the committee without delay.*

The child is insured in the event of an accident. Should an accident occur that is entitled to reimbursement, this should immediately be reported to the committee, upon which appropriate documents regarding the accident will be enclosed.

Costs for health care, at least if they amount to a significant sum, should probably be reimbursed either in whole or in part by the committee.

Do not forget to notify the child's immediate family about his or her arrival in your home and to provide updates about how the child is doing from time to time.

In the beginning *maintain the greatest caution* with food, since Finnish children are not used to nutritious food.

Stockholm,   4 May   1942
Help Committee for
FINLAND'S CHLDREN

Appendix

Facsimile of a document distributed throughout Sweden on behalf of individual Finnish war children. Courtesy of Veijo Paine.

Hjälpkommittén för
FINLANDS BARN
(f. d. Finska Sommarbarn)
HERKULESGATAN 26
STOCKHOLM

Reg.nr 13719

Telefon Namnanrop FINLANDS BARN
Postgiro 19 03 03

Till ....

Överdirektören Hardy Göransson, ordf.
Advokaten Lars Östberg, sekr.
Dr Gunnar Beskow
Docenten Curt Gyllenswärd
Professor Einar Key
Landshövdingskan Margit Levinson
Generalskan Maja Schmidt
Folkskoleinspektören Karl Steenberg

I Eder vård har anförtrotts finska undersåten Pönniäinen, Veijo Kalevi
.... Kotka, Museokatu 9. (Ronkainen)

.... i Finland, som genom Hjälpkommittén för Finlands barn överförts till Sverige för att tills vidare få vistas i Edert hem såsom gäst.

Kommittén framför härmed till Eder sitt varma tack för Eder vänlighet att öppna Edert hem för detta barn. Åtgärden har den största betydelse både för barnet självt och för stärkande av banden mellan Finland och Sverige.

Kommittén anhåller, att Ni ville, taga väl hand om barnets legitimationshandlingar.

Ransoneringskort för barnet erhålles efter hänvändelse till ortens kristidsnämnd mot uppvisande av legitimationshandlingen. Om legitimationshandling för barnet saknas kan ransoneringskort ändock erhållas mot uppvisande av detta mottagningsbevis (enligt Livsmedelskommissionens skrivelse den 10 okt. 1941).

För den händelse Ni behöver råd och anvisningar rörande barnets vård eller i andra liknande angelägenheter, ombedes Ni hänvända Eder till kommitténs ombud ....
Fru Maja Sundström, Sven Erikssonsgatan 17, Borås
.... Ombudet eller annan därtill befullmäktigad person kommer att i mån av tid avlägga besök i Edert hem för att taga del av Edra eller barnets önskemål.

Därest barnets adress skulle bliva ändrad av någon anledning — t. ex. genom flyttning, sjukhusvistelse e. dyl. — *skall detta ofördröjligen anmälas till kommittén.*

Barnet är olycksfallsförsäkrat. Skulle olycksfall inträffa, som berättigar till ersättning, skall detta omgående anmälas till kommittén, varvid erforderliga handlingar rörande olycksfallet skola medsändas.

Kostnader för sjukvård, åtminstone om de uppgå till något större belopp, torde kunna helt eller delvis ersättas av kommittén.

Glöm ej att snarast underrätta barnets anhöriga om dess ankomst till Edert hem och att sedan då och då meddela huru barnet har det.

Iakttag till en början *den allra största försiktighet* med maten då de finska barnen äro ovana vid närande föda.

4.5.
Stockholm den 1942

Hjälpkommittén för
FINLANDS BARN

Bibliography

Almgren, Sinikka Ortmark. *Du som haver barnen kär.* Stockholm: LT, 1989.
———. *Krigsbarns erinran: snäll, lydig och tacksam.* Stockholm: SinOA, 2003.
Andersson, Pentti. "Post-traumatic Symptoms Linked to Hidden Holocaust Trauma Among Adult Finnish Evacuees Separated from Their Parents as Children in World War II, 1939–1945: A Case-Control Study." *International Psychogeriatrics* [Turku, Finland] 23, no. 4 (2011): 654–61.
Bettelheim, Bruno. *The Uses of Enchantment.* New York: Vintage. 1977.
Bonney, Thérèse. "Children in Peril." *Collier's* 112 (July 3, 1943): 21–22.
Bowlby, John. *Attachment and Loss,* 2nd ed. New York: Basic Books, 1999.
Bowlby, John, et al. *Children in War-time.* London: New Educational Fellowship, 1940.
Danielsen, Ann-Maj. *Att inte höra till: ett finskt krigsbarn berättar.* Stockholm: B. Wahlström, 2000.
Edvardsen, Annu. *Det får inte hända igen: Finska krigsbarn 1939–45.* Stockholm: Askild & Kärnekull, 1977.
Engle, Eloise, and Lauri Paananen. *The Winter War: The Soviet Attack on Finland, 1838–1940.* Harrisburg, PA: Stackpole, 1992.
Ericsson, Kjersti, and Eva Simonsen. *Children of World War II: The Hidden Enemy Legacy.* Oxford: Berg, 2005.
Freud, Anna, and Dorothy T. Burlingham. *War and Children.* New York: Medical War Books, 1943.
Gelhorn, Martha. "Death in the Present Tense." *Collier's* 105 (February 20, 1940): 14–15, 46.
Heinl, Peter. *Splintered Innocence: An Intuitive Approach to Treating War Trauma.* London and New York: Routledge. 2001.
Historical Statistics of Sweden, Second Edition, 1720–1967. Stockholm: National Central Bureau of Statistics, 1969.
Jakobson, Max. *Finland Survived: An Account of the Finnish-Soviet Winter War, 1939.* Helsinki: Otava, 1961.
Jowett, Philip, and Brent Snodgrass. *Finland at War: 1939–45.* Oxford: Osprey, 2006.
Jutikkala, Eino, and Kauko Pirinen. *A History of Finland,* rev. ed., trans. Paul Sjöblom. New York: Dorset, 1988.
Kähönen-Wilson, Lempi. *Sisu Mother.* St. Cloud, MN: North Star, 2002.
Kavén, Pertti. *70,000 små öden.* Stockholm: Sahlgrens, 1985.
———. "Under the Shadow of Humanity." PhD diss., University of Helsinki, 2010.
Kinnunen, Tiina, and Ville Kivimäki, eds. *Finland in World War II: History, Memory, Interpretations.* Leiden and Boston: Brill, 2012.

Korppi-Tommola, Aura. "War and Children in Finland during the Second World War," *Paedogogica Historica* 44, no. 4 (August 2008): 445–55.

Littonen, Greta. *Centralized Voluntary Relief in Finland*, English summary. Helsinki: Suomen Huolto, 1949.

Lundin, Leonard C. *Finland in the Second World War.* Bloomington: Indiana University Press, 1957.

Nicholas, Lynn. *Cruel World: The Children of Europe in the Nazi Web.* New York: Alfred A. Knopf, 2005.

Parsons, Martin, ed. *Children: The Invisible Victims of War—An Interdisciplinary Study.* Denton, Peterborough: DSM, 2008.

———. *War Child: Children Caught in Conflict.* Gloucestershire: Tempus, 2008.

Rosnell, Kai. "The Complexity of the War Child Movement from Finland to Sweden and Denmark, 1939–1946." *New World Finn* 13, no. 1 (2012): 22–26.

Rossi, Tapani. *Räddade till livet: om en stor svensk hjälpinsats för Finlands barn 1939–1949.* Höör, Sweden: self-published, 2008.

Saffle, Sue. "Children, War, and the Rhetoric of Remembrance: The Stories of Finland's War Children." *Children in War* 1, no. 4 (November 2006): 97–103.

———. "'A Happier War Child Story': One Finnish War Child's Exceptional Memories and Circumstances." In: *Children: The Invisible Victims of War—An Interdisciplinary Study*, ed. Martin Parsons (Denton, Peterborough: DSM, 2008), 213–24.

———. "The Stuff of Fairy Tales: Finnish War Child Rauni Janser Remembers." *Children in War* 1, no. 7 (February 2010): 85–92.

———. "Toward a Collection of Finnish War-Child Stories: The Reminiscences of Seppo Mälkki." *Children in War* 1, no. 5 (January 2008): 25–31.

———. "Understanding Backwards: The Story of Finnish War Child Veijo (Pönniäinen) Paine." *Children in War* 1, no. 6 (February 2009): 77–84.

Serenius, Mona. "The Silent Cry: A Finnish Child during World War II and 50 Years Later." *International Forum of Psychoanalysis* 4 (1995): 35–47.

Tatar, Maria, ed. *The Classic Fairy Tales.* New York: W. W. Norton, 1999.

Virkkunen, Sakari. *Suomen presidentit.* Helsinki: Otava, 1994.

Virtala, Irene. "Identity Processes in Autobiographies by Finnish War Children." In: *Entering Multiculturalism: Finnish Experiences Abroad*, ed. Olavi Koivukangas (Turku: Institute of Migration, 2002): 240–47.

———. Summary Abstract, *Finnish War Children in Literature* (Web Reports No. 5). Turku: Migrationsinstitutet, 2004. Unpaginated.

War and Children in Finland during the Second World War. Tampere: Department of History and Philosophy, University of Tampere, 2008.

Index

Aalto, Alvar, 89
Äänekoski (Finland), 150
Åbo (Swedish name for Turku), 291. *See also* Turku
Agrarian Party (Finland), 220
Ahvenanmaa, 215. *See also* Åland Islands
air raids. *See* Finland at war
Alajärvi (Finland), 72, 75
Åland Islands (Finland), 132
Alexander I, Czar of Russia, 212n1
Almgren, Sinikka Ortmark, 2, 4, 16, 21–22
American-Finnish newsletters, 22–23
Amerikabreven ("American Letters"), 171
Ann Arbor (Michigan), 253
Andersen, H[ans] C[hristian], 44
Andersson, Pentti, 19, 140n–141n
Ange (Sweden), 235
Ångermanland (Sweden), 81
Anjala (Finland), 85
Arctic Circle, 152
Arctic Sea, 215–16
Arcturus (Swedish ship), 10, 20, 43, 86, 122, 130, 150
Arizona (United States warship), 173
Artjärvi (Finland), 36
Artjärvi (Finnish lake), 34
Arvika (Sweden), 285–87
Asterix (comics character), 214
Auran (Finnish river), 295
Australia, 22, 54
Austria, 9

Baltic Fair (Estonia), 170
Baltic Sea, 99, 104, 138, 150–51

Barron, Marja Hultin, 13, 15
Basel (Switzerland), 184
Båstad (Sweden), 177
Battle of Rukajärvi. *See* Karelia
Bettelheim, Bruno, 18–19
Bible, 200, 291. *See also* Old Testament
Bible (and missionary) schools, 213, 219
Bobrikov, Nicholas, 204, 212
bombs and bombings. *See under* Finland at war and Soviet Union at war
Bonney, Thérèse, 7
Boras (Sweden), 65
Boston, 121, 278
    Bank of Boston, 121
    Copley Plaza Hotel, 278
Bothnia. *See* Gulf of Bothnia
Bowlby, John, 8, 18, 25n26
Boy Scouts and scouting, 173, 299, 301–302, 306
Brenäs (Sweden), 150
Broström, Martti Kalervo, 13
Buddhism, 293
Burlingham, Dorothy, 8

Canada, 22, 57–58, 112–13, 160, 170
Center for Help in Finland, 9
Central Organization of War Child Associations (Finland), 21
Chalmers University, 292
Chicago, 184
child transports, 2, 5, 9. *See also* Kindertransport, Operation Pied Piper, and Peter Pan children
Christianstad (Sweden), 138. *See also* Kristianstad

Christmas. *See* holidays
Churchill, Winston, 7
Cold War (1950s–1960s), 4
Conservative Party (Finland), 220
Continuation War (July 1941–September 1944), 2, 6–10, 35, 43, 46, 70, 71, 79, 96, 105, 149, 150, 176, 195, 215, 219, 255, 260, 279, 281, 284, 300
Convention of Children's Rights, 21
Copenhagen, 43, 46, 50
Cuba, 2
curfews, 157

Dalarna (Sweden), 131
Dammert, Erja, 20–21
Danielsen, Ann–Maj, 4
Day for the Children of War. *See* holidays
Death Valley, 117
Den bästa av mödrar ("Mother of Mine"; film), 20
Denmark, 1–4, 8–10, 12–13, 21–22, 43, 46–51, 70, 76, 166, 177, 187, 212, 291, 295, 300
desanis (Estonian parachutists). *See* Finland at war
Donald Duck, 214, 291
Dragsfjärd (Finland), 304

Edvardsen, Annu, 2
Emory University Medical School, 33
England, 2, 12, 22, 41
English Channel, 117
Ero ("Separation"; statue), 20
Espoo (Finland), 272
Estonia, 6, 25, 70, 149, 170, 291–92, 300–301, 303
Eurajoki (Finland), 225–26
European Union, 70

Falkenburg (Sweden), 52–54
Films about war, 41. *See also* Den bästa av Mödrar
Finland at war
  18th Separate Infantry Battalion (also ErP18), 296, 299
  air raids and bomb shelters, 19, 29, 32, 39, 42, 88, 92, 106, 121, 128–30, 142, 144, 153, 176, 180, 186, 195, 221, 234, 241, 250, 255, 295–97
  bombs and bombings of, 5, 7, 39–40, 42–43, 51, 52, 55, 71–72, 86, 92, 95, 107, 114, 128–31, 133, 142, 166, 185, 186, 196, 199, 202, 205, 207, 223, 231, 233–34, 241, 250–51, 255, 259, 295–96, 297
  boy soldiers (sotilaspoika) of, 169, 172
  casualties of, 7
  Civil Guard (Suojeluskunta) of, 299, 301, 304
  fighter planes of, 296
  horses used in battles by, 149n4, 180, 250, 271, 288, 297
  Karelia briefly regained by (1941), 7
  machine guns and gunners of, 34, 143, 288
  parachutists (also desanis), 149n3
  planes shot down by, 160n1
  Russians, ambivalent attitudes toward, 185n1
  troops, 7, 32–33, 146, 199, 259, 297, 302, 305
Finlandia Foundation, 220
Finland (or Finnish) Aid Organization, 44
Finland's independence from Russia (1917–1918), 6
Finnish Aid Center (Sweden), 222
Finnish Civil War (January–May 1918), 204, 212n2
Finnish Defense Forces, 303
Finnish Supreme Court of Justice, 21
Finnish war children. *See* war children
Finnish War Child Society (Sweden), 173–74
Finnish War Child Transport Committee, 9
Finska Krigsbarn (Swedish war–child magazine), 21, 230
Freud, Anna, 8, 18

Garveda (Sweden), 182, 184
Gävle (Sweden), 151, 188, 260

Gelhorn, Martha, 8
General Assembly (Finland), 21–22
Geneva Convention, 167
Germany and Germans, 6–7, 9, 17, 24–26, 51, 68–69, 170, 174–75, 212, 269, 300
    Anti–Semitic attitudes of, 170
    concentration camps of, 19
    Nazi Party and sentiments concerning, 170–71, 174n3
    offers to accept Finnish war children, 9
Germany at war
    aid to and cooperation with Finland, 7, 269
    destruction of houses in Finland, 271–72
    iron ore supplied by Sweden, 174
    in Kuusamo, 270
    occupation of Denmark, 51n2, 166, 300
    occupation of Norway, 51, 300
    troops, 6, 174, 300, 302–303, 305
Gone with the Wind (novel), 117
Göteborg (or "Götheborg; Sweden), 64, 168–70, 174, 182, 201, 219, 226, 285
    University, 292–93
Göteborgs Handels– och Sjöfartstidning (Swedish newspaper), 174n2
Gotland (Sweden), 176, 215
Gräbo (Sweden), 171
Graninge (Sweden), 267
Graningebruk (Sweden), 261–62, 264
Graningeverket (Swedish forestry and energy company), 265–66
Gray, Zane, 117
Grimm, Wilhelm and Jacob, 18, 98
Gulf of Bothnia, 10, 18, 122, 132, 221, 229, 299
Gulf of Finland, 25, 70, 150, 249, 300
Gustav XVI, King of Sweden, 20

Hagfors (Sweden), 298
Hakkapelitta (Finnish army periodical), 149
Halonen, Tarja, 20
Hamburg (Germany), 300

Hämeenlinna (Finland), 34, 70, 242–43, 259, 262–63, 266–67
    War-child association of, 5
Hankkila, Juha, 11, 19
Hanko (Finland), 160
Hanko Peninsula (Karelia), 25
"Hansel and Gretel" (Grimm Brothers story), 18, 87, 98
Haparanda (Sweden), 10–11, 31, 35, 99, 151, 176, 183, 199–200, 223, 239, 255, 267, 298
Härnosand (Sweden), 260–61
Haukivuori (Finland), 113, 115
Heimdall (Swedish ship), 10, 227, 307
Heinl, Peter, 17–19
Heino, Karina, 15
Heinola (Finland), 63–64, 66–67
Help Committee for Finland's Children (Swedish organization), 197
Helsingin Sanomat (Finnish newspaper), 20, 225
Helsinki (Finland), 6, 8, 29, 39–40, 46, 62, 63, 71–72, 75, 83–84, 85, 93–94, 120, 128–31, 133–35, 137–40, 142, 145, 148, 150, 152, 159–60, 175–76, 178, 183, 212, 230, 232, 238–39, 249–51, 253, 255, 257–58, 260, 277, 281, 284–85, 287, 289–90, 292, 294–95, 297, 300, 304–306, 308
    airport, 277
    apartments and apartment buildings, 39, 128–29, 139, 175–76, 249–50, 257, 287, 289
    bus station, 128
    Forum (department store), 128
    Hietaniemi Cemetery, 159
    Lutheran cathedral, 212
    market hall, 291
    National Museum, 249
    newspaper. *See* Helsingin Sanomat
    old church and park, 249
    Olympics (1952), 178, 305
    railroad station, 64, 257, 305
    shops, 130
    Sollentuna Church, 159
    Stockman's (department store), 289
    University, 62, 93–94, 148, 258
Herrljunga (Sweden), 64
Hibbing Junior College, 76

Index

Hirvensalo (Finland), 214, 217–18
Hitler, Adolf, 3, 79, 170–71, 174, 225, 230
Holback (Denmark), 43
holidays
    Armistice Day, 279
    Christmas, 28–29, 53, 56, 60–61, 73, 85, 109–111, 116, 118, 121, 138–39, 151, 152–54, 157, 182, 193, 205, 207–209, 223, 227, 231–32, 244, 251, 258, 262–63, 276, 282, 287
    Day for the Children of War (proposed), 22
    Gustav II Adolf Day (November 6 in Sweden), 307
    May Day (May 1), 263, 276–77
    Midsummer Day (c. June 21–25; also Juhannus), 275, 282–83
    St. Lucia's Day (December 13), 60, 109, 207–208, 212n5, 253, 257
    Swedish Day (November 6 in Finland), 307
Holland, 9
Holopainen, Veijo, 15
Horred (Sweden), 198, 201
Huaröd (Sweden), 97, 104
Hufvudstadsbladet (Swedish newspaper), 225
Hungary, 9

Iilomantsi (formerly Karelia, now part of the Russian Federation), 113
Iisalmi (Finland), 113, 117–18, 120
Iitti (Finland), 305
Imatra (Finland), 42–43, 46–47, 49, 51n1, 166, 230, 299
Inkilä (Karelia), 63
Inkinen, Veikko, 3, 5, 11, 21, 248n1
Interim Peace (between Finland and the Soviet Union; March 1940–June 1941), 7, 29, 299
Ivesoksa, Soile, 14

Jaakkola, Eric, 14
Janser, Rauni, 18
Järvenpää (Finland), 179
Jewish war children. *See* Kindertransport
Jokipii (Finland), 198, 201
Jokispilä, Markku, 22
Jönköping (Sweden), 35, 37, 246, 248n2
Juhannus. *See* holidays
Juntunen, Rauno, 17

Kaila, Martti (Finnish psychologist), 68
Kajaani (Finland), 96, 99, 102, 105
Källeberg (Sweden), 198
Kallinge (Sweden), 73
Kalmar (Sweden), 182
Karelia (formerly part of Finland, today part of the Russian Federation), 7, 10, 28, 31, 34, 42, 49, 51, 59–60, 63, 83, 92, 113, 146, 149, 152, 166, 171, 180, 216, 245, 247, 250, 295, 299, 302
    Battle of Rukajärvi, 92
    evacuations and refugees from, 10, 40, 69, 121, 216, 270, 299–300
    inhabitants considered Russian by some Finns, 70n3
Karelian Isthmus. *See* Karelia
Karlajan kannas (Karelian region), 241
Karleby, 59. *See also* Kokkola
Karlskoga (Sweden), 242
Katrineholm (Sweden), 150–51
Kaukinen, Sirpa, 16
Kavén, Pertti, 3–4, 11, 16–17
Kemio (also Kimito; Finland), 304
Kerava (Finland), 295
Kindertransport (Jewish children), 2, 8, 12
Kinnala (Finland), 273, 281
Kinnunen, Tiina, 22
Kivik (Sweden), 104
Klaralven (Swedish river), 298
Koivisto, Helena Nyqvist, 123
Kokkola (Finland), 59, 61, 78–79, 122, 126, 130, 132, 305
Kokkoselka (Finland), 297
Kontiomäki (Finland), 99
Korppi-Tommola, Aura, 2, 7, 14, 94n3, 185nn1–2
Kotka (Finland), 85–87, 91, 94, 142, 144, 195–96, 201, 203, 308, 310
    harbor, 142
    Union Bank of Finland branch, 308
Kouvola (Finland), 142, 297

krigsbarn ("war child" or "war children" in Swedish). *See* war children
Kristianstad (Sweden), 96, 103
Kungshamn (Swedish resort), 29–30
Kuopio (Finland), 55, 113, 125, 166
Kuusamo (Finnish district), 268, 270, 303
Kuusankoski (Finland), 142
Kyminlinna (Finland), 86

Ladoga (or Laatokka; Karelian lake, today part of the Russian Federation), 42, 59, 70, 216, 241
Lahti (Finland), 34, 36–37, 52, 231–34, 237, 239
Lake Bluff (Illinois), 184
Lapland (Finland and Sweden), 6, 156, 160, 220, 268, 272
Lapland War (September 1944 – April 1945), 2, 7, 25, 72, 191, 219, 305
Lappeenranta (Finland), 47
Lapua (Finland), 62, 127
Latvia, 6, 25, 169–70
Lemetti (Finland), 299
Lempaala (Finland), 295
Levämäki (Finland), 99
Lindgren, Astrid, 137
Lindgren, Eeva, 5
Linköping (Sweden), 86–87, 94
Lithuania, 6, 25
Little Women (novel), 117
Lottas. *See* Lotta Svärd
Lotta Svärd (Finnish women's voluntary national defense force), 47, 51n3, 54, 122, 146, 203, 205, 297–98
Louhimo, Pekka/Peter, 13, 15
Loviisa (also Lovisa; Finland), 295, 297, 300
Lund (Sweden), 60–61, 94, 134, 139
Luoma, Marja, 11
Luumäki–Taavetti (Finland), 259

machine guns and gunners. *See* Finland at war and Soviet Union at war
Mälaren (Swedish lake), 125
Mälkinkyla (Finland), 166
Mälkki, Seppo, 15, 167, 173–74, 174nn2–3
   and soldier–brother Jorma, 172

Mannerheim, Carl Gustav Emil, 9, 174, 225, 230n1
Mäntyharju (Finland), 115
Mariehamn (Åland Islands), 132
Marquette (Michigan), 253
May Day. *See under* holidays
Medlems nytt (periodical), 244
Mickey Mouse, 146
Midsummer Day. *See under* holidays
Mikkeli (Finland), 115, 117
Miller, Eine, 11, 15
Ministry of Social Affairs (Sweden), 59
Minneapolis (Minnesota), 76
   University, 203
Möhkö (formerly Karelia, now part of the Russian Federation), 113
Mölndal (Sweden), 291
Moscow Peace Treaty (between Finland and the Soviet Union; 21 March 1940), 96. *See also* Interim Peace
music and musicians, 31, 33, 89, 117–18, 131, 175, 178, 191, 256, 264, 277, 284, 293, 299, 304, 307
Myrdal, Alva, 10

Nädendal (Finland), 284
Nashwauk (Minnesota), 76
National Center for Disease Control (Atlanta), 33
Nazi Party. *See* Germany and Germans
Netherlands. *See* Holland
New World Finn (magazine), 308
New York City, 76, 184, 278
Nicholas II, Czar of Russia, 212
Night Wanderers in Sweden (organization), 174
Niinistö, Sauli, 21
Nilsson, Helena, 11, 15
Nora (Sweden), 240
Nordic Assistance Center (Finland), 9
North America, 298
Northwestern University, 309n4
Norway, 51n2, 212n4, 285, 300
Nyköping (Sweden), 213–15, 219

Oakville (Ontario), 160
Odensvi (Sweden), 222
Oihonna (Finnish steamship), 260, 299
Old Testament, 219

100,000 Dollars for a Wife (musical comedy), 307, 309n4
Onge (Sweden), 236, 239
Operation Pied Piper, 3, 9, 12
Ostrobothnia (Finnish region), 122, 221
Oulu (Finnish town), 99, 268, 271, 300
Oulu (Finnish river), 270

Paasikivi, J. K., 309n3
Paine, Veijo Pönniäinen, 11, 15
    letter of, 200
    war child administration form of, 311–12
Pälkäne (Finland), 245
Palos, Virve Kaisu Kyllikki, 16, 23
Parainen (Finland), 28
Pargas (Finnish island), 284
Paris Peace Treaty (1947), 308
Peter Pan children, 2
Pied Piper children. *See* Operation Pied Piper
Pienpero (Finland), 28
Pirkanmas (Finland), 245
Pops and Moms in the Street (Swedish organization), 174
Pori (Finland), 168–69, 225, 227
    College of Nursing, 184
Porkkala (Finnish region), 305
Poronvesi (Finnish lake), 119
Porvoo (Finland), 160, 295
propaganda, 3, 143, 185
Punkaharju (Finland), 107
Pyhäjärvi (Karelian lake), 42, 49

Raate (Finland), 300
Råda (Sweden), 298, 304
Radetsky March, The (novel), 139
radio operators, 50, 105
radios and radio broadcasts, 25, 31, 45, 78–79, 89, 98, 103, 117, 128, 130, 156, 174, 179, 181, 240, 250, 256, 269, 307
Rahkonen, Ossi, 15
railways. *See* trains, train stations, and train travel
rationing and ration coupons, 9, 29, 38, 55, 79, 82, 90, 98, 102, 116, 125, 130–31, 157, 176, 197–98, 205, 207–209, 212, 276, 302, 305–306

Rauma (Finland), 225
Red Cross (international organization), 10, 133, 183, 188–89, 234–35, 237, 239
    Swedish branch, 285
Red Guards. *See* Finnish Civil War
Rehula, Lea, 15
Riihimäki (Finland), 199, 297
Rimmi (Finland), 122, 124–26
Ristijärvi (Finland), 99
Ronneby (Sweden), 72–73
Rosnell, Kai, 3, 9, 14, 16, 18, 21
    honored for work with war children, 21
Rossi, Tapani, 11–13, 21
Rotebro (Sweden), 155, 157
Rukajärvi. *See* Karelia
Rullander, Gertrud, 15, 23, 240
Runeberg, J. L., 223
Ruovesi (Finland), 270–71
Russification, 212n1, 212n3
Russia. *See* Soviet Union
Russian Federation, 7
Rydh, Hanna, 9
Ryselin, Gerda, 307
Ryti, Risto, 309n3

Saarinen, Eliel, 305
Saint (St.) Lucia Day. *See* holidays
Salla (Finland). *See* Winter War
San Diego (California), 185
Sandler, Maya, 9
Santa Claus, 263, 276
saunas, 49, 87, 99–100, 106, 115, 117, 119–20, 269, 275–76, 282, 292–93, 294, 296, 306
Savo (also Savolaks; Finnish province), 166, 195, 298
Sea of Bothnia. *See* Gulf of Bothnia
Secret Garden, The (novel), 117
Segerstedt, Torgny, 174n2
Seinäjoki (Finland), 127, 149, 151, 198, 221–23
Serenius, Mona, 19, 22
Sibelius, Jean, 89, 179, 293
Siberia, 144
Siilasvuo, Hjalmar (Finnish Lt. General), 300
Silja (Swedish lake), 65

sisu (Finnish for "determination" or "endurance"), 176, 256, 292
Skåne (Swedish county), 60–61, 96, 178
Skarpö (Swedish island), 157–59
Slätmon (Sweden), 87
Småland (Sweden), 35
Söderberg, Bodil Nordman, 19–20
Södertälje (Sweden), 177, 285
Soivio (Finland), 268
Soiviojärvi (Finnish lake), 269
Sollefteå (Sweden), 261–63, 266
Sordavala (Finland), 297
sotalapsi ("war children" in Finnish). *See* war children
Soviet Union, 6, 10, 24–25, 69–70, 96, 105, 108, 132, 174, 215, 230, 245, 254, 269, 284, 294, 300, 303
   border with Finland, 42, 79, 96, 143, 182, 270, 302
Soviet Union at war
   bombs, bombers, and planes, 6, 29–30, 39–40, 42, 55, 64, 71, 128–29, 133, 142, 144–46, 166–67, 176, 180–81, 195, 199, 204, 213, 222, 235–36, 245, 249, 255, 269, 284, 288, 294, 296–97, 300–302, 304
   casualties, 7, 105
   Communist coup d'etat in Finland suspected of, 309n
   demands, including war reparations, 8, 148, 305, 309n3
   destruction of the Soviet embassy in Helsinki, 253n1–254n1
   machine guns and gunners of, 6, 160n1
   occupation of Estonia, 291
   prisoners of war, 79, 146, 181, 185, 250, 270, 300
   punishment of suspected Finnish guerilla forces, 309n
   seizure of Karelia, 49, 247, 270
   spies of and for, 144, 147, 301
   submarines of, 10
   troops, 6
Spanish Civil War children, 9
sparks. *See* radio operators
Stalin, Josef, 79, 147, 288
Steffenstorf (Sweden), 60

Stenius-Aarniala, Brita, 12–13, 21
Stockholm, 4, 10–12, 30–32, 37, 43, 54, 60, 66, 72, 81, 86, 88, 96, 99, 110, 119, 122–23, 126, 129–31, 133–34, 138–39, 150–51, 154–55, 157–60, 168, 173–74, 178, 191, 194, 197–98, 204–206, 208–210, 213–15, 222, 225, 237, 240, 244, 245–46, 250, 257, 260, 267, 285, 287, 290, 298–99, 307, 310
   airport, 139
   apartments and apartment buildings, 30, 131
   Gröna Lund (amusement park), 210
   harbor, 30, 154, 260
   Hotel Anglais, 11
   National Archives, 226, 230
   Olympic Stadium (1912), 307
   railway station, 260
   Royal Castle, 307
   Skansen (amusement park), 307
   University, 37, 94
Stockholm (Swedish ship), 201
St. Petersburg (Russia), 70, 169, 216, 300
Strängnäs (Sweden), 108, 205, 306–307
Sunswaal (Sweden), 235
Suojärvi (formerly Karelia, now part of the Russian Federation), 180
Suojeluskunta. *See under* Finland at war
Suomenlinna (Finnish island), 133, 230
Suomi-American magazine, 23
Suomussalmi (Finland), 96, 99
   battle of, 104, 229
Svenska Dagbladet (Swedish newspaper), 20
Sweden and Swedes
   accidental Russian bombings of, 212n4
   admirers of Hitler and fascism, 174n2
   volunteers who fought with Finland, 160n2
   war child programs of, 260
Switzerland, 9

Tähtinen, Marja, 13–14
Tainionkoski (Finland), 297
Tammisaari (Finland), 249

Tampere (Finland), 23, 160, 204, 209, 211–12, 259–60, 270, 295
Tapanila (Finland), 71, 74–75
Tarto Negotiation (between Finland and Russia, 1920), 70
Tatar, Maria, 18
theater and theatrical performances, 139, 175, 194, 307
"Time of Flowers is Approaching, The" (hymn), 137
Toijala (Finland), 297
Topelius, Zachris, 137, 223
Torneå (Sweden), 151, 267
Tornio (Finland), 10, 31, 34, 99, 108, 125, 152, 183, 188, 259, 223, 255, 297–99
trains, train stations, and train travel
　collision of (March 1940), 10
　electric locomotives, 260
　rail gauges of, 11, 38n1, 188
　railway stations, 43, 47, 66–67, 84, 86–87, 99, 110, 122, 126, 152, 155, 168, 180, 187, 189, 197–98, 209, 227, 234–35, 255, 267, 272, 285, 287. *See also* Helsinki and Stockholm
　steam-powered trains, 260–61
　train travel, 5, 11, 31–32, 35, 43, 47, 52–54, 56, 59–60, 64, 72–72, 80, 83, 86–87, 96, 99–100, 107–08, 110, 118, 122, 125–26, 129–30, 133, 138–39, 150–52, 155, 167–68, 176, 182–83, 187–89, 191, 197–99, 208, 213–14, 226–27, 234–35, 237, 241–43, 245, 250, 255, 257, 260–61, 267, 271, 285, 287, 291, 295, 297–98, 302, 305
　used to transport alcohol, 272
Treaty on Adoption (Nordic countries, 1931), 13–14
Trent, Rita, 14
Turku (Finland), 10, 28–29, 31–32, 43, 86, 96, 106–108, 122, 127, 129–30, 152, 157, 160, 168, 186–87, 191–92, 197, 204–205, 208, 213–18, 237, 243, 250, 257–58, 260, 267, 284, 291, 294–97, 299, 301–305, 307–308
　apartments, 217–18, 295
　Auran silta (bridge), 295
　harbor, 152–53, 168
　Institute of Migration (Studies), 160
　old cemetery, 33
　Svenska Klassiska Lyceum, 299
　University, 127
Turku archipelago, 304

Udby (Denmark), 43, 45
Uddevalla (Sweden), 19, 250–53
Umeå (Sweden), 255–57
Union of Soviet Socialist Republics. *See* Soviet Union
United Nations
　Convention on the Rights of the Child, 22
　High Commissioner for Refugees, 271–72
United States, 1–2, 22–23, 29, 31, 33, 54, 69, 75–76, 80, 84, 116–17, 121, 168, 170–71, 175, 185, 200–202, 220, 253, 278–82, 294, 301–302, 309
　Amerikanpaketti (care packages sent to Finland and Sweden), 48, 75, 116, 146, 302–303
　athletes of, 305
　Bay of Pigs military fiasco (1961), 2
　Marshall Plan, 69, 309n3
University of Espoo (Finland), 272
Uppsala (Sweden), 123–26, 182, 250–51
　apartments in, 123, 125–26
USA. *See* United States
USSR. *See* Soviet Union

Vaasa (Finland), 125, 204, 222
Värmeln (Swedish lake), 285
Värmland (also Varmland; Sweden), 242, 285–86, 298
Vestra Götamanland (Sweden), 64
Veteli (Finland), 122
Vetlanda (Sweden), 35
Viipuri (also "Vipuri"; Karelia), 52, 70n1, 146, 149n3, 160, 166, 259
Virolainen, Johannes, 121n1
Virolathi (Finland), 149
Virtala, Irene, 3, 18

Volvo (Swedish car corporation), 239, 261, 286
Vuoski (Finnish river), 48, 51n1
Vyborg. *See* Viipuri

Waija (Sweden), 81
War Child Memory Project, 21
war children
    adoptions of, 9, 13–14, 16, 30–31, 34, 36–37–, 53–54, 57, 68, 99, 114, 140, 169, 173, 182, 192–93, 239, 279, 291
    avoidance as survival strategy by, 140n–41n
    collecting stories of, 2, 17, 22–24
    definitions of, 1–2
    feelings of guilt, 4
    film about. *See* Den bästa av mödrar
    as "hired help" (farm work, maids, etc.), 14, 32, 56, 117, 127, 227, 257, 279–81
    illnesses and injuries of, 11–12, 36, 39, 46, 72, 105, 107–109, 120, 123, 134, 142, 150, 177, 182, 188–89, 199, 255–56, 279, 291
    letters and postcards sent or received by, 124, 194, 206, 211, 252–53, 294–97, 299–301, 303, 305–306, 308
    medical examinations of, 11–12, 35, 60, 81, 123, 150, 171, 188, 200, 213, 222, 225, 242, 260, 298
    nametags, cards, and labels worn by, 10, 20, 35, 62, 86, 123, 153, 167, 176, 182, 188, 197, 234–35, 256
    and polytrauma, 17
    and Post Traumatic Stress Disorder (PTSD), 19
    punishments, humiliations, and traumas of, 1, 5, 11, 14–15, 44–45, 48–49, 74–75, 116, 118, 123, 125, 127, 137, 227, 280, 288–90
    statue commemorating. *See* Ero
Wartsila-Patsola (also Wartsila; formerly Karelia, now part of the Russian Federation), 180, 287
war widows, 7, 29, 32, 277
Washington (state), 308
Westerberg, Norman, 309n3
Wild West stories, 214
Winter War (November 1939 – March 1940), 2, 6–8, 34, 39, 51, 52, 59, 71, 75, 79, 83, 85, 96, 105, 106, 112, 113, 118–19, 121, 122, 128, 143, 149, 152, 157, 167, 176, 186, 195, 204, 219, 221, 223, 228, 241, 253, 255, 259, 269, 271, 273, 288, 299, 302, 308
    Salla, Battle of, 7
wireless operators, see "radio operators"
World Bank, 220
World War I (in Europe; 1914–1918), 9, 79, 212n2, 260
World War II (in Europe; 1939–1945), 1–2, 5–6, 9, 13, 17, 22, 24, 143, 160n2, 185n1, 225, 260, 265, 288, 291. *See also* Continuation War, Lapland War, and Winter War

Zealand (Denmark), 43